THAT ONE
GLORIOUS SEASON

Leominster's Little League Representatives who presented Ted Williams, Red Sox slugger and member of the Jimmy Fund committee, with a check for $362.17 at the Red Sox-Washington Senators game in Boston last Thursday, are pictured above. The two youngsters were selected to make the presentation of the fund collected on donations taken up by members of the Little League as they collected the largest sum. The Little Leaguers were guests of the Red Sox for the game. Richard Letarte, 6 Orchard Street, left, Williams, in the middle, and Clifford Richards, 300 Lincoln Street, as they visited with the great Red Sox slugger after making the presentation. Williams is shown in the picture holding the check made out to the Jimmy Fund which he accepted in behalf of the committee. [Original caption from the *Leominster* (Massachusetts) *Enterprise*, August 1954.]

THAT ONE GLORIOUS SEASON

BASEBALL PLAYERS WITH ONE SPECTACULAR YEAR

1950–1961

RICHARD H. LETARTE

Dear Jean,
Please enjoy some of
baseball's best
moments!
Rich Letarte

PETER E. RANDALL
PUBLISHER LLC
Portsmouth, New Hampshire 03802
2006

© 2006 by Richard H. Letarte

ISBN:1-931807-51-5
ISBN13: 978-1-931807-51-7

Library of Congress Control Number: 2006905227

Published by
Peter E. Randall Publisher LLC
Portsmouth NH 03802
www.perpublisher.com

Book design: Grace Peirce

Cover photo: Photocopy of photograph showing the interior of Shibe Park, Philadelphia, Pennsylvania, also known as Connie Mack Stadium. This was taken on September 10, 1963 during a game between Phillies and Mets. Courtesy of Library of Congress, Prints and Photographs Division, Historic American Buildings Survey or Historic American Engineering Record, Reproduction Number: HABS, No. PA-1738-11.

Dedication

This book is dedicated to the ballplayers of the mid-twentieth century who were the heroes of so many youngsters who grew up during that time. They were an eclectic, colorful group who, in their own way, encouraged many of us to strive to achieve our goals, whatever they were. Thank you.

Contents

Acknowledgments

A collective thanks to every individual who uttered the encouraging words: "When are you gonna be done with that book?" I wish that I could remember you all, but seeing as it took over seven years from start to finish, my aging memory does not serve quite that well.

A special thanks to Dick Monfils, who found the baseball cards used for the book; the patient librarians of Lunenburg and Fitchburg, Massachusetts, who provided me with long-out-of-print books and day-by-day newspaper copy; Tim Wiles and his staff at the Baseball Hall of Fame in Cooperstown, New York, who quickly retrieved player folders and other pertinent information. In addition, they located a video copy of Happy Felton's Knothole Gang for my driving companion, Joe Gunther, who wished to recall his youth in and around New York City. In one of the hall's viewing rooms we watched an episode in which Jackie Robinson, of the Brooklyn Dodgers, gave fielding tips to a trio of Little Leaguers.

Ed Glotch and Joe Giovino helped me with editorial comments, as did Russ Wolinsky of the Hall of Fame staff. Steve Priest gave me tips on publishing as well as editorial comment. Shipmate Dan Corbett encouraged me with positive feedback after reviewing parts of the project; other ancient mariners from our old USS *Mauna Kea* crew repeatedly asked about publication at every reunion. Howard Clark assisted me with key contacts.

Dusty Rhodes and Bob Shaw were very generous with their time when we visited them both in Florida. Mary Konstanty and Jeanne and Hank Sauer sent me materials from which I added to my research. Al Rosen wrote back with a series of books and publications that I used for information. Ned Garver assisted me with a phone interview. I made numerous calls to Katharine Jensen and she helped me with details concerning her husband.

My daughters, Marie and Evelin, their husbands Mark Mueller and Carter Ross, and my son, Greg, constantly supported me to get on with this project. Finally, I could not have completed this book without the encouragement from my wife MaryEllen, who, since 1998, has been determined to manage a book tour to the thirteen cities highlighted in this work, along with its numerous signings and visits to the local high spots. As this has been a hobby for me, a joyful labor surrounding the game I loved as a kid, I will be more than happy to let her take over that function.

Preface

The 1950s have long been eulogized as a period of tranquillity, stability, and general satisfaction with life. So it was in the world of baseball. Major League baseball, with a few exceptions, revolved around the Northeast, and its successes centered on the city of New York. A World Series took place in Gotham in every year of the 1950–1960 period except 1959, and that season's champions, the Dodgers, had been residents of Brooklyn as recently as 1957.

I have enjoyed baseball since my first encounter at Braves Field in Boston in 1950 at the age of seven. In those days, almost all of the games were played during the day, and teams did not draw fans like they do today. Attendance of a million fans annually was considered a bonanza and a very successful season. On sleepy August afternoons, the Braves and the Red Sox both opened their grandstands to Little Leaguers, figuring that the seats would go unused anyway, so they might as well sell some ice cream, peanuts, and souvenirs while providing thrills to the youngsters.

I remember buying a major league yearbook at that first game that was crammed with facts and statistics pertaining to the 1949 season. I loved the statistics so much that I begged a second-grade teacher to instruct me in long division even before I could properly subtract in order that I might compute batting averages. I also remember taking a ride with my father in late September of that

year and we listened to a rebroadcast of the Philadelphia Phillies–
Brooklyn Dodgers game in which Dick Sisler, Richie Ashburn, and
Robin Roberts brought the Phillies' fans their first flag in thirty-five
years. I recall my dad, a real Braves fan, becoming very excited as
the Dodgers were ousted from a return trip to the World Series.

My first significant media experience was listening to the 1951
Giants–Dodgers three-game playoff. I arrived home from school
just in time to catch the last few innings of each game, and believe
me, I was not disappointed. I had followed the miracle of Coogan's
Bluff through September in the now defunct evening *Boston Traveler*. I searched for the area in a map of New York City that I had
found at our home. It did not take me long to realize that Yankee
Stadium was a mere stone's throw across the Harlem River from
the historic Polo Grounds and that the Bronx was actually a place
where people lived. My knowledge of things pertaining to baseball
grew exponentially. My mother remarked more than once that if I
knew my lessons in history and geography like I knew the subjects
relative to baseball, she would have an "A" student on her hands
of whom she could be proud instead of a sports-statistics-spouting
preadolescent.

The 1952 season saw Ted Williams depart Boston for the
regions unknown in the western Pacific and 1953 brought him back
amid renewed hopes for a Red Sox resurgence after the Braves' shift
to Milwaukee. The Yankees won their fifth consecutive World Series
and we ten-year-olds from anywhere other than New York looked
forward to our favorites finishing second to Casey's Stenglemen.

The 1954 season brought a new type of slugger to Fenway Park
in the person of Jackie Jensen, a strong man who could perform in
the field and on the base paths as well as hit with power. However, I watched in awe as the Cleveland Indians took twenty-one of
twenty-two games from the Red Sox and then were swept away in
the World Series by the New York Giants with their clutch hitting,
great fielding, and good pitching. The Yankees and the Brooklyn
Dodgers were back in 1955 and 1956 and the Yanks looked good

in 1957, until the Milwaukee Braves express derailed them in game two of the World Series.

Wait a minute! At this point in our brief lives, when was the last time a team from other than New York City won a World Series game? It had last happened in 1948, when no team from the Big Apple appeared in the series. The facts showed that forty-six consecutive World Series games were played from 1949 to 1957 and no team wearing a uniform other than one representing the city won a game until the upstarts from Wisconsin in October 1957. In the two instances in which teams from outside the city made it into the fall classic during the period (the 1950 Philadelphia Phillies and the 1954 Cleveland Indians), they were swept away by the New York entry.

I had always been enamored of the 1954 Giants and their distinctive flash-in-the-pan status. This was a truly average team whose players jelled at the same time to collectively produce their finest performances and, sparked by the great Willie Mays, brought the borough of Manhattan its final world baseball triumph. This team, with its upset of the Indians in the fall classic, was named by *Sports Illustrated* in a special edition (1999) one of the top twenty teams of the century.

I had always wanted to be an author of something other than a term paper so I began to ponder players who, like the occasional team, rose above all for one shining moment as a sort of phoenix. The Giants roster contained a number of players who truly experienced that one glorious season . . . Johnny Antonelli, Don Mueller, and Ruben Gomez, to name just three. I settled on Dusty Rhodes, as he truly shone then as never before and never would again. I tried to limit my work to the pre-expansion period of 1950 to 1960, which I knew best. There would be no Hall of Famers or any Rookies of the Year. In order to gather perspective of the respective feats, I put together a brief history of each team leading up to *that one glorious season.*

The process then got easier: Jim Konstanty and the 1950 Phillies Whiz Kids, twenty-game-winner Ned Garver of the last-place

1951 Browns, MVPs Shantz and Sauer of the 1952 Athletics and Cubs, respectively, and Al Rosen with his huge year for the Indians in 1953. These were easy choices. Rhodes took the honors for 1954, but 1955 proved to be difficult.

I decided to use Vic Power's 1955 season. Power never played a game with the New York Yankees but had been the first man of color signed by the Bronx Bombers. He was peddled to the Athletics prior to the 1954 season amid much controversy among the Yankee faithful. He finished second to Al Kaline in batting in 1955, hitting .319 for the newly transplanted team in Kansas City. I could use him for the short Yankees history and easily follow him to KC. Don Newcombe, of the Dodgers, was a foregone choice in 1956 with his 27-7 record and his MVP, which went along with the first-ever Cy Young Award. Lew Burdette of the 1957 world champion Braves, MVP winner Jackie Jensen of the 1958 Red Sox, Bob Shaw of the 1959 White Sox flag winners, and the 1960 Pirates MVP Dick Groat rounded out the decade.

I had players from twelve teams with the finest displays of their lives. Why not go for all sixteen? I was missing representatives from the Senators, Tigers, Cardinals, and Reds. Bob Porterfield went 22-10 in 1953 for Washington and was a key cog in their last .500 season before their departure for Minneapolis, while teammate Mickey Vernon beat out Al Rosen to collect his second bat crown. Harvey Kuenn won the American League batting championship crown for Detroit in 1959 prior to his departure for the Indians in exchange for home-run-king Rocky Colavito. Two to go . . . That left the Cardinals and the Reds.

The St. Louis Cardinals of the 1950s had Musial, Slaughter, and Schoendienst, all residents of Cooperstown. Ken Boyer? His greatest year in 1964, so no go. Harvey Haddix went 20-9 in 1953 but appeared in seven games in 1952. Was he a rookie? The powers of baseball said no and Jim Gilliam of Brooklyn took those honors in 1953. Thinking about it, Harvey Haddix, as a member of the Pittsburgh Pirates in 1959, pitched the finest game ever thrown in the history of baseball and lost it. He has always sparked a lot of interest among fans and writers.

What about the Reds? In 1956, they had come from nowhere to make a three-way race against the Dodgers and the Braves, powered by Ted Kluszewski and company. They also won the last 154-game pennant in history in 1961 and were paced on the mound by Joey Jay with his twenty-one wins. Why not?

I then decided to add a few players as they enjoyed their finest performances and complemented the primary subject. Del Ennis, John Antonelli, Vern Law, and Jim O'Toole were added to the flag winners in 1950, 1954, 1960, and 1961. Mickey Vernon joined Porterfield in the Senators' last decent season, in 1953.

The big difference in baseball then and baseball now besides the high salaries and pampered egos was that the majority of games were played during the day, pitchers aimed to complete their starts, and the doubleheader was a Sunday staple. The length of the games today is tied directly to the media and the necessity to pay their bills. Ned Garver pitched a 10-9 complete game in 1951 in two and a half hours. The players seemed to have fun, and time between innings was not dictated by network whims. The owners and management were shown the way by such diverse personalities as Branch Rickey and Bill Veeck. The absence of specialists and the expansion of the pitching staff plus the experiment called the designated hitter have changed the game, and not necessarily for the better. How many Hall of Famers have made it aided by longevity and batting statistics gathered while not having duty in the field?

So much for editorials. I have enjoyed doing the research for the book. I have tried to send each player a copy of his essay in order to catch any omissions and/or errors. Mrs. Jim Konstanty sent back a copy full of red marks. Dusty Rhodes sat with me for a few hours and was quite gracious. He encouraged me to get on with the project "because we ain't gettin' any younger." Bob Shaw welcomed me into his office and was very helpful in my getting his piece right. I had the pleasure of spending time on the phone with

Ned Garver, Hank and Jeanne Sauer, Al Rosen, Katharine Jensen, and Mary Konstanty, all of whom were of great assistance.

Please enjoy reading it as much as I loved putting it together.

1

*1950: J*IM *K*ONSTANTY *& D*EL *E*NNIS

P*HILADELPHIA* P*HILLIES*

One day before the start of the 1950 World Series, at Shibe Park in Philadelphia, a photographer assembled four pitchers, starters all, for a pre-series photo. One of the four, either future Hall of Famer Robin Roberts, Bubba Church, or Ken Heintzelman and Russ Meyer, both veterans, would start the opening game against the American League champion New York Yankees. But who? Then, from out of the blue, came a startling announcement. Jim Konstanty, baseball's best relief pitcher, who had started nary a game in more than four years, would open the series for the Philadelphia Phillies, champions of the National League.

The tall, bespectacled right-hander stood on the mound on that warm Wednesday afternoon, October 4, 1950. It was the first game of the World Series and Konstanty was indeed warming up for the home team. Most people thought Jim Konstanty was the premier reliever in the early fifties and perhaps the primary reason that the

Phillies were in the series. Yes, he was all of that, but his team had barely squeaked out a pennant against the hard-charging Brooklyn Dodgers on the last day of the season. The starting pitchers were dog-tired. Roberts had started three games during the last five days of the season and pitched the ten-inning pennant clincher on the final day, beating the Dodgers at Ebbets Field for his twentieth win of the season. Church had faded late in the campaign. Heintzelman and Meyer showed their age.

Konstanty wound up on the short end of a 1-0 shutout at the hands of Yankees right-hander Vic Raschi. Konstanty toiled eight innings that day, giving up just five base hits. The Yankees' lone run was the result of a fourth-inning double by Bobby Brown and two long fly balls. Jim went on to pitch in three of the four games, solidifying his reputation as one of that year's best pitchers.

It was reminiscent of an earlier October day, in 1929, when another surprise Philadelphia starter, Howard Ehmke of Connie Mack's powerful Athletics, faced the Chicago Cubs in the first game of that year's classic. The results were similar, yet distinctly different. Ehmke gave up eight hits but won his start, striking out a then series record thirteen batters along the way.

The Yankees swept the Phillies in the series but that did not diminish the accomplishments of the 1950 squad, nicknamed the Whiz Kids. As recently as 1948, the Phils had finished in the second division, a position very familiar to the club. In 1949, they surprised the sports world by reaching third place for their highest finish since 1917. The team took thirty-two of its last fifty-six games to edge the 1948 champion Braves for the third slot by six games. It was only the eleventh time the Phillies had finished above fifth place in the previous fifty years.

The Phillies' turnaround had its roots set during the throes of World War II. In early 1943, after the last of five consecutive cellar finishes, the league took over the franchise and sold controlling interest to a New Yorker named William Cox. Cox seemed unaware that gambling, particularly on your own team, was less than enthusiastically condoned by the powers of major league baseball. When his misdeeds were exposed, he was promptly relieved of his parcel of the Phillies and subsequently barred from baseball.

While rumors abounded that Bill Veeck wanted to purchase the team, baseball commissioner Kennesaw Mountain Landis quietly put greasy skids under that transaction. Veeck, who would earn fame as one of the sports world's most innovative entertainers, let it be known that he intended to stock the team with some of the Negro Leagues' brightest stars. Landis apparently feared that the quality of Veeck's players could turn the sport on its ear. He did not allow the deal and brought in his own candidate for ownership.

Robert M. Carpenter, an heir to a portion of the du Pont fortune, purchased Cox's interest. He promptly turned over the team to his twenty-eight-year-old son, who had been quite an athlete in his own right. Young Bob Carpenter had played on Duke University's Rose Bowl entry and also pitched on the school's baseball team. He recognized that he was a novice in the sports business, so his first move was to hire Herb Pennock, the former Red Sox and Yankee pitcher and future Hall of Famer, as his general manager.

Prior to the arrival of the Carpenter family, the Phillies were known to be a supermarket for ballplayers at good prices. The perennially cash-poor Phillies management was always happy to make a deal for one of the few good players to grace the home field, particularly in exchange for cash. Only two of the Phillies' outstanding players, outfielders Chuck Klein and Cy Williams, retired in Philadelphia. Klein, perhaps the finest pre-1950 Phillie, was sold twice prior to his final stint in Philadelphia.

Pennock, who served as a Red Sox coach and administered its minor league system, quickly changed the Phillies' way of doing things. His observations, while a player in the 1920s, of the descent of the Red Sox and the emergence of the Yankees transcended into policy under Bob Carpenter. The Phils now sought quality players and did not generate working capital by offering them at a tag sale. They shocked the baseball world in 1947 when they bid against virtually every other team for the services of Curt Simmons, a left-handed high school pitching sensation. What's more, they signed him for $65,000, a record at that time. The following year they signed right-handed pitcher Robin Roberts. The team also began to get serious about developing a farm system and made other acquisitions of legitimate major leaguers.

The Signing of Del Ennis

Though Pennock installed discipline and determination into the development of the team, an important acquisition was made just before his arrival, that of outfielder Del Ennis.

Ennis grew up in Philadelphia and was playing baseball for the Olney High School team in 1941 when Phillies scout Jocko Collins traveled to the school to observe a young pitcher. He got sidetracked, however, watching Ennis powder the ball all over the field. Del, at sixteen years old, already exceeded 180 pounds and stood six feet tall, with the build of the fullback he was during the gridiron season. Collins forgot about the pitcher and made an effort to get to Ennis after the game. He asked if Del would like to play for the Phillies. Ennis, with an amazing degree of modesty, didn't feel his skill level warranted that kind of attention. Perhaps he just didn't want to associate with the Phillies, given their history through 1942. In any event, his father convinced him to graduate before considering any move into baseball. The Phillies agreed, and he stayed in school.

Ennis graduated from high school and, true to his word, signed with his hometown team. The club assigned him to its Class D squad in the Canadian-American League for the 1943 season; before he reported, however, the league disbanded. The Phillies then reassigned him to their Trenton team in the Class B Interstate League. He proceeded to rip apart the circuit, batting .346 with eighteen homers and ninety-three RBI. He entered the Navy immediately after the season and spent 1944 and 1945 in the service. In the military, he played ball against the likes of Johnny Vander Meer, Virgil Trucks, and Hall of Famers Billy Herman and Johnny Mize.

Like many other young Americans, Del Ennis left the service in late 1945. He ventured to a big-league spring-training camp in the spring of 1946. Ben Chapman, manager of the Phillies, liked what he saw in the twenty-year-old outfielder and kept him on the parent squad. Del batted .313 with seventeen home runs and seventy-three RBI. The *Sporting News* named him Rookie of the Year. He excited the fans of the City of Brotherly Love as no outfielder had since the days of Chuck Klein.

As Del Ennis experienced the limelight of major league stardom, the Phillies continued to seek out quality players in search of respectability. They acquired the services of Jim Konstanty in 1946. Konstanty, a 1939 graduate of Syracuse University, had signed a minor league contract with the Syracuse Chiefs, who promptly sent him to Springfield, Massachusetts, where he toiled in the Eastern League, leading the circuit in losses. Konstanty was primarily a starter and pitched so unconvincingly that he considered returning to education and utilizing his degree in physical education as a coach. He stuck with baseball, however, and in 1944, his performance continued to improve.

The Cincinnati Reds, so desperate for pitching that year that they signed a fifteen-year-old schoolboy named Joe Nuxhall, purchased his contract. Jim started twelve games with the parent club, worked in twenty, and posted a creditable 6-4 record with a 2.80 ERA. After a year in the service, he attended the Reds' spring-training camp in 1946 and was traded to the Boston Braves on the trip north. The Braves were a struggling young team stocked with enough potential that they would win a league championship in 1948. Manager Billy Southworth had to make a decision between Konstanty and a left-hander named Warren Spahn. He chose Spahn, who went on to a Hall of Fame career. Konstanty was subsequently reassigned to Toronto, of the International League. He was once again considering calling it quits and heading back to the classroom, but he decided to take one more shot at the big leagues.

The Undertaker and the Mystery Pitch

During the off-season, Konstanty coached at Westfield Central School and at Worcester New York Central School. He had a student catch for him as spring approached each year. In early 1947, Jim went to look up his battery mate and discovered he had graduated the previous spring. He asked a local undertaker, Andy Skinner, to be his receiver. Although the two men had been acquaintances for a number of years and Skinner was a baseball fan, Andy had not really played much baseball.[1]

Konstanty began to throw his assortment of pitches, a curve here, a fastball there, but nothing consistent. The fastball was slow and the curves barely broke. On occasion, however, a curve would get by Andy with no explanation from Jim. After many pitches and an analysis of each, the two men determined that Jim gripped the ball in a slightly different manner, providing the ball with additional movement. He threw it overhand, similar to a fastball, but it broke away nicely. It became his slider, a pitch upon which he came to depend.

Whatever it was, the slider, palmball, or sinker joined the rest of Konstanty's assortment of pitches and he headed to Toronto and the International League to give his career one last chance. He prided himself on his control, the result of his dogged perseverance.

He persisted for one more season and finished 13-13 and was encouraged to try again. Toronto had become an affiliate of the Phillies in 1948 and Eddie Sawyer held the team manager position. Jim continued at a .500 (10-10) pace, but he proved to be consistent and reliable. Sawyer liked the slow curves, sinkers, and sliders that Konstanty brought with him to the mound.

Bob Carpenter was grooming Sawyer to be the next manager of the Phillies. His assignments included an analysis of the budding youngsters on the farm and to develop relief pitching. Konstanty became the answer to his bullpen needs. While at Toronto, Sawyer instructed Jim to warm up during every game. The big New Yorker would diligently get up, pitch, and sit down when not needed. He informed Sawyer that he felt he would injure his arm with a daily, vigorous workout. Eddie insisted on the routine but let Konstanty

---

1. *Sport Magazine*, May 1951, 19. "Jim Konstanty, All-Time Fireman," by Andy Duncan.

work at his own pace. Jim followed orders, sort of. He never complained but got up, began throwing at a leisurely pace, and watched the game between pitches. He developed an uncanny sense as to when a starter was faltering and instinctively would pick up his warm-up routine. He always stayed mentally in the game, and he could be ready in just a few moments. Powered by Ennis, the Phils finished a surprising fifth in 1946 but slumped back to seventh in 1947. Ennis tailed off in 1947, dropping to .275, but managed to drive in eighty-one runs. The team appeared to be heading for familiar territory in 1948 when Carpenter fired manager Ben Chapman halfway through the season and replaced him with Eddie Sawyer.

The two men's styles could not have been more different. Chapman was brash, rude, and impatient; Sawyer was scholarly and soft-spoken. Sawyer did his disciplining in private and usually did it by making a point. He was blessed with a remarkable memory and often taught by recalling a similar incident and elaborating from there. His goal was to manage ballplayers who could think on their feet and learn from their mistakes. Ennis responded to the managerial change with thirty homers to go with his ninety-five RBI.

The remainder of 1948 was not an instant turnaround for Sawyer and his ballplayers. However, the seeds of success had been sown. A nucleus of very young players had been formed, hence the moniker Whiz Kids. (The team was nicknamed after a late-1940s radio show *Quiz Kids*, in which smart children answered difficult questions.)

The 1949 season gave Sawyer a chance to assemble his troops and give them some necessary experience before the race of 1950. Ennis complemented his fine 1948 performance with twenty-five home runs. He had been joined in the outfield in that year by Richie Ashburn, a speedy leadoff man who also provided great defense. The catching was spearheaded by power-hitting Andy Seminick. The infield learned to play together and operated like a fine-tuned instrument. Veteran pitchers Ken Heintzelman and Russ Meyer both produced seventeen victories. The Phils had had only one other seventeen-game winner since 1934. Youngsters Roberts and Simmons added fifteen and four victories, respectively. Sawyer led them into third place with an 81-73 record.

After Sawyer had moved up to the Phillies in mid-1948, he brought along Konstanty late in the season. Jim appeared in six games, all in relief. Sawyer continued to work with the big junk-baller, and in 1949 Konstanty appeared in fifty-three contests. The two-hundred-pound right-hander responded with a 9-5 record, an earned run average of 3.25, and seven saves in the Phils' first winning season in thirty-two years. He helped set the table for one of the most exciting seasons in National League history.

The most bizarre event of 1949, however, happened off the field. Slick-fielding first baseman Eddie Waitkus was hitting .306 after fifty-four games when he was shot in a Chicago hotel by an ardent, but deranged, female fan. He sat out the remainder of that season and was replaced by Dick Sisler. He recovered fully in time to play every game of the season at first base and hit .284 for the 1950 Phillies. Bernard Malamud based his book *The Natural* on Waitkus's unusual experience.

The long-suffering fans of Philadelphia were not prepared for that magical 1950 pennant race. In the forty-seven baseball seasons from 1902 through 1948, the Philadelphia Phillies clearly laid claim as the worst team in the National League. They finished first once, in 1915, and achieved the first division during just ten other seasons.

1950: The Philadelphia Phillies' Whiz Kids

The 1950 pennant race began with the Phillies picked to finish fourth by the writers polled by the Associated Press. The team possessed an overall abundance of youth and exuberance and truly felt that it could take it all. Arthur Daley predicted in his Sunday column in the *New York Times* just prior to opening day that the Phillies would finish second behind Brooklyn, only because they were "too young to win it all."

The Whiz Kids' infield averaged twenty-six years of age and the number stood that high only because first baseman Eddie Waitkus turned thirty-one during that hectic September. Mike Goliat and Willie "Puddin' Head" Jones, the regular second and third basemen, respectively, were but twenty-five years old; Granny Hamner, the hustling shortstop, was only twenty-three.

The outfield of Ennis, Ashburn, and Dick Sisler, all under thirty, provided top-notch defense as well a balanced offense and experience. At their tender ages, Ashburn and Ennis were starting their third and fifth big-league seasons, respectively.

The ages of the pitching staff starters ranged from Simmons at twenty-one to ace Roberts at twenty-three. As noted, there also existed a thirty-three-year-old in this sea of babes. Jim Konstanty became the reliever of relievers in 1950, and an unlikely predecessor to the modern mop-up man.

They opened at home and won, perhaps a portent of things to come. Roberts beat Brooklyn Dodgers ace Don Newcombe 9-1. The next day Konstanty made his first appearance of the season and pitched the last two innings in a 7-5 loss to Brooklyn.

At the same time, Mildred "Babe" Didrikson Zaharias won the first stage of the women's transcontinental Weathervane series at Pebble Beach with a 158 for thirty-six holes. The tourney consisted of a total of 144 holes at four courses spread across the country and ending at White Plains, New York. The prize to the ultimate victor would be five thousand dollars.

The Phillies stayed with the pack through April, playing .500 baseball and in early May found themselves at the top of the National League. By the first weekend in May they had improved to 11-8 and trailed the Dodgers by half a game. Roberts and Simmons combined for five wins while Konstanty had appeared in seven games.

At the Kentucky Derby on May 6, Middleground, an 8-1 shot, took the classic ridden by an eighteen-year-old apprentice named Bill Boland. Hill Prince, the favorite, pulled in at second place, a scant one and a quarter lengths behind. Two weeks later, Hill Prince turned the tables on Middleground at the Preakness, winning by five lengths in a six-horse shootout.

On May 7, in a widely followed PGA tourney, Ben Hogan scored a twenty-one-under-par 259 for seventy-two holes, taking the Greenbriar

Open in White Sulphur Springs, West Virginia, by ten strokes over Sam Snead. Hogan thus took his first tourney victory since a near fatal auto accident in February 1948. His prize amounted to $1,250.

On May 10, Philadelphia backed into undisputed possession of first place when Cincinnati defeated Brooklyn and the Phils were rained out in Pittsburgh. The next day, when the showers ended, Roberts took the mound and beat the Pirates 3-2. Puddin' Head Jones supplied all the runs with a first-inning, three-run round-tripper.

The Phils completed a successful 7-2 road trip and returned to the friendly confines of Shibe Park, taking the first of a series with the New York Giants, 7-1, behind Simmons as Ennis and Sisler poked home runs. On Sunday, May 14, they split a doubleheader with the Giants, with the second game called due to the Pennsylvania Sunday curfew. Bobby Thomson powered the Giants with a home run in the opener to snap the Phils' six-game win streak. Konstanty relieved Ken Heintzelman in that game after seven innings and allowed nothing to New York. After Roberts beat the Reds 1-0 for his fifth win, there were two days of rain and the Cubs then came into Philadelphia.

The Phils lost to the Cubs and thus allowed the Dodgers to retake first place, as they beat the Pirates twice. In the split of a Sunday twin bill, Philadelphia lost the opener to the St. Louis Cardinals. Konstanty mopped up after Roberts suffered a shelling in a mere two and two-thirds innings in a 6-5 loss.

Later that week, the Phillies toppled the Pittsburgh Pirates with a six-run, late-inning rally at Philadelphia. Konstanty relieved Bubba Church in the eighth inning and was the beneficiary of the scoring outburst, winning his second game.

In New York on May 27, a day after Roberts beat the Giants 3-2 by driving in the go-ahead run in the seventh inning, Konstanty preserved a Simmons victory when he came into the game with Alvin Dark and Thomson on base in the eighth. He gave up a run-producing single to Don Mueller and then got the last six batters to save Simmons's sixth success. In the first game of a doubleheader on Sunday, Jim pitched five innings of shutout one-hit relief as the

Phils scored three in the eleventh inning on Mike Goliat's three-run blast to win 5-2. Konstanty did not appear in the second game and the Giants prevailed 3-1. The Phils ended May with a 22-15 mark, a scant half game behind the Dodgers.

Konstanty again came to Simmons's rescue with a one-and-two-thirds-inning stint against the Cubs at Wrigley Field to start June in fine fashion. Ennis, who had recently returned from a brief layoff due to a leg injury, but leading the league with twenty-seven runs batted in, started a five-run rally in the second inning with a single.

Curt Simmons and Robin Roberts headed up the starting pitching for the Phillies. Both had shown great promise but were rough in many facets of their game. Arthur Daley, in his *Sports of the Times* column on Sunday, June 4, described how Sawyer recruited Benny Bengough, a former New York Yankees reserve catcher. Benny could reach into his memory and equate physiques and styles from the past with pitchers of the present. Bengough worked with the young pitchers and altered their deliveries to fit their physical makeup. He observed Simmons's herky-jerky motion and taught him the art of a graceful pivot similar to that of Earl Whitehill, a 218-game-winning left-hander who toiled mainly for Detroit and Washington. Roberts loved to tinker with various pitches, such as the slider and knuckleball. Bengough had him concentrate on his curve and blazing fastball, emphasizing his remarkable control. In addition, Bengough succeeded in slowing him down and controlling his impatience on the mound, having him work deliberately like Hall of Famer Lefty Grove.

Roberts apparently listened; he whipped the Cards 6-5, giving up thirteen hits on June 5 as the Phils took over second place, just behind the Dodgers. At the end of eight innings, the score was 3-2 in favor of the Phillies and Ennis appeared to ice the game with a three-run homer. The scrappy Cardinals put together three scores in the bottom of the frame, but came up a tally short. Two days later, rookie Bob Miller improved his record to 4-0, allowing the Reds only seven hits in a 4-0 blanking.

In the racing world, Boland and Middleground bounced back from their defeat at Pimlico to take the Belmont Stakes, with favorite Hill Prince a distant seventh. Meanwhile, old-timer Ben Hogan continued his remarkable comeback by taking the U.S. Open in a playoff with George Fazio and Lloyd Mangrum. Hogan won the playoff by four strokes with a sixty-nine.

After a loss to the Reds on the road, the Phillies were rained out for two games and then split a Sunday doubleheader with Pittsburgh at Forbes Field. Konstanty pitched a pair of frames in each outing and won his fourth game in relief of Robin Roberts in the opener.

While Philadelphia sat out rainy days and played even-up baseball, St. Louis went on a tear, and by midweek led the Dodgers by three. They visited Philadelphia and handed the Phils a 6-3 setback, sinking Simmons with a six-run sixth inning on June 13. The Redbirds took the next game 4-2 for their seventh in a row. Even Konstanty's scoreless inning and two-thirds could not stop the streaking Cardinals.

Two more rainouts and a Roberts complete-game victory over the Reds gave a boost to the Philadelphia mound corps. On Sunday, June 18, they swept the Reds behind Miller and Simmons. Ennis contributed home run number thirteen in the first game. After another soaker, Russ Meyer earned his first victory of 1950, defeating the Pirates 7-3 with help from Willie Jones's home run. Both Meyer and Ken Heintzelman had won seventeen games in 1949, but each had suffered six losses before tasting victory in 1950. Roberts then lost to the Bucs, so the Phils still trailed the Cards by a game and a half.

Over in the American League, on June 21, Joe DiMaggio became the eighty-eighth player in major league history to attain the two-thousand base hits milestone, nailing a single against the Indians in Cleveland.

On June 24, Konstanty came to the mound for the twenty-fourth time in fifty-six games, this time to save Meyer's second win. He entered the game in the sixth inning with the score 5-4 with two on and nobody out. Konstanty shut the door. Philadelphia stood at

33-23, one game behind Brooklyn. The Dodgers had just played a game that was suspended in the eighth inning because of the Saturday night–Sunday curfew with the football-sized score of 19-12. The game was scheduled to be completed on August 1.

The Phillies took over first place in Boston after a split with the Cubs. Konstanty preserved Simmons's ninth win with a hitless final two-thirds of an inning. The team then dropped two to the Braves, losing to Johnny Sain and Vern Bickford.

While the Phillies tangled with the Braves and got ready to travel to Brooklyn for a key series with the Dodgers, the United Nations Security Council found North Korea guilty of violating peace agreements with South Korea. President Harry Truman met with his top aides in Washington and June 27, 1950, and ordered the U.S. Army and Navy to the western Pacific to aid South Korea, putting General Douglas MacArthur in charge. The Korean conflict had begun, and would eventually have an impact on the 1950 National League pennant race.

June 1950 came to a close and the Phillies headed the pack in the National League with a very modest 36-26 record. On the last day of the month, in a key series with Brooklyn, Konstanty relieved in the sixth in a Newcombe–Roberts duel. The Phils got to Newk for twelve hits. Although Konstanty picked up the win, it was not one of his better outings. He gave up a go-ahead home run to Gil Hodges in the top of the eighth but the Phillies rallied for four to bail him out and secure the victory. That same day the Dodgers recalled an outfielder from their St. Paul affiliate, Cal Abrams. Abrams would play a key role in the theatrics of the season's finale.

The very next day, Konstanty came in again against Brooklyn, this time to preserve Bob Miller's seventh straight victory with two and a third innings of shutout relief. On Sunday, July 2, he made another appearance, in the nightcap of a twin bill, which was ultimately suspended due to the Pennsylvania curfews. On July 4, Konstanty proved he was not invincible, serving up a grand slam to the Boston Braves' Sid Gordon, and was saddled with the loss in a 12-9 downer.

The Phillies moved on to Brooklyn, where on July 7, Simmons won his tenth decision with a 7-2 complete game. Roberts and Newk went at it the following day. With the game tied 1-1, Sawyer pulled his ace after he gave up a leadoff single to Roy Campanella in the bottom of the eighth. Konstanty came in and shut down the Dodgers for the last six outs. Bill Nicholson, a veteran slugger who had made his mark with the Cubs in the 1940s, poled a three-run homer in the top of the ninth to win it for Konstanty. In the final game before the All-Star break, the Dodgers salvaged the last game of their series 7-3. The Phillies led the league by one game.

The National League took the All-Star Game 4-3, in a fourteen-inning thriller. Roberts got the start and was followed by Newcombe, with Konstanty appearing for an inning.

Championship play resumed on July 13, and the Phils beat the Cardinals 3-2 behind Simmons and solo home runs by Granny Hamner, Andy Seminick, and Dick Sisler. They then dropped a pair to the Cardinals, and then lost a twin bill to the Cubs in Chicago. At the exact midpoint of the campaign, the Philadelphia Phillies had a 45-32 record. Jim Konstanty had appeared in thirty-eight of the team's games, sporting a 7-4 mark.

On July 18, a three-way tie occurred when the Braves routed the Pirates to match the Cardinals and Phillies with identical 46-34 records, one and a half games ahead of Brooklyn. Over in the junior circuit, the Detroit Tigers held a three-and-one-half-game edge over the New York Yankees. The Phillies then split a doubleheader with Pittsburgh, with Konstanty appearing in both ends of the twin bill. He came in with one out in the ninth to save Simmons's twelfth win in the opener 3-2 and pitched the final frame in Meyer's 4-2 loss in the finale.

As July progressed, Sawyer constantly called upon Konstanty. Jim began to tire and picked up a few problems with his mechanics. Thus, down from upstate New York came his old off-season catcher, Andy Skinner, the undertaker. Andy and Jim worked on the slider and soon things were humming again.

After another split with the Pirates and a Saturday split in Cincinnati, the Phils swept the Reds on Sunday, July 23, behind Simmons and Meyer and regained the league lead. Two days later, they solidified that lead with a double-shutout sweep over the Chicago Cubs. Roberts took the nightcap 1-0 as Richie Ashburn singled home the winner in the bottom of the ninth; Church had prevailed in the opener, 7-0. They would not relinquish the top spot for the remainder of the season, although they came mighty close. The next day, Konstanty went the last three innings to preserve another win. With the Phils behind 4-0 in the bottom of the sixth, Del Ennis doubled home Eddie Waitkus to start a six-run rally.

Ennis, who had been driving in runs but struggled with his average, heated up at the right time. He drove in seven runs in a 13-3 win to nail down Simmons's fourteenth win, and the team went on to take four more. After a setback inflicted by the Pirates, they embarked on two more victories by sweeping the Bucs in a two-timer, 10-0 and 4-2. Ennis provided the margin in the second game with a two-run homer after poking a grand slam in the opener. Konstanty earned his eighth win with a pair of shutout innings in the nightcap. The Phils led the Cardinals by three games at the end of July, having won fifty-eight against thirty-nine losses.

The Phillies suffered from a severe lack of depth. The regulars other than catcher averaged 150 games played. Dick Sisler, son of Hall of Famer George, enjoyed his busiest season and played "only" 141 games. That was the fewest of all the everyday players. Mike Goliat appeared at second base for 145 games. This was the only year in his career in which he played regularly. The other three infielders, Waitkus, shortstop Granny Hamner, and third baseman Willie "Puddin' Head" Jones, all played the entire season. Ashburn and Ennis each appeared in more than 150 contests. Dick Whitman, a spare outfielder, saw the most reserve action, coming to bat 132 times in seventy-five games. Andy Seminick, the home-run-hitting catcher, required the most relief. He caught in 124 games, whereas Stan Lopata saw action behind the plate in fifty-one contests.

On July 31, Curt Simmons received notice that his military unit would be called up because of the crisis in Korea. He had just finished a two-week stint with the group and had been granted a special pass to arrive in time to pitch the second game of a Tuesday doubleheader. The news must have disturbed him, as he lost to the Reds 4-1 after Miller and Konstanty nailed down a 6-4 win in the opener, with Ennis leading the way with a home run and three RBI. Del poked another dinger the next day as Church drove in the first run in a 2-0 whitewash of the Reds.

On August 4, Roberts matched Simmons, winning his fourteenth game over St. Louis, 4-2, with Ennis again pacing the offense with three hits, including a triple and two runs scored. The Phils followed that up with a victory over the Cards for their eleventh victory in thirteen games. Mike Goliat, who had been married in nearby Reading, Pennsylvania, the previous day, provided all the runs with a two-run shot in the fifth inning. Konstanty came in with one on and one out in the ninth to save Meyer's sixth win. After dropping a pair to the Cards in a Sunday twin bill, the Phils rallied to take the finale in the five-game set, 9-0, on Monday, August 7.

After a successful series in Brooklyn, the Phillies returned home to face the Giants, the hottest team in baseball. Konstanty gained win number nine when he arrived in the eighth inning of a tie game, which was decided in the tenth, 6-5, when Hamner scored on Seminick's single. The Phils split the next two games. Konstanty went the final four innings for his tenth win on August 12. He came in to start the seventh inning and stuck around for the 5-4 decision. Stan Lopata, who smashed a triple in the eleventh, came home on Waitkus's sacrifice fly. After a Sunday loss to the New Yorkers to split the series, the Phils remained five games up on the Braves. Over in the American League, the Tigers retained a three-and-a-half-game spread over the Yankees.

The second-place Braves arived in the City of Brotherly Love and in the first of two, Konstanty came into the contest with one out in the ninth to preserve Curt Simmons's fifteenth win. The next day, Ennis propelled a home run to ease the way for Roberts to get win number sixteen, a 5-1 victory over Vern Bickford, who had no-hit the Dodgers in his previous start.

After Brooklyn swept a twin bill from New York to climb back into second, the Phillies traveled to the Polo Grounds in northern Manhattan. The Giants were all over Meyer in the first game of the series, but after a rainout, Simmons notched his sixteenth win with a four-hit, 4-0 shutout.

While the Phillies were in New York, Henry Fonda appeared as Lt (jg) Doug Roberts for the one-thousandth time in the Broadway hit Mr. Roberts. *Fonda had not missed a single performance and seemed to be the Great White Way's answer to the durable Konstanty.*

On August 23, Konstanty saved Bob Miller's eleventh win, a 6-4 squeaker over Cincinnati. Jim came in with two on and two out in the ninth and induced Joe Adcock to fly out to end the game. The next day, Simmons started against the Pirates at Forbes Field. He lasted until the fifth inning, and in the seventh Jim Konstanty trudged to the mound with the score 6-6. The Phils went on to win in the fifteenth, 9-7, and Konstanty was still on the mound, emerging as the victor. The one run he gave up was a solo home run by Ralph Kiner after the Phils had gone ahead by one in the visitors' half of the inning. In the top of the fifteenth, he was at the plate with Puddin' Head Jones on third. Cliff Chambers, on in relief for the last-place Pirates, uncorked a wild pitch and Jones rushed home as Hamner hustled over to third base. Hamner then scored on Konstanty's timely single with an insurance run.

Konstanty made his fifty-sixth appearance against the Cubs in Chicago on August 27 and preserved a 4-4 tie in a game that was called on account of darkness. He pitched three and two-thirds innings of no-hit ball. The next day the two teams split a double-header, with Konstanty coming in with one out in the fifth with the score 5-5. He remained until the game was finished, and in the seventh, Ennis got things going with a single. He also slammed a two-run homer to pace the 9-5 win.

The team's next stop was St. Louis, where Konstanty saved Roberts's eighteenth win. He came on in the ninth with the score

5-3 and two runners on and promptly slammed the door shut. Stan Musial had gone three for four and was leading the league in batting with a .359 mark, second in the majors only to the Red Sox's Billy Goodman's .374. That same day, Don Newcombe took his fifteenth victory, 8-2 over the Cubs.

In the meantime, Althea Gibson became the first African-American to play in the U.S. Lawn Tennis Association championships at the West Side Tennis Club in the Forest Hills section of Queens, New York. She impressed her followers but lost to Louise Brough in the final.

The Phils ended August on a sort of reversal. Konstanty, in his usual role of reliever, ran into difficulty against the Cardinals. Curt Simmons came to his rescue after Jim gave up two runs in the eighth inning. That broke a streak in which Konstanty gave up but one run, the homer by Kiner on August 25, in his previous forty-two and a third innings. The Phillies entered September at 78-47, up by five and a half games. Del Ennis had driven in forty-one runs during August as the Phillies went 20-8 that month and increased their lead by two and a half games. Meanwhile, the Yankees took over the lead in the American League with a doubleheader sweep of the Cleveland Indians.

On September 2, Simmons secured his seventeenth win, shutting out the Braves while Newcombe kept the Dodgers within striking distance of Philadelphia with win number sixteen. After a rainout in Boston, the team flew home, and more than 30,000 fans greeted them at Philadelphia's International Airport. Eddie Sawyer addressed the crowd and thanked them profusely. He also reminded them that the season was not yet over and that they had serious work to do. Sawyer's words would prove to be prophetic. The red-hot Giants put a damper on the celebration with a double whitewash, beating Roberts and Miller. The Dodgers followed up with another sweep but the Phils' lead remained at five and a half games. Sawyer called on Konstanty in both games against Brooklyn. Jim took the loss in the nightcap as he gave up three runs in the top of the ninth and the Phillies squandered a 2-0 lead. Roberts lost the next game but this time Meyer halted the slide, going the route and beating Brooklyn 4-3.

The Phils then took on Boston, and Jones ended a two-for-twenty-seven drought with the game winner in the ninth to beat the Braves 7-6 on September 9. Johnny Sain got the Braves even in the series with his eighteenth win, beating Church 3-1. Roberts then won his nineteenth with a 1-0 complete-game victory over the Cubs, and on September 12, the Phils went back up by six and a half games. In the American League, the Tigers clung to a half-game lead over the Yankees as Fred Hutchinson won his sixteenth.

On September 10, Phils ace lefty Curt Simmons left for military duty. Curt was on his way to Germany and was lost for the remainder of the season. He was 17-8 at that time and had been in and out of the Army throughout the season, missing four starts to this point. He would miss at least four more, putting additional pressure on an already drained pitching staff.

The Phils' lack of depth had really begun to show. Bubba Church, the twenty-four-year-old right-hander, who contributed eight clutch victories to the cause, was struck in the face by a line drive off the bat of Cincinnati Reds slugger Ted Kluszewski. Bubba was out of commission for a week, adding to Sawyer's pitching woes.

On the evening of September 15, the Phils took the field against the Reds for a twi-night doubleheader. They won the first 2-1, and with the score 5-5 after eight frames in the nightcap, Konstanty came in and pitched the next ten innings. He gave up two runs in the top of the eighteenth on a Ted Kluszewski single. In the bottom of that frame, Del Ennis doubled and Dick Sisler singled and both later scored. Ennis, who went five for thirteen in the two games, drove in the winner the next inning. The Phillies sported a seven-and-a-half game lead with fifteen to go. Ewell Blackwell shut out the Phils 2-0 the next day, but no damage was done as Brooklyn also lost.

The Pirates came to town and Konstanty came in to mop up and preserve Russ Meyer's ninth win, 5-3. Granny Hamner led the way with a three-run blast. The Braves inched into second place when Spahn won his twentieth game and the Dodgers lost to the

Cubs. However, on September 19, the Dodgers swept the ever-handy Pirates while Hank Sauer of the Cubs beat Roberts 1-0 with a home run in the top of the fifth. The next day Konstanty came in for his sixty-eighth appearance, this time in the sixth inning with the score tied 4-4. He earned his sixteenth win of 1950 as Mike Goliat hit a two-run homer in the bottom of the eighth, his second of the game, to provide the winning runs in a 9-6 game.

The Dodgers then arrived and once more it was Don Newcombe versus Robin Roberts. Both pitchers wound up with 19-10 records as Newk bested Roberts in a 3-2 game. The Dodgers then clobbered the Phillies 11-0, but the Whiz Kids still led Brooklyn by five games, with only nine contests left.

The Phillies traveled to Boston and split a doubleheader on September 25. Konstanty went three and two-thirds innings in the nightcap but suffered his sixth setback as opposing pitcher Max Surkont drove in the winning run to beat him 5-3. The next day, Ennis hit a three-run homer in the top of the seventh to make the score 5-2 in a 7-6 victory. Konstanty was obviously feeling the strain of a long season, giving up three hits in two-thirds of an inning in that game. The Phillies hung on to win. Brooklyn also won but Philadelphia maintained a five-game lead with only seven games left to play. But hold on, folks. The season was not yet over!

The three-game series at Braves Field in Boston had brought two victories in three tries for the Phillies and a bit of breathing room. The train ride south to New York was extremely tense as their next opponent was the Giants, a team whose record since the All-Star break surpassed that of all other teams in the majors. Adding pressure, two consecutive doubleheaders made up the series schedule. The Giants swept all four games from the dog-tired Phils. The Phillies did not lose easily to the Polo Grounders; three of the games were decided by two runs or less. Konstanty gave up a single to Al Dark in the bottom of the tenth to lose the first game 8-7. Robin Roberts then suffered a tough loss to Sheldon Jones, 3-1, on Whitey Lockman's bloop single. Roberts had let a fastball get away and Lockman merely ducked, trying to avoid the errant pitch, and poked it into the outfield, scoring two runs.

In the meantime, the Dodgers split a doubleheader with the now eliminated Braves, and Philadelphia had backed into at least a tie for the flag. On September 29, an off day for the Phils, Brooklyn took two more from Boston and headed home to meet the Phillies for the season's final two. The lead was down to two games with two to play . . . against the Dodgers . . . at Ebbets Field . . . in Brooklyn. The Dodgers needed to win both, and given their momentum and the lackluster performance of the Phillies in recent weeks, the Whiz Kids were nobody's favorites. They had lost seven of their last nine games while the Dodgers had roared to twelve wins in their last fifteen outings. This was the most crucial two-game series in Philadelphia Phillies history. On the road, no less, and, to repeat, at very unfriendly Ebbets Field in Brooklyn.

Miller started the Saturday contest, which soon evolved into a no-contest as Duke Snider and Roy Campanella struck for home runs en route to a 7-3 victory. The Phils' lead had shrunk to one game with one to go. A Dodger victory would result in a tie and force a playoff. Sawyer chose Robin Roberts to start the finale; Burt Shotton, the Dodger manager, decided on Don Newcombe. Both pitchers sought their twentieth victory.

Roberts took the mound, starting his fourth game in Philadelphia's last eight; he was going to work on two days' rest. This was his sixth attempt to pick up win number twenty. He had pitched magnificently, but his teammates had given him scant support. Sawyer's rationale in giving Roberts the ball centered on the right-hander's superb control and that he had thrown few pitches. In 1950, Robin pitched 304 innings, walking only seventy-six. It was the first of six consecutive seasons in which he won more than twenty games and pitched three-hundred-plus innings in each. Over that span he won 138 games, exhibiting extraordinary control. In 1952, for example, he appeared in 330 innings, walking forty-five batters on his way to twenty-eight victories.

On a beautiful early-autumn Sunday, on October 1, 1950, the teams matched each other for five scoreless innings. The Phillies scored first in the sixth but the Dodgers countered in the bottom of the inning. The score remained 1-1 to the ninth when the Phillies went down in the top half of the inning. In the Dodger half, rookie Cal Abrams led off with a walk and Pee Wee Reese singled with Abrams stopping at second. Duke Snider hit a scorcher to center, but Richie Ashburn, playing dangerously close to the infield with a slugger like Snider at the plate, handled it perfectly on one hop. He fired the ball to the plate and Abrams was out by fifteen feet, Lopata applying the tag. Roberts was out of one jam, but with first base open, he walked Jackie Robinson intentionally before getting Carl Furillo on a pop-up and Gil Hodges on an outfield fly.

Roberts, a good hitting pitcher, led off the top of the tenth with a single. First baseman Waitkus then blooped a Texas leaguer into center with Roberts holding at second. Ashburn attempted to sacrifice, but Roberts was forced at third. Dick Sisler came up. He already had three singles for the day. The count went to 1-2 when Sisler hit a fastball to left with enough on it for the ball to make into the stands. Roberts set down the Dodgers in order in the bottom of the tenth, and the Phillies ended a thirty-five-year pennantless drought. They took the train home for the one-hundred-mile journey south, where 25,000 delirious fans awaited them at Philadelphia's Pennsylvania Station. Not surprising, the team led the National League in attendance with nearly 50 percent more trips through the turnstiles than in 1949.

Pitching proved to be the cornerstone of the Phillies' success. The team led the league in earned run average and saves. The staff walked the fewest runners in the league. Robin Roberts came through with the first of six consecutive twenty-victory, twenty-plus complete-game seasons. Roberts proved to be an iron man, particularly toward the end of the season.

Simmons and Roberts combined for 40 percent of the Phillies' ninety-one victories. Rookie Bob Miller started twenty-two games, completing seven and winning eleven. Another rookie,

Bubba Church, added eight victories and a 2.73 ERA to the equation, making up the remainder of the Phillies' big four. In eight succeeding seasons, Miller never reached ten victories again and Church was out of the majors by 1955.

The starting pitchers completed fifty-seven games, with Roberts and Simmons contributing twenty-one and eleven, respectively. In the remaining ninety-seven games, Konstanty appeared in seventy-four and hurled 152 innings. He won sixteen games and saved twenty-two, then a National League record. The entire circuit recorded only 135 saves, and Konstanty owned 16 percent of them.

The save did not become an official part of baseball's statistics until 1969. The complete game was still the objective of the starter. In 1950, major league pitchers finished more than 40 percent of all starts. Konstanty was the middleman, long man, and the closer all wrapped into one during the Philadelphia Phillies' dream year, but few recognized his importance until the pressure began to build. As interest in the Phils' success heightened, a local tabloid began to highlight a player a day. Jim's picture and stories about him appeared more often as his consistent performances helped the Phillies cause. According to Mary Konstanty, Jim's widow, one day before a game, the wife of a regular was heard to say to another Phillie wife, "Why all the publicity about Jim Konstanty? Why, he's only a relief pitcher." [2]

Until then, relievers usually had starting experience behind them and were mopping up as their careers wound down. Prior to Jim Konstanty, relievers had had outstanding seasons, but none had been groomed for the job as he had been, nor did any other play such a singularly important role in the outcome of a pennant race. Konstanty made fans all over the country more aware of the necessity of a good relief pitcher as the Phillies captured the imagination of newfound fans everywhere. In the previous year, lefty Joe Page of the New York Yankees world champs appeared in sixty games and saved twenty-seven. Page was an important ingredient in that

---

2. Personal commmunication with Mary Konstanty, 1998.

team's efforts, but the Yankees had depth in their lineup and other support for their pitching. Those back-to-back seasons helped put the bullpen on the map as something other than a resting place for old and weary starters. Konstanty was an ideal man for the key position of overall reliever. His exercises and constant toil in the minors under the tutelage of Eddie Sawyer gave his arm a certain resiliency, and he reacted rapidly to an emergency on the field. He needed only about twenty pitches to be ready for duty and he and his inventory of do-nothing, no-speed pitches could be called upon with little notice.

Konstanty had a degree of confidence and a very unemotional personality as he approached the mound. He appeared to be unconcerned and sometimes so cool that he annoyed those around him. But in 1950, this detachment provided the impetus for a lot of wins for those hungry, eager Phillies. His control that season was nearly flawless. He walked fewer than three batters per nine innings, giving opponents scant opportunity to score free runs. At one point during the season he allowed no runs and just seven hits in twenty-two innings of relief. Konstanty was the ubiquitous fireman. His resilient arm and self-assurance made Sawyer's decisions as to whom to use in relief virtual no-brainers.

Konstanty finished that magical 1950 season with a 16-7 record, twenty-two saves, and a 2.66 ERA in a then record-setting seventy-four appearances, a mark that would stand until 1964. He was directly involved in thirty-eight of the Phils' ninety-one victories. He finished sixty-two of the seventy-four games he entered and usually did not require relief.

The Phillies won the pennant as a team, but the pitching got the press. However, the regular players responded with some of the best years of their careers. Ennis led the league with 126 RBI to go with his .311 batting average and thirty-one home runs. Puddin' Head Jones contributed twenty-five homers and he, Sisler, and Hamner all drove in more than eighty runs to complement Ennis. Ashburn batted .303 and led the circuit in triples with fourteen while pilfering fourteen bases. Sawyer provided good, quiet governance and usually made the right decisions.

As is the case with so many exciting pennant races, the World Series became anticlimactic. The Yankees swept the Phillies in four games, but that did not mean that Philadelphia was blown away. On the contrary. Each of the first three games was decided by one run, and the final game, in the Bronx at Yankee Stadium, was taken by the New Yorkers by a 5-2 margin. The two teams combined for a total of sixteen runs scored in the four games played. The Phillies batted .203 as a team and their staff allowed only 2.27 earned runs per game. The Yankees managed a .222 batting average but their pitchers held the opposition to a meager 0.73 earned run per game.

Konstanty appeared in three games, starting and losing the first, 1-0, going eight innings. He relieved in the third and fourth games. He enhanced his iron-man reputation as he pitched fifteen innings and gave up 2.40 runs per game during the World Series. He had not started a game in the major leagues since 1946 and would not start another until Sawyer became desperate in 1951. On November 8, he was elected the Most Valuable Player in the National League; Del Ennis finished fourth in the balloting.

In the glow of that magical season, the Phillies went to spring training the next year confident of a repeat performance. However, the persistent lack of depth and the shortage of good starting pitching to assist Roberts proved their undoing. They finished under .500, in fifth place, and never contended.

Jim Konstanty followed the team downward. He labored through a 4-11 season with only nine saves and a 4.05 ERA. He stayed with the Phillies through 1954, winning fourteen games in 1953. His position continued to be general relief although that year he started nineteen games. The New York Yankees purchased his contract in August 1954. He had been waived out of the National League within forty-eight hours of being put on the list by the Phillies. The Yankees were about to finish in a position other than head of the class for the first time since 1948. Ironically, they won 103 games, the most in the twelve-year reign of manager Casey Stengel. Konstanty appeared in only nine games for New York, going 1-1.

Konstanty proved to be one of Casey's famous late-season, National League veteran pickups. Following in the tradition of Johnny Sain and Johnny Mize, Jim provided the Yankees with experience and know-how. As was his habit, he worked at his own pace in the spring of 1955 and was in fine shape as the season began. His easy approach to pressure situations was reminiscent of the Whiz Kid days. This time, his team's talent extended deep into the dugout and he had help in the bullpen. He was joined by another righty, Tom Morgan, and they combined for twenty-one saves. Jim went 7-2, and allowed only 2.32 earned runs per game.

Konstanty did not appear in the 1955 World Series, the only championship won by the Brooklyn Dodgers in nine tries. A most unusual move prevented him from helping the Yankees in that series. On August 14, the Yankees recalled two pitchers, one of whom was Bob Grim, from the Richmond International League club, and to make room sent down Konstanty and Bobby Richardson. They were not recalled until September 6, rendering them ineligible for the World Series. Grim, the Rookie of the Year in 1954 with twenty victories, had struggled in 1955. Stengel hoped the minor league assignment would help rehabilitate him. Upon his return, however, someone had to go and that someone was Jim Konstanty. True to form, Jim went down with no complaints, appearing in eight games for Richmond.

Considering Konstanty's prior World Series performances and Richardson's MVP performance in the 1960 fall classic when he batted .367 with twelve runs batted in, it makes one wonder if the wrong players made it to the Yankees' series roster. But, then, Brooklyn fans needed one championship before being abandoned by Walter O'Malley for the golden hills of California.

As he approached forty years of age in 1956, Jim pitched briefly for the Yankees, and was dealt to the St. Louis Cardinals in mid-season. He appeared in twenty-seven games for them and went 1-1. This was the last stop in his major league career. Over the course of eleven seasons in the majors, he worked for three teams, posted a lifetime 66-48 record with an ERA of 3.46, and saved seventy-four games.

Konstanty had opened a retail outlet, Jim Konstanty's Sporting Goods, in Oneonta, New York, in 1947, when he seriously considered not returning to baseball. He also served as athletic director for nearby Hartwick College from 1967 through 1973. He did not coach, although he assisted with the baseball program. One of his pupils was Dave Lemanczyk, who went on to pitch in the American League. He considered all sports to be of equal importance but saw the coming of soccer as a major force in North America. He built a program that resulted in an eventual championship. He continued to be active in Oneonta, working with several civic organizations as well as the downtown retailers. Jim Konstanty developed liver cancer and died in June 1976 at the young age of fifty-nine.

His widow, Mary Konstanty, remained active in the business and later it was run by her daughter and son-in-law. They sold the store in 1990, but it remains in business to this day. I have been in contact with Mrs. Konstanty over the years and found her stories about the Whiz Kids so fascinating that I didn't want to let her off the phone. I would like to thank her for providing me with a number of fine anecdotes as well as a few grammatical corrections to this piece. I think she remembers that marvelous pennant race better than anyone else. But, then, she should, for her husband, Jim Konstanty, certainly enjoyed *that one glorious season.*

Del Ennis continued to knock in runs for the Phillies. He slumped with the rest of the team in 1951, struggling through his worst season, knocking home just seventy-three runs. He rebounded the following year with 107 RBI and followed up with 125 in 1953. In the 1951–56 stretch, he managed to knock in 639 runs, an average of 106 per season. In eleven full campaigns with Philadelphia, he drove in 1,124 runs. Prior to the start of the 1957 baseball season, the Cardinals traded outfielder Rip Ripulski and infielder Bobby Morgan to Philadelphia for Ennis. He did not disappoint, belting twenty-four homers while driving in 105 runs, complementing Stan

Musial and his 102 RBI. The Cards climbed from fourth to second and won eleven more games with his assistance.

Ennis faded quickly and retired from baseball in 1959. In a fourteen-year period he batted .284 with 288 home runs and 1,284 RBI. Ennis produced more homers and RBI than any other Phillie before the arrival of Mike Schmidt.

Ennis then ran Del Ennis Lanes, a bowling alley in Rockledge, Pennsylvania. He owned the facility with John Wise, former Phillies traveling secretary. Over the years Del dabbled with the horses. In the mid-1960s, he became a partner in the Shamrock Hill Farms stable of Lumberville, Pennsylvania. The trotters and pacers raced at Liberty Bell Raceway in Philadelphia and at Freehold in New Jersey.

Del Ennis became a fan favorite after his retirement. He happily signed autographs and refused payment for them. He had his detractors during his career and, like many heavy hitters, drew a chorus of boo-birds in the home stands. Still, he respected them and merely worked harder.

He died in February 1996 of complications from diabetes. For all his accomplishments and remarkable consistency in his decade-plus in the big leagues, no year could compare with Ennis's and his teammates' fabulous 1950 performance, certainly *that one glorious season.*

DEL ENNIS

Outfield—Philadelphia Phillies
Born: Philadelphia, Pa., June 8, 1925
Height: 6 ft.   Weight: 195
Bats: Right   Throws: Right

Big Del was the leading batter for the 1950 pennant winners, hitting .311 in 153 games. His 185 hits included 34 doubles, 8 triples and 31 homers. He paced the League in runs batted in with 126. Began in organized ball with Trenton, 1943. On Phils' roster, 1944-45, though in service. Hit .313 for Phils, 1946, first year in majors. Slumped to .275 in 1947. But batted .290 in 1948; .302 in 1949.

No. 4 in the 1951 SERIES

BASEBALL

PICTURE CARDS

©1951 Bowman Gum, Inc., Phila., Pa., U.S.A.

JIM KONSTANTY

Pitcher—Philadelphia Phillies
Born: Strykersville, N. Y., Mar. 3, 1917
Height: 6-1½   Weight: 195
Bats: Right   Throws: Right

Set a modern major league mark for pitchers in 1950 by appearing in 74 games. Set another mark by finishing 62. Won 16 and lost 7. Saved many games for the young Philadelphia pitching staff not shown in own record. Earned run average, 2.66. Voted the National League's most valuable player. In 3 World's Series games. Drew a starting assignment in one. Dropped heartbreaker.

No. 27 in the 1951 SERIES

BASEBALL

PICTURE CARDS

©1951 Bowman Gum, Inc., Phila., Pa., U.S.A.

2

1951: N*ED* G*ARVER*

S*T.* L*OUIS* B*ROWNS*

On Sunday, July 1, 1951, the St. Louis Browns took the field to play the Chicago White Sox at Chicago's Comiskey Park. The teams split a doubleheader. The White Sox won the first game 2-1 in eleven innings. In the nightcap, Browns right-hander Ned Garver held Chicago to a mere two hits in posting a 3-1 victory. At the time, the Chicago American League representative was tied with the New York Yankees for the circuit's lead and Garver had given them a quick trip into second place. The White Sox would eventually finish a surprising fourth, gaining twenty-one victories over 1950's sixth-place 60-94 record. The Pale Hose were at the beginning of a seventeen-season run during which they finished in the first four positions in the standings sixteen times, culminating in a pennant in 1959. On that same day, the first of July, future Hall of Famer Bob Feller, of the Cleveland Indians, threw the third no-hitter of his career, beating the Detroit Tigers by a score of 2-1.

Five days later, also in Chicago, the American League offices announced the roster for the All-Star Game, to be played in Detroit on July 10. Casey Stengel, manager of the American League champion New York Yankees, chose Ned Garver of the St. Louis Browns as one of the pitchers. Meanwhile, back in St. Louis, Garver once again victimized the White Sox with a 4-1 win for his eleventh success against a mere four losses. While his record was certainly All-Star Game material, the circumstances of his success proved to be extraordinary. You see, his Browns resided in last place, twenty-three games behind the league front-runners, having recorded a pathetic 22-50 mark to date. The aforementioned split of the Sunday twin bill had afforded them a very successful afternoon and Garver owned exactly half of his team's victories.

Ned Garver had been the high point of the Browns' woefully inadequate minor league pipeline, having been recruited by his semipro coach. Garver's skills were formidable and it is quite possible that he could have been an everyday player. He had been playing in a semipro league based in Fort Wayne, Indiana, when big-league opportunity struck him at the age of eighteen.

In 1925, Ned Garver had come into the world in tiny Ney, Ohio, a Christmas present. He grew up on his father's farm in the northwest corner of the state and pursued tilling of the soil as an avocation in addition to baseball. His older brothers played catch with him at an early age and he quickly learned to dispel all fears of the tossed ball. He played high school baseball, but because of the size of his school, his real experience came in the semipro sort of way. During his schoolboy days, he played baseball for the Fort Wayne, Indiana, City Lights. Both Garver and his high school catcher played for the Lights and made a twice-weekly forty-mile trek from Ney to Fort Wayne. Due to wartime gas rationing, the boys had to hitchhike every other trip, and one night trudged more than fifteen miles to get home.[3]

He pitched, and he filled in at third base, shortstop, and the outfield. Not only was he an accomplished hurler, but he was

---

3. *Sport Magazine*, July 1955, page 82. "How Ned Carver Found His Arm Again," by Furman Bisher.

potent with the bat as well and possessed good speed. The City Lights squad took the state title and then proceeded to Youngstown, Ohio, for the National Amateur Baseball Federation tournament, where an array of scouts from various teams gathered to evaluate the youngsters.

The City Lights made it to the national semifinals in that summer of 1943 and Ned batted .407 during the tournament, while playing third base and in the outfield. He won the only game he pitched. Four teams showed genuine interest in the lad but World War II was raging and Garver had a date with the U.S. Naval Air Corps. He entered active duty in November; foot problems, however, resulted in an early discharge and Ned found himself back in Ney the following spring. His manager with the City Lights, P. L. McCormick, now scouted for the St. Louis Browns and Ned sought his advice about pursuing a career in baseball and with whom. Garver signed with the Browns before contacting any of the other clubs that had expressed an interest. McCormick steered him that way, figuring he might have a better chance to reach the big time earlier with a team that had so many holes to fill.

Garver went to spring training in 1944 with the eventual American League champs, but wound up with their Newark, Ohio, affiliate of the lowly Class D Ohio State League after a short stint with the Toledo Mud Hens of the American Association. He relieved in his first appearance and held the opposition scoreless after coming in with an eleven-run deficit.

His manager at Newark, Clay Bryant, saw that Garver had fine natural skills as well as a good attitude. Bryant, who had pitched for the Chicago Cubs, took the youngster under his wing and taught him how to throw an effective changeup to add to his pitching repertoire. Garver, an eager and bright student, posted a 21-8 mark with an earned run average of 1.21 in his initial campaign. He led the league in most key pitching categories, and when he was not pitching, Bryant positioned him in the outfield; Garver was also used to pinch-hit. He drove in more runs than the regular catcher and batted .407 for the season.

The following season he returned to the Mud Hens, where he pitched in more than thirty games and played left field. He then toiled for San Antonio, of the Texas League, during the 1946–47 seasons and went 17-14 for a seventh-place team in the later campaign. It became apparent that Ned performed well with a loser and appeared comfortable in that disagreeable role. The Browns' farm system mirrored its futile parent team and Garver had learned early to deal with the frustrations of playing for untalented teams. The Browns, who had returned to their natural second-division habitat after their war-weary success, brought him up to the majors in time for the 1948 pennant race.

Many people today have either forgotten or are unaware that the city of St. Louis, Missouri, ever had a team representing them in the American League. The Browns of the twentieth century epitomized the height of futility in their hopeless organization. From the inception of the American League in 1901 to their final season in St. Louis in 1953 prior to their move, and eventual success, to Baltimore, the Browns managed to reach the first division just twelve times. They achieved that landmark seven times in the 1920s, led by first baseman and Hall of Famer George Sisler in the field and Urban Shocker on the mound. They did not see the light of the first division again until 1942 and won their only pennant in 1944, falling to their Sportsman's Park tenants, the Cardinals, in six games in the World Series.

Given the scarcity of talent on the St. Louis Browns roster, it is very puzzling that Ned Garver remained in the team's farm system for four years. He went to training camp in California in the spring of 1948 but was not wildly touted despite his record in the high minors. During spring training one day, Cliff Fannin, manager Zack Taylor's choice to start a game against Cleveland, could not be located, so Garver started in his place. He hurled three no-hit innings against the Indians, and allowed only one hit against the Chicago Cubs in a start a few days later. Thus, twenty-two-year-old Ned Garver was up to stay with the Browns in time for the 1948 season.

The Browns, of course, did not make it into the run for the laurels that year, but Garver debuted with a modest 7-11 record and paced the team with a 3.41 ERA, finishing fifth in the league in that category. He relieved on twelve occasions, picking up five saves. He also batted .288. The 1949 and 1950 campaigns brought 12-17 and 13-18 records, respectively, and in 1950 he posted the league's second best ERA at 3.39. One run decided thirteen of his thirty-one decisions that year. He led the Browns in hitting, batting .286 in ninety-one at bats.

The Browns had won 170 games over the 1948–50 years, averaging not quite fifty-seven victories per season, about 37 percent of their games played. Garver notched thirty-two of those wins and posted an ERA of 3.59 for a team that gave up more than five earned runs per game during the same span. He tied Cleveland ace Bob Lemon in 1950 for the league lead in complete games, finishing twenty-two of his thirty-one starts. In addition, he relieved in six games.

Garver had consistently hit well in the minors. As noted earlier, while toiling in the Browns farm system, Ned was used as an outfielder and a pinch hitter. He hit .255 during his first three years in the majors, although management realized early that, unlike Babe Ruth, he was more valuable on the mound than in the field.

While their play on the field lacked consistency, ownership of the team had remained in the DeWitt-Barnes families since 1935. Bill DeWitt and Donald Barnes had formed a syndicate and purchased the team from the estate of previous owner Phil Ball between the 1935–36 seasons. They had sold shares to the public to raise operating funds in the early years, as fans did not storm the gates to support the team. As a matter of fact, they stayed away in droves. Throughout the entire decade of the 1930s, fewer than one million people watched the Browns. A game in 1934 drew thirty-four attendees, and in 1935 a total of 84,000 fans spun the turnstiles. The Cardinals had become St. Louis's team and DeWitt and Barnes knew it, although it took DeWitt sixteen years to acknowledge the unsavory truth. Over the years, the Cards outdrew the Browns by a margin of six to one. Bill DeWitt had owned the Browns since 1933 and had watched as the team rose from the depths to the pinnacle of the American League in 1944, only to fall back to the dungeon with a resounding thud. In 1949, his brother, Charles, bought out Barnes's successor, making it a DeWitt family affair.

The Browns' high-water mark as far as attendance is concerned goes way back to 1922, when just over 700,00 fans stormed Sportsman's Park to view the best team ever fielded by the franchise. As was typical of the St. Louis Browns, they finished second that year.

The DeWitt brothers tried everything to make the Browns a winner. In 1950, they hired David Tracy, a psychologist with a doctorate in metaphysics. The team employed him to hypnotize the Browns and perhaps provide them with the confidence to eke out a better performance with the ultimate hope of a rise in the standings.[4] Dr. Tracy had achieved success in helping people with smoking and drinking problems but, as the results indicate, he did not have much luck with inept baseball players. The Browns finished a poor seventh, forty games behind the New York Yankees.

In June 1951, after much soul searching, the DeWitts arranged to sell the team to a syndicate headed by former Indians owner Bill Veeck. Veeck was legendary in his pursuit of paying customers and St. Louis would be no exception. His Cleveland entries of the late 1940s drew fans by the millions because of the quality ballplayers who graced the grounds of Municipal Stadium, but Veeck remained ever the showman with his giveaways and special effects. Veeck had built the Indians into a world champion in 1948, utilizing a solid foundation in pitchers Feller and Bob Lemon, in outfielder Larry Doby, and in player-manager Lou Boudreau. What he found in St. Louis was Ned Garver. Veeck then quickly produced Eddie Gaedel.

---

4. *Sport Magazine*, August 1951, page 71.

Ned Garver and the 1951 St. Louis Browns

The St. Louis Browns of 1951 were en route to nowhere. Zack Taylor, a former catcher who played primarily in the National League, was serving his fourth and final full season as manager of the Browns. He had not been blessed with an outstanding cast of characters, and none of his entries ever won more than fifty-nine games. Besides Garver, his quality players were catcher Sherm Lollar, who would eventually toil for the 1959 American League champion White Sox, and 1949 Rookie of the Year Roy Sievers. Sievers slumped badly for three years after batting .306 in his initial effort in the majors. Perhaps he merely wanted to leave St. Louis and could not be serious with a nonperforming club. His next stop, however, was Washington and he starred there as a slugging outfielder with a poor team for six years before being traded to the White Sox just prior to the 1960 season.

Considering the offense and defense with which he had to work, Garver had proved his worth with a decent overall performance during his first three seasons. He had received little support and often was the offense as well as the defense. However, on April 17, in the 1951 campaign's opener at Sportsman's Park, he was neither of these as the Chicago White Sox and Billy Pierce handed him and the Browns a 17-3 pounding. Garver had lasted a mere inning and two-thirds and had surrendered five hits during his brief sojourn on opening day.

A week earlier, President Harry Truman recalled General Douglas MacArthur from leading the American troops in Korea. Truman fired MacArthur for insubordination, and the nation's eyes and ears were riveted on the hearings and the innuendo surrounding the dismissal.

Garver quickly turned around and won his next three decisions. He defeated the Indians and Lemon 9-1 at Cleveland on April 21. He picked up a victory in relief against the Tigers in Detroit. The Browns returned home and Garver improved to 3-1 with a 6-3 success over Early Wynn and the Indians. The Browns also improved, to 3-8.

On May 1, Yankee rookie Mickey Mantle hit his first major league home run against the White Sox in Chicago and knocked in three runs to pace New York to an 8-3 win. Garver lost a 2-0 game to Willard Nixon and the Boston Red Sox at home before 2,495 fans on Sunday, May 6. The Browns were 5-15 and mired in seventh place.

On May 5, at Churchill Downs in Louisville, Kentucky, Count Turf, sired by 1943 Kentucky Derby winner Count Fleet, followed in Dad's hoofprints and took the Run for the Roses by four lengths. Count Turf went off at 15-1 and won handily over Royal Mustang, whose odds were 53-1. Count Turf, ridden by Con McCreary, prevented legendary jockey Eddie Arcaro from achieving his fifth Derby triumph.

On May 13, Garver pitched a 13-10 complete-game victory against the Tigers, improving to 4-2. He allowed eleven hits and three walks and his teammates added to his woes with two errors. Garver went two for four with a pair of singles. An interesting sidelight was that this slugfest took only two hours and thirty-six minutes to complete, although Detroit used five pitchers.

That same day golfer Sam Snead took the Greenbrier Open by four strokes over Jim Ferrier by shooting a 64 in the last round to finish with a 263.

Two weeks after the Derby, Bold, with Arcaro aboard, prevailed in the Preakness by seven lengths over Brookmeade. Count Turf did not run at Pimlico and Arcaro took home his fourth win in that classic.

On May 22, Garver lost to Allie Reynolds, 6-1, at Yankee Stadium. Five days later, Ned improved to 6-3 by beating the Tigers in Detroit 8-3. He contributed two hits to the attack, which was highlighted by Jim Delsing's two-run homer. Garver's next victims were the Red Sox, whom he shut out 4-0 on eight hits on June 1. He drove in the first two Brownie runs in the fourth inning to snap a ten-game Boston win streak.

On June 4, the New York Times *noted that liberal arts and engineering graduates commanded between $225 and $300 monthly. Recent degree recipients anxiously awaited those offers. Larger employers who were interviewed did not appear to be concerned with a potential loss of personnel to the draft despite the Korean War.*

Ned beat the Athletics 10-1 the next day in St. Louis and led the offense with a single and double and an RBI in four at bats. He then pitched a complete game in a 10-9 win over the Washington Senators on June 10, a game that lasted only two and a half hours. He gave up eighteen hits, all but one a single, and his teammates supplied their usual support with three miscues. But the Browns were streaking. At that point they had won four of their last five games and were considered extremely hot in the circle in which they ran. They had left the cellar to the Philadelphia A's and were in rapid pursuit of the Senators in the race for sixth place, and had risen to a mere eighteen games behind the front-running White Sox. The Browns then endured three rainouts, in New York and Boston.

On June 16, the skies cleared in time for the running of the Belmont Stakes, on Long Island. Counterpoint, a horse who had been considered for the glue factory a year before due to a cracked anklebone, took the third leg of racing's Triple Crown. Counterpoint, also sired by Count Fleet, easily outdistanced his sibling Count Turf by twenty lengths. Counterpoint's jockey, David Gorman, had also risen from horse racing's scrap heap of the previous year. He had ballooned to 142 pounds and thus had not worked in the profession. After a huge effort at regaining his former diminutive stature, he emerged as a winner at Belmont Park.

That same day, June 16, the Red Sox got even for the whitewash inflicted on them two weeks earlier by Garver. They roughed him up to the tune of six extra-base hits to go with an uncharacteristic seven walks as Boston won 10-5.

Less than a week later, the United States House of Representatives voted to increase personal income taxes by 12.5 percent. They did not raise the top rate and it stayed at an incremental 91 percent for incomes over $80,000. They also created a "head of family" category to minimize the impact on poorer, single-parent taxpayers.

As mentioned earlier, Garver had handcuffed the White Sox in both Chicago and St. Louis on July 1 and July 6, respectively. Between those games, Bill Veeck completed the deal in which he took over the DeWitts' interest in the Browns. By the time the All-Star break rolled around, Ned Garver had won 50 percent of his team's twenty-two victories. He had four consecutive complete-game victories over a fourteen-day period in late May–early June. Manager Taylor figured that a lead was safer with a tired Garver than with a fresh pitcher from the bullpen. Given that the Brownies' relief corps produced a total of nine saves that year and an ERA in excess of five runs per game, the skipper's skepticism was surely well founded and not questioned.

Ned had notched his eleventh victory just before the mid-season classic between the league's premier players. Through July 10, he had appeared in fifteen games and completed ten. He tied with lefty Ed Lopat of the Yankees for the league lead in games won. Garver was the only St. Louis representative on the American League squad and manager Casey Stengel picked him as the starting pitcher. He was in very good company; a total of seventeen future Cooperstown residents were listed on the rosters of the two leagues for the game.

Ned Garver went the maximum three innings allowed in the 1951 classic, which was played in Detroit that year, shutting down the Nationals on one hit. His star shone the brightest although the senior circuit eventually took the contest 8-3, hitting four home runs to the American League's two.

The season resumed after the All-Star festivities, and on July 15, Garver beat the Red Sox 3-1, allowing only three safeties in the opener of a home twin bill to improve his record to 12-4. Boston held first place at this time but would eventually finish third, eleven games behind the New York Yankees, but were giving their ever-burdened fans something to cheer about at midseason.

On July 20, the Yankees arrived in St. Louis for the start of a four-game set. Manager Taylor called on his ace to open the series. Garver gave up just six hits while hurling his fourth consecutive complete game; however, his teammates could garner only three safeties against Tom Morgan, and the Browns went down 1-0. Before the game, the Yankees' touted rookie Mickey Mantle was sent down to their Kansas City affiliate, as his performance toiling for the parent club was found wanting. Ned continued his steady, winning ways as July came to its end. The team traveled east and opened its road trip with a two-game series against the A's. Philadelphia was pulling away from the Browns in the battle for last place. The 1951 season was the first that someone other than A's owner Connie Mack managed the team. Jimmy Dykes had his hands full, but he managed to outdo Mr. Mack by eighteen games won and two places in the standings, but the A's, like the Browns, were counting the days in the place of their residency for the last half-century.

Garver was doing his best to make it a race between the also-rans. He started the first game of the short set and beat the A's 5-4 on July 25 in yet another complete-game effort. With this victory, Ned improved his record to 13-5, in comparison to the Browns' stark 28-62 mark.

Garver then took the mound on July 31 against the Red Sox at Fenway Park. He left in the fifth inning after surrendering a single to Vern Stevens. Ned was leading 3-2, as he had driven in two runs in the top of the frame, but had pulled a leg muscle while rounding first base. He was relieved by timeless Satchel Paige, who had jumped at the chance to work again for Veeck after being released by the Indians. Satch got the win as the Brownies outlasted the Sox, 8-6.

Garver's exploits with the bat may have gone unnoticed, but he often helped himself offensively. He had a lifetime average of .218 with seven home runs. Veeck quickly recognized a potential twenty-game winner in Garver and encouraged manager Taylor to move Ned up in the order, as he was leading the team in batting. Garver also pinch-hit at a .400 pace in 1951. He compares favorably to three other solid-hitting hurlers of that era: Warren Spahn, of the Braves; Don Newcombe, of the Dodgers; and Bob Lemon, of the Indians.

Back in action a week later, Garver lost to the Yankees in New York 6-2, again going the distance. Five days later he beat the Tigers 4-2, allowing seven hits, going four for four at the plate. He now stood at 14-6, trailing just Eddie Lopat, of the Yankees, and Mike Garcia, of the Indians, both of whom had logged fifteen wins. Cleveland's Bob Feller was 18-4 and would go on to lead the league in victories with twenty-two. At this point in the season, August 11, the Yanks and the Tribe were locked in combat for the American League lead and had posted identical 68-39 records. The Browns' 34-74 record made Garver's accomplishments that much more noteworthy.

The next day the Yankees lost a doubleheader to the Philadelphia A's, leaving them one and a half games behind Cleveland, while the New York Giants of the National League took two from the Philadelphia Phillies, placing them a seemingly insurmountable twelve and a half games behind the Brooklyn Dodgers.

Unwittingly, Garver became a passive participant in two of Bill Veeck's most famous escapades in August 1951. The legends surrounding Veeck up to that time revolved mainly around his zeal to please fans and provide a stellar product. Bill Veeck's father had been an executive for the Chicago Cubs in the 1930s and Veeck cut his promotional teeth at age fourteen selling peanuts at Wrigley Field. In fact, the legend is that young Veeck, as a summer worker, planted the famous ivy that still graces the outfield walls of that venerable ballpark. Veeck rose to club treasurer in 1940 but, convinced that the Wrigleys would block further advancement to a non-family employee, left the team.

Veeck proceeded to invest in the Milwaukee minor league franchise. The team had few prospects, but that did not deter the strong-willed Veeck and his partner Charlie Grimm, whose primary concerns were good baseball and memorable entertainment. He turned a listless franchise into a winner both on the field and at the box office. He started games at 8:30 in the morning to accommodate night workers and personally roamed the stands, similar to the Wrigleys' habits in Chicago. He did this while serving in the Marines during World War II, where he lost his right leg.

Veeck sold the Brewers after leaving the service to pursue the acquisition of the Philadelphia Phillies. However, commissioner Kennesaw Mountain Landis rebuffed his efforts to purchase the Phillies when he got wind of the rumor that Veeck intended to stock the team with the cream of the Negro leagues.[5] Not to be deterred, Veeck merely waited until Landis departed and then went after another club, this time the Cleveland Indians. His mastery continued in Cleveland, where, in 1948, his philosophy and antics produced a world champion and an attendance record. He sold his share of the Indians in 1949, in part to finance a divorce and in part to move on to greater challenges.

Challenge was what Veeck found in St. Louis. While both Milwaukee and Cleveland were one-team towns, the Browns were poor cousins to the Cardinals and needed unique excitement to drum up a following. Veeck had not owned the team a month when, in July 1951, he installed usherettes in the stands and entertained the fans with vaudeville and circus acts.

On Sunday, August 19, the Yankees and Indians were once again in a deadlock and the Dodger lead had shrunk to nine games over in the senior circuit. However, on that date, St. Louis was the place to be. At Sportsman's Park, Garver started and lost the first game of a doubleheader to the Detroit Tigers, 5-2. During the break between games, a celebration was held commemorating the American League's fiftieth birthday and featured a huge papier-mâché cake complete with a midget wearing an especially tailored Browns uniform featuring the number 1/8. The little man jumped from the cake as the fans cheered. Major league baseball was about to meet Eddie Gaedel, pinch hitter par excellence.

The second game started soon after the end of the festivities and any student of the history of baseball can recount what happened next. The Tigers went scoreless in the top of the first inning and the Browns came up for their turn at the plate. Frank Saucier, the 1950 batting champion of the Texas League, was scheduled to bat leadoff. Immediately after introducing Saucier, the announcer startled the patrons with "Batting for Frank Saucier, number one-eighth, Eddie Gaedel." The paid attendance on that day exceeded 18,000 fans, and undoubtedly each and every one wondered who

---

5. *Encyclopedia of Major League Baseball, National League,* 412.

Eddie Gaedel was. It did not take them long to get an answer. Eddie Gaedel had most recently been seen as the midget whose only previous major league experience had been during the doubleheader break. His job had been to burst through the papier-mâché cake. As he approached the plate with his short, determined strides, a roar came from the stands. Veeck's new weapon warmed up his forty-three-inch, sixty-five-pound frame by swinging three toy bats. Tiger manager Red Rolfe roared from the visitors dugout and conferred with the plate umpire. Brownie skipper Zack Taylor slowly moved to join the conference and produced an official American League contract. Veeck had anticipated such a protest and was prepared with the proper paperwork. Eddie Gaedel was, indeed, a bona fide major-leaguer.

Gaedel took a turn at bat and walked on four straight pitches. Veeck also foresaw the ensuing executive howling and counter-complained about tall men such as Ted Williams of the Red Sox and Larry Doby of the Indians, and threatened to pursue the overturning of Gaedel's (and other little people's) eventual banning from professional baseball by American League president Will Harridge. Eddie displayed a bit of showmanship to match that of Veeck. He later told reporters that he hoped the fathers of baseball would soon clear up the matter because "Mr. Veeck has plenty of work for me over the rest of the season."[6]

Five days later, Garver started against the Philadelphia A's before 3,925 fans, 1,115 of whom sat behind the plate and participated in another Veeck scheme, known as grandstand manager's day. The fans held signs with a side saying yes and a side for no. Manager Taylor sat in the box-seat section, where many were available, lounging in an easy chair, joined by the A's venerable Connie Mack. Taylor then watched as five of the Athletics' first six batters hit safely. After Garver had been touched for these hits, the public address announcer asked the fans if the Browns should warm up a new pitcher. Realizing that their meal ticket was on the mound, the

6. The Sporting News *Selects Baseball's 50 Greatest Games*, 1986, 165.

fans issued, via their signs, a collective and resounding NO. Ned stayed in the game and rewarded their loyalty and confidence by allowing only two more hits as he completed the game and won 5-3 for his fifteenth victory. It was his eleventh straight conquest of the ever-handy A's, dating back to June 1949.

Garver then started against the Yankees and was shelled as the New Yorkers ran up a 15-2 laugher. This game marked the end of Ned's August, and he stood at 15-9, with a month to go, pitching for a last-place team. The Browns had twenty-nine contests remaining and Garver could look to six to eight starts in pursuit of twenty victories.

His next start brought him another loss when the Indians hit three consecutive home runs against him and won 5-1. Harry Simpson started the barrage with an inside-the-park two-run job and Al Rosen and Luke Easter followed with solo shots. With this victory, Cleveland drew to within half a game of the Yankees. Five days later, on September 7, Ned got even with the Tribe and beat them and "Big Bear" Mike Garcia 4-2, knocking the Indians from the top of the American League. Ned slammed a double off the soon to be twenty-game winner and scored a run to boot. Cleveland regained the lead as the Browns topped the Yankees twice in New York on September 12. Garver was not involved in either of those contests.

On September 13, in Boston, he succumbed to the Red Sox and Mel Parnell, 5-4, in the opener of a doubleheader and it was beginning to look doubtful that he would attain twenty victories. He stood at 16-12 and the Browns had only sixteen games to play. He won his seventeenth in Washington on September 18, beating the Senators 3-2 in the second game of a twin bill. Ironically, Browns lefty pitcher Tom Byrne, used as a pinch hitter, singled home the winning run in the ninth. Byrne had started and hit a grand slam in the first game and easily beat the Nats, 8-0. In Byrne and Garver, the St. Louis Browns had two of the majors' best hitting pitchers on their roster. Byrne, who achieved a modicum of success with the Yankees both before and after his stay with the Browns, batted .238 with fourteen home runs over the course of his career.

On September 22, with season's end fast approaching, Garver prevailed over the White Sox 5-1 and singled on his own behalf to improve his record to 18-12. However, the attention of the sports world now concentrated on New York City. The Yankees finally secured first place and stood one game up over the Indians, never to trail again. Meanwhile, over in the senior circuit, the Giants closed to within three games of the Dodgers, with six to play.

Garver's next start proved to be successful as he beat Detroit at home 7-1, collecting a single in the process. He now had four days to prepare for his last appearance in 1951. It would be against the White Sox and he was seeking to make history as the most successful hurler for a most inept franchise.

As Garver took the mound on that final Sunday of the 1951 regular baseball season, the focus of the camera was nowhere near St. Louis. Unfortunately for Ned, the eyes of the sports world were now riveted on the two National League teams from the city of New York. On the morning of September 30, the Giants and the Dodgers had identical records with one game each to go, and later that day, they wound up tied for first place with 96-58 records. This deadlock, as any student of the game will remember, resulted in the unforgettable "shot heard 'round the world" playoff.

Even Veeck, the promotional mastermind, could not control the events that unfolded in Gotham as his ace warmed up. However, a faithful 12,000 fans appeared at Sportsman's Park to see if Garver could do the unbelievable and capure win number twenty. If more people had been aware or had been watching the Browns–White Sox contest, they would have appreciated Garver's performance.

He actually did it all, good and bad. He committed two errors and gave up five runs, but he also went two for four at the plate and put his team ahead in the fourth to stay with his first home run of the year. He had done it! He won twenty games for a last-place team and lost just twelve in the process. The last time the majors saw that happen was in 1924, when Hollis Thurston of the White Sox went 20-14. It would be another twenty-one years before another hurler toiling for a cellar dweller would take twenty. The baseball world waited until 1972 when lefty Steve Carleton won an astonishing twenty-seven games for the beleaguered Phillies. However, Garver accomplished a feat that to this date has yet to be matched. No other pitcher has ever won twenty games for a last-place team that lost more than one hundred games.

Garver posted an ERA of 3.79 on a team that gave up 5.17 earned runs per game. The Browns finished last in fielding that year, so it can be assumed that some of Ned's earned runs allowed were a product of a very leaky infield. He appeared in thirty-three games, starting in thirty. He led the league in complete games with twenty-four and was 2-1 in relief. He received the decision in thirty-two of his thirty-three appearances. He batted .305 in ninety-five at bats.

Garver and manager Taylor spoke kindly with regard to each other. Taylor once boasted that Garver was not only his best pitcher but also his best hitter, fielder, and baserunner. He used him as a pinch hitter and a pinch runner. Garver, for his part, acknowledged Taylor's tough role as skipper of the hapless Browns and was thankful for the faith Taylor had in his abilities.

Ned Garver's performance attracted many glances among the sportswriters who selected the league's Most Valuable Player. There was no clear choice among the position players, so Ned was definitely in the running. When the final votes were tallied, he finished second to the Yankees' Yogi Berra, 184 points to 157. A strange thing was noted, however; no New York writer included Garver as one of his choices.[7] The way the scoring went in pre-expansion days was that each of three writers from every city in the league voted for ten choices, with the first pick receiving fourteen points, the second nine points, the third eight points, and so on. Had Garver merely placed second among the Gotham scribes, he would have shared the MVP with Yogi. He had been notified by the wire services that he had won before the Gotham votes were received, but it was not to be.

In reality, in 1951 Ned Garver was worth much more to the Browns than Berra was to the talent-rich Yankees. Had the Browns

7. *One Shining Season*, Michael Fedo, 59–60.

been capable of winning even forty games without him? The team's record without their ace came in at 31-91.

Ned Garver earned the highest salary ever paid to a member of the St. Louis Browns, a whopping $25,000, in consideration of his efforts in 1951. Nevertheless, he was one of the first outspoken critics of baseball's reserve clause and felt a particular pain for those players who spent the good part of a career as backup to a star. He penned a letter to New York Congressman Emmanuel Cellar, who led a review of the teams' apparent ownership of players' movements.

The commencement of the 1952 campaign brought two quick shutouts against Detroit and Chicago. Just before his next start, Garver was pitching batting practice when he was struck in the back of the neck by a ball thrown by a teammate shagging flies, resulting in an injury to a cervical disk. Still, he did not miss a start and had another shutout going through the seventh inning of his next outing. The following day, however, he could not straighten his arm. The nerves had been damaged, but four days later he still pitched against Boston, although he lasted only five innings.

He kept trying to pitch because there was not a great deal of pain, although he knew there was something wrong. He had his elbow X-rayed, but nothing appeared to be amiss. His arm merely felt weak and tired, as though he had already pitched a complete game. On August 14, 1952, with a 7-10 record, he was traded to Detroit in an eight-player deal. He started one game for the Tigers, beating the Browns, but his season was over abruptly. He managed to turn in a 3.60 earned run average despite the problems that befell him physically.

In 1953, he produced an 11-11 record for the sixth-place Tigers. He improved to 14-11 in 1954 and had the best ERA of his career, 2.81. The Tigers were rebuilding, and in 1955 Garver would enjoy playing for a team whose winning percentage exceeded .500. Detroit won four more than they lost and his teammates included outfielder Al Kaline, who won the batting crown that year and would make it to Cooperstown. In addition, third baseman Ray Boone tied for the league lead in runs batted in and shortstop Harvey Kuenn, another future bat champ, rattled out 190 base hits and a .306 batting average. Garver went 12-16 with a respectable 3.98 ERA and placed third in the league with sixteen complete games. In 1956, Detroit finished fifth at 82-72, but Ned appeared in only six games. He was traded to the Kansas City A's in December 1956 in another eight-player trade. Basically, he and fellow hurler Virgil Trucks went to the A's in exchange for infielders Jim Finigan and Eddie Robinson.

Playing for Kansas City felt a bit like being part of the Browns again, although the fans were still attending games, as the novelty of major league baseball had not yet worn off in that midwestern city. The Philadelphia A's had moved to Missouri when the team was sold by the Mack family after finishing last in 1954. The financial and field successes achieved by the Boston Braves after their move to Milwaukee prompted changes in locale by both the A's and the Browns, who had one season earlier become the Baltimore Orioles. Of course, neither American League entry had the talent of the Braves at the time of the transfer, and both continued to flounder at the bottom of the American League.

Garver put together another winning season for KC in 1958, going 12-11, and went 10-13 in 1959 along with a .282 batting average and two home runs. As expansion loomed for 1961, however, he was left unprotected by the A's and the brand-new Los Angeles Angels drafted him for their staff. He appeared in twelve games for them in 1961 and was eventually released.

Ned Garver pitched in the major leagues over a fourteen-season span. He won 129 games and lost 157, posting a career earned run average of 3.73. He was not a strikeout pitcher, nor did he give up a lot of walks. His control got better after his arm injury in 1952, as he learned to substitute craft for talent. Over the course of his career, he averaged slightly more than three walks and three strikeouts per game and gave up just under a hit per inning. His strength was his stamina. He completed more than 46 percent of his starts, comparing favorably to Hall of Fame contemporaries Warren Spahn, Robin Roberts, and Whitey Ford, all of whom enjoyed better support. In his first four seasons, Garver completed sixty-nine of 117 starts, a better than 60 percent rate. Of course, manager Zack Taylor had far more confidence in Garver than in all his other pitchers combined, particularly his bullpen corps.

Ned Garver never played with a first-division finisher although the Tigers of 1955–56 did exceed the .500 mark, winning a total of fourteen more than they lost over the two-year span. However, the luckless Garver missed most of the latter year with injuries. The teams for which Garver toiled during the 1948–61 period performed at a .411 winning percentage and only the Tigers of 1954–55 posted a team ERA of less than four runs per game.

After his release by the Angels in 1961, Garver went home to Ney, Ohio, and farmed with the family for a year or so before taking a public relations job with a local meatpacker. He worked there until he retired in 1980, but he owned and managed two farms with a total of 240 acres. He served as mayor of Ney for seven years and also spent time as a long-term member of the town council. He had married his high school sweetheart, Dorothy Sims, right after graduation, and they have two children, Donald and Cheryl.

So where would Ned Garver have been had he pitched for a better team? Given his lifetime winning percentage of .451 versus that of the teams for whom he played, I believe the statistics tell us pretty definitely that he would have been a true force to be reckoned with during the fifties, not just the owner of *that one glorious season.*

NED FRANKLIN GARVER

212 Pitcher: St. Louis Browns   Home: Ney, Ohio
Born: Dec. 25, 1925, Ney, Ohio   Eyes: Blue   Hair: Black
Ht.: 5'10"   Wt.: 180   Throws: Right   Bats: Right

☆   Ned was the first American League pitcher since 1924 to win 20 games for a last place team. In doing so, he won 38% of the Browns' victories in 1951. He also led the League in Complete Games with 24 and pitched a 2-hitter. His first year of pro ball was 1944, when he won 21, pitched a no-hit game and had the best ERA (1.21) in the Ohio State League. The Browns brought him up in '48 after he won 17 for San Antonio in '47. In '50 his 3.39 ERA was 2nd best in the League.

MAJOR LEAGUE PITCHING RECORD

	Games	Innings Pitched	W	L	Pct.	Hits	Runs	Strike Outs	Walks	Ern. Runs	ERA
PAST YEAR	33	246	20	12	.625	237	114	84	96	102	3.73
LIFE-TIME	149	928	52	58	.473	946	452	314	401	374	3.63

© T. C. G.   ☆ **TOPPS BASEBALL** ☆   PRTD. IN U.S.A.

3

1952: BOBBY SHANTZ

PHILADELPHIA ATHLETICS

In mid-November 1952, six weeks after the end of the regular baseball season, the Baseball Writers Association of America announced that Bobby Shantz, the five-foot six-inch, one hundred-forty-pound left-hander of the Philadelphia Athletics, had been voted Most Valuable Player in the American League. The result came as no surprise to followers of the game as Shantz had won twenty-four games against a mere seven losses for a weak fourth-place team. The A's boasted the batting champion in first baseman Ferris Fain, and outfielder Gus Zernial ranked with the leaders in both home runs and runs batted in, but the diminutive Shantz certainly proved to be the difference in the team's performance.

It was rather ironic that the team would leave Philadelphia within two years and settle in the midwest enclave of Kansas City, Missouri. The fans of the City of Brotherly Love had embraced the National League entry, the Phillies, during their exciting run for the flag in 1950, and never seemed to pay much attention to the A's after that, unless, of course, Bobby Shantz was slated to pitch.

Whenever Bobby was the scheduled starter that season, home attendance always numbered more than 15,000 fans. He appeared at Shibe Park, the ancient ball field used as home by both the A's and the Phillies, sixteen times during the 1952 season. The rest of the year, the A's averaged about sixty-four hundred faithful. The management turned away thousands of fans on August 5, the night Bobby nailed victory number twenty. The house sold out on at least one other occasion.

Shantz's appearances kept the team solvent for one more year and helped immensely toward a winning season. His presence provided over 40 percent of the patrons in about 20 percent of the games.

Bobby was a humble individual whose stature and success made him the darling of baseball during that season. He grew up in Pennsylvania and graduated from high school in 1943. He was not yet eighteen years old, nor had he yet reached five feet in height. However, he possessed enough talent to play center field on the Pottstown High School team.

Due to the war, his family moved to Philadelphia, as his father worked at Cramp's Shipyards. Bobby snagged a job shining saws at a local Disston plant. While toiling for Disston, he was rejected for military service because of his size, so he returned to his job in Philadelphia. There, he played baseball for the Holmesburg Ramblers while waiting to grow a bit in order to serve Uncle Sam. He often pitched batting practice and manager Alton Cuthbertson noticed that his hitters had trouble connecting with his servings, in particular his curve ball.

He eventually made it into the Army, serving for fourteen months in the Philippines, where he concentrated on his mound skills with the division baseball team. He stayed in the Army through 1947, having grown to five feet six inches, and eventually weighed in at 140 pounds. After his discharge, he returned home and played semipro baseball in the Eastern Pennsylvania League, where he once beat future Philadelphia Phillies lefty ace of the Whiz

Kids, Curt Simmons. With this and numerous other performances, he displayed sufficient talent to merit a tryout with the A's.

In his only full season in the minors, Shantz compiled an 18-7 record for Lincoln, Nebraska, in the Western League, where he and future Chicago White Sox second baseman Nellie Fox led the Class A entry to a successful season. His tenure in the Cornhusker State was rather brief, but Bobby made the most of his stay. While he rested his arm on an off day, he ventured to the Capital Beach Pool for some relaxation and was introduced to a recent graduate of the University of Nebraska Teachers College. Bobby was smitten with Shirley Vogel, and the couple married in January 1950.

By the time he and Shirley exchanged vows, Bob had already experienced the American League for a full season. Just prior to the start of the 1949 campaign, the A's abruptly promoted him to the parent club, shortly after he reported to Buffalo, of the International League. He had been scheduled for more seasoning under former backstop and future White Sox manager Paul Richards. Before Bobby could unpack and get fitted for a Buffalo uniform, however, he was ordered to Detroit to meet the A's for a series with the Tigers. Two of the varsity pitchers had come down with weak arms and Bobby looked like the best bet in the pipeline.

On arriving in Detroit, he wasted no time gaining some experience as he was called in to relieve the very next day in the third inning. He made a mark for himself by shutting down the Tigers and not allowing a hit for the next nine innings. He gave up a run and two hits in the thirteenth, but the A's had scored in the top of the frame and he earned the victory. He went 6-8 during that season and posted a respectable earned run average of 3.40 as the A's finished fifth, eight games over .500. The Athletics' 1949 season was only the second time the club won more than it lost since 1933. That season also saw the first Philadelphia A's hurler to achieve twenty victories since the great Lefty Grove notched twenty-four in 1933. Shantz's road roommate, lefty Alex Kellner, accomplished the feat with a neat 20-12 record.

Shantz watched as the team fell apart in 1950 and dropped into the cellar. Kellner's twenty wins became twenty losses and the A's managed to produce a 52-102 record, finishing six games behind the pathetic St. Louis Browns. Bobby struggled to an 8-14 mark but began to experiment with a changeup and knuckleball and saw real progress with these toys, although they did not show up immediately in his won-lost record. He had good control, but during 1950 he worked to make it better. Because of his diligence, his bases on balls per nine innings dropped rapidly over the next three seasons. Bobby, aware that his stature was a big factor against his potential success, also worked on his fielding, base running, and hitting. Manager Connie Mack was not overly impressed by Shantz, for he felt that Bobby wouldn't have the stamina to perform well over a long season. He did, on the other hand, see a craftsman in the making with a secure grasp on the fundamentals. However, the venerable Mr. Mack would not be around to share the glory the diminutive lefty would enjoy.

The Shibe and McGillicuddy (Mack) families had been the principal owners of the Philadelphia Athletics since the early 1900s. The Macks had become the majority shareholders upon the death of John Shibe in 1937. Connie Mack was the only manager the A's had known through the first half of the twentieth century. He announced his retirement at the end of the 1950 season at the age of eighty-eight. Unlike today, no media barrage or constant publicity accompanied the event. The majority of the players learned of his departure by reading about it in the newspapers or hearing it on the evening news.

The truth was, though, that the A's were nearly broke and dissension raged within the Mack family in regard to assigning responsibility for the financial failure. The patriarch became the ultimate victim as well as an obvious accessory. In the past, Mr. Mack had twice broken up world champions simply because he feared that the cost of paying his players would outpace the revenues they generated at the gate.

The team owned Shibe Park, the field that was home to the A's; to the 1950 National League champions, the Phillies; and to professional football's Eagles. The ballpark made money, but by 1952 the A's were grossly overshadowed by the rejuvenated Phils, and their attendance began to fade.

To try to halt the negative cash flow, the family took a mortgage on the previously unencumbered property and leased the concessions to the Jacobs brothers, who would soon make a name for themselves in the food and entertainment industries.

These drastic moves generated a quick fix, but a further decline in attendance only depleted the already strained revenue stream. The sons of Connie Mack had argued for years over their father's capabilities, and after only one first-division finish in seventeen seasons, the elder Mack quietly rode off into retirement as unobtrusively as he had arrived. He was replaced by Jimmy Dykes.

Dykes had been a particular favorite of Connie Mack's, for he was happy to play anywhere and did anything to win. He came up with the Athletics in 1918, was traded to the Chicago White Sox in 1932, and returned as a coach for Mack, and became only the club's second manager when he succeeded the elderly gentleman after the 1950 season.

Dykes took over as manager in February 1951 and promptly put the team through the physical grinder during spring training. He was determined to have a capable, fundamentals-based squad that could win games with an extra bit of stamina and heads-up play. He encouraged rumors that trades were in the offing, in particular one that had Bobby Shantz heading to the Red Sox with Ferris Fain and three guys named Joe for Boston's slugging outfielder Ted Williams. He felt that uncertainty kept the players alert and fighting for positions.

The season started poorly for the Athletics; they lost twelve of their first thirteen games. On April 30, 1951, outfielders Dave Philley and Gus Zernial arrived in Philadelphia in a three-way deal with the White Sox and Cleveland Indians. By early July, the Athletics were mired in familiar territory, seventh place, showing a 28-44 record. At that point, Bobby Shantz did sport a 7-6 mark, although his earned run average hovered over 5.00. Things began to jell at that point as the Athletics won forty-two of their last eighty-two contests to finish 70-84 and only three games behind the fifth-place Tigers.

Shantz was selected to the 1951 American League All-Star team but did not appear in the game. He was not pitching with consistency and the hitters seemed to wait on him, acknowledging his control and knowing a good pitch would eventually come their way. Manager Dykes spoke to him privately and questioned why Bobby, with his superb mastery of pitches, insisted on pitching to the outside corners. Shantz did not surprise Dykes with his answer, expressing concern for the possibility of hitting a batter. Jimmy sized up the situation and encouraged Bobby to use the inside corners to his advantage. Batters were well aware of Shantz's control and confidently dug in while at the plate. Bobby began to use the corners to keep hitters on their toes, and thus to win ball games. Dykes was also aware that Bobby worried and slept fitfully the night before a scheduled start. Jimmy decided not to tell his pitcher of his assignment until game day. Shantz had more than an inkling of his turn in the rotation, but the lack of an official notice seemed to relax him. Over the remainder of the 1951 season, he went 11-4 and lowered his ERA to 3.95 for the year.

During that 1951 season, Bobby went from experimentation with the knuckleball to using it with his curve as his two best pitches. He credited pitching coach and former A's ace Chief Bender with developing his knuckler as well as with slowing him down on the mound. Bobby worked exceptionally fast and once pitched a nine-inning complete game in under an hour and thirty minutes. Bender taught Bobby to pace himself and the result was that he was often as strong in the ninth inning as he was in the first, as his inventory of pitches did not force him to rely on a strength-draining fastball.

The 1951 season ended for Bobby Shantz with a respectable 18-10 record for a sub-.500 team. The onset of the off-season found him on a tour of the Orient with a group of big leaguers headed by Lefty

O'Doul. He was accompanied by such luminaries as Joe and Dom DiMaggio, Red Sox lefty Mel Parnell, and teammate Ferris Fain, who had just captured his first batting title at .344. The Americans stayed in the Far East for more than a month, had a few laughs, played and taught baseball, and made some friends. When they arrived home, Bobby Shantz immediately began preparing for 1952.

The American League's Most Valuable Player in 1952

The Athletics were not expected to reach any heights in 1952. After their first eleven games, they seemed to prove the prognosticators correct: The team stood at 2-9. In the second game of the season, Shantz had gone the distance with a 3-1 victory over the Yankees and Ed Lopat before 3,860 fans in Philadelphia. He lost to those same Yankees four days later, giving up five runs, but was victimized by a Gus Zernial miscue. On April 30, he beat the Cleveland Indians 3-1 in Philadelphia, and this was the start of a personal eleven-game winning streak that would not end until the same Indians toppled him 2-1 in Cleveland on June 24.

On May 4, he whipped the last-place Detroit Tigers and their best pitcher, Virgil Trucks, 10-6 in the first game of a Sunday-doubleheader sweep in Philadelphia. Again at home on May 9, he proceeded to down the Washington Senators 9-3 for his fourth success. The A's hit the road and Shantz defeated the St. Louis Browns 5-1 on May 13, then shut out the Indians and Bob Feller 2-0 in the opener of a twin bill five days later. Bobby had improved to 6-1 and was virtually single-handedly keeping the A's afloat as they floundered in seventh place with an 11-15 mark.

In between the Cleveland games, Bobby beat every team in the league except the Red Sox and the only reason they did not succumb was that he did not face them in the rotation. He won games with his glove and his bat as well as his arm. He was blessed with luck and heads-up management.

As an example, Jimmy Dykes's knowledge of local rules won a game for Shantz and the A's on May 30 in New York. The Athletics were facing the Yankees in a Memorial Day twin bill. Before the start of the games, ceremonies at Yankee Stadium included a wreath laying in center field at the monuments to honor Babe Ruth, Lou Gehrig, and Miller Huggins. Connie Mack, Bill Dickey, and Casey Stengel were chosen for the honor of placing the wreath.

Shantz then started against the Bombers. He pitched a fourteen-inning thriller, winning 2-1, going all the way in less than three hours and forty-five minutes. However, he might have lost the game had Dykes not been alert. With the Athletics leading by a run with one out in the fourteenth, Mickey Mantle, who had earlier provided the Yankees with their lone tally in the third with a home run, hit a screamer off Bobby to center field. The ball hit the bleacher rail before bouncing into the stands. The local fans howled with glee, thinking their heroes had pulled a gold piece out of the sandbox. The Philadelphia manager roared out of the dugout, however, waving his arms at the umpires. He showed them the ground rules and Mantle was sent back to second base, as his hit was reduced to a ground-rule double. The next two Yanks went out and Mickey saw the game end while still on second.

Bobby Shantz was a pitcher whose mind was always in the game. Unlike his Brooklyn left-handed counterpart Billy Loes, who once reputedly lost a grounder in the sun, Shantz at all times knew the score, the number of men out, and the location of the ball. Facing Detroit in Philadelphia during his winning streak and leading 4-2 in the top of the ninth, a strike to the dangerous Vic Wertz got past catcher Joe Astroth. Johnny Groth, on second base at the time, alertly raced home while Astroth spun in circles in search of the ball. Shantz spotted it immediately and raced from the mound to retrieve it and then stared down Joe Ginsberg so he stayed put at third. Bobby coolly threw a strike past Wertz to end both the inning and the game. On June 2, the New York Giants' close-shaving ace Sal Maglie lost to the St. Louis Cardinals 5-4, snapping his personal win streak at nine and giving him a 9-1 record. Shantz was 8-1 with seven in a row and would beat the Detroit Tigers two days later to bring his record up to that of Sal the Barber's. At this juncture in the young season, the Athletics had won eighteen games against nineteen losses. Shantz owned half of the team's victories.

The following day, the U.S. Supreme Court overruled President Harry Truman's seizure of the steel industry on April 8. The Court, in a 6-3 decision, ruled that the president had usurped Congress's legislative powers. Truman had taken over the mills in order to avoid a strike of their 600,000 employees.

Shantz won his tenth game on June 8, beating Cleveland 12-4 in the first game of a Sunday twin bill before nearly 22,000 home fans, and, in doing so, became the first American League pitcher that year to hit double figures. The Athletics were now playing decent baseball and the team had closed to five and a half games behind the league-leading Indians and were only one game shy of .500.

Bobby won two more before losing to Cleveland and ending his 11-0 streak. Over the seven-week period, he pitched 119 innings and walked only thirty batters while fanning seventy and allowed just 1.64 earned runs per game. In his final appearance in June 1952, Bobby held the Yankees to two hits and shut them out at Yankee Stadium 12-0. Besides blanking the Yanks, he drove home a run with a squeeze bunt, poked two hits, and made a great fielding play on Jim Brideweser's bounder up the middle. That prompted Yankee manager Casey Stengel to describe Shantz as a guy who "is the best pitcher, fielder, and bunter in the American League. A guy who can beat you a dozen different ways." Those lessons learned during the dog days of 1950 sure were coming in handy against the competition in 1952.

Shantz had two more starts before the All-Star game, which was ironically to be played at Shibe Park in Philadelphia. Bobby beat the Senators but suffered a loss to New York. Pains across his chest forced him to leave the game on the short end of a 4-2 contest at home before 31,935 fans. He entered the midseason break with a 14-3 record. The loss to the Yankees was the first time in fifteen tries that he did not complete his start.

American League All-Star manager Casey Stengel had teased Bobby before the start of Sunday's game and assured him that his Yankees would provide him with an early exit in order to be ready for the year's classic matchup. Bobby did gain an early exit, but the Bronxmen did not really precipitate it.

Casey did not start Shantz in 1952's midsummer classic but brought him into the game to pitch the fifth inning with the Nationals leading 3-2. Chicago Cubs slugger Hank Sauer had hit a two-run homer in the fourth inning to provide the one-run margin. Shantz continued to show that it was truly his year to shine. With the weather threatening, Shantz struck out the Giants' Whitey Lockman and then proceeded to mow down future Hall of Famers Jackie Robinson and Stan Musial, getting them both to whiff on his specialty curveball. The Americans had not scored in the first half of the inning, so the Nationals entered the rain delay ahead. Bobby anxiously paced the clubhouse while the skies opened up, as he couldn't wait for another chance at the rival league's best. He was not aware of Carl Hubbell's five-strikeout feat in the 1934 classic. In the first inning of that contest, Hubbell fanned Hall of Famers Babe Ruth, Lou Gehrig, and Jimmy Foxx. In the second frame, Al Simmons and Joe Cronin went down for the count before Bill Dickey broke the streak with a single. Could Shantz have continued his spell? Pure speculation at this point, as Sauer, Roy Campanella, and Enos Slaughter were scheduled for the sixth.

On July 11, in Chicago, the Republican Party nominated Gen. Dwight Eisenhower on the first ballot to be its nominee for president of the United States. He handily defeated Sen. Robert Taft of Ohio, who had sought the nomination for the third time. General Eisenhower was joined by Sen. Richard Nixon of California, who was chosen by acclamation for the vice presidential spot. Two weeks later, also in Chicago, Illinois Governor Adlai Stevenson took the Democratic Party nomination.

After the excitement of hosting the All-Star game was over, the Athletics resumed the day-to-day chore of winning ball games. On July 15, Shantz shut out the White Sox with the help of two home runs by Gus Zernial. Zernial had joined the Athletics on April 30,

1951, in the trade that sent Minnie Minoso to the go-go White Sox. Zernial proceeded to lead the league in round-trippers and RBI with thirty-three and 129 respectively. Combined with first-sacker Fain's batting title, the A's swept the triple crown. Zernial continued to produce in 1952, whacking twenty-nine homers and driving in one hundred runs. Fain took his second bat crown although he dropped seventeen points to .327.

Ferris Fain was a hard-charging, slick-fielding first baseman who preferred to hit singles and doubles rather than swing for the fences. In 1952, in addition to his bat title, Fain led the majors with forty-three doubles. He always seemed to get his bat on the ball; his nine-year career produced a lifetime .290 average and a strikeout only once in every sixteen at bats. Fain often made interesting copy for the sportswriters and fans. After his successful 1951 season, he returned his unsigned contract to the club and criticized the team for being a "shoestring operation." He also made comments about the reserve clause and its general inequity to professional athletes.

In 1952, Fain started very slowly, going twenty-one at bats without a hit, generating discussion about whether his prior year's success had been a fluke. By the end of April he was hitting a minuscule .121, but May saw an improvement to .245. On June 17, he started to hit and by July 13 he had secured a hit in twenty-four consecutive games, raising his average to .324. In the process, on July 15, the day Bobby Shantz won his fifteenth game of the season with a shutout of the White Sox, Ferris Fain's hit streak came to an end. In January 1953, he was traded to the White Sox, primarily for power-hitting first baseman Eddie Robinson, and never again achieved the lofty marks that he had for Jimmy Dykes in the 1951–52 era, though he hit .302 on a part-time basis in 1954.

Fain retired from baseball after the 1955 season due to leg problems and returned home to central California. By the mid-eighties he had suffered health problems ranging from arthritis to leukemia and, in a strange series of events, was arrested twice for cultivating marijuana on his Georgetown, California, farm. In an article on Sunday, April 20, 1986, in the *San Jose Mercury News*, reporter Charles Bricker told the sorry tale of Fain's physical woes and subsequent legal problems.

With the All-Star Game behind him, Shantz proceeded to beat the Browns in his next two starts, 3-1 and 3-2, with battery mate Joe Astroth providing a two-run homer in the latter game. He then knocked off the White Sox and the Tigers for the third time each. It was not August yet and Bobby had already recorded nineteen victories against a measly three losses.

On August 5, 1952, Bobby Shantz took the mound at Shibe Park in his first appearance of the season against the Boston Red Sox. The crowd began to gather around the park hours before the gates were to open. The tickets went early and it was estimated that nearly 10,000 fans were turned away, as all of Philadelphia was fanatically following Shantz's progress and successes. The 35,673 who watched in person witnessed, in Bobby's words, "a very ordinary game." In addition, they sat through a rain delay of more than an hour, but when it was over, Shantz had his twentieth victory, a seven-hit 5-3 triumph, overcoming a Red Sox lineup that included eight right-handed hitters.

It was somewhat overlooked, but Bobby had just notched his sixth straight win. His record was 20-3 and he had earned a decision in every game in which he appeared. He had beaten every team in the league except the Red Sox at least three times. Through August 5, Shantz had started twenty-three games and completed twenty-one while posting a sparkling ERA of 1.54. If he had hung up his spikes for the year after his win over the Red Sox, he still would have been a contender for MVP. But he didn't. He had more work to do. The A's had climbed to 51-48 and were playing solid baseball. They trailed the Yankees by eight and a half games.

The Phillies also played their home games in Shibe Park, and they had a strong right-hander who would reign as the National League's premier hurler and eventually make his way into Cooperstown. Robin Roberts was 16-6 and won his seventeenth game the day after Shantz nailed his twentieth.

Bobby then lost to Washington 4-2 but won against them and the Browns during the next two weeks. His 9-0 whitewash over St. Louis was half a doubleheader sweep that found the surprising A's in fourth place, six games above .500 and a mere six games out of first place.

To demonstrate the excitement that a Shantz appearance generated, on August 20, teammate Carl Scheib beat the Tigers at home before 4,487 fans. Two days later, Shantz started and beat the Browns 9-0 and then went nine innings against Bob Feller and the pennant-chasing Indians on August 26, leaving in favor of a pinch-hitter with the score 3-3. The Tribe won in the eleventh, 6-3. These two games drew nearly 60,000 fans into the Athletics' ballpark. The Red Sox got even with Bobby as he made his final appearance in August and had to leave after seven innings on the short end of a 6-1 score.

Kemmons Wilson, a Tennessee contractor, opened his first motel on the main road connecting Memphis and Nashville. The accommodations, restaurant, and swimming pool were built in ninety days. He called it Holiday Inn.[8]

In his first September appearance, the Yankees pounded Bobby for eleven earned runs in a 12-2 shellacking. These two home games with Boston and New York drew another 50,000 fans into Shibe Park. At Cleveland on September 9, the streaking Indians beat Shantz and the Athletics 6-1. Bobby had not won since August 22. His record was now 22-7.

Two days later, Robin Roberts beat the St. Louis Cardinals for victory number twenty-four en route to a 28-7 year. Neither Shantz nor Roberts would lose again in the 1952 season.

It was during this stretch of seeking the elusive twenty-third victory that Shantz received some unwanted notoriety, as the recipient of a life-threatening letter. The postwar, early-1950s era produced a few disturbing moments in baseball. Just prior to the start of the decade, Phillie first baseman Eddie Waitkus had been

---

8. *The Fifties*, David Halberstam, Willard Books, 173–79.

shot by a deranged fan who claimed she was in love with him. The decade itself brought threatening letters to Pittsburgh Pirates slugger Ralph Kiner, Dodger reliever Joe Black, and Boston Braves lefty ace Warren Spahn. Shantz also became the target of a crank-letter writer, receiving three missives in August 1952, all warning him not to appear against the Red Sox at Fenway Park in Boston. He discarded the first two and happened to show the third to a team-mate when a Philadelphia sportswriter heard about it, obtained it, and published it. The police and the FBI got into the act, but, as in the case of the other threats, nothing came of the incident.

Shantz made three futile attempts to pick up victory number twenty-three. Finally, on September 14, he whipped the ever-handy Browns 10-5. He followed up that performance with a four-hit, 2-0 shutout of the Yankees in the Bronx ballyard before nearly 38,000 fans who were unsure of whether to root for the home team or Bobby and the A's. Shantz helped his own cause by poking a single against Vic Raschi to start a rally that produced the only runs scored in the game. The Yanks were neck-and-neck with Cleveland in a race in which they would eventually prevail, but Bobby beat them for the fourth time in 1952, running up a twenty-nine-inning score-less streak at Yankee Stadium.

The American League, on September 18, 1952, boasted six teams that had won more games than they lost. After 147 contests, the sixth-place Washington Senators stood at 74-73 and trailed the first-place Yankees by a mere sixteen games. It turned out that the Red Sox finished in that sixth spot with a 76-78 mark. All the teams feasted on both the Browns and the Detroit Tigers, as those squads held on to the bottom rungs.

With two, possibly three, starts left in the season, Dykes gave Shantz the ball on September 23 against the Senators. He was leading 3-0 in the bottom of the second when he came up to the plate against right-hander Walt Masterson. Although Shantz threw left-handed, he batted right, exposing his pitching arm to opposing fastballs. Masterson threw Bobby a bit tight and Shantz instinctively raised his left arm to protect his face. The result was a clean break in the wrist, and his season, and effectively that of the Athletics, was over.

But what a season it was! Bobby Shantz started all thirty-three games in which he appeared and completed twenty-seven, finishing one behind Cleveland's Bob Lemon for the league's best. He won twenty-four and lost seven and posted a 2.48 ERA. He threw five shutouts and beat every team but Boston at least three times. He pitched nearly 280 innings, walking just sixty-three while fanning 152. It was the only time in a sixteen-year career that he exceeded one hundred strikeouts in a season.

The break in his wrist disappointed Bobby and his fans in numerous ways. It deprived him of a shot to win at least twenty-five games as well as another chance to face the Yankees in Philadelphia. The Yanks finally nosed out the Indians, but by a margin of only two games. Another victory by Shantz might have turned the tide in the direction of the Tribe. The big loser was really the Mack family, as a final New York–Shantz matchup would most surely have pulled in a full house.

The A's finished in fourth place at 79-75, sixteen games behind New York. It was their last hurrah in the city of Ben Franklin and the birth of our nation. In 1953, they slipped to seventh place with Shantz a mere shadow of his former self, turning in a lackluster 5-9 record with a 4.09 ERA. Bobby tore a tendon in his right shoulder, which put him out of action for the second half of the year. On opening day of 1954, he tore it again. He made but two appearances in 1954. Bobby moved to Kansas City with the A's after that season and floundered for another two years as a spot starter and reliever, although he showed flashes of his former brilliance.

In late April 1955, in Kansas City, Shantz and the newly relocated A's beat the Yankees 6-0. It was Bobby's first complete game since 1953 and his first shutout since his two–zip whitewashing of these same Yankees for victory number twenty-four back in 1952. He controlled the game in all respects, allowing only three free passes and three singles. A real bonus to this performance was that his brother Bill worked the receiving end of the battery.

They worked a few games together and formed the first sibling pitcher-catcher team since the St. Louis Cardinals' Cooper brothers of the early 1940s. Bob's two-year stint in Kansas City resulted in a total of only seven victories, but Casey Stengel, long an admirer of Shantz, saw more in his record than met the eye. In 1956, Bobby had appeared in forty-five games and pitched 101 innings, allowing only ninety-five hits and thirty-seven bases on balls. Was he back?

Stengel acquired Shantz for the Yankees in February 1957 and he stayed with them for four years, winning thirty games and pitching in a total of six World Series games for the Bombers. His 11-5 record earned him Comeback Player of the American League in 1957, as he also nailed down the league's ERA title, allowing 2.45 runs per game. Ironically, Hank Sauer, his National League MVP counterpart in 1952, now toiled for the crosstown Giants and took home comeback honors in the senior circuit that same year.

Defensive prowess was finally officially recognized in the form of the Gold Glove by position in 1957. Shantz, as noted earlier, worked on every aspect of the game, and received the first-ever Gold Glove presented to a pitcher. He continued to dominate around the mound and picked up the honor every year until he retired after the 1964 season.

He moved on to the Pittsburgh Pirates prior to the 1961 season and also pitched for the brand-new Houston Colt 45's, St. Louis Cardinals, and Chicago Cubs before winding up his career with the Philadelphia Phillies for fourteen contests in 1964.

Over a sixteen-year span he won 119 games and lost ninety-nine while posting a lifetime ERA of 3.38. The truly sad part is that in the prime time of his stay in the big leagues (1953–56), he suffered from injuries and won only thirteen games.

After hanging up his glove, Bobby Shantz returned to Pennsylvania, taking over a bowling alley owned by Joe Astroth, his primary battery target with the A's. He eventually sold it to start the Bullpen Dairy Bar in nearby Chalfont. There, for twenty-two years, he covered all the bases: he acted as the prep man, cook, general manager, and janitor. He and Shirley brought up four children and, at this writing, have five grandchildren. He also played golf and, like many other good athletes, became adept at the game, scoring regularly in the 70s.

I wrote to Bobby Shantz, as I did to all my subjects. As usual, I enclosed a self-addressed stamped envelope and asked if I could either do a phone interview or perhaps take a ride to Pennsylvania. He quickly answered the letter with a very polite note that he was not able to assist me with my project but wished me luck. Hey, I had his autograph. I had to rely on the printed word, however, but there was oodles on Bobby Shantz, particularly about that memorable 1952 campaign, *that one glorious season.*

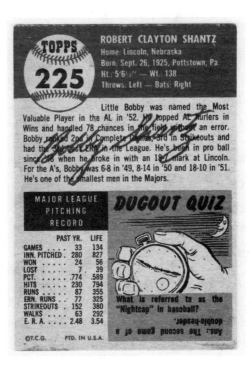

4

1952: Hank Sauer

Chicago Cubs

Philadelphia's old Shibe Park was the site of baseball's 1952 All-Star game, with the Nationals hosting the classic. While history will show that it was the first and only game called on account of rain, it was far from the least significant contest. It began twenty minutes late, but a near capacity crowd of 32,785 fans waited patiently for the game to begin. When it did, and for its brief duration, the participants treated them to a sterling contest.

The American League had, through 1949, virtually owned the midseason interleague series, winning twelve of the first sixteen games. The Nationals took both the 1950 and 1951 games and looked to add to their recent success on July 8, 1952. However, Mother Nature had other plans, and the rain came down intermittently and in buckets. The dugouts, in which the players waited by game time, had become wading pools.

The game did go on and the senior circuit added to its streak with a five-inning, 3-2 victory on a mere three hits, two of which were home runs. The game-winner was stroked by Chicago Cubs slugging right-fielder Hank Sauer in the fourth inning with the St. Louis Cardinals' Stan Musial on base. Stan the Man had reached first via a pitched ball between the shoulder blades. Sauer did not hit an ordinary home run. This was a 430-foot blast that cleared the left-field wall and then some, crashing against the front of a brick house across the street. It did the trick, as no American League runs crossed the plate in the fifth.

The heroes for the respective teams were Sauer, whose timely hitting proved to be the ball game, and the Phillies' diminutive Bobby Shantz, who provided fifth-inning thrills by consecutively striking out Whitey Lockman, Jackie Robinson, and Musial.

Then the skies opened and the rains poured down. After nearly an hour, the umpires mercifully called the game and awarded a third consecutive "W" to the Nationals.

This left fans to forever wonder if Shantz would have equaled or bettered Carl Hubbell's feat of five straight strikeouts in the 1934 contest or if Sauer could stroke another home run. You see, in 1952, Sauer and Shantz played for teams that had finished eighth and seventh, respectively, the previous year but both their teams were performing at levels that far exceeded expectations, flirting with the first division throughout the season. In 1952, these two men were directly responsible for the relative successes of their clubs and, as a result, both were elected the Most Valuable Player of their league.

Hank Sauer was born in Pittsburgh in 1917, the fourth child of Hungarian immigrants. His parents had actually left Europe in 1913 but went back to Budapest as homesickness set in. However, they wanted to provide their young family with the seemingly endless opportunities here, so they returned to America when the elder Sauer, a skilled mechanic, secured employment with a company that manufactured taxi meters.

The family purchased a four-acre plot in nearby Ross Township. There they raised a few animals and tended to a large vegetable garden. A small portion of the acreage was reserved for play and it was here that Sauer had his first exposure to baseball. Hank's oldest brother, Fred, played catch with him and devised a makeshift glove from an old boxing mitt. Another brother, Eddie, was born in 1920 and eventually the four Sauer boys made up a good part of a local baseball team, the Quaill A.C. Hank, the largest brother, usually played shortstop.

Hank entered high school in 1932. His father, suffering from ill health, wanted to move his family back to Hungary. Hank's mother prevailed and she and the boys remained in the United States. Julius Sauer departed for Europe that year and the family never saw him again.[9]

Young Hank Sauer played baseball in the semipro Pittsburgh City League after high school, holding down first base for the Immaculate Heart team. Paul Kritchell, a New York Yankee scout, offered him a contract for one hundred dollars a month for the duration of the summer. Hank took it.

Thus, Hank Sauer broke into professional baseball in 1937 as a first baseman in the New York Yankees farm system. He played for the Butler entry of the Penn State League for half of 1937 and all of 1938, when he tore up the league, batting .351 to pace the circuit. He then proceeded to move up the ladder to the Class C Mid-Atlantic League with the Yankees' Akron, Ohio, entry, where he enjoyed another fine season, hitting .301 and leading the league's first-sackers defensively. He also drove in more than ninety runs in 127 games.

It was while playing for Akron that Sauer caught the eye of one Frank C. Lane, at that time the farm director for the Cincinnati Reds. Lane, who would later be the architect for the go-go Chicago White Sox of the 1950s, liked what he saw in the big youngster and was able to acquire him for the Reds organization before the 1940 campaign. Sauer spent the next two years playing as a Cincinnati farmhand for the Birmingham (Alabama) Barons in the Southern Association. He performed well, appearing in 114 games and batting a respectable .292.

---

9. *Most Valuable Player Series, Hank Sauer*, 34.

A more important event happened to Hank Sauer during his sojourn in Dixie. He developed a strange affinity for soft drinks at the Birmingham YMCA and in doing so met, fell in love with, and married the young lady who worked at the soda fountain at that venerable institution. Her name was Esther Tavel and she and Hank were married in December 1940. Hank Sauer was not yet twenty-two years of age.[10]

Sauer remained in Birmingham through the 1941 season, spending the year at first base and hitting .330 while driving in 114 runs. His work around the bag progressed and the parent club rewarded him for his efforts with a September trip to Cincinnati. Sauer was a big, lumbering man and not at all a natural defensive player. He worked hard in the field, taking great pride in his slow but eventual mastery of the area around first base. Upon arrival at Crosley Field, Sauer was immediately designated by Reds skipper Bill McKechnie to be an outfielder. The Rhinelanders had a more than adequate first baseman in Frank McCormick, who had sent home 127 runs during the Reds' 1940 world championship season and continued to shine in 1941. Left field, on the other hand, had given McKechnie fits since his arrival in Cincinnati in 1938. He thought Hank might be the solution to his problem as he hit hard, and played well enough around first base. McKechnie's reasoning told him that Sauer should be adept in the outfield.

Sauer's nine games in the big leagues in 1941 provided a glimpse of the reputation that would follow him throughout his career. He hit well and in a timely fashion, driving home five runs and poking five two-base hits. He batted .303. He had a tough time in left field, however. During one game, as he ran up Crosley Field's unique incline just before the left-field wall, he caught his spikes in the grass and wound up parallel to the turf.

Despite his miscues in the outfield, Hank was instructed the following spring to report to Tampa, Florida, for spring training, where he continued to impress with his bat, although he seemed

---

10. Ibid. 45–48.

lackluster in the field. McKechnie kept him with the parent club
after the season's start but played him sparingly. After a mere seven
games and twenty at bats, Hank headed to the Triple A Syracuse
Chiefs, where he played exclusively in the outfield. There, he hurt
his ankle and had the worst year in his career to date. He appeared
in only eighty-two games and could manage just eleven homers to
go with a pathetic .213 batting average.

Sauer was not quite twenty-four and he and Esther decided
to remain in Syracuse for the winter of 1942–43, as Hank took a job
in a defense plant while waiting to enter the service. World War II
had already begun to rear its ugly head in full force and other ballplayers had to make similar decisions, as did all other able-bodied
Americans. Esther became ill, however, and Hank received a temporary reprieve that allowed him to play in 1943.

Due to wartime travel restrictions, baseball's commissioner
Kennesaw Mountain Landis had decreed that all teams train in an
area north of the Mason-Dixon line and east of the Mississippi River.
The Cincinnati team located its camp at the University of Indiana
in Bloomington. After a couple of weeks, Sauer was sent back to
the Syracuse team, where he played the entire season alternating
between first base and the outfield and batting a solid .275. His consistent bat and noticeably improved defensive skills were significant
contributions to the Chiefs' league championship that season.

To assist in the war effort, Sauer joined the U.S. Coast Guard,
enlisting in October 1942. He did not report for full-time active duty
until a year later. After basic training, he was assigned to Curtis
Bay, Maryland, where he remained until his discharge in August
1945. While there he was able to play on the station's baseball team,
and usually batted fifth in the lineup behind Sid Gordon, a rising
New York Giants slugger. Upon his discharge, he went directly to
Cincinnati and performed well both at first base and in the outfield,
hitting .293 with five home runs in thirty-one games. Three of these
round-trippers came in a single game against the Boston Braves.

The Cincinnati entry in the mid-1940s did not instill fear in its
National League rivals. After the powerful squads that took pen-

nants in both 1939 and 1940, the Reds began a downward trek that was exacerbated by the war and the drain of talented personnel. By the end of hostilities, the Reds' returnees had by then grown old and feeble and the players of the 1945–47 era became second-division teams with adequate pitching, average defense, little power, and the worst batting averages in the senior circuit. It seemed very strange to many people that an organization with a young, strong player with skills sorely needed would continue to deny that player a chance to help the team. In particular, when Sauer was given an opportunity, he certainly did not embarrass himself. In fact, Hank hit a cumulative .290 in his prior trials and his fans saw marked improvement in the field. Thus, it was a surprise to all when, once again, McKechnie sent him back to Syracuse for the 1946 season with instructions to concentrate on the outfield.

Hank Sauer spent two more full seasons in the International League, and after 1947 he had seen the last of the minor leagues, as he virtually annihilated Triple A pitching with a .336 batting average and fifty home runs. Hank had experimented with a huge bat, a forty-ounce war club, as opposed to his former thirty-five-ounce model. His six-foot four-inch frame and awesome strength were a perfect match for the oversized shillelagh, and his performance reflected that. The Syracuse Chiefs, led by Sauer and manager Jewel Ens, took the league championship, beating the Buffalo Bisons and their manager, Paul Richards, the future skipper of the Chicago White Sox. It was during this series that the announcement was made that Sauer's contract had been purchased by the Reds for yet another tryout.

Hank finally stuck with the Reds in 1948, playing mainly in left field with an occasional game at first. He supplied the team with the power it lacked, belting thirty-five homers and driving in ninety-seven runs. In the field, he led all National League outfielders with six double plays. He was leading the majors with twenty-seven homers by mid-August, when he hit his inevitable slump.

Throughout his career Sauer had been a streaky hitter, but this time the slump overcame him in total. Between the dog days of summer and an all-out effort on his part to break the miserable routine, Sauer lost nearly twenty pounds, and with the sapping of his strength came a mere eight round-trippers over the last six weeks of the year. Still, it had been a very rewarding season and he went to spring training determined to make 1949 an even better year. However, he performed poorly in Tampa, and the new Reds manager, Bucky Walters, seemed to want him to prove himself all over again. He opened the season with two hits as the Reds took the first game of the year, but that did not last. On June 15, 1949, after playing in forty-two games for Cincinnati, in which he batted a whispering .237 with four homers and sixteen RBI, Sauer and center fielder Frank Baumholz were traded to the Chicago Cubs for Peanuts Lowrey and Harry Walker. Hank had to wonder . . . was he going from bad to worse?

The Chicago Cubs had fallen on hard times in the days after World War II. However, they had been a league powerhouse in the early 1900s and were consistently in the thick of things from the late 1920s through 1945. The club was one of the original eight teams comprising the National League upon its formation in 1876.

The team has had a gloried and storied past, from the classic "Tinker to Evers to Chance" infield trio of the early 1900s to the managerial guidance of Joe McCarthy in the late 1920s. Its home field was constructed in 1914 for play in the outlaw Federal League and the Cubs took it over in 1916. By 1921, William Wrigley, of chewing-gum fame, became majority owner. From 1906 through 1945, the team took ten league flags but won the World Series in only 1907 and 1908. In 1945 the Cubs won a war-torn flag, fielding the best squad in a run-down league.

Nineteen forty-six produced the last winning season the Cubs would enjoy until 1963. From 1947 through 1951 they held up the league in the fight for the final three spots in the standings. In 1949, on their way to an eighth-place finish, they traded for Hank Sauer, and with him came Frank Baumholtz. It ranks as one of the best deals Wrigley and his hirelings ever made.

When Hank Sauer learned of the trade, he was overjoyed. His younger brother Ed had toiled in the outfield for Chicago during the war years and had been treated most fairly. Hank could not wait to get to Chicago and he knew the Cubs sorely needed his bat. They were in the first of a three-season stretch in which they had the worst cumulative record in the National League. They had hit the least homers in the league during the previous campaign and their pitching staff competed with the Pirates to see who could give up the most earned runs in 1949. Hank stepped right up to the plate, poking two doubles in his first appearance as a Cub. He also threw out a runner at the plate. He hit .291 to go along with twenty-seven homers and eighty-three runs batted in while appearing in only ninety-six contests for the Cubs.

Just before Sauer's arrival in Chicago, Frank Frisch replaced longtime Cub Charley Grimm as field manager. The team's overall ineptitude proved to be frustrating to Frisch. Frisch had played his entire nineteen-year career with the New York Giants and the St. Louis Cardinals, participating in eight World Series along the way. He was effusive as the 1950 season got under way. However, he harbored no illusions that this club would be a clone of his 1934 St. Louis Cards' Gashouse Gang, nor that he would even find his squad in the thick of things. He felt that they would prove pesky and could liven things up in the National League race.

Bob Rush, a big right-handed pitcher, had come up to the Cubs in 1948. Although his losses exceeded his wins, his performances continuously merited inquiries from other teams. In 1950, Rush posted a record of 13-20, topping the circuit in losses. However, he completed nineteen of his thirty-four starts and recorded a respectable ERA of 3.71. Fred Hiller, a Yankee castoff, enjoyed his one season in the sun, going 12-5 with a team-leading ERA of 3.53. These two hurlers were an important cog in the Cubs' race with the Reds for the capture of sixth place. The Cubs proved to be an exciting team to watch, as their home-run output rose from ninety-seven in 1949 to 161 in 1950. Sauer nailed thirty-two round-trippers to go with 103 RBI and a respectable .274 batting average. Center fielder Andy Pafko also produced a fine season, hitting .304 and sending thirty-six balls sailing out of the park. Both Cub outfielders were chosen for the All-Star game, which was to be played on July 11 at Chicago's Comiskey Park.

In the weeks prior to the classic, Sauer found himself in the center of an All-Star controversy. Hank had finished third in the outfield in the fans' voting behind the Cardinals' Enos Slaughter and the Pirates' Ralph Kiner. This was, at that time, carried out in concert with over three hundred newspapers and radio stations from all big-league cities and beyond. The game rules stated that the manager must abide by the will of the fans for at least three innings. Burt Shotton, skipper of the 1949 champion Brooklyn Dodgers and, therefore, in charge of the 1950 All-Stars, wanted to put his own Duke Snider in center. His reasoning was that the fans did not elect a center fielder, thereby jeopardizing the chances of his team to prevail in the game. As you might imagine, an uproar ensued. Shotton's critics came from all angles, including opposing manager Casey Stengel, of the Yankees. Shotton was overruled and Sauer started the game at his familiar right-field position. Hank played four innings in right and came up to bat twice, sending Slaughter home with a sacrifice fly in the second and grounding hard to third in the fifth. The Nationals won the game in the fourteenth on the Cardinals' Red Schoendienst's home run.

Sauer had fond memories of the 1950 season. For example, he touched Phillies ace left-hander Curt Simmons for three home runs in a game on August 28. That gave the flag-bound Phils a shock from which they promptly recovered before nearly handing the Dodgers the pennant. Hank was murder at home but his production dropped dramatically once the Cubs hit the road. He, Pafko, and company helped lure the fans into Wrigley Field, however, as the Cubs drew 1.2 million in 1950 while fielding a seventh-place team.

The Cubs had trained at Wrigley's Catalina Island since 1921 with the exception of the war years, and the team headed there for spring training in 1951. Hank and Esther had moved to Inglewood, California, after the 1948 baseball season at the prodding of Hank's brother Eddie, who thought he was in heaven after playing in Los Angeles with the Cubs' Pacific Coast farm team. Ordinarily, Hank's wife would accompany him to Chicago, but she stayed on the West Coast for an addition to the household was on its way. Hank Sauer was not a happy-go-lucky guy to begin with, but the separation and worry about his family put pressure on him and he slumped badly. Sauer was a streaky hitter, but in the spring of 1951, he experienced a streak of a slump. The drop in his output became so severe that Sauer tried anything suggested to rid himself of the demons. He gave up golf and pipe smoking, and changed his stance in order to hit to the opposite field with more frequency. To make matters worse, Pafko was traded to Brooklyn on June 15 and this gave opposing hurlers a chance to bear down on Sauer, as they no longer had to contend with a hitter of Pafko's caliber following him at the plate.

Sauer posted his worst numbers to date in 1951. Sure, he hit thirty homers and drove in eighty-nine runs, but his average dropped to a weak .264 and he was unable to lead the team out of an eighth-place finish. Admittedly, he had little help, although first-year third baseman Randy Jackson provided some punch with sixteen homers and a .275 batting average. The Cubs tailed off in the power department, the pitching got worse, and Frisch was replaced as manager by longtime Cub first baseman Phil Cavaretta after eighty games. Cavaretta then generated a worse record than Frisch had realized in his half-season.

Bob Rush once again produced a fine season under the circumstances, winning eleven and dropping twelve with a respectable 3.83 ERA, and Dutch Leonard provided capable bullpen assistance. Rush, like the Browns' Ned Garver, was a top-notch pitcher who had the misfortune of playing for a team with perpetually inadequate support. He toiled for the Cubs from 1948 through 1957, a period in which his team finished higher than seventh only twice. Still, he managed to win 110 games against 140 losses, exceeding an ERA of 4.00 only three times. After perhaps his worst season with the Cubs in 1957 (6-16, 4.38 ERA), he was traded to the newly crowned world champion Milwaukee Braves, for whom he turned a neat 10-6 trick in 1958. He started a World Series game but fell the victim of a shutout by the Yankees' Don Larsen–Ryne Duren duo.

In 1951, however, he was wrapping up a credible performance and about to embark on a great year one season hence.

The National League's
Most Valuable Player in 1952

The Cubs broke camp and started the 1952 season on seemingly a new note. They had abandoned Catalina Island for new digs in Mesa, Arizona. Cavarretta emphasized defense and the infield appeared to tighten. The team committed thirty-five fewer errors in 1952 than in 1951. Cavarretta worked on the pitching and, with the help of Cub mound legend Charlie Root, assembled a decent staff who lowered their ERA from 4.34 to 3.58.

By April 23, the team stood at 5-2 and Hank Sauer had already knocked in ten runs. On April 19, he had sparked a rally with a single as the Cubs came from a 4-1 deficit to win, and helped beat the Pirates two days later, going three for four with an RBI. Four days later, he beat the Reds in Chicago with a two-run homer in the seventh in a 7-3 victory. On April 28, the Cubs nailed their fifth win in six tries as Sauer drove home all the Chicago tallies in a 4-3 squeaker against the Cardinals.

As May began, the Cubs had already won nine games and Hank had driven in seventeen runs. The team went into the new month confident and upbeat; ballplayers who never had smelled the air far above the musty cellar liked the new and unusual scent.

On Saturday, May 3, jockey Eddie Arcaro rode favored Hill Gail to a two-length Kentucky Derby win.

The Cubs continued the beat as Rush went ten innings to put away the Brooklyn Dodgers 3-2 on enemy turf. The next day, the Cubs ventured across the river to the Polo Grounds but lost to the Giants in ten innings, 6-3. Sauer went four for five and delivered a home run, keeping the Cubs in the game against the defending league champs. Later that month he led the Cubs to a doubleheader sweep over the Giants at the Polo Grounds, driving in three runs, including a tremendous blast off Jim Hearn in the second game.

May 24 found the Cubs in Pittsburgh against the cellar-bound Pirates. Sauer's ninth homer of the season in the second inning started the rally that resulted in a 7-5 win. The Cubs took on the Cardinals at Wrigley Field on May 28 and Hank poked a double and drove in one run in aid of his team's 7-2 win.

That same day Willie Mays played his last big-league game until the magical 1954 season, as he left for the Army, and Don Newcombe, the Dodger ace, was found fit to serve by his draft board and prepared to leave for the Army as well.

In the last series in May against the Reds, Sauer went five for seven in a twin-bill sweep. He hit a two-bagger and even stole a base before 35,999 delirious Cub fans. May 1952 ended with the Cubs at 23-16 and Hank batting a torrid .338 with ten home runs and forty-five RBI. During the month, he had driven in twenty-eight runs to lead his team to a 14-12 record. On the last day of May 1952, coach Charlie Grimm left the team to take over as manager of the Boston Braves. The Braves would be Grimm's only other employer in baseball besides the Cubs after Charlie was acquired by Chicago in 1925.

Betsy Rawls took the LPGA Cross-Country Weathervane Tournament with a 144-hole score of 590 strokes, winning a five-thousand-dollar purse. The four-course tourney started on February 16 at Normandy Shores Country Club in Miami, Florida, and ended on June 1 at the Scarsdale Golf Course in Hartsdale, New York.

The Cubs continued to perform above all expectations, and Sauer led the attack. Early June brought more success with decisive victories over the Giants and Braves in consecutive series. He drove in runs when needed and made key hits to set up other hitters in clutch situations. By June 8, Hank had hit fourteen home runs and driven in fifty-four runs and the Cubs were ten games over .500 at 29-19, a mere six and a half games behind the Dodgers. This came from a team with no significant change in personnel and that had won ball games at a .403 clip during 1951.

Eddie Arcaro rode the winner in the Belmont Stakes on Saturday, the seventh. He was not on Derby winner Hill Gail, a nonparticipant in *the third leg of racing's Triple Crown. Arcaro was aboard One Count in a six-horse race. One Count paid $27.60 to win, nosing out Blue Man, the Preakness winner and odds-on favorite.*

On June 11, Sauer touched Phillies lefthander Curt Simmons for three home runs in a 3-2 victory at Wrigley Field. He repeated a hat trick performed in 1950, also against Simmons. Simmons had, on May 13, celebrated his release from the Army with a 6-0 whitewash over the Cubs in Philadelphia. Hank ended the game batting .352.

The Cubs slipped a bit, winning nine of the remaining twenty games played in June, and thus stood at 38-30 at month's end. Sauer had gone through a none-for-twenty-four stretch and his value to the team stood out during this tough period as the team struggled without his clout. However, the Cubs still held third place and Hank was leading the league in both home runs and RBI with twenty and sixty-two, respectively, while sporting a .305 batting average.

The Cubs played nine games between the first of July and the sixth, winning four. Sauer added three round-trippers to his résumé and drove in seven more ribbies. Although the team had tailed off a bit from its June 8 high, the Cubs stayed nine games behind the pennant-bound Dodgers and were 42-35 at exactly the midpoint of the season.

Note that the Cubs played nine games in six days. Some of the apologists for the baseball players of today point out that the majority of games were played during the day until the 1960s and that there was no coast-to-coast travel during the pre-expansion era. That may be so, but nearly every Sunday produced a preponderance of doubleheaders and the train did not get from New York to Chicago in two hours.

The All-Star Game showcased some stellar Cubs representation as Sauer won the rain-shortened contest with a homer in the fourth and Bob Rush relieved Curt Simmons in the same inning, pitching two innings to pick up the victory.

The next ten games brought the Cubs back down to earth as they began to play familiar baseball and went 3-7. They continued to falter and on Sunday, July 27, dropped to .500 by losing a double-header to the Phillies.

On Saturday, July 26, California's Bob Mathias won the decathlon after twelve hours of competition at the Summer Olympic Games, held in Helsinki, Finland. Mathias retained the iron-man title he had first earned in the 1948 London games.

By the end of July, the Cubs had regained some momentum and were two games above .500, at 50-48. Hank Sauer's home run production had tailed off a bit during the heat of the summer, as he hit but five homers in the month, but he continued to send runs home, driving in twenty-one. On July 31 he still paced the circuit, with twenty-five homers and eighty-three RBI.

August started well for the Cubs. On the first, they beat the Dodgers 6-1 and handed Preacher Roe his first loss in 1952. He would go on to produce a record of 11-2 for the Bums after a remarkable 22-3 in 1951. The Cubs continued to play seesaw baseball and on the tenth took two games from the Pirates. Sauer led the charge in the 9-5 first-game win, going two for five with a two-run homer and two other RBI. The fifteenth saw a loss to the cellar-bound Pirates, which dropped the Cubs below .500 for the first time in 1952. That same day, the Wrigleys extended manager Cavarretta's contract through 1953. Ralph Kiner, of the Pirates, who had either led or tied for the lead in home runs in every season since 1946, hit his twenty-sixth and began to gain on Sauer. The next day Chicago split two games with the Bucs as Sauer poked number thirty-one. Bob Rush won his twelfth game after two consecutive 1-0 losses.

By the end of August, the Cubs headed the second division and had dropped to 65-67. Sauer still led the majors in homers and RBI with thirty-four and 114, respectively. On the first of September, Sauer blasted a 425-foot home run at Pittsburgh's Forbes Field. That hit propelled the Cubs to a 6-0 victory in the first game of a twin bill. By the tenth it appeared that the Cubs were in the process of finally doing what was expected of them: to lose consistently. They had fallen to five games under .500 when Hank led them to an 11-7 victory over the Dodgers at Ebbets Field, banging out three

hits including a double and his last home run of the year, his thirty-
seventh. His performance seemed to light a final fire under the
Wrigleymen and their 9-4 record over the last weeks of the season
brought them to a very credible 77-77. Kiner finally caught Sauer
in the homer derby, tying him for the league lead on September 27,
giving him his seventh straight home-run title.

With Phil Cavarretta supplying the capable management and
Hank leading the way for most of the season, a number of the Cubs
enjoyed the best year of their careers. Right-fielder Frank Baumholtz hit .325 and finished runner-up to Stan Musial's .336 batting
championship. Bob Rush went 17-13 and Warren Hacker and Paul
Minner contributed fifteen and fourteen wins, respectively. The
Cubs posted the third lowest ERA in the National League and won
fifteen more games than in 1951. In addition, Sauer and company
drew the fans into Wrigley Field. Total major league attendance
slipped nearly 9 percent from the exciting 1951 season, but the Cubs
drew more than one million patrons, an increase of over 130,000
fans or almost 15 percent.

On November 20, 1952, the same day his son Hank was born,
Hank Sauer was chosen by the Baseball Writers of America as the
Most Valuable Player in the National League. The voting was close;
Sauer polled 226 votes against Phillies ace Robin Roberts's 211
votes and Dodgers rookie reliever Joe Black's 208. Within hours,
a firestorm erupted, for it was discovered that one writer omitted
Roberts despite his 28-7 record and three forgot about Black. Criti-
cism was aimed at Sauer's final .270 batting average, his September
swoon, and his team's fifth-place finish. In an article in the *New
York Herald Tribune* the following day, Harold Rosenthal suggested
an anti-eastern sentiment among the twenty-four members of the
Baseball Writers Association.

The votes were in, however, and no one dared to say that the
modest success of the 1952 Chicago Cubs was not due in great part to
the tremendous year a gentle giant named Hank Sauer put together.

As was that of fellow 1952 American League MVP Bobby
Shantz, Hank's 1953 performance was marred by injuries. He was

relegated to 108 games and slipped to nineteen homers as the Cubs won only sixty-five games and finished seventh. In 1954, he hit a personal high of forty-one round-trippers and batted .288, but the Cubs stayed mired in seventh. He was traded to the Cardinals for the 1956 campaign in exchange for Pete Whisenant, and in that one-season span became fast friends with Stan Musial. After the end of that season, the Cardinals released him and he found himself in New York in a Giants uniform. He had appeared at bat only 151 times for the Cards in 1956, but in New York he found a second life, slamming twenty-six home runs and being voted the National League's Comeback Player of the Year. Ironically, Shantz earned the same award across the Harlem River with the Yankees.

Hank moved west with the Giants after they abandoned Gotham with the completion of the 1957 season. He stayed with the Giants in San Francisco through 1959, then hung up his spikes at the age of forty. He worked for the Giants as a full-time coach and scout, retiring after thirty years. He discovered and signed Barry Bonds. He ran the Giants' instructional league camp in Arizona, where he had the ignominious responsibility of releasing his son Hank, who had been a farmhand in the San Francisco organization. During his retirement, he found himself playing more and more golf, and excelled on the links. He purportedly could shoot below his age when he turned eighty in 1997. Ironically, Hank suffered a fatal heart attack while on the Crystal Springs Golf Course in Burlingame, California, on August 24, 2001, at the age of eighty-four.

Hank's size, easy disposition, and good looks brought him bit parts in movies with Ronald Reagan and Doris Day. He and Peanuts Lowrey (for whom he was traded to Chicago in 1949) were once fired for missing a film shooting. They were busy buying golf clubs and lost track of the time. He was often a guest on Bay Area sports-talk shows. His likable personality often involved him in banter with the show hosts. As his slowness afoot was legendary, an announcer once wondered in an interview in the late 1990s if

Hank had ever hit a triple. Sauer feigned annoyance but was ready with his answer: "Nineteen, and eleven stolen bases."[11]

Besides Hank Jr., Hank and Esther had a son and a daughter, and the family took root in California. Esther passed away in 1979 from the ravages of cancer and Hank married Jeanne in 1980. She had been a patient with Esther. I had the pleasure of interviewing them on the phone and they supplied me with a number of anecdotes and interesting facts, most of which have been recounted in this chapter.

During the summer of 1998, Hank Sauer was inducted into the Syracuse Wall of Fame. His records from the overpowering season he enjoyed in 1947 have yet to be surpassed by any subsequent member of the Syracuse Chiefs. But as good as 1947 was, it will never match his accomplishments and leadership of *that one glorious season* of 1952.

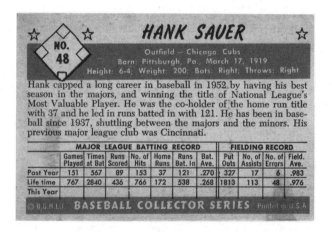

☆ ◇ ☆   **HANK SAUER**   ☆

NO. 48

Outfield — Chicago Cubs
Born: Pittsburgh, Pa., March 17, 1919
Height: 6-4; Weight: 200; Bats: Right; Throws: Right

Hank capped a long career in baseball in 1952 by having his best season in the majors, and winning the title of National League's Most Valuable Player. He was the co-holder of the home run title with 37 and he led in runs batted in with 121. He has been in baseball since 1937, shuttling between the majors and the minors. His previous major league club was Cincinnati.

| | MAJOR LEAGUE BATTING RECORD | | | | | | | FIELDING RECORD | | | |
	Games Played	Times at Bat	Runs Scored	No. of Hits	Home Runs	Runs Bat. In	Bat. Ave.	Put Outs	No. of Assists	No. of Errors	Field. Ave.
Past Year	151	567	89	153	37	121	.270	327	17	6	.983
Life time	767	2840	436	766	172	538	.268	1813	113	48	.976
This Year											

© B.G.H.L.I   **BASEBALL COLLECTOR SERIES**   Printed in U.S.A

---

11. Conversation and correspondence with Hank and Jeanne Sauer at various times during 1998.

5

1953: HARVEY HADDIX

ST. LOUIS CARDINALS

Harvey Haddix's career spanned the period from 1952 through 1965. He won 136 regular-season games, yet was most famous for a game he lost. In 1959, he pitched what was perhaps the finest single-game performance in the history of baseball. That game's score was 1-0 although it should have been 3-0 except for a mistake on the part of a future member of the Hall of Fame. Haddix won two World Series games in 1960, yet was overshadowed by Bill Mazeroski's seventh-game, last-inning clutch home run. He won twenty games in 1953, his first full season in the majors, but confusion reigned as to whether he was eligible to be considered for the Rookie of the Year award because he had appeared in seven games during the previous season. The powers thought not and this particular controversy would soon help to define the term *rookie*. The man who beat him in the "greatest game" in 1959 nearly ruined his career in 1954, when he was on his way to an even better year than the previous one. So where do we start?

Harvey Haddix Jr. was born in May 1925 in Medway, Ohio, and played baseball as a youth, learning the intricacies of the game from his father, who had played semipro ball. Haddix Senior encouraged Junior and his three farm brothers in the sport and often played ball with them on their spread in the central part of the state, about thirty miles west of Columbus. Harvey attended Catawaba High School, where he played primarily shortstop and pitched when the need arose. He batted and threw left-handed. By the time he graduated, in 1943, he had grown to about five feet six inches but never seemed to be able to put on weight, topping off at about 140 pounds. After his graduation, Harvey's parents accompanied him to a tryout at Columbus, where he caught the attention of two of the American Association team's scouts.

Harvey had completed his registration in a general way, listing himself as a first baseman/outfielder/pitcher. Walt Shannon, a Columbus employee, took one look at him and decided that this slight kid could not do all three, at least not at once. Haddix threw fastballs and curves during the tryout and impressed Shannon so much that he was offered a contract that day. However, a Philadelphia Athletics scout expressed interest and Haddix wanted to give him the courtesy of a response, but no offer came and Harvey signed with Columbus.

Haddix spent the remainder of the season with the AAA team but did not appear as a player. He also anxiously awaited the call from his draft board, as World War II still raged in Europe and in the Pacific. The call came several months later and the draft board assigned him to stay on the 430-acre farm; in their opinion, he could help the country there more than on any front.

Thus, he stayed close to home during the war. Soon after, he and brothers Ed and Ben played semipro ball on the Jeffersonville team that took the Ohio state championship in 1946. After that, and with the appearance of stability in the country, he went to Daytona Beach, Florida, to the Columbus team's training facility and was assigned to Winston-Salem in the Class C Carolina League. By this time, he had grown to five feet ten inches and put on nearly ten pounds.

The Columbus Red Birds were affiliated with the St. Louis Cardinals, and their association with Winston-Salem resulted in many Cardinal organization personnel working with the two clubs. The 1946 Cardinals had just taken the world championship and the pitching hero of the series had been Harry "the Cat" Brecheen, to whom Haddix bore a remarkable resemblance. They both threw left-handed, were slight of build, and possessed similar pitching characteristics: Haddix became "the Kitten."

As a young man accustomed to the openness of farm life, Haddix suffered from the claustrophobia of city-living surroundings. He also suffered from tonsillitis, and in June 1947 left the team to have the family doctor remove his tonsils. He returned a month later, and by then had put on solid poundage. The extra weight and stamina helped him make an impressive professional debut in the Carolina League despite the medical leave. He won nineteen games while losing just five and led all other pitchers in earned run average with 1.90. He completed nineteen of his starts and struck out 268 batters in 204 innings, and tossed a no-hitter and a nineteen-strikeout one-hitter. For that season's performance, he earned the league's Most Valuable Player award.

As Haddix had been an all-around player in high school, he retained his everyday player skills. He proved to be an adept fielder and handled the bat fairly well. Once, during his stay in Winston-Salem, his folks traveled from Ohio to watch him play. They did not tell him of their journey and, with them in the stands, he belted a pinch-hit home run. Later in the season, he hit two homers in one game.

He spent the next three years in Columbus but did not really excel until 1950, when he went 18-6 with an ERA of 2.70. He took the league's pitching triple crown, topping all hurlers in wins, ERA, and strikeouts with 160. He had developed into a pitcher with finesse and an inventory of variety. Coach Ira Hutchinson, who had pitched in the National League, worked on his curveball and manager Rollie Hemsley, who caught nearly 1,500 games over an eighteen-year span in the majors, taught him the changeup. Harvey's intelligence, as well as his additional weight and his strong wrists, which came from years of farmwork, made him an apt and eager student. Hutchinson also worked on Harvey's game form in order to preserve his stamina for the later innings.

On August 16, 1950, Haddix had his first brush with weird no-hit-type games. He retired twenty-eight batters in a row. However, the succession did not start with batter one. Haddix started and pitched eleven innings, with the twenty-eight consecutive outs coming after the first hit. Incidentally, he won that game for himself by singling in the winning run. The Cardinals purchased his contract in September 1950 but within two weeks of that call he received another . . . from Uncle Sam.

Now, you'd think that he did his duty by staying on the farm as instructed back in 1944, and that no further time would be required by the U.S. government. But this was 1950 and Harvey Haddix had not yet served any formal military time, so he did not question the call. He went off to Fort Dix, New Jersey, where he suffered from claustrophobia in the barracks until his release in August 1952. He went directly to St. Louis upon discharge from the Army and appeared in seven games over the final five weeks of the season. He won two and lost two with three complete games in six starts. He impressed the Cards' hierarchy with a 2.79 ERA and thirty-one strikeouts against ten walks in forty-two innings.

The St. Louis Cardinals that Haddix joined had been a National League powerhouse since the early 1920s, commencing with a World Series victory in 1926. They then took eight more pennants and five series victories over the next twenty seasons and featured such players as Dizzy Dean, Pepper Martin, Frankie Frisch, and Stan Musial. Since 1950, though, they had been in a period of decline and no longer commanded the respect of a league leader.

After their World Series win in 1946, the St. Louis Cardinals remained a force in the National League and finished second each year through 1949. By then the absence of former general manager Branch Rickey began to show what a keen eye for talent the man possessed. Rickey had put together the Cards' farm system and pipeline to the parent club, producing nine league champion-ships in twenty-one tries. They finished second six times and in the second division just twice. Only the New York Yankees produced more success over the period.

By 1947, Cardinals owner Sam Breadon had developed cancer and was doing less and less in running the team. In late November of that year, he sold the club to Fred Saigh and Bob Hannegan, who was also ill and who sold his share to Saigh one year later. Saigh enjoyed his short sojourn as owner of the Cardinals, but because of problems with the Internal Revenue Service, he sold the club to the Anheuser-Busch Brewing Company in 1953. The city of St. Louis should be forever indebted to him, for it is because of his honor and love for his home that the Cardinals reside in Missouri. He sold the team to Anheuser-Busch for three quarters of a million dollars less than he could have reaped from groups representing Houston and Milwaukee.[12]

As Rickey's strategies fueled his new employer, the Brooklyn Dodgers, the Cardinals began to wane. Despite the presence of Musial and fellow Hall of Famers Enos Slaughter and Red Schoendienst, the Cards managed to slip to third in both 1951 and 1952. By 1951, Solly Hemus had replaced defensive whiz Marty Marion at short and Marion took over as skipper, with a weak third-place finish.

Eddie Stanky replaced Marion and he, too, brought in the team at third, but with seven more victories, at 88-66. During the tail end of the campaign, a young left-hander named Harvey Haddix came directly to St. Louis after his release from the Army in August 1952. On August 20, Haddix won a game that was called after seven and a half innings due to rain. He joined a group of young arms, led by Gerry Staley, who showed a great deal of promise for the Cards. Haddix pitched in eight games in the winter leagues to further pre-pare him and give him some of the experience he had missed in 1951–52.

---

12. Peter Golenbuck, *The Spirit of St. Louis*, "The Saigh Era," 395.

Harvey Haddix and the 1953 Season

After a successful spring training, Haddix opened the season at home against the Cubs and shut them out. By the end of April he had won two games against one loss and the Cardinals were competitive at 7-4. On May 15, he beat the Brooklyn Dodgers 9-3 and snapped Preacher Roe's ten-game win streak against his team. He won his fifth game, 6-3, against the Cubs in the first game of a twin bill on May 26. Red Schoendienst, putting together his finest season, belted a homer to seal the win. Teammate Wilmer "Vinegar Bend" Mizell was knocked out in the second contest with one out in the sixth inning despite having struck out nine Cubbies.

On June 14, Haddix and Mizell combined for a two-complete-game sweep of the Giants at the Polo Grounds. Haddix shut out the New Yorkers 1-0 to improve his season to 7-3 while Mizell stood at 6-2. Four days later, in the sweltering Missouri heat, Haddix lasted five innings but triumphed against the Dodgers for his eighth win. On June 23, at home, he hit a home run with three runs batted in to pace the team to a 15-8 complete-game win over the Giants. Although he gave up three round-trippers, the game took only two hours and forty-one minutes. Still in St. Louis on June 27, he pitched the nightcap in a twin bill and beat the Philadelphia Phillies 4-3 for his tenth win, as the Cardinals closed to within one game of the pace-setting Dodgers and Milwaukee Braves.

Dodger manager Chuck Dressen picked Harvey and fellow Card Gerry Staley for his All-Star Game pitching staff, but neither appeared in the contest as the Nationals took their fourth straight midseason classic from the rival Americans. Dressen stuck with starter Robin Roberts and followed with veterans Warren Spahn, Curt Simmons, and Murray Dickson.

At this stage in the season, the Cards were in a tie with the Phillies for third place, a mere four games behind Brooklyn at 48-35. Haddix stood at 10-3. The last two weeks of July saw the Cards win five and lose nine while Haddix went 2-1.

Harvey won only those two games during the month, both over the Pirates by identical scores, 8-2. He pitched well against the Cubs on July 3 but suffered from a lack of support. He left in the sixth inning, behind 2-1, having surrendered only three hits. His teammates tied the game in the top of the eighth but the Cubs erupted for seven runs in their half of the inning and won going away, rendering Harvey decisionless. On July 28, Al Simmons and Cardinal legend Dizzy Dean entered the halls of Cooperstown as the sixty-third and sixty-fourth inductees. The next day, Haddix won his twelfth game of 1953 but on the last day of the month the Cards had fallen to eleven behind the Dodgers.

July 1953 proved to be a critical month politically. Sen. Joseph McCarthy's witch hunts were gathering serious opposition from his colleagues and from the press. Internationally, India and Pakistan reached an agreement whereby Kashmir would be split but its residents were to have no say. The conflict in Korea appeared to come finally to an end and a truce was signed on July 27.

August arrived and the Cardinals and Haddix hosted the Brooklyn Dodgers in a searing Midwest heat that reached 110 degrees for the third straight day. Haddix took the mound and recorded his third win of the year against the flag-bound Bums, limiting them to six hits in a 10-1 victory. Four days later he shut out the Phillies 2-0 on a mere two singles for his fourteenth victory and fifth straight complete game.

He knew that his good fortune and performances had to hit a bump in the road and on August 10, they did. The Braves, in front of their adoring home fans, chased him in the fifth inning after he gave up seven runs, although only three were earned. Haddix's teammates committed three miscues, leading to an early shower and his fifth loss. On August 15, Haddix went seven and a third innings, beating the Reds 10-4 for his fifteenth win.

The National Football League's 1952 champions, the Detroit Lions, played the College All-Stars in the twentieth annual such contest at Soldier Field in Chicago. Bobby Layne, of the Lions, completed nineteen passes for one touchdown as he led the pros to their twelfth success in the series.

On August 22, a spokesperson for the North American Aviation Company reported that its F-100 had been flying at a rate that exceeded the speed of sound, about 660 miles per hour. Although not the first airplane to achieve that milestone, the F-100 was the first fighter to attain it while flying at a level altitude, not heading down.

Haddix shut out the Cincinnati Reds 4-0 at Sportsman's Park on August 22, assisted by a home run from first baseman Steve Bilko and two RBI on the part of Schoendienst. Four days later, he gave up the first of Dusty Rhodes's three home runs as the Giants shelled the Redbirds 13-4 in New York. Haddix took the loss and his record dropped to 16-6. The Cardinals and Haddix faced the Dodgers on August 30 in the sixth straight day of a ninety-plus-degree heat wave. Carl Erskine, also on track to a twenty-game season and tied with Haddix for second in the league with sixteen wins, opposed him. Harvey fell victim to two Redbird miscues and allowed six runs. The Dodgers routed the visitors 20-4. On September 3, Harvey fell victim to Phillies' ace left-hander Curt Simmons, losing 2-1.

By September 13, Harvey had picked up two more victories and, in a 17-3 rout of the Phillies, he went two for five, scoring two runs and driving in another. On September 17, he faced Erskine again, this time in St. Louis. Once again, the Dodgers got even for Harvey's early-season success against them and won 4-3. The Dodgers had clinched the flag and now ensured Erskine's twentieth win.

On that same Tuesday, New York voters ousted Mayor Impellitteri in the primary and Robert Wagner was elected the next mayor of the city.

Haddix went on to win his last two starts and finished at 20-9 with an ERA of 3.06. He completed nineteen of his thirty-three starts and topped the league with six shutouts. The Cards' pitching deteriorated after him and Gerry Staley, who contributed an 18-9 mark with an ERA of 3.99. In addition, the left side of the infield proved to be rather porous. Both shortstop Solly Hemus and third baseman Ray Jablonski ranked among the league leaders in errors. Jablonski did drive in 112 runs but his .932 fielding percentage offset a lot of that offense. That does not consider those balls he could not reach.

St. Louis finished fourth, twenty-two games behind Brooklyn, but the team looked forward to 1954.

Haddix had been considered by some pundits to be in line to be the National League's Rookie of the Year. However, those pesky seven games in 1952 in which he appeared for the Cards became an impediment in the voting. He was ruled a second-year player and second baseman Jim Gilliam, of the Dodgers, took the honors.

The 1954 preseason columns highlighted the Cardinals' weaknesses, such as lack of pitching depth other than Haddix as well as a weak defense. New shortstop Alex Grammas tightened up the infield but did not wield the bat of his predecessor, Solly Hemus. Enos Slaughter moved to the New York Yankees in exchange for pitcher Vic Raschi. Nonetheless, the Cards were picked to contend with Philadelphia for the bottom of the first division.

Haddix opened the 1954 campaign on April 13 against the Cubs and lasted into the third inning as Chicago routed the Redbirds 13-4. Two days later, he pitched two innings of relief and dropped another, this time to the Braves. Rip Ripulski's misplay of Danny O'Connell's single proved to be the difference as speedy Bill Bruton scampered home with the winning tally. Harvey picked up his first victory of 1954 the next day, beating the Reds 6-3. He went eight innings, giving up seven hits.

On April 17, thirty-seven-year-old Martha Raye took her fifth groom, Thomas J. Begley, in Arlington, Virginia. Begley, seven years her junior, had worked as a dancer on her television program.

On April 24, fellow left-handed member of the 1953 twenty-win circle Mel Parnell, of the Boston Red Sox, suffered a broken bone when he was hit by a pitch thrown by former teammate Mickey McDermott. In the meantime, Haddix went out and threw his first complete game of the year, a six-hit 7-3 win over the Braves. With that, he evened his record at 2-2. On April 29 he struck out thirteen Pirates but they overcame him to take a 4-3 victory. Harvey ended April 1954 with a 2-3 record and an ERA of 4.15 while the Cards checked in at 8-6.

On May 2, Stan Musial belted a record five home runs at Sportsman's Park in a doubleheader that the Cards split with the Giants. Stan the Man went six for eight on that big day. Three days later, Haddix fell victim to an error by rookie first-sacker Tom Alston that led to three unearned runs in the seventh, and with that gift, the Phillies went on take a 14-10, eleven-inning slugfest. Haddix had not had his usual stuff and manager Stanky took him out in that fateful seventh inning.

On May 8, Haddix went the distance and beat the Reds at Crosley Field. He gave up three runs in the first inning but shut down the Cincinnati sluggers for the remainder of the contest, winning 7-3. Stanky used a four-man rotation and Haddix took the mound again on May 12. This time, the Cards backed him with twenty-one hits, two of which were his, and rolled to a 13-5 triumph over Pittsburgh. Haddix picked up win number four.

In Brooklyn, Cardinal nemesis Erskine won for the ninth time in ten tries over St. Louis on May 15. This was a squeaker, as the Brooks got their run on an error by third baseman Jablonski in the second inning. In Philadelphia the next day Haddix went seven and a third innings to conquer the Phils, 7-3. After a no-decision, he beat the Cubs at Wrigley 7-3 with a complete game on May 25, contributing a triple and an RBI. The Cards moved on to Milwaukee for a series with the Braves. Haddix was pitted against Warren Spahn in a battle of lefties. Harvey triumphed over the Hall of Famer with a 3-2 victory, ending May at 7-3.

Haddix made his first June appearance on the fourth and promptly took down the Phillies with a complete-game, 5-2 victory. Musial, who was on his way to thirty-five home runs, helped Harvey with two round-trippers and four RBI. On June 9, Haddix shut out the Dodgers 3-0 on three hits for his ninth win. Four days later he matched that with another three-hitter, a 5-0 whitewash of the Pirates in the first of a St. Louis twin bill. Musial hit a homer in the second game but helped Haddix once again with two RBI in the opener. The Cardinals moved on to the Polo Grounds, and Haddix shut out the first-place Giants 5-0 on four hits. Once again, Musial was instrumental to the victory, with a home run and two RBI. The Giants had won six in a row and Haddix halted their surge with his third consecutive whitewash.

On June 23, Haddix again went the route and beat the Pirates 7-1 on five hits. Dick Cole broke his scoreless streak at thirty-seven innings when he scored on an infield out after tagging Haddix for a triple in the bottom of the sixth. Harvey rang up his tenth consecutive success. His record stood at 12-3 and he had lowered his ERA to 2.58. Over his ten-game win streak, Haddix allowed a scant 2.09 earned runs per outing while tossing three scoreless games and completing his last seven starts.

All good things must come to an end, and the Dodgers roughed him up for ten hits and five home runs in six and a third innings on their way to an 8-6 victory. At the end of June, Haddix led the league in victories with twelve against four losses while the Cards floundered in and out of fifth place at 33-36.

July opened in Milwaukee with Haddix on the mound against the Braves. He gave up a run in the first inning, but by the start of the fourth, he appeared to be in command. Joe Adcock led off the home half of the inning and promptly hit a screamer off Haddix's leg. Harvey faltered, then limped over to scoop the ball and get Adcock at first. He then fell to the ground and left the field on a stretcher. The Redbirds went on to win 9-2, but Haddix did not fare so well. He won his next game in Cincinnati 2-1 but left after seven innings. At the All-Star break he was tied for the most wins in the National League at thirteen with the Giants' John Antonelli. Haddix had lost just four. The Cardinals still looked upward at the .500 mark at 40-42.

The remainder of the season Haddix went 5-7 and completed only four games, ending the year at 18-13 with a 3.57 ERA. He threw one more shutout but seemed to favor his injured leg, reminiscent of Dizzy Dean and his midseason injury suffered in the 1937 All-Star Game. In 1956, the Cards traded him to the Phillies; he then went to the Reds in exchange for Wally Post. He moved to Pittsburgh in time to start the 1959 campaign.

The Game

Harvey Haddix took the mound in Milwaukee against the Braves and the powerful bats of the National League champions on May 26, 1959. The 1958 Braves had taken the Yankees to the seventh game of the World Series for the second consecutive year. They had won it all in 1957, only to lose the championship the next year. Nonetheless, they were powered by the likes of Hall of Famers Hank Aaron and Eddie Mathews, with lefty Warren Spahn leading the pitching corps. Haddix sought his fourth win against two losses, opposing Milwaukee right-hander Lew Burdette. Haddix felt a tickle in his throat and feared a cold coming on. To make matters worse, the weather was damp and raw, as May evenings have a tendency to be. He quickly disposed of the first nine batters, striking out three. He continued in the same vein inning after inning. After nine frames, he had held the Braves scoreless, hitless, and devoid of baserunners. After nine innings, he had thrown a perfect game, twenty-seven men up, twenty-seven men down. He then retired the next nine batters.

Burdette, however, had kept up with Harvey and prevented the Pirates from scoring despite allowing twelve hits over the course of the game. Neither pitcher had walked a batter unintentionally through twelve and a half innings and the score still stood at 0-0. In the home half of the thirteenth, Felix Mantilla, who had replaced second baseman Johnny O'Brien in the eleventh, reached base on a throwing error by third baseman Don Hoak to give Milwaukee its first man on. Eddie Mathews then sacrificed Mantilla to second. Pirate manager Danny Murtaugh instructed Haddix to walk Hank Aaron in the hopes of forcing a double play. With two on and one out, old nemesis Joe Adcock strode to the plate. Adcock, still a fearful hitter, had not hit the ball past the infield all night. Adcock propelled Harvey's second pitch just past right-fielder Bill Virdon's glove for a home run. Mantilla scored from second but Aaron thought the ball hadn't cleared the fence, so after seeing Mantilla score, he tagged second and headed for the dugout. Adcock, running with his head down, passed second and, technically, Aaron. Hank then returned to the field and completed his trip around the sacks, but then controversy erupted around the Braves victory. What was the score? Was it 3-0, 2-0, or 1-0? League president Warren Giles finally put the matter to rest by declaring it a 1-0 game. Still, it was a loss for the man who threw the finest game ever pitched.

Thirty-two years later, in 1991, a committee defined the rules pertaining to a no-hit game. The committee declared that a pitcher must pitch the entire game without surrendering a base hit in order for the game to be considered a no-hitter. So the rules continued to go against him. He lost out on Rookie of the Year in 1953 and credit for hurling the greatest game ever pitched in 1959, albeit three decades later.

Haddix finished 1959 with a modest 12-12 record and a credible 3.13 ERA. The next season he went 11-10 in the Pirates' world championship drive. He started the fifth game of the World Series and went six and a third innings to secure the win. He relieved Pirate ace Bob Friend in the ninth inning of the seventh game and was the beneficiary of Bill Mazeroski's last-of-the-ninth clutch home run, which gave all the marbles to Pittsburgh.

He won another twenty-two games for the Pirates through 1963, then was traded to Baltimore, where he spent two years shoring up the bullpen. As an American Leaguer, he appeared in seventy-three games and garnered eight victories and eleven saves. He retired after the 1965 season with 136 career wins against 113 setbacks and posted a lifetime ERA of 3.63.

In addition to being a good hitting pitcher, Haddix fielded his position exceptionally well. He won Gold Glove awards in 1959 through 1961. Over his career, he was often called upon to pinch-hit and picked up seven hits in twenty-eight at bats in that capacity. As did many other mid-twentieth-century players, Haddix had the misfortune to have been called to military duty just as he blossomed, despite his willingness to serve in 1945. The loss of 1951–52 possibly cost him thirty to forty victories.

After his active days, Haddix stayed in baseball as a pitching coach. He did tours with the New York Mets in 1966–67, the Reds in 1969, the Red Sox in 1971, and the Indians in 1975–78. He returned to Pittsburgh for the 1979–84 stretch, when his expertise provided the pitching staff with enough savvy to post the best ERA in the league at 3.11 despite finishing last in the National League's Eastern Division in 1984. Harvey Haddix, who often smoked in the dugout during games, died on January 9, 1994, of emphysema.

Haddix, in a quiet way, bred his share of controversy. He had a great first year, or was it his second? In his second (or was it his third?) season he dominated the league's hurlers until Joe Adcock nailed him with a line drive, effectively making him an ordinary pitcher. Five years later, he pitched the finest game ever thrown, only to lose it to that same Joe Adcock. Then a committee took away his no-hitter. *Glorious game* or *glorious season*, Harvey Haddix kept the rule makers in a state of speculation, unfortunately never coming down on his side.

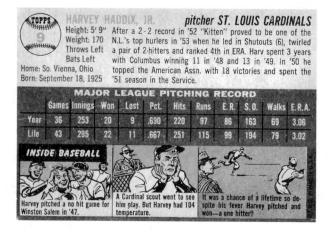

6

1953: BOB PORTERFIELD & MICKEY VERNON

WASHINGTON SENATORS

On September 25, 1953, right-handed pitcher Bob Porterfield of the Washington Senators won his twenty-second game of the season against only ten losses with a 1-0 victory over the Philadelphia Athletics. No Senator pitcher had won as many since the team's last pennant triumph back in 1933, when Alvin (General) Crowder took twenty-four and Earl Whitehill twenty-two. The triumph marked the pinnacle of Porterfield's baseball career and he was honored as the *Sporting News* Pitcher of the Year in the American League.

While Porterfield savored the moment, left-handed-hitting first baseman Mickey Vernon battled Cleveland Indians slugger Al Rosen to win his second batting title. Vernon had led the league for most of the season and did not deviate very far from his eventual final mark of .337. Rosen, who put together a whale of a year, had been chipping away at Vernon's lead and in the waning days of the 1953 season had closed the gap to .001 more than once. As Porterfield left the mound on his big day, Vernon had struggled through a zero-for-four day and saw his average shrink to .333. Al had posted a four-for-six performance against the Tigers and was red-hot, improving to .332. Manager Al Lopez had been batting him at leadoff in order to generate more at bats for his slugger. Then, the last two days saw Rosen go five for nine and end at .336, whereas Vernon went five for eight to finish with .337 and deprive Rosen of his triple crown.

Bob Porterfield began life in August 1924 in Radford, Giles County, Virginia, as Erwin Coolidge Porterfield, the youngest of six children, and soon became "Bob." His three older brothers all excelled at sports and young Bob followed in their footsteps, working on the family farm and participating in hometown athletics. They played as a family in the local church leagues, as only six years separated the oldest from the youngest. Like many other farm boys who became pitchers, Bob Porterfield honed his skills by throwing rocks. He played baseball while attending high school in Radford and started as a catcher until his coach, one J. A. Copenhaver, observed his throwing prowess and insisted that he spend some time on the mound.

After high school, he entered the Army and here the reports become a bit muddy. In article after article in publications such as the *New York Times,* the *Washington Post,* the *Sporting News,* and *Sport Magazine,* Bob Porterfield is depicted as an 82nd Airborne Division paratrooper who jumped on D-Day and participated in four other jumps, including one at Berlin. A later article, in the August 14, 1954, issue of the *Saturday Evening Post,* disputes his service record, insisting that it was inflated and that no jumps occurred in Berlin. A *Washington Star* piece written after his death in 1980 supports the earlier version. In either case, he left the Army in early 1946 and returned to rural Virginia.

He went to work for his father as a plumber's apprentice and pitched for the Radford team in the newly organized Blue Ridge League, going 7-5. It was there that he met his wife-to-be, Vera Jean.

They married in August 1946. During his courtship of Vera Jean, Bob was being courted by the New York Yankees, who bought his contract and saw enough talent to assign him to Norfolk, of the Class B Piedmont League, for the rest of the season. He stayed on through 1947, going 17-9 with a 2.37 earned run average. He completed twenty of his thirty-two starts and led the league in strikeouts with 208. The Yankees promoted him to Newark of the AAA International League and there he went 15-6, with a league-leading ERA of 2.17 and 133 strikeouts. The parent club beckoned to him in early August 1948.

Yankee manager Bucky Harris, in the middle of a pennant race, insisted he needed pitching help, and he wanted Porterfield. He argued long and hard with general manager George Weiss and eventually got his man. Porterfield went 5-3 over the final seven weeks of the season but the Yanks still finished third. Weiss gave Harris his walking papers at the end of the campaign and the sports scuttlebutt generally attributed his dismissal to the Porterfield incident.

In his first start for the Yankees, Bob faced the pennant-bound Cleveland Indians before more than 73,000 fans at Municipal Stadium. He pitched into the seventh inning and allowed only four hits, one of which was an Eddie Robinson solo home run. In the seventh, pinch hitter Hal Peck hit a screamer back to the mound that badly bruised the index finger on Porterfield's pitching hand, putting him temporarily out of action. This was the first of many hard-luck, bizarre injuries for the young man from Virginia. In 1949, he appeared in only twelve games for the Yankees and five for Newark as he twice tore a muscle below his right elbow. The next year, while pitching batting practice in Boston, a line drive caromed off his leg and sent him to the hospital. Later in the year, Paul Calvert of Detroit beaned him, again putting him out of action, this time with a broken jaw. In 1951, after joining the Senators, he was lighting a cigarette when the box of matches flared up, singeing his eyelashes and eyebrows.

Bucky Harris, now Washington manager, and Senators owner Clark Griffith traded lefty Bob Kuzava to the Yankees for Porterfield and two other players. Yankee manager Casey Stengel wanted Kuzava as a southpaw reliever. Harris wanted to be reunited with Porterfield and was ecstatic when the deal went through. Porterfield further boosted Harris's confidence in him, going 9-8 with a 3.24 ERA for the 62-92 Senators. His record slipped to 13-14 in 1952, but his ERA also dropped, to 2.72. He threw three shutouts, but he had to, for while he pitched, the Nats were shut out seven times, three times by 1-0, including a no-hitter by the Tigers' Virgil Trucks.

Mickey Vernon: Veteran Senator

James Barton "Mickey" Vernon enjoyed the admiration of none other than President Dwight D. Eisenhower. Ike considered him his favorite ballplayer. Vernon was born in April 1918 in Marcus Hook, Pennsylvania, making him just four months older than Ted Williams. He shared a distinction with Williams, that of being a four-decade man. Both started in the majors in 1939 and both retired after the 1960 campaign.

Mickey Vernon did not play baseball until later in his grammar school days and at that time was taken under the wing of his uncle James McAbee. McAbee had played first base for various amateur teams and had been a student of the mechanics around the sack. McAbee took the lad to watch games at Shibe Park in nearby Philadelphia and young Mickey soon became enamored of the sport. Vernon did not play in high school; his family feared for his health, as he had grown so rapidly. He played in the local industrial leagues, often with men quite older and more experienced than he was. He entered Villanova in 1936 on a baseball scholarship with the intention of pursuing a career in medicine. After a semester in which he realized that doctoring would not be in his future, he played eighty-three games with Easton (Pennsylvania), a St. Louis Browns affiliate. He batted .287 but the Browns severed their arrangement with Easton and did not pay Vernon at the end of the season, as they promised. Doc Jacobs, a part owner of the Easton team and a mentor of Vernon's, sold his contract to a Senators affiliate in Salisbury, Maryland.

Vernon impressed the Senators during a tryout at Salisbury and they assigned him to Greenville, South Carolina, in the Class B Sally League in time for the 1938 season. He eventually made his way to Springfield, Massachusetts, in 1939 and the Class A Eastern League, where he batted .343 in the first half of the season. He spent the remainder of the year in Washington and hit .257 in seventy-six games.

Despite a favorable showing, Vernon found himself back in the minors for all but five games during 1940. He came up for good in time to start 1941, and hit .299 with ninety-three RBI. Perhaps the life of a newlywed agreed with Mickey. In March 1941, he had married Elizabeth Firth, whom he met in high school. They began to see each other more frequently as he climbed the minor league ladder, and tied the knot when it became apparent that Mickey would make it to the big time.

In 1942 he contributed another eighty-six RBI, although his bat mark slipped a bit to .271. After a .268 performance in 1943, he spent the 1944–45 seasons in the Navy, where he served as a chief petty officer. While in the service, his duties included acting as a physical training instructor and among his charges were Billy Goodman, a future American League batting champ, and future Cleveland outfielder and Hall of Famer Larry Doby, who would twice lead the American League in home runs, and in RBI in 1954.

Vernon left the service in time for the 1946 campaign and promptly hammered the ball as never before. He led the league with a .353 mark and pounded fifty-one doubles within his 207 hits, driving in eighty-five runs in the process. The team ended in fourth place, its last first-division finish while in Washington.

Vernon struggled with the bat over the next few years, plummeting to .242 in 1948. Prior to the start of the 1949 season, he was traded with Early Wynn to the world champion Cleveland Indians for Eddie Robinson and two other players. He regained his batting eye for the Tribe, bouncing back to .291 with eighteen homers and eighty-three runs batted in. He started the 1950 season in a terrible slump and soon made his way back to Washington once Luke Easter became the Indians' first baseman. Vernon snapped out of his slump and hit .281 for the year. He followed that up with .293 in 1951 but dropped back to .251 for 1952. His daughter Gay Anne was born in July 1952, perhaps competing with baseball for Mickey's concentration.

While Bob Porterfield sent signals of optimism with his low ERA in 1952, Vernon, at thirty-five years old, began to question his skills and value as a major league first baseman and an effective hitter for the Washington Senators. The Senators of the 1940s and early fifties fielded good and bad teams; they mirrored the history of big-league teams that had resided in the District of Columbia since the inception of professional baseball. The representative of our nation's capital had been blessed with the services of Hall of Fame pitcher Walter Johnson, a winner of 416 games in a twenty-one-year span. The team had won pennants in 1924–25 and 1933, but they were better known for second-division finishes, having achieved that ignominious honor thirty times in the American League's first half century of play. The Senators did finish a strong second to the Detroit Tigers in the war-scarred year of 1945.

Mickey Vernon returned from the service a bit heavier and more confident. In 1946 he and outfielder Stan Spence combined for 170 RBI as they led Washington to a 76-78 fourth place. As noted, Vernon hammered out fifty-one doubles and took the circuit bat crown with a .353 mark, besting Ted Williams's .342. He posted a .508 slugging percentage despite hitting only eight round-trippers as the Washington Senators eked out the last first-division finish in the city's baseball history.

Early Wynn, the Hall of Fame pitcher who made his name with the Indians and the White Sox, began his big-league career with the Senators. He came up for two quick tryouts, in 1939 and 1941, before sticking with the team in 1942. He won eighteen games in 1943 but dropped seventeen the following year. He went 17-15 in 1947 and followed with an 8-19 mark in 1948. He pitched for Washington for six full seasons and compiled a 72-94 record. In forty-five of those losses, his team produced no runs to support his efforts.

He and Vernon moved over to Cleveland after the 1948 campaign in exchange for three players, most notably Eddie Robinson. Wynn went on to appear in two World Series and took Cy Young honors in 1959.

Manager Ozzie Bluege lasted through the 1947 season and turned over the reins to Joe Kuhel, a member of the Senators' final pennant-winning infield in 1933. Kuhel spent two years in the depths of the American League and was relieved of his duties by owner Clark Griffith after a 50-104 record in 1949 andd replaced by none other than Stanley "Bucky" Harris, no longer the Boy Wonder. Harris had managed the team to its first two pennants while in his twenties and was now in his third stretch as skipper. Harris led the team to a surprising fifth in 1950 although it finished twenty games under .500. The American League that year had a very clear definition of the "haves" and the "have-nots." The Yankees took the flag at 98-56 and the Indians finished fourth with a 92-62 record; the Senators placed a weak fifth, going 67-87.

Still, Harris guided them to seventeen wins more than in the previous year. Vernon returned during the season to bat .306 for the Senators after the Indians replaced him at first with the slugging Luke Easter. Third baseman Eddie Yost batted .295 and led the league with 141 bases on balls. Vernon posted another good year in 1951, batting .293 and leading all other American League first basemen in fielding. Eddie Yost hit .285 and walked 126 times. During the season, a twenty-eight-year-old right-handed pitcher named Bob Porterfield joined the team and won nine games.

Eddie Yost had become the Senators' regular third baseman in 1947, playing 115 games before he turned twenty-one years of age. He was a fixture for the team at the hot corner through 1957, when the Tigers traded for him during the off-season. His extraordinarily keen eye enabled him to receive more than sixteen hundred free passes in addition to banging out 1,863 hits. He led the league in walks six times during his career, vying with either Ted Williams or

Mickey Mantle for that honor over the 1947–60 period. Yost stood only five feet ten inches tall yet had an air of durability about him. He once played in 838 consecutive games, only to be stopped in 1955 by tonsillitis and its accompanying fever. His defensive prowess enabled him to lead all third basemen in putouts eight times and he still ranks among the leaders in lifetime putouts for his position.

Harris's first five-year sojourn, over the 1924–28 period, produced one world championship, two pennants, and five first-division finishes. His last effort in that span garnered a fourth-place finish but with a team that was below .500 by four games. His second go-around, over the 1935–42 era, showed a noticeable decline in performance, one fourth-place team and seven assorted bids resulting in fifth-place, sixth-place, and seventh-place finishes. Between those two stops in Washington, Harris skippered mediocre Tiger and Red Sox squads. He also piloted a poor Phillies entry for two-thirds of a season in 1943. He struck gold in 1947, leading the Yankees to a world championship, but found himself out of a job after a third-place finish in the hard-fought campaign of 1948. Griffith pounced on him in time for the 1950 season and for the third time Bucky Harris was manager of the Washington Senators.

As mentioned, the 1951 version of the Senators finished a poor seventh, eight games behind the Athletics. Only Bob Porterfield (9-8; 3.24) and Connie Marrero (11-9; 3.90) posted winning records. On May 3, 1952, Washington engineered trades with the White Sox and Yankees. The Senators sent outfielder Irv Noren to New York in exchange for outfielder Jackie Jensen and pitcher Spec Shea, and Sam Mele went to the White Sox for the fleet Jim Busby. Jensen and Busby provided defense and speed in the outfield. Jensen hit .286 in Washington and drove in eighty runs for the season. He led all American League flychasers with seventeen assists while playing right field. Busby led his peers in putouts and total chances.

The Senators posted the league's fourth best ERA with a 3.37 average in 1952. Porterfield went 13-14, tossing three shutouts, and led the squad with an ERA of 2.72. Marrero added eleven victories and a slick 2.88 ERA and Shea went 11-7 with a 2.93 ERA. Vernon's bat mark dropped to .251 but he drove in eighty runs and played his usual excellent first base. Harris brought the team in at a respectable fifth with a 78-76 record, one game out of fourth place.

1953: The Washington Senators' Final Respectability

The Washington Senators entered the 1953 season relatively optimistic. After all, they had performed reasonably well over the previous campaign and spring training proved positive. The pitching appeared very capable and Busby and Jensen had bolstered the outer defense. Slugger Clyde Vollmer had been reacquired from the Red Sox in late April and he replaced the light-hitting Gil Coan in left.

Whirlaway passed away on April 8, 1953. The big Thoroughbred, racing's Triple Crown winner in 1941, became the first horse to exceed $500,000 in winnings. He had been hobbled by a leg injury in 1943 and was forced into the world of an equine gigolo. Whirlaway won thirty-two of the sixty races he entered and finished out of the money only four times.

Rain forced a postponement of the traditional opener in the nation's capital against the Yankees on April 11. However, Milwaukee rejoiced as its new team, the Braves, thrilled their new fans and beat the Cincinnati Reds 2-0 for the city's first major league win since 1901. The following day the Senators were snowed out in Boston, and they went back to Washington to prepare for a doubleheader against the Yankees.

Bob Porterfield took the mound for the belated opener and was reached for eleven hits and four walks in the New York 6-3 win. The following day, lefty Chuck Stobbs started for the Senators and he gave up Mickey Mantle's famous 565-foot home run in the fifth inning. Stobbs had issued a walk to Yogi Berra, and Mantle promptly brought him home with his rocket, which could have gone farther had the ball not caromed off a scoreboard fifty feet high and 460 feet from home plate. Mantle followed that blast with a drag bunt that went untouched until it stopped in front of second base. The bunt took the starch out of the home team; the Yankees scored three in the eighth inning and went on to a 7-3 victory.

Sunday, April 19, brought the Senators a 4-0 win over the Red Sox at Fenway Park. Vernon went two for four and scored a run in the first game of the annual Patriots Day doubleheader. Two days later, back home, Vernon went two for two in a 5-1 win over the Athletics before a meager crowd of 3,742. He followed that up with two hits and an RBI in a 7-4 loss to Philadelphia the next day.

On April 24, Porterfield faced the Yankees and lefty Eddie Lopat in New York. Lopat prevailed against the Nats with a 4-1 win. Lopat had not lost to Washington since June 1951, winning six straight decisions. Porterfield dropped to 0-3 and wondered when he would record his first win of 1953.

The next day, the Senators fell once again to the Yankees, this time by a 4-3 score. Vernon found himself doubled up as Mantle made a running catch of Pete Runnels's blooper. He then rifled a shot to Johnny Mize when Vernon wandered too far from the safety of first base.

The Senators traveled west and Porterfield finally achieved his first win, giving up five hits and shutting down the White Sox 3-0. On April 30, the Senators struggled at 4-9 and held up seventh place, and Porterfield, the team's purported ace, checked in at 1-3.

May began with accusations flying that the North Koreans had somehow brainwashed American prisoners of war held in that country. Although these allegations were vehemently denied by all parties, they never left the minds of many Americans as some of their countrymen languished in a land half a world away.

On Saturday, May 2, the Senators beat the Browns 5-4 in St. Louis; Vernon led the way with two hits and an RBI in front of a sparse crowd of 3,342. Three days later, in Detroit, Porterfield hit a grand slam, his big-league first, to pace a six-run sixth inning in a 14-4 laugher over the Tigers. Vernon added an RBI and two hits, one a double. Porterfield gave up sixteen hits in his complete-game victory. The next day, Vernon went two for three in a loss to the Tigers' Ned Garver while the St. Louis Browns' Bobo Holloman tossed a no-hitter against the A's in his first major league start. Bobo went on to record two more victories in his brief stay in the majors.

Walt Masterson, a big right-hander, limited the A's to two hits, allowing no runs in a 6-0 victory at Shibe Park. Vernon picked up two hits and scored the first run in the second inning. Porterfield followed that performance with a one-hitter of his own, shutting out the A's 8-0. Athletics shortstop Eddie Joost spoiled the bid for immortality with a single in the seventh inning. Porterfield walked Kite Thomas in the ninth but he, like Joost, was doubled up, so Porterfield faced only twenty-seven batters. Once again, Bob helped his own cause with a home run, a double, and three RBI. Vernon went three for five with a stolen base and two runs scored. With that outing, Mickey reached tenth place in the young batting race at .309.

On May 17, Porterfield improved his record to 4-3 with a 6-0 whitewash of the Browns at Griffith Stadium. He had two hits in four trips to the plate in front of a scant crowd of 3,906. That same day, Brooklyn Dodger manager Charlie Dressen benched first baseman Gil Hodges. Hodges, a favorite of the fans, had gone none for twenty-one in the 1952 World Series and continued to struggle at the plate, batting a mere .187 a full month into the season. His prolonged slump prompted his church pastor to forgo a Sunday sermon, encouraging the faithful to "go home and pray for Gil Hodges." It must have helped, as Hodges rallied to hit .302 for the 1953 season.[13]

The next day Vernon went two for three, aiding Connie Marrero to win his third game and post another shutout over the Browns. The whitewash was the Senators' sixth such success in the past fifteen games. Washington had won eleven of its last seventeen games and now stood in fifth place at 15-15. Two days later, Mickey stroked four hits including a two-bagger and contributed an RBI

---

13. *The 1988 Baseball Card Engagement Book,* by Michael Gershman, September 3, 1988, "The Gentle Giant."

in an 8-3 win over the Indians before a home crowd of more than 22,000 fans.

On May 22, Porterfield continued to hit as well as he pitched, going two for five with a double and allowing the Yankees eight hits in a 12-4 victory. He combined with Vernon and Pete Runnels to turn Irv Noren's screaming line drive into a triple play in the ninth inning.

Vernon banged out three hits and drove in two runs as the Nats took two of a three-game series from the Athletics. The team then traveled to New York and fell to its old nemesis Eddie Lopat 3-1 on May 27 for its eighth consecutive setback at his hands. Vernon, however, continued to hit and after a two-for-four game was leading the American League in batting at .346. On May 28, Whitey Ford took advantage of a five-run Yankee sixth inning to stop two Senator streaks, Porterfield's four victories in a row and Vernon's twenty-game batting streak. Mickey went hitless in four tries in a 7-2 loss.

On Memorial Day, Bill Vukovich took the Indianapolis 500.

The Senators split a Memorial Day doubleheader with the Red Sox in Washington. The next day the same two teams took the field at Fenway Park, where the Senators swept the home team behind Porterfield and Spec Shea, both going the distance. Porterfield improved to 6-4 with his 5-4 squeaker. Vernon went three for five during the twin bill with a run scored and an RBI. At the end of May, his batting average stood at .339 and the team rested in fourth place at 23-20.

The Senators traveled on to St. Louis and Vernon contributed an RBI and two hits in a 3-2 win on June 3. The next day he belted a home run in a 10-1 victory. In Chicago, on the fourth, Vernon led the Senators into third place by beating the White Sox 8-4. Mickey nailed two hits and scored two runs.

Wes Santee, a University of Kansas student, ran the fastest American mile to date, clocking in at 4:02.4 at the Compton, California, Invitational Meet on June 6. He missed the world mark, held by Gunder Haegg of Sweden, by exactly one second.

The Senators held on to their lofty perch as Porterfield won game one of the next day's doubleheader 16-2 to record his seventh victory. Bob picked up two hits and drove in a run; Vernon abetted the attack with a three-for-five day and four runs batted in.

On Tuesday, June 9, the worst tornado to hit New England in more than a century sailed through central Massachusetts, targeting Worcester and leaving in its wake ninety-two dead.

On June 14, Vernon, Jackie Jensen, and Eddie Yost all poked home runs to lift Shea to a 6-1 win over the Tigers at Briggs Stadium. Two days later, the Senators succumbed to the White Sox 7-3, despite Vernon's two RBI. Mickey drove in the only run of the game the next day as Masterson overcame Chicago's excellent pitching with a shutout of his own. Vernon continued to lead the league in batting with a .335 mark. On June 20, he went two for four with two RBI and a double as Porterfield took his eighth decision with a complete-game, 7-3 victory over the Indians. As was often the case in 1953, Bob helped his cause with a base hit.

In his next start, against the Browns four days later, Porterfield stroked two hits including a double and drove in three runs. It was not enough, as St. Louis took the win 7-6, handing Porterfield his seventh loss. The Browns completed a sweep of the Senators as Vernon hit a stone wall with his bat. His average had dropped to .319 and Washington now topped the second division at 32-34, as Detroit extended the losing streak to six games. On June 27, Vernon coaxed a walk in the bottom of the ninth to start a three-run rally to eke out a 6-5 victory over the Tigers. He had kept the team in the game with two earlier hits and an RBI. The next day held a typical Sunday doubleheader for the faithful; Vernon went three for six while the Tigers split the twin bill with the Senators.

As June ended, Porterfield took the mound against the Athletics and did what he would do nine times over the course of the 1953 campaign. He threw a shutout while topping the A's, 3–0. He belted a two-run homer in the top of the ninth, thus providing himself with a cushion. He improved his record to 9-7 while the Senators hung on to their fairly consistent flirtation with .500 at

35–36. Vernon checked in at .327 behind Boston's Billy Goodman in the batting race.

The first of July brought the news from the U.S. Treasury that the country spent $9.4 billion more than it took in through taxation in the fiscal year just ended. The deficit was the highest (peace-time) in the nation's history and brought about a chorus of criticism, albeit from the usual quarters, those who directed the spending.

On July 3, the Senators faced the Red Sox at Fenway Park. Both teams committed four errors but three of Boston's miscues occurred in the first inning and gave the Nationals a quick two runs. Vernon contributed two hits to assist Spec Shea in reaching 7-1. Porterfield picked up his tenth win on July 5, in a double-header sweep at home against the Yankees, shutting them out 4-0. Vernon helped his cause with a run and two hits. The twin bill marked the Senators' season midpoint and they continued to stay close to .500, now with a 40-37 mark. Vernon was batting .322 with ninety-seven hits.

Over in the National League, Preacher Roe, in his eleventh season in the majors, smashed a home run that represented only his third extra-base hit in more than five hundred at bats. That round-tripper also helped the Dodgers set a league record as they hit at least one home run in twenty-one consecutive games. They went on to hit home runs in twenty-four straight games, falling one game short of the major league standard set by the 1941 Yankees.

In the meantime, the Marine captain and erstwhile Red Sox slugger Ted Williams arrived in San Francisco and checked in to Oak Knoll Naval Hospital, as he had suffered from audio problems at high altitudes. He was back from the Korean War, in which he had flown thirty-nine combat missions. He had been hit twice by enemy fire and once made a crash landing. Williams ruled out any return to baseball during the 1953 season and wondered out loud if the Red Sox were even interested in a thirty-four-year-old former slugger.

On July 10, Porterfield lost to the Yankees 6-1, as Eddie Lopat continued his mastery over the Senators. At this point in the campaign, Bob had beaten the Bronx Bombers twice but had suffered four setbacks. He was 8-4 against the rest of the league. The All-Star

Game was played and the National League won its fourth straight contest on July 14. The Senators had dropped to 42-42 but were in solid command of fifth place, fifteen games behind New York.

Porterfield started the first game after the break and lost his ninth to the White Sox 5-4 on an Eddie Stewart two-run homer in the eighth inning. As the second part of the season was under way, he stood at 10-9 and Vernon was batting .314. The White Sox went on to sweep a four-game set against Washington as they climbed to second place, only four games behind New York. The Senators were now four games under .500 when they moved on to St. Louis, where the ever-handy Brownies anxiously awaited their arrival.

On July 19, Vernon went four for eight in a doubleheader split with St. Louis. He hit a double and drove in two runs over the afternoon. Two days later, the team lost to Detroit in the tenth inning, 7-6, but it was not because of failure on the part of either Vernon or Porterfield. Bob had to leave in the sixth inning with a leg injury and Vernon gave the Senators the lead in the ninth with a three-run homer. The Tigers clawed back, however, tying the game in the last of the ninth and winning in the tenth. The team traveled to Cleveland and Mickey battered the Tribe's vaunted pitching with a double and a triple to go with three RBI in a 6-4 Washington victory.

On July 26, news of a truce in Korea flashed across the nation.

Bob Porterfield beat the Indians 4-3 in the first game of a Sunday split at Cleveland on July 26. He again helped his own cause at the plate, rattling a double. Vernon scored the winning run in the first game, pounding a single in the ninth and coming around on Busby's sacrifice fly. He drove in three runs in game two but Washington came up on the short end of a 7-6 decision.

After a loss to Detroit on July 28, the Senators hit the lowest point of the season, falling to 45-53. On July 30, Vernon produced a hit in his eighteenth consecutive game and was now hitting .330. The next day, Porterfield took the mound against the White Sox at Griffith Stadium and tossed a three-hitter, winning 2-0. Jackie Jensen drove in Eddie Yost in the first inning, and then Busby chased him home. That was all Bob needed for his twelfth victory against nine setbacks. As July ended, Vernon stood at .330 with ten home runs and seventy-three RBI.

The world watched as the first wave of United Nations prisoners left North Korea on August 5, 1953. Seventy Americans were among the initial 394 released.

Cleveland right-hander Mike Garcia won his thirteenth game on the fifth, blanking the Senators 3-0. Vernon achieved his third consecutive one-for-three game. The Nationals remained mired in fifth place, seven games below .500, at 49-56. Porterfield countered Garcia's shutout with a whitewash of his own as he beat the Indians 11-0 the following day. He stroked two doubles and knocked in a run and Vernon poked three hits. The next day Marrero shut out the Browns and Mickey added two more hits.

Although he had expressed reservations about returning to baseball, Ted Williams did, indeed, come back, and hit a pinch-hit home run in a 9-3 loss to the Indians in his second at bat after reactivation. That same day, August 9, the Senators split a twin bill with the Browns as Vernon continued his consistent hitting, going three for nine during the two games with a double and an RBI. The next day he picked up three more hits and was key in a 2-0 Porterfield victory over the Red Sox at home. He started the scoring in the first inning and drove in Eddie Yost with an insurance run in the eighth. In improving to 14-9, Porterfield tossed his eighth shutout of the season. Now he had blanked every team in the American League except the Tigers. Two days later, in a real laugher, the Yankees tore up Griffith Stadium with twenty-eight hits in a 22-1 outrage.

On the fifteenth, in Boston, Bob Porterfield followed a 5-2 Chuck Stobbs victory with a 4-2 win of his own. As usual, he contributed offensively, this time driving in Jim Busby with the go-ahead run in the eighth. The Red Sox broke his streak of twenty-nine consecutive scoreless innings. Three days later, Vernon got two hits and four RBI in a 10-8 win over the Yankees. Mickey stroked a bases-loaded triple to pace a seven-run, ninth-inning rally to overcome the Yankees in the Bronx. He was batting .331 with eighty-four RBI, but the Indians' slugging Al Rosen began to creep toward him, at .320.

The Yankees got even the next day with a 7-0 victory as Eddie Yost's fourth-inning, two-out miscue added to Porterfield's woes and hastened his early departure. As usual, Lopat was the beneficiary of the Senators' largess, and he rattled off his eleventh straight win over Washington.

The Senators returned home and hosted the Red Sox, splitting a doubleheader on August 21. Vernon led the attack in the opening 9-1 victory with two doubles and an RBI. In the nightcap, Ted Williams paced the Boston lineup with four hits, including a three-run homer, in a 7-0 victory. Williams's Marine Corps colleague Yankee second baseman Gerry Coleman left Korea that day, having flown sixty-seven combat missions, primarily in an F-4 Corsair. That was added to the fifty-seven missions he was credited with in World War II. Williams celebrated Coleman's discharge with a two-for-three, three-RBI performance the next day as Vernon went two for five in a 4-3 Boston victory.

The Senators took two and lost one until Porterfield took the mound and beat the Indians 8-4 at Municipal Stadium on August 25, his sixteenth victory. Vernon contributed two hits and Porterfield held Al Rosen of the Tribe to none for four. Two days later, up in the Motor City, Vernon banged out two hits in a 12-5 win over the Tigers and followed up that display with three dingers including a home run and a pair of RBI in a 7-4 victory. Porterfield started against the Tigers on August 29 determined to rack up a shutout, but settled for a 7-2 showing for win number seventeen. Vernon drove in a run with one of his two hits. August ended with Mickey going one for eight in a split with the Browns. Don Larsen threw a shutout, winning the opener for St. Louis, 3-0. Chuck Stobbs took the nightcap for the Nats, 9-3.

Porterfield lasted into only the sixth inning while posting his eighteenth win at Comiskey Park. He fielded a grounder and threw out of position trying to get the runner at first. He pulled a back muscle on the play and left the game after finishing the inning. He departed with the White Sox scoreless. At Shibe Park, four days later, he improved to 19-10 with a 6-3 win over the Athletics.

Although he gave up thirteen hits, Bob Porterfield notched his twentieth game of the season on September 12 with a 4-3 win over the Indians before the home fans. Vernon assisted with two hits and an RBI. Porterfield became the team's first twenty-game winner in eight years and only the third since the Senators' last league championship, in 1933. The Senators lost the next two to the Tigers but salvaged the series' final game for a split. Vernon continued to hit, going nine for fourteen over the four-game set. The last game drew only 1,257 fans and Mickey left that contest at .339, ten points ahead of Al Rosen.

On September 15 the U.N. Assembly elected Madame Vijaya Pandit of India as its president. A sister of Prime Minister Nehru, she defeated Prince Wan Waithayakon of Thailand for the position.

That same day, a Dodger farmhand named Bill Sharman announced that he was through with baseball and would concentrate on basketball with a team called the Boston Celtics. He had suffered a broken wrist and an ankle injury in addition to contracting the measles while a member of the Mobile Bears in 1953.

Porterfield racked up win number twenty-one, 3-2, over the White Sox and their ace, Billy Pierce, while Vernon dropped to .336. Three days later, on Sunday, September 20, Mickey went three for nine in a double loss to the A's at Shibe Park. Rosen managed two hits in a split in Detroit.

On September 25, Mel Parnell of the Red Sox won his twenty-first game and his fifth against the Yankees in 1953. He had shut out the Bombers in four of those five victories and posted an ERA of 0.64 against New York. Porterfield also won that day, taking his league-leading twenty-second victory, 12-1, against Philadelphia. Vernon went five for twelve in his last three games; Indians manager Al Lopez batted Rosen at leadoff to generate more at bats. Al went nine for fifteen over the three games to close at .336.

Vernon won the bat crown with a .337 mark but it will be forever tainted, as teammate Mickey Grasso got himself casually picked off second in the eighth inning. With Mickey due up fourth, the first three ninth-inning batters—Kite Thomas, Eddie Yost, and

Pete Runnels—went down with little effort to ensure that Vernon would not have to come up to the plate. Vernon sort of backed into his second batting crown.

The Senators finished the 1953 season at 76-76 for fifth place. The efforts of Porterfield and Vernon contributed mightily to a poor team's credible showing. Porterfield started thirty-two games and completed a league-leading twenty-four. He also led in shutouts with nine, and his twenty-two wins topped the league. He posted an ERA of 3.35 and batted .255 with three home runs in ninety-eight at bats. He went 10-1 over the August–September stretch.

Vernon appeared in all his team's games and hit .337. His performance was consistent; he rarely strayed far from his season's average. He paced the league in doubles with forty-three and belted eleven triples and fifteen home runs. He finished second with 205 base hits, and with 115 runs batted in trailed only Rosen in that category. His 315 total bases gave him a slugging percentage of .518.

After 1953, the Senators went downhill quickly. In 1954 they dropped to sixth, and spent the remainder of the decade alternating between seventh and last. Vernon and Porterfield went to the Red Sox in a November 1955 trade. Vernon batted .310 in 1956 and went back to Cleveland, where he hit .293 in 1958. He finished his career with Pittsburgh, playing nine games in 1960 before calling it quits. He posted a lifetime .286 batting average and garnered 2,495 base hits.

Porterfield again led the league in complete games in 1954, with twenty-one while going 13-15. His ERA was a sharp 3.32 but the Senators failed to support him in the same manner as they had in 1953. As noted above, he joined Vernon on the trip to Boston but Bob never regained his 1952–54 form, going 3-12 in 1956. He was out of baseball by 1959, retiring with an overall record of 87-97 and a career ERA of 3.79.

Porterfield coached for the Syracuse Chiefs during the early 1960s but eventually migrated back south and settled in Charlotte, North Carolina. By the time he and Vera Jean moved to Charlotte, they had three children: Robert, Sandra, and Cynthia. Bob took a job with Westinghouse and worked there until his premature death from cancer in April 1980.

Mickey Vernon became the first manager for the expansion Senators after Griffith moved the old team to the cooler but greener pastures of Minnesota. He stayed for almost three years but could never guide the team past ninth place. After being replaced by Gil Hodges in May 1963, he coached for the Pirates, Cardinals, Montreal Expos, and Yankees. He also served as a batting instructor in the Dodgers' and Kansas City Royals' organizations. He managed in the top-rated Pacific Coast and International Leagues. He still lives in Pennsylvania and is active in old-timers' appearances and is often the most-sought-after former Senator.

These two players, along with Jensen, Yost, and others, sought to provide our nation's capital with the best brand of baseball before Calvin Griffith abandoned the city for Minnesota. Old Senators faithful will always remember 1953 and thank Bob and Mickey for that last *one glorious season.*

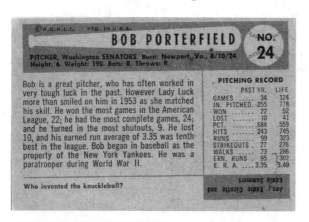

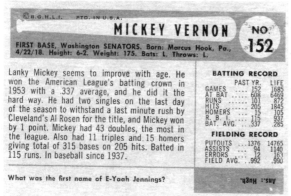

7

*1953: A*L *R*OSEN

C*LEVELAND* I*NDIANS*

The Cleveland Indians opened the 1953 championship season on April 14 at Municipal Stadium, their home park. They approached the start with a certain degree of confidence and enthusiasm. In both 1951 and 1952, they had finished runners-up to the New York Yankees in the chase for the American League pennant. In the latter year, they had held the lead in a seesaw battle with Casey Stengel and his troops before finally losing the flag in the last week of the season by a mere two games. In both years, the Cleveland pitching had produced three twenty-game winners and, in total, completed more than 50 percent of games started.

This, however, was a new season, and right-handed ace Bob Lemon took the mound at home against the Chicago White Sox and promptly picked up where he left off. He had posted a 22-11 record in 1952, and on that cool April day in 1953, he limited the Pale Hose to one hit before nearly 54,000 Indian rooters. Al Rosen, the Cleveland third baseman, went one for three with a key run batted in. On that same day, the *New York Times* displayed a picture of New

Orleans native Mel Parnell, the Boston Red Sox ace left-hander, wearing skis and throwing snowballs in Beantown's Fenway Park. A freak storm dropped over a foot of the white stuff on the East Coast, delaying the season openers by up to five days and giving southerners such as Parnell their first glimpse of Mother Nature's white rain.

The weather continued to create havoc all over the baseball map. On April 19, in Chicago, the Indians and White Sox were forced to postpone a doubleheader because of the cold. They had played to an 8-7 Chicago victory the day before. In that game, the Sox had four hits and the Tribe but three. The Indians' usual pitching control was sorely lacking; their staff gave up eleven bases on balls. The White Sox hurlers' generosity loomed larger as they issued fifteen free passes. There were errors galore, two by usually glue-fingered Cleveland catcher Jim Hegan and one by White Sox slick-fielding first-sacker Ferris Fain. It was chilly out there in Comiskey Park, and not only was it difficult to hold on to the ball, but the impact of a swinging bat against a fastball gave batters' hands quite a jolt as well.

Al Rosen did not hit his first home run of 1953 until April 23, but he chose his spot well, with first baseman Luke Easter aboard, to lead the team to a 4-1 victory over the Detroit Tigers. Mike Garcia, affectionately known as the Big Bear, was the recipient of that blast and recorded his first win of the year. He had gone 22-11 with a 2.37 earned run average in 1952.

On April 24, Rosen singled home the game-winner in the eighth inning in a 4-3 squeaker over the Tigers to give Early Wynn his first victory of the young season. Wynn had gone 23-12 the year before with a 2.90 ERA, placing second to Philadelphia Athletics lefty Bobby Shantz in victories. In a span of a mere ten days, Rosen had contributed mightily to the first victory of the season for each of the Indians' Big Three. And that was just the start.

As a matter of fact, Al Rosen had been a determined and competitive individual from the very beginning. He was born in Spartanburg, South Carolina, in 1924. His parents split up when he was at an impressionable age. His mother and grandmother provided the love and structure for him and his brother, Jerry. Al suffered from bronchial asthma and was a rather sickly child, and his mother heeded the family doctor's advice and encouraged as much outdoor play as possible. The family moved to the Miami, Florida, area and young Al attended a baseball school in addition to regular studies and chores.

By age thirteen, he played softball in an adult men's church league and quickly made a name for himself as a budding talent and fierce competitor. He enrolled at the Florida Military Academy and became a participant in four sports including baseball and boxing, excelling in both. He won the state schoolboy middleweight championship. According to Jack Torry, in his book *Endless Summers,* about the Cleveland baseball franchise, it was at the academy that Rosen got the nickname "Flip" from his habit of flipping the ball toward home plate. In *The Jew in American Sports,* by Harold and Meir Ribalow, however, the authors claimed that he earned the moniker on the basketball court. Wherever it was, it was not on the golf course or at the racetrack.

Rosen entered the University of Florida after a poor showing at a tryout held by the Indians' Wilkes-Barre Class A farm team. He had been offered a contract to play in their North Carolina State Class D League and decided to further his education after mulling over the offer, which, at seventy-five dollars per month, he considered a pittance. Prior to eventually turning pro, Al Rosen earned his degree at the University of Miami, playing football and boxing on the intercollegiate level. Baseball, however, continued to beckon. In 1942, he signed a minor league contract for ninety dollars a month, having been turned down after a tryout with the Red Sox. He wound up at Thomasville, North Carolina, in the circuit he had earlier rejected. The manager, Jimmy Gruzdis, worked with him on both hitting and fielding as he observed that Rosen, although possessing immense talent, brought a tremendous liability in the form of inexperience, particularly in the field.

Gruzdis recognized the potential in Rosen but nearly dismissed him for lack of hustle. Rosen was devastated when the manager told him that his efforts were not up to Gruzdis's standards, and he was determined to earn a reputation as a hard and diligent worker, not that of a slacker. Over the course of his career, Al Rosen achieved renown in baseball circles as one of the sport's most dedicated and hardworking athletes. Rosen had long been regarded as a powerful hitter but a weak fielder at best. His grit and determination to overcome that label eventually brought him respect and admiration for his work around the hot corner.

With the war now raging, Rosen joined the Navy after his brief stint in professional baseball in 1942 and earned a commission as an ensign. He was assigned to Camp Shelton in Virginia, where he got a chance to meet a few professional ballplayers before being assigned to a ship in the South Pacific. He served as a small-boat officer, eventually rising to full lieutenant. Baseball was found infrequently among the islands and atolls unless another ship happened to be in port and they had enough personnel to field a team.

The end of the war saw Al back in the Indians camp along with 246 other returning veterans. After a weeding-out period, Rosen was sent to a Cleveland affiliate in Pittsfield, Massachusetts, where he played in 1946, after which he moved on to Oklahoma City for the 1947 campaign. That year he hit .349 and was named the best player in the league. This performance earned him a trip to Cleveland, where he appeared in seven games at the tail end of the year. In 1948, he was invited to training with the parent club, but he did not impress manager Lou Boudreau. He proceeded to Kansas City, of the American Association in AAA baseball. He continued to pound the ball, hitting .327 with twenty-five home runs. He went up to Cleveland for another look-see, but the Indians were in a battle for the pennant with the Red Sox and Yankees, so Rosen's opportunities were limited. Besides, Ken Keltner, a Cleveland icon, virtually owned third base and showed no signs of wear and tear.

It seemed that the ubiquitous Keltner would never slow down. He had not yet turned thirty-two and had been a key element in the chase for the elusive flag, producing his best all-around year en route to the 1948 world championship. Injuries took their toll in 1949 and limited him to eighty games. Before the 1950 season, the Tribe's general manager, Hank Greenberg, sold his contract to the Red Sox, where Keltner appeared in just thirteen games and then decided to call it a day.

In the meantime, Rosen had impressed the parent team with another fine season in the minors, this time with San Diego, of the Pacific Coast League. Greenberg was ferociously in Rosen's camp and lobbied for his advancement. Although Keltner's deterioration was sudden, it was quite obvious to both management and fans. Greenberg's dilemma revolved around the replacement by a Jewish general manager of an immensely popular player with a new, talented, but untried Jewish youth.

On opening day of the 1950 season, before nearly 66,000 home fans, Rosen came to bat with the Tribe behind 6-4 in the bottom of the eighth. There was a runner on base and Al promptly tied the score with a two-run home run. He managed to hit eight round-trippers in April alone and had accumulated twenty-five by the fourth of July, and the memory of Keltner swiftly faded from the minds of the Indians fans.

As described in *Endless Summers,* during his rookie year Al suffered through periods when he was tormented by verbal taunts and physical abuse from both fans and opponents. The patrons and opposing players often jeered him by making anti-Semitic remarks. On one occasion, a Boston player unrelentingly hurled ugly epithets at him. Rosen took it quietly for part of the game, but eventually called time and left the field to head for the opposition dugout. Apparently, the unnamed player was unaware of Rosen's pugilistic skills but his teammates had heard of them. Bobby Doerr and Johnny Pesky quickly got to their loud-mouthed teammate before Rosen could inflict serious pain upon him.

Rosen's clutch hitting and consistent bat moved manager Boudreau to change his position in the batting order and place him in the cleanup spot. He produced admirably, pacing the American

League in home runs with thirty-seven while knocking in 116 runs. He played third base more than adequately and led the league's "hot-corner men" in assists. He also batted a respectable .287 and would probably have been Rookie of the Year had not Walt Dropo of the Red Sox hit thirty-four homers and knocked in 144 runs.

The Cleveland Indians of Al Rosen's era were a force to be reckoned with. They had outstanding pitching as well as excellent everyday players. The Tribe won two flags and one world championship in the ten seasons in which Rosen was affiliated with the team. However, from the inception of the American League in 1901 until the end of World War II, Cleveland's entry could be best described as acceptable but was generally mediocre. The Indians had won just one pennant and World Series and that happened in 1920. On the other hand, the Indians had finished in last place only once, in 1914. Respectable it was, but it was devoid of the multiple championships, color, and failings of the Philadelphia Athletics and of the utter, laughable incompetence of the St. Louis Browns. Cleveland fans, until the appearance of one William Veeck, simply possessed a workingman's team that, on occasion, had its moments. The team mirrored life, players going to the job every day, pursuing their trade, punching out, going home, and, every once in a while, exceeding the expectations set for them.

Before the advent of Veeck, by mid-1945 the Sherwin brothers, partners with Indians president Alva Bradley, were itching to leave the battles of baseball. The team played in two parks within the city. League Park had the dimensions of a cigar box with close fences and Municipal Stadium was built symmetrically with respectable 320-foot foul lines but with a 470-foot dead center and nearly 90,000 seats. These logistical facts and the eventual arrival of Bill Veeck would put Cleveland in the center of the baseball world for an all-too-brief period starting in 1946. Veeck, ever the promoter, made Municipal Stadium the permanent home of the Cleveland Indians and then began to do what he did best.

Wartime ball had not been profitable, and the majority of the front-line players in both leagues were off in the service. Veeck had served in the U.S. Marines and lost his right leg in the process. Prior to joining the Marines in 1942, he and Chicago Cub legend Charlie Grimm purchased the American Association's Milwaukee Brewers and turned every game into an adventure. A great many of his stunts were unannounced, for the creative Veeck was constantly in touch with his fans, relying on them for input. He heard the comments firsthand: He, like his mentor Bill Wrigley of the Cubs, sat in the stands with the patrons. He started games at 8:30 A.M. to accommodate the folks coming off the industrial graveyard shifts, which were supporting production in the fight against the Axis powers. He cleaned up the ballpark, making it a great place to bring a date or a family. He held on to the Brewers throughout the war, then, after his discharge, sold the team. He heard about the discontent in Cleveland and set his sights on the Tribe. He led a syndicate of ten individuals and purchased the team in early 1946.

Veeck saw to it that the Indians had constant exposure. He scheduled lots of night games and ensured that all games were broadcast. He handed out free tickets at truck stops and encouraged one and all to attend. He hired comedians as coaches and put music in the stands—something for everyone. The end of the war brought fireballing right-handed pitcher Bob Feller back from the Navy, along with great expectations. However, Veeck's first year as owner saw a disappointing sixth-place finish in 1946.

Lou Boudreau, then a twenty-four-year-old shortstop, had been named to replace manager Roger Peckinpaugh after the 1941 season. Boudreau was overwhelmingly opposed for the job by the powers of the team, but his lone board supporter convinced the rest of the brass to surround him with an experienced coaching staff and hope that the rest of the squad would absorb his youthful exuberance. During the war years, Boudreau did not have the horses to produce a great team. He was the best player on the Indians both on the field and at the plate, winning the league batting crown in 1944. Like most of his predecessors, his teams were respectable but plain vanilla, producing a third-place, a fourth-place, and two fifth-place finishes.

After the purchase of the team by Veeck and his consortium, which included Cleveland native Bob Hope, it became clear to Boudreau that his job was in jeopardy. Veeck respected him as a player and field leader but expressed verbally his misgivings about Lou's qualifications as a manager. On June 14, 1946, his team was edged 11-10 by the Boston Red Sox on the strength of Ted Williams's three home runs and eight RBI. Boudreau had just set a record with five-extra base hits in five at bats, but he was fuming at the difficulty in getting Williams out. His coaching staff maintained charts showing that Williams pulled the ball to right field about 95 percent of his at bats, so he devised the "Boudreau shift" in which the shortstop played in back of second base. The Indians kept statistics on their success and claimed that they got Williams out more often than those teams not employing the "shift."

Veeck recognized Boudreau's intelligence and strategic strengths and stuck with him as skipper. Lou then converted Bob Lemon from an outfielder into a pitcher. Lemon went along with the experiment reluctantly but he won four quick games. Feller notched twenty-six wins in 1946 despite his team's poor finish. He set an American League strikeout standard, fanning 348 batters. The following year Veeck acquired second baseman Joe Gordon and pitcher Gene Bearden, and outfielders Dale Mitchell and Larry Doby soon followed. Lemon responded with a neat 11-5 record to go along with Feller's 20-11. The Tribe inched up to fourth but won twelve games more than in 1946, setting the stage for 1948.

After the arrival of Jackie Robinson in Brooklyn in 1947, Veeck immediately went to work to sign good black ballplayers. At that time, the Negro leagues had high-quality players but the lure of the major leagues soon enticed the cream of the crop to abandon their former teams and opt for fame and more money. The big-league clubs that employed the Negro leagues' graduates quickly rose to the top of the standings in their respective leagues.

Larry Doby arrived in Cleveland on July 5, 1947, the second black man to appear in a major league uniform. He was used sparingly by the Tribe and appeared in only twenty-nine games that year. Veeck had long eyed the stars from the Negro leagues as an untapped professional-sports gold mine. In 1944 he had secretly plotted to purchase the Philadelphia Phillies and stock the team with Negro league all-stars. Veeck had been rebuffed in this quest by Commissioner Kennesaw Mountain Landis, but that was not to be the case in Cleveland. By 1947, Landis had departed the earth and Branch Rickey, of the Dodgers, had broken the ice in Brooklyn. Doby played regularly in 1948 and for the Indians through 1955. He batted .301 in the 1948 pennant year and won the fourth World Series game with a home run off Boston Braves ace Johnny Sain. He took two home run titles, topped one hundred RBI five times, and was enshrined at Cooperstown in 1998.

The aftermath of World War II brought great prosperity to the United States, particularly to the heartland, with industrial centers such as Cleveland leading the lot. The ironworks and mills were humming and Veeck brought the city a proud baseball organization. His player acquisitions proved fruitful and everything clicked in 1948. The Indians won the pennant in a three-team struggle culminating in a one-game-playoff win against the Boston Red Sox, and followed that up with a World Series triumph over the Boston Braves. Lemon and Beardon each won twenty games and Feller added nineteen. Manager Boudreau was voted the league's Most Valuable Player, batting .355. The Indians set a major league attendance record with more than 2.6 million fans passing through the turnstiles.

Lost in the euphoria of the championship team was the arrival of Hank Greenberg as a team executive. Greenberg had retired from baseball after finishing his Hall of Fame career with Detroit and a one-year stint with the Pittsburgh Pirates. Bill Veeck hired Greenberg before the 1948 season, and by 1949 he headed the farm system and rose to general manager. Unlike Veeck, he shunned sportswriters and felt they disliked him. He fired Boudreau after a fourth-place finish in 1950 and replaced him with Al Lopez. Meanwhile, third base was becoming an issue as Keltner was beginning to show signs of age. Keltner had enjoyed a thirteen-year career in which he and Boudreau anchored the left side of the Cleveland infield. His most productive year was the 1948 championship season, in which he hit .297 and knocked in 119 runs, including three in the playoff game against Boston. He was most remembered, however, for the night of July 17, 1941, when he took away two sure hits from Joe DiMaggio to end the Yankee Clipper's fifty-six-game hitting streak before more than 67,000 Cleveland fans. Keltner became an icon in Cleveland and seemed to be a fixture at third base. Al Rosen was waiting in the wings, anxious to get a chance to prove his skills, but Keltner's devoted teammates and fans made it difficult for Rosen to follow as his successor. In 1949, Al played in twenty-three games but failed to impress anyone, so he was sent to San Diego for more experience. Meanwhile, Keltner abruptly showed his age that season, and Greenberg sent him walking before the 1950 campaign.

Veeck had sold the Indians in November 1949 to a group headed by Cleveland resident Ellis Ryan. Veeck was in the midst of a messy and expensive divorce and needed the money to settle his affairs and move on to his next challenge. He might also have been too successful for his own good, for he began to appear bored. He turned over much of the day-to-day operations to Greenberg, and while the two men had similar philosophies regarding baseball, they were the antithesis of each other in personality. Veeck was informal, always sporting an open-collar shirt and insisting on first names. He enjoyed a good relationship with the public and the press and made himself available for meaningful copy. Greenberg, on the other hand, appeared aloof and felt that the fourth estate looked to him as a scapegoat.

Despite ninety-two victories in 1950, the Tribe finished six games behind the Yankees. The staff led the league in earned run average and the offense paced the league with 164 home runs, but the pieces of the puzzle were not fitting quite properly. Veeck and Greenberg were responsible for much of the team's success from 1947 through the late fifties. They concentrated on good prospects and building a sound pipeline from the minor leagues. Their trades, although not frequent, usually ended up in favor of Cleveland. However, their most important contribution was in their efforts to integrate the Indians. In replacing Boudreau with Lopez after the 1950 season, management could not have chosen a better man to lead the team of eclectic individuals. Lopez, the son of Spanish immigrants, grew up in Tampa, Florida, and worked his way through school in cigar factories. He knew firsthand the meaning of racism. Lopez, one of the best defensive catchers ever to grace the major leagues, cajoled and supported his players until the assimilation was reasonably complete. By spring training of 1951, the teams that had brought on the most black players were the Indians, Chicago White Sox, Brooklyn Dodgers, Boston Braves, and New York Giants. Besides the Yankees, who virtually reeked with talent, these teams proved to be the most successful in the decade of the 1950s, winning eleven of the thirteen league championships not captured by the Yankees.

Lopez emphasized speed, defense, and pitching. He was a quiet man who observed intently and thought constantly about ways to strengthen his team. He admired men who gave their all without complaints or excuses. He managed the only teams to finish ahead of the Yankees in the American League during the 1950s. Those teams were Lopez squads—speed, defense, and pitching—the 1954 Indians and the 1959 Chicago White Sox. He was elected to the Hall of Fame in 1970, a dual choice, as one of the finest defensive catchers and as a manager.

Al Rosen was a Lopez-type player who made it a point never to show a sign of weakness. When hit by a pitch, he would ignore the hurt and simply trot to first base. He once insisted on playing after being hit in the face by a line drive, and usually returned from an injury too soon. He was not a big man as athletes go, standing five feet, ten and a half inches and weighing a solid 180 pounds, but he was always ready to play. He was a strong man who, while not blessed with blazing speed, ran the bases with intelligence and managed to take liberties and enhance the position of his team in key situations.

After his sterling rookie performance, he slumped to .265 in 1951 but still drove home 102 runs while drilling twenty-four homers, as Lopez guided the Tribe into second place, five games behind the Yankees. Indians pitching produced three twenty-game winners in Feller, Wynn, and Garcia, with Lemon chipping in with another seventeen. The following year saw Cleveland lose out to the Yanks in the last week of the season, finishing just two games behind. Lopez's catcher Jim Hegan handled the staff just as Lopez would have done in his heyday. Lemon, Wynn, and Garcia each recorded twenty wins under his guidance. Rosen rebounded to hit .302 and led the league in RBI with 105. He hit twenty-eight home runs, four behind teammate Larry Doby.

Al Rosen and His 1953 Most Valuable Player Season

Rosen contributed handily to assist the team's three ace pitchers in gaining their first victories of the young 1953 season, but had hit only one home run by the third week of April. In a doubleheader sweep of the Detroit Tigers on April 25, he hit another homer, scoring both runs in a 2-1 win in the first game and driving in four in the second.

Native Dancer, a three-year-old colt, was having no trouble piling up racing wins. On Saturday, April 25, he took the Wood Memorial for his eleventh victory in as many tries. He went off as a 1-10 favorite and was the consensus horse for the following week's Kentucky Derby.

On April 29, Joe Adcock, of the newly relocated Milwaukee Braves, put a 475-foot blast into the center-field bleachers of the Giants' Upper Manhattan home, the Polo Grounds. It must have been the eastern air that spring: Twelve days earlier Mickey Mantle hammered the 565-foot job that cleared everything in Washington. Mantle's tape-measure home run prompted Yankee catcher Yogi Berra to remind Mickey that he still got credit for only one no matter how far he hit the ball.

On April 30, 1953, the New York Times *ran a feature article noting that thoroughbred and harness tracks, with nearly forty-six million paying fans, outdrew all professional baseball teams by more than five million patrons in 1952. Ironically, two days later, on May 2, Dark Star, a 25-1 longshot, handed Native Dancer his first career loss in twelve starts. Unfortunately, that upset happened at Churchill Downs in the Kentucky Derby.*

In the 1950s, Sunday usually meant church for many Americans and a doubleheader for baseball fans from April through September. On Sunday, May 3, the Cleveland Indians swept two games from the Washington Senators, winning 7-0 and 4-3. Rosen, still searching for that elusive third home run, paced the Tribe with five hits in the twin bill and drove in a run in each game. A week later, he hit two round-trippers and drove in three runs as the Tribe beat the Browns 12-3 in St. Louis. He was hitting .362, second in the league, and had now hit four home runs, but did not yet appear among the leaders in either home runs or RBI. The Indians were tied with the Yankees for first place with a 13-6 record.

On Friday, May 15, heavyweight champion Rocky Marciano knocked out challenger Ezzard Charles at 2:25 of the first round of their fight in Chicago. More than 13,000 fans attended the event with a gross gate of $332,000. Marciano's take was in excess of $160,000.

Earlier on May 15, longtime Boston Red Sox center fielder Dominic DiMaggio announced his retirement from the game at age thirty-five, the last DiMaggio brother to hang up his spikes. The next day, Dimaggio's former teammates eked out a 1-0 squeaker over Cleveland at Fenway, handing the Indians their fifth straight loss and dropping the Tribe to fourth place. The Indians then moved on to Philadelphia, where the Athletics, who were a mere shadow of their competitive 1952 team, gleefully dropped a twin bill to them.

The following Saturday, Rosen and Larry Doby each hit two two-run homers in a 5-1 win over the ever-handy Browns in Cleveland. Al was beginning to appear among the leaders in both home runs and RBI while maintaining his lofty average.

On May 23, Native Dancer, ridden by jockey Eddie Arcaro, rebounded from his stunning defeat in the Derby by racing to a victory at Pimlico Racetrack in the Preakness. Dark Star, his nemesis from Churchill Downs, finished fifth and thus assured the public that there would be no Triple Crown champion in horse racing in 1953. As an aside, an article in the

New York Times on June 1, 2003, entitled "The Gray Ghost Is Haunting the Triple Crown," by Alfred G. Vanderbilt Jr. spoke about gelding Funny Cide and his prevalence in the 2003 Derby. Funny Cide succeeded at the Preakness but failed in the Belmont and, as in every year since 1978, denied racing fans a Triple Crown winner. However, the article also noted that every entry in the 2003 Kentucky Derby was a descendant of Native Dancer, merely solidifying the power of that particular horse.

Al Rosen continued to lead his team with clutch hitting and timely production, chasing a different triple crown. On May 24, he drove in three runs and hit a homer off former teammate Satchel Paige in the first game of a 5-1, 9-8 sweep over the Browns. Two days later, he went two for four with two RBI as the Indians took the Tigers 9-8. They then moved on to Chicago, where they won two of the first three games against the White Sox, with whom they were neck-and-neck in the race behind the Yankees. Rosen won the Friday-night game with a solo shot in the sixth as the Indians hung on for a 2-1 win. On Saturday, before nearly 42,000 fans, the teams split a twin bill as Rosen drove in another five runs. At this point in the season, he was now first in home runs with ten, second in batting at .341, and second in runs batted in with thirty.

On June 2, 1952, Al Rosen celebrated the coronation of Great Britain's Queen Elizabeth II by driving in four runs with a double and a home run to solidify Mike "Big Bear" Garcia's victory over the Red Sox 7-3 in Boston. The next day the Bostons showed their English heritage with a 4-3 win, but Rosen poked another homer and drove in all the Cleveland runs. Al's bat began to cool off, and over the next weekend he began a nothing-for-ten stretch, although the Tribe won all three games.

The following Saturday, Native Dancer won the Belmont Stakes to take the final two-thirds of the Triple Crown and leaving the Kentucky Derby as the only blemish on his remarkable record.

The weekend of June 12–14 saw the Yankees come into Municipal Stadium and take four straight contests, with the Sunday doubleheader drawing nearly 75,000 fans. The Yanks made the Tribe their eighteenth consecutive victim with a 3-0 win in the second game. They led the American League by ten and a half games.

Of all teams, it was the St. Louis Browns that snapped the Yankees' win streak the next day, beating them 3-1. As it was a Monday, the Indians had the day off and licked their wounds, hoping to gear themselves up for a pennant race. The Tribe won three of their next four appearances; Al led the way with two homers and six RBI. Throughout his career, opponents regarded Rosen as most dangerous in clutch situations. He provided his team with timely leadership.

A week later in Yankee Stadium, the Indians were in the middle of a three-game weekend sweep, handing the Yanks their fifth, sixth, and seventh consecutive losses before crowds totaling more than 100,000. They now trailed New York by only six games.

The Yankees would eventually lose nine in a row, ending this ignominious streak by being four-hit and shut out by Boston ace left-hander Mel Parnell. Parnell would go on to record five wins over the Yanks in 1953, four of them whitewashes. More than 50,000 fans in Detroit on June 30 watched as the Indians took a 6-4, rain-shortened game from Ned Garver and the Tigers, with Rosen hitting his seventeenth homer and driving in two runs. He was hitting .317, placing second in round-trippers, and leading the league in runs batted in with fifty-six.

July brought the intense heat of summer and Rosen responded by hitting home runs in five straight games. On July 8, Bob Lemon beat the Browns 9-1 for his eleventh win and the Brownies' twenty-first consecutive defeat in their home park, a new big-league record for ineptitude. At the same time, the league office announced that Al Rosen would be the starting third baseman in the midseason All-Star Game. He had received a quarter of a million votes more than George Kell of the Red Sox.

A week before the All-Star break, the Indians stood at 46-31. They were six and a half games behind the Yankees at the exact middle of the pennant campaign. Rosen led the league in home runs and RBI with twenty-one and sixty-six, respectively, and was batting .317 to boot. On Sunday, July 12, the Indians lost a twin bill to the White Sox. They entered the All-Star break in third place, with Chicago sneaking into second.

Rosen was hitless in the summer classic as Ted Williams stole the show at Crosley Field in Cincinnati. With the Korean War coming to an end, Williams had finished his tour as a pilot in the Marines, earning three air medals in the process. He threw out the first ball amid a deafening roar worthy of a returning hero. The Nationals beat Casey Stengel for the fourth consecutive time, winning 5-1.

Rosen and the Indians promptly got back to business two days later with Al belting a double and a round-tripper and sending home four runs to beat the A's for Garcia's eleventh win against six losses. The next day Rosen hit two singles as Lemon beat Bobby Shantz 5-0, for his twelfth success.

Back in Cleveland for a key series with the Yankees over the July 21–23 period, Rosen went six for thirteen with two homers and four RBI. The Tribe swept the series, which was highlighted by complete-game victories by Lemon, Wynn, and Garcia. The Indians held third place, eight games out.

On the lighter side, the subway fare in New York City increased from a dime to fifteen cents effective July 25. Within a week, ridership had decreased more than 10 percent and the use of slugs in place of coins peaked that weekend; nearly forty-four hundred of the counterfeit coins clogged the turnstiles. The Transit Authority quickly set to work redesigning the tokens to preclude any more free rides, as one of every 980 patrons evaded his rightful toll on that day.

Mike Garcia won the middle game of that set and now stood at 12-6. He would eventually finish the season at 18-9, sporting an earned run average of 3.25. Over the 1951–54 stretch, the Big Bear won seventy-nine games against forty-one losses and in 1954 paced the league in ERA with a 2.64 mark. He was a workhorse, and during that period completed sixty-eight of his 135 starts and led the league in shutouts in both 1952 and 1954. Mike was an important element in the Tribe's powerful pitching staffs in the Lopez era, but his accomplishments over that four-year span paled in comparison to the careers of Feller, Lemon, and Wynn, all of whom are enshrined in Cooperstown. He retired in 1961 with a lifetime of 142 wins against 97 losses.

On July 25, Rosen hit a two-run, tenth-inning homer to beat the Senators 6-4. The following day, the Indians split a twin bill with the Nats at home, then headed north to Yankee Stadium for a three-game series. This time, on enemy turf, they salvaged the finale in the set, then headed to Philadelphia, where, on the last day of July, they took the first game from the A's, 12-6. Al contributed three hits, including a triple, and an RBI.

An article in the August 1 issue of the *New York Times* noted that the Pacific Coast League had all but given up hope of becoming a third entry in the major leagues. Instead, the prominent cities, notably Los Angeles and San Francisco, would pursue existing franchises. Browns owner Bill Veeck correctly predicted that this scenario would take place sooner rather than later.

Meanwhile, in Philadelphia, Al Rosen paced the Indians to complete a three-game sweep of the A's, driving in four runs with five hits including home run number twenty-seven. Later that week, on the final stretch of the road trip, Rosen went two for five against the Red Sox to provide Garcia with the punch necessary to improve to 14-6. Boston had taken the first two games at Fenway Park, where more than 27,000 fans showed up in hopes of seeing Ted Williams return to action. Although they might have been disappointed at the loss, Williams hit a pinch-hit home run in his second at bat since returning to the Red Sox.

Back home, beginning on August 11, the Indians entertained the White Sox, who led them by five games in the race for second place. The Tribe then proceeded to lose two games of the three-game set. In the last contest, they were beaten by Virgil Trucks, a lifetime winner of 177 games who was heading for his first and only twenty-victory season. Trucks, who had toiled for the Tigers since 1941, had been obtained by the White Sox via the Browns. Virgil had won only five games against nineteen losses for the last-place 1952 version of the toothless Tigers. Despite that record, his ERA was a respectable 3.97 and two of his five wins were 1-0 no-hit games, one against the Yankees and the other against the Senators.

The Indians continued to flounder, losing two of three to the Browns in St. Louis. Rosen was six for thirteen in the set, keeping the Tribe close with two RBI in each of the losses. On August 20, paced by Rosen's three-for-six, three-RBI performance, the Indians bounced back to down Detroit 13-7. They now stood at 65-52, fifteen games behind New York and six in back of the White Sox. Since July 25, Cleveland had gone 11-12 and Rosen had a hand in most of the wins. In the process, he raised his average to .321 and poked six homers while driving in twenty-two runs.

At home, on August 21, the Indians began to show the talent that would propel them to the heights in 1954. They swept four from the Browns with Rosen banging three home runs with eleven RBI and took three more from New York before more than 78,000 fans. Al went five for twelve in the series with two homers and three RBI. His shot in game two tied the score at 2-2 in the sixth inning. The Indians went on to win 3-2. He continued his rampage when Boston came to town, going three for eight in a twin-bill sweep before nearly 35,000 fans on August 30.

Native Dancer won the Travers at Saratoga, going off at 1-20 and paying $2.10 to win. It was Dancer's sixteenth win in seventeen outings. A week later, on August 22, he would win in Chicago by two lengths with Eddie Arcaro in the saddle; he paid $2.40 on that wager. In that race, he carried 128 pounds, eight more than any other entrant.

On August 31, Ted Williams's three-run homer snapped the Tribe's six-game winning streak, putting the Indians in third place. They were eight and a half games behind the Yankees with twenty-two contests remaining. Rosen still led the league in home runs and RBI with thirty-five and 122, respectively, and was batting .325.

September began well for the Tribe, as Rosen's homer and three RBI paced the team in a 13-3 pounding of the Red Sox and Early Wynn took home his sixteenth victory. They continued to play exceptionally well, with the culmination coming in Cleveland with a 4-2 triumph over the White Sox. All Indian scores came from two-run home runs, the first by Rosen in the fourth with Dale Mitchell on base, the second by Larry Doby in the sixth inning. This victory put them in undisputed possession of second place. On Labor Day they swept the Browns, with Rosen contributing homer number thirty-nine. The Indians completed a stretch where they went 18-2.

On the road in Boston, Garcia shut down Williams and held the Red Sox to one run while Rosen supplied the firepower. He drove in both runs in a 2-1 victory with his fortieth round-tripper. Since returning to the lineup, Williams had started in fifteen games and hit safely in all of them until confronted by the Big Bear. The Tribe moved on to the Bronx, where the Yankees celebrated the return of second baseman Gerry Coleman from the Marines with two quick wins, the latter clinching the pennant. The following day, with Dodger manager Chuck Dressen observing in preparation for the World Series, Bob Lemon took his twentieth win, 1-0 over the Yanks. Rosen drove in the game's only run with a single.

With both league champions having been decided by September 13, the main race shifted to Rosen's pursuit of the Triple Crown. On September 24, Al, now hitting .331 along with forty-one homers and 140 RBI, trailed Mickey Vernon in the batting race by .003 and Gus Zernial of the A's by one in the home-run race. He had the RBI crown wrapped up as Vernon, his closest rival, trailed by twenty-five in that category.

The season's final weekend arrived and manager Lopez had Rosen batting leadoff to generate more times at bat. In the final three games with the Tigers, Al went nine for fifteen with two homers and five RBI. However, he lost the bat crown to Vernon by .001, .337 to .336, as Mickey's teammates helped protect his average with questionable baserunning. He did beat out Zernial by one with forty-three round-trippers while driving home 145 runs. Remarkably, he struck out a mere forty-eight times in 599 official plate appearances.

During that last weekend in September 1953, Notre Dame's Fighting Irish football team won over Oklahoma 28-21. The Sooners would rebound from that setback and win forty-seven consecutive games before being upended by the same Irish with an entirely different set of players in 1957.

The Indians served as bridesmaids for the Yankees for the third consecutive season. They won ninety-two games, and their "big four" pitching staff picked up sixty-six of those triumphs. The staff completed eighty-one games and the sluggers, led by Rosen and Doby, led the circuit in homers with 160.

The final thirty-seven games of the 1953 season were a harbinger for 1954. The Cleveland Indians played at a 28-9, .757 pace and Rosen paced that stretch by hitting .373 with fourteen home runs and forty runs batted in. When his performance that year is analyzed, it shows that Al did not enjoy any huge individual day. Rather, he consistently banged out timely hits that resulted in many Cleveland victories. For his contributions, Al Rosen became the first unanimous choice in the annals of electing a most valuable player.

Cleveland won the pennant in 1954 and, in the process, recorded 111 triumphs, setting a league standard for team victories that lasted until the Yankees topped it in 1998. In that championship season, Rosen batted an even .300 with twenty-four homers and 102 runs batted in. By the end of May, however, he was leading the league in both home runs and RBI and was neck-and-neck with teammate Bobby Avila in the batting race. Al broke the index finger on his throwing hand stopping a drive hit by Chicago's Jim Rivera on May 25, but stayed in the lineup until June fifth. He returned after a ten-day hiatus but was never the same.

Rosen and Larry Doby provided the power on a very well balanced team whose staff completed exactly half of their starts and let up a mere 2.78 earned runs per game. On the eve of the World Series, the Indians were overwhelming favorites to claim victory over the flash-in-the-pan New York Giants. However, Dusty Rhodes and Willie Mays had other thoughts, and the Tribe was swept away in a never forgotten four-games-to-none humiliation.

After the season, Rosen quarreled with Greenberg, his former mentor. His 1954 performance, which would have been the envy of most of his contemporaries, drew a cut in pay from the general manager. Al accepted the cut but not without emphatically informing Greenberg of his displeasure. Greenberg seemed to resent Al for his popularity and standing in the Cleveland community. Their relationship would deteriorate further before Rosen hung up his spikes.

Al Rosen's right index finger was crushed by a line drive in early 1955 only months after his car had been rear-ended by an old Ford Model A. In that accident, he suffered injuries to his back and neck. He pulled a hamstring early in the year. These ailments affected his play and his average dropped to .244 with twenty-one homers. In 1956, he appeared in only 121 games and seemed to be losing his powerful stroke. He was not meeting his own standards and the specter of a trade loomed large, so he retired from the game, at the age of thirty-three, before the start of the 1957 campaign. He played for only seven full seasons and batted .285 over that span. He hit 192 home runs and drove in 712 tallies, an average of nearly 102 RBI per season. In his all-too-brief stay in the majors, Al Rosen was known as a hardworking, no-nonsense player who demanded excellence from those around him, both teammate and foe.

Al Rosen had gone through life on the offensive. As a youngster, he endured torments primarily because of his sickly nature and his Jewish religion. He did not seek, nor did he back down from, confrontation. As his skills and reputation as a pugilist grew, he had to use his fists less often and it was usually the tormentor who decided that a beating at the hands of this young man was just not worth it. Rosen was proud of his heritage and who he was and grew more so as life progressed. His skills at third base improved with hard work and lots of practice and he was as demanding of himself as he was of teammates. He hit the ball hard and played with a fierce desire to win. Opponents preferred almost any other Indian at the plate in a clutch situation.

Rosen had prepared himself for life after baseball. He had earned his stockbroker's license and had a growing clientele at the Cleveland office of Bache. The company accommodated him with his unusual work schedule and he had an immense loyalty to the company and the city. His children were born there and he was involved in many community activities.

In 1978, fellow Clevelander George Steinbrenner hired Rosen to be the Yankees' general manager. He left the Yankees the following season and accepted a position with Bally's Casino in Atlantic City, New Jersey. While there, he hired Willie Mays for publicity and goodwill. At once, baseball commissioner Bowie Kuhn gave Mays an ultimatum: baseball or Bally's. This applied to Rosen as well.

From 1980 through 1985, Al supervised the rebuilding of the Houston Astros, resulting in the 1986 Western Division title. By the time the Astros made it to the playoffs, Rosen was remaking the San Francisco Giants. His first move involved bringing in former pitcher Roger Craig as the field manager, and the Giants made it to the earthquake-tainted 1989 BART (Bay Area Rapid Transit) World Series against the Oakland Athletics.

Al Rosen can surely be called a success. He is an educated man with strong opinions who always gives the most he can. His accomplishments, however, from his home run title in 1950 to his successes in business and as a shrewd general manager in his post-playing years, pale in comparison to his awesome performance in 1953, *that one glorious season*.

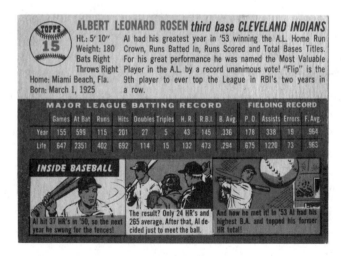

8

1954: DUSTY RHODES & JOHNNY ANTONELLI

NEW YORK GIANTS

A t about midnight on June 29, 1954, at the Polo Grounds in New York City, the hometown Giants, inhabitants of that symmetrical, horseshoe-shaped ball field, played hosts to the Brooklyn Dodgers for an elongated baseball game. It was the bottom of the thirteenth inning and the Giants were at bat trailing 3-2 with runners at every base. A pinch hitter named James Lamar "Dusty" Rhodes strode to the plate ready to go home or, better yet, somewhere cozy for a cold one.

He took two quick strikes from the Dodgers' Billy Loes and waited for Loes to throw again. Loes's next pitch became the game's last as Dusty swung hard and lined it into center field, scoring two of the three runners and giving the New Yorkers a 4-3 victory. The team, which had finished in fifth place in 1953, thirty-five games behind the pennant-winning Dodgers, increased its lead to two games over the Bums. This series and this victory in particular were crucial to the cause, for they never again pursued a leader after that game.

Nine days earlier, also at the Polo Grounds, Rhodes had hit a pinch home run, the third consecutive Giant round-tripper, to overtake the St. Louis Cardinals in a 7-6 victory. His was the second New York pinch homer in the inning. Left-handed pitcher Johnny Antonelli then came on for his first relief appearance of the season and kept the Cards at bay to preserve the victory.

James Rhodes began life as the fourth child of eight, born in 1927 to a Mathews, Alabama, farm family. As a youngster, he traveled eight miles to school and, as legend has it, was demoted to the ninth grade while in the eleventh. He left school and began his working days with a grocery wholesaler and soon found himself the shortstop on a local Montgomery softball team.

Rhodes, then sixteen years old and ready to leave for a tour of duty in the Navy, had teamed up with a pair of friends, James Hayes and Elmore Ward, who were on their way to watch a baseball game in a local church league run by a Father Rafferty in Montgomery. When two players failed to show up, the padre asked young Rhodes if he wanted to be the center fielder for the St. Andrew's Gaels.

Now, Jim had come to see a game, not participate in one, and his attire reflected that of a spectator, not a participant. Nevertheless, he removed his shoes and sauntered out to center field and began to play ball. Nothing has ever been said about his performance in the outfield that day, but stories abound that he hit two towering home runs and a triple. That and future displays of his prowess earned him a spot on the team until his departure for the service.

He returned to the Gaels after his Navy stretch. Bruce Hayes, a scout for the Nashville club of the old Southern Association, spotted him and was impressed with his work with the bat. Hayes offered him a contract to play in the Kitty League at Hopkinsville, Kentucky. He required the signature of a parent, however, for Rhodes had not yet attained the age of eighteen. Jim took it to his buddy Elmore, who promptly doubled as a surrogate father and endorsed the document. It was Hayes who dubbed him "Dusty," saying, "All roads are dusty, right?"[14]

---

14. *The 1992 Baseball Card Engagement Book,* by Michael Gershman, August 30, 1992, "Dusty the Fifth."

Complete with his moniker, Rhodes traveled up the minor league hierarchy, starting in 1947. Frank Scalzi, skipper of the Hopkinsville team, took him under his wing and tried to soften the edges in his performance. Scalzi, who had endeared himself to Giant fans with a three-error debut as an infielder in 1939, quickly saw that all Dusty could do with skill was to swing a bat. Scalzi taught him some finesse with the stick and soon Rhodes was placing and pulling the ball at will, and working on his play in the field.

He progressed until he reached Des Moines, a Class A Chicago Cub farm team managed in 1950 by former Cub pitcher Charlie Root. While moving up the minor league alphabet, Dusty acquired a reputation for downing whiskey and ignoring curfews in search of a good time. Root cornered Rhodes early on and warned him that breaking the rules would incur his wrath, and that in doing so, Dusty Rhodes would be walking the dusty roads home. As it turned out, Rhodes and a couple of buddies broke all the rules anyway and one Sunday morning Root caught him returning to the hotel after the sun had come up. While trying to draw a sober breath himself, Root asked his young slugger where he had been. Dusty, seizing the opportunity to escape unscathed, reported that he had just come back from attending an early church service. Charlie was unsure of Rhodes's religious leanings, so he accepted the excuse with a half-grin and departed for bed. Rhodes soon thereafter departed for Grand Rapids, Michigan. After a few games there, he was off to Decatur, Illinois, and eventually found himself in Rock Hill, South Carolina.

Rhodes finished his travels and stayed in Rock Hill for the duration of the 1950 season, batting .303 in the Tri-State League. His work ethic took hold and in 1951 he hit a solid .344 along with thirty-one homers and 140 runs batted in. This performance merited a trip back to Nashville with the Volunteers. At spring training in preparation for the 1952 campaign, Rhodes and a teammate went out in the evening and did not make it back to camp until about four o'clock in the morning, causing a disruption. A greater disruption occurred the following morning when the Vols' skipper, Hugh

Poland, informed Rhodes and his companion that they were not on holiday and that they were hurting their chances of making it to the big time. Rhodes's attitude and hustle began to resemble that of the previous year and by mid-July he was hitting at a .347 clip, along with eighteen homers and sixty-nine RBI. With that done, Dusty Rhodes was on his way to Cincinnati to join the New York Giants.

The Arrival of John Antonelli

John Antonelli came to the Giants by way of the Boston/Milwaukee Braves. As a junior high school student in Rochester, New York, John joined a three-team baseball league and played in the field as well as pitched. He went out for the Jefferson High School team as a freshman and carried a first baseman's mitt with him. Charlie O'Brien, coach of the team, observed his work in the field, and Antonelli's velocity and accuracy impressed him. He switched John to the mound corps despite objections on Antonelli's part. He began pitching as a sophomore and possessed a sharp curve in addition to a blazing fastball. He played football in high school but gave that up when his father, Gus, realized that John might develop into a major league prospect. Antonelli also played American Legion and semipro ball and began to attract the eyes of scouts from many teams.

Gus Antonelli knew that his son had the talent to rate consideration as a genuine big-league prospect. Gus traveled south in the winters and made his way to the baseball training facilities. He talked and observed, but mostly he listened and absorbed all he could about talent and procedure. Before John graduated from Jefferson, Gus penned letters to clubs he felt worthy of his son's talents. He arranged a game and invited the scouts, nine of whom showed up. Lou Perini, owner of the pennant-bound 1948 Boston Braves and a construction man like the senior Antonelli, made the journey to Rochester to observe this young man.

Perini signed John Antonelli for a bonus of $52,000. John headed for Boston amid great publicity, but was in for a letdown. In those days, in order to preclude the rich clubs signing every available prospect, the parent club was forced to carry high-priced, inexperienced talent on its rosters. In the heat of the 1948 pennant race, Antonelli appeared in four games, pitching four innings. He understood his lack of work but many of his teammates did not appreciate his paycheck. A good number were grizzled World War II veterans who came back to baseball only to be confronted with untried high schoolers taking up a place on a contending team, and at a high cost to boot. Johnny Sain, the Braves' right-handed ace who went on to win twenty-four games that year, reportedly went to Perini to complain about salary and left his meeting with a raise.

The following season, the Braves slipped to fourth and John threw ninety-six innings, won three, lost seven, and posted a creditable earned run average of 3.56. Still, he existed on a staff that boasted the likes of Sain, Vern Bickford, and Hall of Famer Warren Spahn.

The next year the team contended until September 1950. Manager Billy Southworth limited Antonelli to fifty-eight innings as he went 2-3 with an unglamorous ERA of 5.93. Spahn, Sain, and Bickford won sixty of the team's eighty-three victories that year. Antonelli had hoped to be the Braves' fourth starter but Southworth never got around to deciding who would play that role. Thus, Antonelli made just ten starts in twenty-two appearances.

Antonelli caught a break in March 1951 when he reported for his active-duty stint of two years with the Army. He spent his brief military career at Fort Myer, Virginia, with the Third Infantry Regiment and played for the post's baseball team. In those days, most young athletes served their two years and, while on active duty, participated in their chosen sport, competing with other units. Antonelli pitched against quality players and basically served his minor league apprenticeship in the Army. He went 42-2 over the two-year span, completed forty-four games, and regained the confidence he had misplaced while riding the Braves bench.

He reported to spring training in March 1953 and the old team had moved on. Spahn, of course, remained but many new players replaced the 1948 squad. Before camp broke and the teams headed north, Perini had received approval from the National League to move the Braves to Milwaukee. The Boston fans had deserted the team and attendance had sagged to under 300,000 in 1952. New manager Charlie Grimm regarded John as another good pitcher, not a liability, and he responded accordingly. Despite an early-season injury and a bout with pneumonia that kept him out for six weeks, Antonelli went 12-12 and completed eleven of his twenty-six starts. His 3.18 ERA came in at fifth best in the league. The Braves reacted positively to the move to the Midwest and to their new, adoring fans, winning ninety-two games and finishing in second place, behind the Brooklyn Dodgers.

While in Boston, Antonelli met and married Rosemarie Carbone, and the couple built a home in nearby Lexington. They did not make a move when the team transferred to Milwaukee and stayed in the Boston area after John's trade to the Giants. However, they did relocate to Rochester in early 1955.

When the Braves moved to Milwaukee, it was often said among the former faithful that the wrong team left Boston. In actuality, the Braves' seventh-place finish in 1952 did not accurately reflect the talent residing in the Braves Field home dugout or waiting in their farm system. The team posted a staff ERA of 3.78. Spahn was the victim of poor support, going 14-19 with an ERA of 2.98. Max Surkont and Lew Burdette rounded out the active staff and Bob Buhl was in the pipeline. Johnny Logan and Hall of Famer Eddie Mathews worked second and third base; Sid Gordon roamed the outfield. In 1953, Joe Adcock, Bill Bruton, and Del Crandall joined them, supplying the team with the foundation to dominate the league in the second half of the 1950s.

Braves management felt that they needed right-handed power and were willing to give up some of their rich pitching talent to achieve that end. The New York Giants, with Willie Mays returning from his two-year Army duty, had the hitting and badly needed left-handed pitching. The two teams struck a deal and on February 1, 1954, the Braves sent Antonelli, lefty Don Liddle, infielder Billy Klaus, and catcher Ebba St. Claire to the Giants for 1951 Giants hero Bobby Thomson and catcher Sam Calderone. The Braves also tossed in $50,000.

Antonelli was elated. The Giants went on to win the pennant by five games and swept the American League record-breaking Cleveland Indians in the World Series. The Giant victory in 1954 was truly a team effort. It is a story about a number of ballplayers who had the seasons of their lives and a fellow named Willie Mays whose performance that year was merely the extension of the 1951 miracle at Coogan's Bluff and the beginning of a long and successful career. The rest of the team seemed to jell at this point in their lives to produce that one last gasp before the abandonment of the city of New York for the gold in the California hills.

Although many of the players were on the fine 1951–52 teams, they had all aged a bit. Pitchers such as Sal Maglie and Jim Hearn had seen better years. Wes Westrum, the starting catcher, could not reach a season average of .200 but manager Leo Durocher stuck with him, primarily for his prowess in handling youngsters like Antonelli and Ruben Gomez. Davey Williams's back ached the entire season, yet he proved to be the glue holding together the infield. He retired the following season. Hank Thompson, Monte Irvin, Whitey Lockman, and Don Mueller faded quickly from the scene after 1954.

The 1954 season was really the culmination of the Giants' life in New York. It proved to be a year when they dominated the league due to heads-up play, a lot of luck, and a group of guys who performed like never before and like never again.

The New York Giants of 1954 approached the end of an era in the city of New York. The team had permanently entered the National League in time for the 1883 season and were solidly entrenched in the National League by 1902, when John McGraw arrived to manage the team. He stayed through a third of the 1932 season, at which point he turned over the reins to Hall of Fame first baseman Bill Terry. McGraw won ten pennants and three World Series during his tenure.

Terry added three more flags as well as a world championship in 1933 and managed through 1941 when another Cooperstown resident, Mel Ott, took over. Ott's Giants of the 1940s were fat, jolly, slow, and losers. His highest finish was third in the war year of 1942. Although his 1947 entry hit a then record 221 home runs, it could manage only a fourth-place result. In contrast, the Giants' cross-borough rivals, the Brooklyn Dodgers, became an exciting go-go team under the tutelage of manager Leo Durocher, who was instrumental in turning the Dodgers from a perennial doormat into a powerhouse.

In 1948, Horace Stoneham, the owner of the Giants, did the unthinkable: He hired the despised Durocher as his manager, replacing Ott sixty-six games in to the season. Ott had been the quintessential Giant. He played for no one else, starting his career with them as a teenager and ending it in 1946 with 511 home runs. At the time of his retirement, he reigned as the National League all-time home-run king and remained so until fellow Giant Willie Mays passed that mark in 1966. Ott was just the third manager of the New York Giants during the modern era. He was a nice guy whose basic strategy was to hope for a walk and hope harder for a home run. His teams were laden with power but lacked speed, good pitching, and defense.

Durocher came from a different mind-set. He had few real playing talents, but he wielded a sure glove in the field and showed an undeniable desire to win. Durocher slowly changed the Giants' way of thinking shortly after taking the reins. However, he made a series of abrupt moves before the 1950 season with the acquisition of Eddie Stanky and Alvin Dark from the Boston Braves. Sal Maglie's return from exile as a result of a sojourn in the outlawed Mexican League provided him with a big-game pitcher and a powerful presence.

During the last months of the Philadelphia Phillies' Whiz Kid championship season of 1950, the New York entry in the National League was easily the best team on the field in the major leagues. In fact, the early line in 1951 made them the favorite to win it all. However, after the first twelve games, they had but one victory, and in May, Durocher called up a twenty-year-old outfielder from Minneapolis named Willie Mays, and with his help the team began to jell.

The season was highlighted by a memorable 37-7 run to come from thirteen and a half games behind the Dodgers on August 11 to tie for the pennant on the last day of regular play. The three-game playoff is, of course, history and well known to any true baseball fan. Bobby Thomson's last-of-the-ninth, come-from-behind "shot heard 'round the world" is among baseball's finest and most exciting moments. To quote Russ Hodges, "The Giants won the pennant," and then met the Yankees in the World Series. They lost that inter-borough encounter four games to two.

Brooklyn reigned in the National League in both 1952 and 1953. New York's entry from north Manhattan performed well in 1952, finishing four and a half games behind the Dodgers for a second-place finish. Destiny did not accompany them that year. The team's respectable finish was a result of skill and desire. Monte Irvin, a vital cog in the 1951 drive, broke his ankle in an exhibition game and was in the lineup for a mere forty-six games in 1952. Willie Mays hung around for only thirty-four games, leaving for the Army in May. At that point, the Giants were in first place with a 26-8 record. It was still a Durocher team, with emphasis on defense and pitching, but with Mays and Irvin unavailable, leadership and a sparkplug were lacking. The team led the league in double plays; that was about all.

Hoyt Wilhelm, a twenty-nine-year-old rookie and future Hall of Famer, joined the team for the season and promptly led the league in winning percentage, earned run average, and appearances, all of which were in relief. He possessed a nearly unhittable knuckle-ball and incredible durability—he pitched regularly until he was forty-seven years old. As a reliever in 1952, he appeared in seventy-one games, posted a 15-3 won-lost record, and saved eleven games along with an ERA of 2.43.

Dusty Rhodes also arrived in 1952 but he did not set the league on fire. He rose from the Southern Association's Nashville entry primarily as a result of Irvin's injury and proceeded to hit a respectable .250 in 176 at bats with ten home runs and thirty-six RBI. He appeared in the outfield in fifty-six games.

The next year was not so kind to Dusty: He appeared in seventy-six games, went a mere five for twenty-nine as a pinch hitter, and hit but .233. Statistics, on the surface, do not always tell the whole story, of course. Durocher read through the numbers and saw that Rhodes had hit eleven home runs and driven in thirty in only 163 at bats. He also produced a slugging percentage of .479. Although this was hardly Ruthian, it certainly commanded a bit of respect when he stepped up to the plate.

Rhodes continued to prove himself a hard-drinking, cigar-smoking, old-fashioned type of ball player who loved a good time as well as a good ball game. He was not particularly an asset in the outfield but this fact did not bother him in the least. He could hit and hit with power, especially in the clutch. Dusty was not one to flinch in the face of a potential conflict. He exuded confidence. Durocher was heard to say that when he would look down the bench for a pinch hitter in a crucial situation, most guys sort of curled up and tried to become part of the concrete, but not Rhodes. Dusty would be up, getting his bat ready, and champing at the bit. He would say to Leo, "What ya waitin' on, Skip? Ah'm your man!"[15] Dusty's attitude would become pervasive during 1954.

After a disappointing 1953 season, in which the Giants fell to fifth place, thirty-five games behind the Dodgers, Durocher and the team toured Japan. Leo noticed Rhodes in the Imperial Hotel lobby one morning at about six o'clock. The furious Durocher quickly questioned Dusty as to his whereabouts in the previous wee hours of the day. Rhodes answered that he had been visiting his sister. Durocher was so incredulous that Rhodes would concoct such a lame story that later that morning he went to owner Stoneham's suite with the intention of mentioning the incident. Although Rhodes was a Durocher-style ballplayer, Leo wanted to ensure that no one would flaunt the manager's rules and then lie about it. Leo was also aware that Dusty was one of the owner's favorites, but he felt that no player should undermine the manager. He knocked

---

15. Noel Hynd, *The Giants of the Polo Grounds*, 371.

on the door and was surprised when he encountered none other than Dusty Rhodes, holding an early-day southern gentleman's eye-opener, playing the butler/bartender for owner Stoneham. Dusty the butler graciously opened the room to his boss. With all due respect accruing to the dandy little manager, Dusty the bartender offered Leo a waker-upper. Apparently he and Stoneham were sharing bread and spirits and discussing baseball, of course. Never to be outdone when it came to a party, any party, any time, Leo joined them and the lobby incident was soon forgotten. As an aside, Dusty's sister was married to an American sailor who was, indeed, based in Japan.

Recently, my wife and I had the pleasure of meeting Dusty Rhodes at his home in Boca Raton, Florida. When I asked him about this particular legend, he confirmed it and told us that he was also a sort of surrogate babysitter for Peter Stoneham, Horace's son. The two had been visiting at the naval station but left early to take part in a walking tour of the off-base gin mills. Rhodes was caught by Durocher because he covered for Pete Stoneham. Dusty didn't think his standing with the team owner would have been so high had Horace followed the two of them around town. He certainly respected the elder Stoneham as a party person, but the feeling on the team was that Horace could not keep up with Rhodes in any category.

That year proved to be somewhat of a transition for the Giants. As often happens when an unlikely team rises like a phoenix, many players have "career" years. The 1953 season seemed to have existed primarily to rid the New Yorkers of any bad baseball remaining in their system before their resurgence in 1954. The 1953 Giants finished fifth with virtually no league leaders except Dark and Wilhelm, who led in at bats and appearances, respectively. Bobby Thomson produced 106 runs batted in but he was traded at the commencement of spring training 1954 to the Milwaukee Braves for a couple of pitchers: John Antonelli and Don Liddle.

The Magical Season of
Dusty Rhodes and John Antonelli

The 1954 season started on a quiet note. The Giants were one of a few teams who trained in Arizona that year. Oddly enough, the Cleveland Indians also used Arizona as their spring base. The two teams saw a lot of each other, as competition was rather scarce. Neither team appeared deep enough to challenge the reigning champs, the Dodgers and the Yankees. However, the Giants seemed loose, confident, and relaxed. A reason was perhaps the return of Willie Mays from a two-year hitch in the Army.

Upon Willie's arrival at camp, it seemed to him that he was surely in a foreign land. No one rushed up to greet him and hail the hero; his idols Monte Irvin and Hank Thompson ignored him; and—most hurtful of all—his mentor Durocher did not seem to realize that he was there. After a short while of this charade, no one could maintain a straight face anymore and the hugs and handshakes and greetings all flowed toward Willie. This sort of easy camaraderie permeated the team for the season.[16]

By April 30 and after fourteen contests, the Giants were a half game behind the Dodgers with an 8-6 record, their latest win a 4-2 extra-inning victory over the Cubs in Chicago.

In the first weekend in May, Determine, ridden by Ray York, won the eightieth running of the Kentucky Derby, beating out favorite Correlation, who finished sixth. Sunday, May 2, proved a historical day for fireworks. Vietnamese insurgents overwhelmed French troops at three Dien Bien Phu strongholds with continuous assaults.

That same day, Stan Musial of the Cardinals slammed five home runs in a doubleheader with the Giants in St. Louis. John Antonelli, seeking to improve on his 2-1 record as a Giant, was touched for four runs in the opener, although Jim Hearn took the loss. The Cards pummeled second-year pitcher Ruben Gomez 8-2 the next day. Two days later, the Cubs roughed up Maglie 7-1 and the Giants slipped to 9-10.

---

16. Lee Greene, *The Baseball Life of Willie Mays*, 85.

On Thursday, May 6, Roger Bannister, a twenty-five-year-old medical student from England, stunned the world by running a mile in 3:59.4 at a meet at Oxford University. This broke the 4:01.4 record set in 1945 by Sweden's Gunder Haegg. Wes Santee, the American record holder at 4:02.4, set his sights on the four-minute mile at meets later in May and early June. It had taken seventy-two years to lop twenty seconds off the 4:19.4 record set by the British Walter George in 1882.

On May 8, Antonelli won his third game to snap a three-game Giant skein by beating Pittsburgh 2-1. Mays poked a home run in the second inning and Antonelli required no more. Starting on four days' rest, Antonelli went the distance to knock off the Reds at the Polo Grounds and improve his record to 4-1. In the American League, the Yankees beat Ned Garver in Detroit 5-3 to maintain a second-place tie with the Indians. Garver, toiling for a poor Tiger entry, had just finished up a forty-inning stretch in which he had not surrendered an earned run.

On Sunday, May 16, the media zeroed in on an eight-for-nine performance by Ted Williams, of the Boston Red Sox, in Detroit. Williams had just returned after suffering a broken collarbone in spring training. While the Red Sox dropped both games at Briggs Stadium, Antonelli quietly won his fifth in a 9-2 victory over the Braves at the Polo Grounds in the nightcap of a twin bill. In the opener, Rhodes appeared for merely the seventh time in the young season, walking for catcher Wes Westrum in a 3-2 loss.

On Monday, May 17, the Supreme Court voted unanimously to ban any form of school segregation in the famed Brown vs. Board of Education case, thus overturning the "separate-but-equal" doctrine set forth by a decision rendered by the Court in 1896. The Court gave school districts a timetable in which to comply.

In consecutive home losses to the Cardinals, Rhodes was sent up to pinch-hit, but without success. After thirty games, Dusty had just eight official at bats. He struck out as Antonelli lost to Robin Roberts and the Phillies 8-1 at Shibe Park on May 21.

At Pimlico, in the Preakness, forty-year-old Johnny Adams rode Hasty Road to victory over Correlation. Adams, who had entered the winner's circle nearly 3,000 times in about 17,000 tries, had finished second in the Derby just three weeks earlier. He nosed out Willie Shoemaker, no slouch in the saddle himself. Up north, Ronnie Perry, a two-sport star at Holy Cross, no-hit the Harvard Crimson. Perry went on to serve as athletic director at his alma mater for many years.

On May 24, Maglie was on the short end of a 4-1 game against Pittsburgh when Mays hit a solo homer in the seventh inning. A few batters later, Rhodes pinch-hit and drove in Ray Katt to bring the score to 4-3. In the bottom of the eighth, Mays poled another, this time with Don Mueller aboard, to secure a 5-4 win for Maglie (known as the Barber, because of his fondness for throwing inside to opposing batters). Antonelli followed up with win number six and was the recipient of a 21-4 hosing of the Pirates as the Giants reached third place with a 20-16 record. John hit his first major league home run in that contest. The team advanced to second with another victory over the Bucs the next day.

On May 29, Wes Santee, of Kansas, made an attempt to better the four-minute mile but fell short, achieving a 4:01.3 run at the Missouri Valley Amateur Athletic Union meet in Kansas City.

The Giants took on the Dodgers that same day and succumbed to Carl Erskine, who allowed only five hits and beat nemesis Maglie 4-2. On May 30, Antonelli got the nod but left after two innings as the Dodgers won again, this time by a score of 5-3. Rhodes struck out in the ninth as a pinch hitter.

Durocher started Antonelli against the Pirates in a Memorial Day twin bill, as he had thrown only two innings the previous day. This time he lasted into the sixth inning. He was relieved by Hoyt Wilhelm, who lost the game in the ninth. Ruben Gomez had shut out the Bucs on three hits in the first game and coasted after Willie Mays provided three runs via a circuit clout in the second inning.

On May 31, the Giants had a 23-19 record and trailed Milwaukee by a game and a half. Antonelli boasted a 6-2 mark, but Rhodes had been used sparingly and had four hits in twelve at bats.

After rainouts in Pittsburgh and St. Louis, Hank Thompson and Mays provided all the runs in a 13-8 slugfest over the Cards.

Thompson poked three homers and Mays hit two, his fifteenth and sixteenth. Hank drove in eight of the runs. Maglie left after being pounded by St. Louis for six scores in the first two innings.

In the news, Sen. Joseph McCarthy claimed to have evidence of a serious Communist infiltration of the CIA, while the Atomic Energy Commission sought to restrict former World War II Manhattan Project chief Robert Oppenheimer from access to certain classified information. At the same time, four U.S. Naval Academy graduates had their commissions held up pending background checks.

The Giants advanced to second place with a Gomez victory over the Reds in the Rhineland. Antonelli followed with a 7-0 whitewash to improve to 7-2, giving New York its tenth win in its last thirteen games. The next day the Reds led 1-0 in the seventh inning when Bill Taylor pinch-hit for Ray Katt and slammed a double. Rhodes then pinch-hit for Davey Williams, driving in pinch runner Billy Gardner with a single. Dusty scored on a two-bagger by pitcher Hearn and the Giants kept winning. The club moved on to Milwaukee, where Antonelli dueled Spahn and drove in the Giants' second run en route to a 4-0 shutout and New York's third straight in Brewville. Don Mueller drove in the first and last New York runs, and his batting average settled in at .365.

Gomez followed Antonelli's whitewash with a 1-0 gem over the Braves to pick up his sixth victory. Bob Taylor pinch-hit a solo homer in the top of the ninth to give Ruben his W. On June 11, Rhodes batted for Westrum and banged out a double in the seventh. Lockman then singled him home in a game at Wrigley Field. The Cubs committed six errors but pulled out a 5-4 win on Eddie Miksis's tenth-inning home run. The Giants returned to their winning ways with a 5-0 victory over the Cubs on June 12. With the score 2-0 in the seventh, Durocher had Rhodes bat for Westrum and Dusty responded with a single, driving in Davey Williams. At that point in the season, the Giants tied with Brooklyn for first with a 32-21 record. Rhodes had appeared only as a pinch hitter but had produced a remarkable seven hits in sixteen at bats for a .437 average.

High Gun, with Eric Guerin aboard, took the third leg of racing's Triple Crown at Belmont Park. With half a mile to go, High Gun was mired in eighth place, twelve lengths behind. He made his move and beat Fisherman, ridden by Hedley Woodhouse, by a neck. That same day, 125,000 golfers entered a nationwide Beat Ben Hogan Day to raise money for various charities. Hogan, however, stymied them all as he scored a 64 at the site of the U.S. Open at Baltusrol Country Club in Springfield, New Jersey.

The Giants took two more from the Cubs on Sunday, 9-3 and 9-4, but Antonelli left in the fifth inning of the first contest. Lockman and Dark committed errors after John walked the bases full. Rhodes once again hit for Westrum, but grounded out in the seventh inning.

On Thursday, June 17, Antonelli gained his ninth victory with a five-hit, 2-1 conquest over the Reds at the Polo Grounds before 4,753 fans. New York managed only two hits and neither figured in the scoring. The Reds' generosity provided both runs via errors and free passes and heads-up New York play.

On the evening of June 17, in front of 47,585 boxing enthusiasts, world heavyweight champion Rocky Marciano took a unanimous fifteen-round decision over challenger Ezzard Charles across the Harlem River at Yankee Stadium. It was Marciano's forty-sixth professional victory without a loss.

On June 20, after grounding out while batting for Liddle against the Cardinals, Rhodes followed Bobby Hofman and Westrum in putting together three home runs in succession in the last of the sixth. Dusty's put the Giants up to stay and the team won 7-6. Two days later, with the Braves up by 2-1, Antonelli yielded to Rhodes and Dusty flied out in the eighth. The Giants came back to score two in the bottom of the ninth to win for Wilhelm, 3-2. The team increased their record on this home stand to 12-2 with a ninth-inning rally to best the Cubs 3-2, and then awaited the arrival of the Brooklyn Dodgers.

The Giants showed no mercy as they swept the Dodgers, starting with Rhodes's two-run pinch-hit single in the thirteenth inning of the series opener on June 29. The following day, Antonelli went seven innings and picked up win number eleven as New York took its sixth straight game. In the series finale on July 1, Rhodes pinch-hit for Monte Irvin and sent two runners across with a single in the eighth to cement Gomez's seventh win as the Giants again prevailed, 5-2.

The team traveled to Pittsburgh and kept the heat high as Rhodes once again batted in the clutch. This time, instead of sending home the key run, he started a five-run rally to overtake the Pirates, 9-5. The Giants had played seventy-two games and Rhodes had appeared at bat only twenty-five times officially, all as a pinch hitter. He had eleven hits for a .440 bat mark, with at least one hit against each of the seven other teams.

On July 5, Dusty Rhodes started both games of a doubleheader against the Phillies at the Polo Grounds. In the opener, he had two hits, one a home run, in helping Antonelli ease to his twelfth win via a 10-0 shutout. In the nightcap, Dusty poked a three-run blast in the fifth inning to put the Giants ahead 4-3. New York held on to take the contest by that same score. The team ventured to Brooklyn and swept three more from the Dodgers, and increased their lead to six and a half games.

June and July were very important months for Rhodes, Antonelli, and the Giants. On June 11, the Giants trailed Brooklyn by one game. On the fifteenth the New Yorkers took undisputed possession of first place, and never relinquished that position. The Giants produced twenty-four victories in twenty-eight games during the month of June. The Dodgers, while not so prolific, managed to keep within striking distance, not really allowing Durocher and company to relax. By the All-Star break, however, the Giants' record had improved to 56-27 and their lead stretched to five and a half games. Antonelli had posted a 13-2 mark and Rhodes was eighteen for thirty-eight for a .474 pace. The three days off for the midseason classic provided a welcome relief.

After an 11-9 victory by the American League in the All-Star Game, the Giants went back to work and took two of three from the Cardinals in St. Louis. Rhodes nailed a pinch-hit single in the middle game but died on base in the eighth inning of a 5-4 defeat. In the series' rubber game, Antonelli had a 9-0 lead in the sixth inning but became unraveled when he failed to cover first base on a routine grounder to Lockman. He then gave up five runs on seven hits before Durocher pulled him from the game. The Redbirds went on to tie the game, but the Giants eventually won the contest. They traveled to Cincinnati and dropped two of three before Antonelli went the route in the series' final game, on July 20, to right the team with a 2-1 victory for his fourteenth win. Rhodes contributed a pinch-hit single in the eighth while batting for Davey Williams. Don Mueller scored, tying the game at 1-1. Whitey Lockman won the game in the thirteenth with a sacrifice fly.

The warring factions in the conflict in Vietnam arranged to split the country at the seventeenth parallel in an accord reached in Geneva. The French agreed to retain a presence in the north for another year in the capital, Hanoi, and the ancient city of Hue. To date, the conflict had claimed more than 300,000 lives.

Also in the news on July 20, nineteen-year-old tennis star Maureen Connolly broke her leg in a freak accident while riding her horse in San Diego. The horse, frightened when a cement truck appeared along the riding path, hit the truck, pinning "Little Mo" against the vehicle and crushing her leg in the process.

The Cubs hosted New York, and the Giants took the opener 2-1 as Rhodes played center field in place of Mays, who had traveled to Alabama for the funeral of an aunt. Dusty handled two chances flawlessly. The Giants' record in one-run games to date stood at 20-12. The Cubs took the next two and New York moved on to Milwaukee, where Antonelli took it on the chin as his former teammates disposed of him in the fourth inning in the first game of a three-game series. The Giants finished their western swing at 5-7 and headed back to New York to play a makeup game in Brooklyn. The Dodgers took that contest 9-0 and beat Maglie for the first time at Ebbets Field. Maglie still maintained a lifetime 21-8 record over the Bums.

The Giants then took the subway home to the Polo Grounds, where on July 28 they hosted the Cardinals. Rhodes banged a solo home run that tied the score at three in the sixth, but St. Louis prevailed despite Dusty's presence in left field and three-for-five day at the plate. The next day, Antonelli went the route to whitewash the Redbirds. Rhodes contributed mightily to the effort with three home runs, two of which foretold the shot for which he will be forever remembered. One of his round-trippers actually grazed the right-field foul pole, making it a 257-foot-eight-inch shot. Mays added his thirty-sixth four-bagger and, at that point in the season, was twelve games ahead of Babe Ruth's pace. The victory put New York two games up on Brooklyn. The Cardinals completed the series with former Yankee ace Vic Raschi throwing an 8-0 shutout, but Chicago kept the Dodgers from gaining with a victory at Ebbets.

Farther north, on the Hudson River, barges floated the first of nineteen spans into place to begin the final stages of what would be the Tappan Zee Bridge on the New York Thruway. The 250-foot metal section was placed on top of steel and concrete pillars and started the river crossing over a three-mile length.

Back in the city, the Dodgers dropped a game to the Braves while the Giants beat the Redlegs 6-1 behind Ruben Gomez, who aided his own cause with a home run. On July 31, Joe Adcock led a 15-7 trouncing of Brooklyn with four home runs and the Giants gained another game with a Maglie–Marv Grissom shutout over Cincinnati in 100-degree heat. At the end of July, Antonelli was 15-2 and Rhodes was batting .415 with eight homers and twenty-one RBI.

Antonelli won his sixteenth game in the first contest of a twin bill on Sunday, August 1, against the Reds. John went seven innings and left for a pinch hitter with the score tied at three. Dusty Rhodes, the pinch hitter, secured the victory with a two-run blast en route to a 9-4 victory. Jim Hearn followed with a 5-0 shutout in the nightcap. The Giants then hosted the Cubs and extended their winning streak to six games. Antonelli went against the Braves and, once again, his former teammates prevailed. Rhodes, now almost a fixture in left, slammed a bottom-of the-ninth homer to make it a 6-5 game, but Dave Jolly came on and retired Mueller to preserve the victory for Milwaukee. Antonelli suffered his first loss since May 21; he had notched eleven consecutive victories. The Giants dropped three more games before Antonelli again snapped the losing string, toiling seven innings in a 2-1 win over Pittsburgh on August 10.

On August 7, Roger Bannister and John Landy ran the "Mile of the Century" in a meet in Vancouver, British Columbia. Bannister beat Landy by a mere five yards and both turned in times under four minutes, with Bannister at 3:58.8 and Landy at 3:59.6.

August 11 saw Ted Williams hit his twenty-second homer of 1954 and the 359th of his career. That blast tied him with Johnny Mize for sixth place on the all-time list. He then trailed Joe DiMaggio by two and would overtake the Yankee Clipper on September 3. The next day, Erskine won his fifteenth game of the season, beating the Giants 3-2 in Brooklyn. The Giants dropped two more to the Dodgers and watched their lead shrink to a mere half game.

In the annual prelude to the football season, the World Champion Detroit Lions pounded the College All-Stars 31-6 at Chicago's Soldier Field. The proceeds, $445,600, went to fund the Chicago Tribune *Charities.*

On August 17, Antonelli won number eighteen over Philadelphia, 8-3, and the Dodgers dropped two. The next day, Rhodes hit two home runs and drove in five runs to give Maglie all the help he needed in a 6-2 win over the Phils. Gomez kept up the pace, shutting down the Phillies while the Dodgers beat the Pirates. Don Liddle shut out Pittsburgh on August 20 and, after a rainout, New York took two from Pittsburgh on Sunday, August 22. Ironically, both Maglie and Antonelli were knocked out early in their starts, but the Giants picked up two runs to win 5-4 in the opener and hung on for a 5-3 decision in the nightcap.

New York had put together another win streak—this time of seven games. After a first-game loss to Chicago on August 25, Antonelli started the nightcap and improved to 19-3 with a 2-1 win, as Rhodes provided the winning hit in the eighth inning and all the team's runs batted in with a two-for-three game. On August 29, Rhodes hit two doubles, two triples, and two home runs to pace a twin win over the Cards. The next day, Antonelli beat the Birds for win number twenty, giving up only four hits in a 4-1 game. Rhodes banged out a key RBI in that game and drove in two more in a 5-3 series finale. With twenty-five games remaining, New York held a three-and-a-half-game lead over the Dodgers with an 82-47 record. Antonelli was 20-3 and Dusty was cruising at .388, with fifteen homers and thirty-nine runs batted in.

An unnamed hurricane made its way up the East Coast and entered New England after crossing Long Island on its way to Quebec. Before it left the United States, it took forty-seven lives and toppled the steeple on Boston's Old North Church, where Paul Revere in 1775 began the ride that announced the Revolutionary War.

September began with the Giants and Dodgers both dropping games on the first. Brooklyn beat the Cubs on September 2, and then they visited the Polo Grounds and the Giants took two of three. Antonelli lost the finale, 7-4. John went five frames and gave up only two earned runs but still absorbed the defeat. The Giants then moved to Philadelphia and split a Labor Day twin bill with the Phillies. Rhodes punched home two runs that afternoon but could manage only a two-for-nine day. Gomez took win number fourteen the next day.

Over at Aqueduct Raceway, jockey Ted Atkinson joined Johnny Longdon and Eddie Arcaro as America's only three-thousand-race winners.

New York returned home for a series with Cincinnati. Whitey Lockman hit the team's sixth grand slam and tenth pinch-hit homer of the season to help Gomez to his fifteenth victory. Antonelli came in and mopped up for the last two innings to preserve the win. On September 13, Rhodes went one for three and drove in the game's only run as Antonelli beat the Cards to improve to 21-5. Dusty sent Mays home with a single after Willie hit a first-inning two-bagger. With twelve contests to go, the Giants maintained their three-and-a-half-game lead over Brooklyn.

They increased that by another on September 16 as Rhodes singled home Mueller in the bottom of the sixth with the score 1-1.

Hoyt Wilhelm went on to win his twelfth game when the Giants scored four more and beat the Braves.

At Yankee Stadium, on September 17, Rocky Marciano won his forty-seventh consecutive decision and knocked out Ezzard Charles in the eighth round of a scheduled fifteen-round rematch.

Across the river, Robin Roberts and the Phillies bested Antonelli and the Giants 4-3. Roberts tied Antonelli for the league lead in victories with twenty-one and would end up at 23-15. That same day, the Cleveland Indians won game number 107 and clinched the American League pennant by beating the Tigers. The Giants won over the Phils 9-1 to move to a magic number of three.

On September 20, Maglie beat the Brooks 7-1 at Ebbets Field and clinched the fifteenth league championship for New York's Giants. Two days later, Antonelli fell to 21-7, losing 3-0 as Dodgers rookie Karl Spooner made his first major league appearance. Spooner struck out fifteen Giants and allowed only three hits. Four days later, he KO'd twelve Pirates in a 1-0 victory. He set a record for first-game strikeouts and strikeouts in the first two games and tied a record for first-appearance shutouts. He went 8-6 in 1955 and appeared in the World Series. He returned to the minors in 1956 and never came back to the majors, despite his brilliant start.

Both Antonelli and Rhodes tailed off after the beginning of September but their performances through that time helped carry the team and complemented the play of their teammates. Antonelli consistently won when a victory was needed and Rhodes was amazing in the clutch. He provided either the winning or the tying tally on nine occasions and started other rallies. Against the Cardinals in two separate series in late August and early September, Dusty had direct responsibility in five victories.

The 1954 campaign was certainly a year for the fans of the New York Giants to remember. It was a season in which nearly everything went right for Rhodes. When a hit was needed, he supplied it. He provided a sort of looseness in the dugout with his ubiquitous confidence and infectious can-do attitude.

The regular season finished for the Giants in a most successful manner. They won the pennant by five games and produced some sterling individual performances. Antonelli came through with a neat 21-7 record and paced the league with a 2.30 ERA and six shutouts. Ruben Gomez, a second-year man, went 17-9 with a 2.88 ERA. Sal Maglie went 14-6. The pitching staff compiled an ERA of 3.09.

Giant fans often remember the 1954 team for its all-around play and hero-a-day displays, but they were more than that. Besides the consistent quality pitching, the team tied Brooklyn for the league lead in home runs.

In the field, Willie Mays won the only batting title in his twenty-two-year career, edging out teammate and fellow outfielder Don Mueller .345 to .342. He had hit thirty of his forty-one home runs and driven in seventy-one of his 110 RBI by July 9. He was batting .332 and manager Leo Durocher instructed him to ease up and get more base hits. It apparently worked, as Willie won the first of his two Most Valuable Player awards and became the day-to-day leader of the Giants with his timely hitting and support in the field.

Mueller, the right fielder, stroked a majors-leading 212 hits and proved a good setup man for Mays and Hank Thompson. Thompson, who had had lost his third base job to Bobby Thomson during the 1951 pennant drive, took it back in 1954. He also slugged a career-high twenty-six homers and drove in eighty-six important runs. Monte Irvin, though showing his age at thirty-six, continued to provide stability and experience both in the field and at bat. He slugged nineteen homers and drove in numerous key runs. Monte holds a special place in the saga of Dusty Rhodes. It was due to his broken leg in 1952 that Rhodes came up to the majors, and he always seemed to be coming to bat in a tight situation when Durocher would call him back and send up Dusty in his place. And Dusty usually came through!

Thompson's neighbors in the infield gave the Giants a very steady defense. Whitey Lockman, a good-fielding first baseman, did not have a good offensive season in 1954. At twenty-eight, his career had seen better days. Whitey had been an outfielder until 1951, but

Durocher, in juggling the ballplayers, imported him to the infield for the chase of the Dodgers. In 1954, his .251 batting average was forty points lower than his lifetime average at that time but he came through in the clutch and anchored the infield despite a stomach ailment that persisted through the season.

Davey Williams sparkled in the field and was easily the league's best-fielding second baseman. On August 6, he bobbled a grounder against the Braves after 261 errorless chances. He collaborated with shortstop Al Dark to turn many a timely double play. He was at the end of his time in the big leagues, as his back consistently gave him trouble. He hung up his spikes after the 1955 season at the age of twenty-six.

But Dusty Rhodes had the season of his life. He told us, "Reaching the top is hard and it's worth it; staying there is tougher." Rhodes appeared in a total of eighty-two games, coming to bat only 164 times. He hit .341 and had a slugging percentage of .695. Fifteen of his fifty-six hits were round-trippers, which led to fifty runs batted in. Durocher used Rhodes sparingly in the outfield; Dusty was not known for his fielding prowess. Apparently, Leo felt that the huge center field at the Polo Grounds was enough for even a young wizard like Mays to cover and he didn't want to burden Willie by having him play right or left in addition. Dusty played only thirty-seven games in the outfield.

Rhodes's specialty that season was the pinch hit. He came up in many clutch situations and accumulated fifteen hits in forty-five pinch at bats during the regular season. His pinch hits resulted directly in at least four Giant victories. He started rallies with clutch off-the-bench hits on at least two other occasions. Rhodes hit two homers in his pinch-hitting appearances. The Giants, as a team, poked a record ten pinch-hit home runs that season and averaged .253 in 182 official pinch at bats. Eight of the ten aforementioned home runs won ball games; the other two gave the Giants a tie at that moment in the game.

The World Series

Rhodes is most fondly remembered by Giants' fans for his pinch-hit home run off Bob Lemon of the Cleveland Indians in game one of the 1954 World Series. That hit followed by two innings Willie Mays's famous catch of the rocket hit by the Indians' Vic Wertz at the 460-foot mark in deepest center field in the Polo Grounds, and gave the Giants a shocking first-game 5-2 victory en route to a sweep of the Tribe.

The Cleveland Indians of 1954 won an American League–record 111 games against only forty-three losses. They boasted a pitching staff that completed half the games they started and allowed only 2.78 earned runs per game. The Indians' big three, comprising Bob Lemon, Early Wynn, and Mike Garcia, won sixty-five games against only twenty-six defeats. Bob Feller and Art Houtemann added twenty-eight wins, losing only ten. The team's elite relief corps managed thirty-six saves with Ray Narleski leading the pack with thirteen. The pitching staff included four future Hall of Famers: Lemon, Wynn, Feller, and Hal Newhouser.

The Indians also boasted a potent lineup. Their second baseman, Bobby Avila, won the batting title with a .341 average and Larry Doby, the center fielder, led the league in home runs and runs batted in with thirty-two and 126, respectively. The infield was anchored at third by Al Rosen, who had been the unanimous choice for the 1953 Most Valuable Player. During the 1950s, Rosen led the league in home runs twice. Other key Cleveland players were Al Smith in the outfield; Jim Hegan behind the plate; and Vic Wertz, who played in the outfield and at first base.

The Indians were unaware that their humble opponents, the New York Giants, were a team dating destiny. This was a group of men who shone brighter together than at any other time in their lives. With the exception of Mays, Irvin, and Wilhelm, there were no Hall of Famers. Durocher, like Billy Martin after him, had the uncanny knack of pulling 100 percent efforts from his players. He responded to them and figuratively went to bat for them and they produced for him. Unlike Martin, however, Leo was able to provide stability to his players for more than a season and this also enabled him to build and shape a team to his liking. The 1954 Giants may have been the most underrated ballplayers who rallied and had the year of their lives at the same time.

In the eighth inning of the first game of the last World Series ever played in Manhattan, the Indians' Vic Wertz strode to the plate with the score tied 2-2 to face reliever Don Liddle, who had just replaced starter Sal Maglie. In 1954, Wertz was a twenty-nine-year-old ball player who had starred for the Detroit Tigers during the 1947–52 period. He went on to post a lifetime .277 average with a career total of 266 home runs.

He will always be remembered more for this one out than for any of his home runs. Wertz hit Liddle's only pitch into the no-man's land in the Polo Grounds known as center field, where the distance from home plate reached 460 feet. In addition to a lot of room, there also existed a crack center fielder by the name of Willie Mays. As the ball soared, Willie ran toward dead center, back to the plate, looked up, and ran some more. Upon the descent of the ball, he reached out, made a clean over-the-shoulder catch, slammed on the brakes, and fired a shot to the infield. This fielding play is one of the most analyzed in World Series history and certainly made Vic Wertz famous.

The catch seemed to take the fight from the Indians. Marv Grissom, the Giants' ace relief man that year, took over from Liddle and pitched through the tenth inning, giving up one hit. In the bottom of the tenth, with one out, Mays coaxed a walk from starter Bob Lemon. Lemon had gone 23-7 over the season, sharing the league's highest victory total with teammate Early Wynn. Apparently sensing something, Willie promptly stole second and baseball strategy told Al Lopez to set up a double play by walking the next batter, Hank Thompson. Durocher sent Rhodes to pinch-hit for the right-handed Irvin. It didn't take long to ice the cake. Dusty, prepared to wait out Lemon, swung at the first pitch, hit it off his fists, and the ball was pulled into right field. He did not take a full swing, as his objective was to get a good piece of the ball and either advance the runners or drive one home. Avila, playing second, began to backpedal onto the outfield grass. Dave Pope, the right fielder, set himself at the base of the wall and leaped as the fly came down and landed in the first row, about 260 feet from home plate, for a game-winning home run. The ball game was over, and rumor had it that Lemon threw his glove farther than Dusty hit the ball. With the New Yorkers winning 5-2, the World Series was effectively over after that hit; the Indians never recovered from the double shock of Mays's catch and Rhodes's home run.

In the clubhouse, the Indians complained about pop-fly home runs and 460-foot outs to the press and anyone else who would listen. The following day, Arthur Daley pointed out in the *New York Times* that the fences were as close for the Indians as they were for the Giants. He also wrote of the trepidation felt by both base runners after they realized the ball cleared the fence. Mays, ever so cautious, made sure all three Giants touched the bases and made doubly sure that neither Thompson nor Rhodes passed him on the base paths.

The Giants won the next game behind Antonelli 3-1. Rhodes was once again called on to pinch-hit for Irvin in the fifth, with Mays on third and Thompson on first and the Indians leading 1-0. Starter Early Wynn, who went 23-11 during the regular season, had handcuffed the Giants until he walked Mays. Dusty did not disappoint the faithful. He lined a single up the middle scoring Mays to tie the game, as center fielder Larry Doby was playing a bit too deep. That brought life back into the Giants. Antonelli helped himself by hustling to beat out a likely double play and the lead run crossed the plate. Rhodes stayed in the game and in the seventh inning poked a solid homer with no one on for the final run and a cushion for Antonelli's victory.

The scene changed in the third game as the teams traveled to Cleveland's cavernous Municipal Stadium. Here, Durocher waited until only the third inning to bring in his premier pinch hitter. Rhodes once again hit for Irvin, this time with the bases loaded against the Indians' Big Bear Mike Garcia, 19-8 for the season. Before a highly partisan crowd, Rhodes once again came through, lining a clutch two-run single to ignite a three-run rally. The Giants won this one 6-2 behind Gomez. The Indians, however, could take solace—Rhodes struck out in his last two at bats.

In the fourth game, Durocher did not require the services of Rhodes, as the Giants took a 7-0 lead before surprise starter Liddle ran out of gas. The final score was 7-4, and the Giants were the champions of the baseball world. Although Rhodes provided the wallop and Mays the unbelievable, this was truly a team effort with an emphasis on defense, pitching, and fundamentals. Wertz, the victim of Mays's robbery in the first game, stood out as the Indians' stalwart, batting .500 with eight hits, one a home run. Bob Lemon pitched a splendid first game. The Indians were dominated by a Durocher team, which beat them in every way possible way: power, pitching, speed, and defense. When the cunning of Leo and company was thrown in, the Indians' long journey home became inevitable.

Dusty Rhodes went four for six in the 1954 World Series and produced ten total bases for a slugging percentage of 1.667. He drove in the go-ahead run in two of the three games in which he appeared and the tying run in the third. He struck out twice in the third game, ironically after the game was safely in the Giants' camp and with no one on base. Apparently, since there was no necessity, he didn't bother to deliver. Antonelli threw the only complete game for the victors and relieved Liddle in the fourth game. He was 1-0 with an ERA of 0.84 and recorded twelve strikeouts in ten and two-thirds innings.

Rhodes's heroics came one year too early, in a way; in 1955, *Sport Magazine* began an award of a Chevrolet Corvette to the most valuable player in the World Series. Johnny Podres of the Brooklyn Dodgers took home the first Vette for his performance in Brooklyn's only world triumph.

In 1955, the Giants slipped to third place during the Dodgers' world championship season. Rhodes batted .305 but managed only six home runs while driving in thirty-two runs. He continued to be a successful pinch hitter, going eleven for forty-four. However, there would never be another 1954 for Dusty Rhodes. He played major league baseball until 1959, toiling only for the Giants.

After spending the 1958 and 1959 seasons with the newly relocated and renamed San Francisco Giants, he played three more years in the Pacific Coast League, enjoying the West Coast as he had enjoyed the East. The PCL was nearly as tough as the majors, and Dusty, true to form, worked hard and played equally hard.

Rhodes returned to New York to get on with his life as an unassuming civilian and took to working on tugboats in New York Harbor, where he was somewhat of a celebrity. He served on a 1,000-horsepower tug whose function was to transfer barges in the New York and New Jersey harbors. He started out as a deckhand, performing every function aboard the vessel from steerer to cook, and eventually ran his own tug. His schedule differed greatly from when he played baseball. He became a morning person, rising at five rather than getting home at that time.

His wife owned a bar, Ginger's Tavern, beside the docks in Staten Island and he helped out, lending his gregarious personality when not on the barges. Dusty, like other tugboatmen, worked one week on and had a week off. He worked mainly on the *Peter Callinan*, a tug for the Manhattan Oil Transportation Company. He was legendary for liking a drink, and that reputation was deserved. While still working the tugs, Dusty Rhodes one day decided to stop drinking. He told us that he drank because he was afraid that life would lose its luster. He said it took him no time to realize that this was not so. He was still the same old Jim Rhodes, drunk or sober, and life's zest followed him in and out of port, home and away.

Dusty Rhodes is now retired and lives, at this writing, in Henderson, Nevada. He spends a good deal of his time playing golf and he admits to being better than a duffer. His stories abound, interspersed with laughter, and he can talk a blue streak, particularly about *that one glorious season*.

Antonelli stayed with the Giants, always a consistent performer. He slipped to 14-16 in the 1955 plummet but posted a respectable ERA of 3.33. He bounced back to win twenty games in 1956, and after a dismal 1957, he moved with the team to San Francisco. He continued to be the staff's ace and won sixteen and nineteen games in 1958 and 1959, respectively. He retired after the 1961 season with a lifetime 126-110 mark and a career ERA of 3.34.

Before the start of the 1955 campaign, John moved back to the Rochester area and invested in a tire center. His baseball fame and good business sense provided the foundation for a long and successful post-baseball career. His business grew into a chain that encompassed more than twenty outlets. He still appears at Boston Braves reunions and remains a popular figure in Beantown. He attributed his success and ability to compete to his days in baseball.

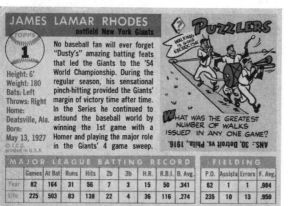

Basically, it all started with *that one glorious season.*

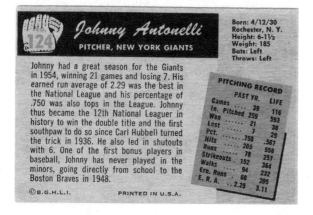

DEL ENNIS

JIM KONSTANTY

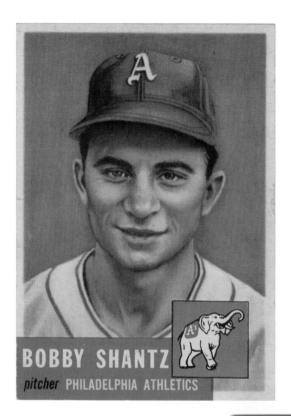

BOBBY SHANTZ

pitcher PHILADELPHIA ATHLETICS

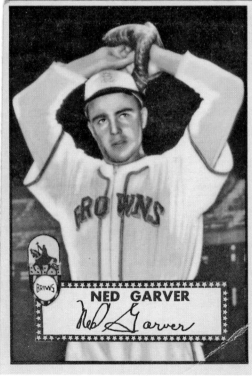

NED GARVER

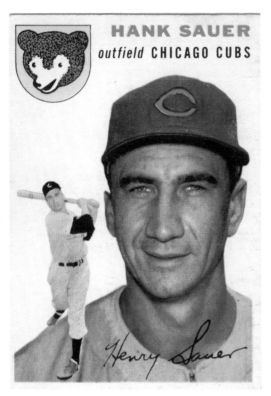

HANK SAUER
outfield CHICAGO CUBS

Henry Sauer

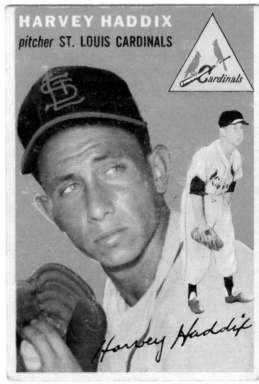

HARVEY HADDIX
pitcher ST. LOUIS CARDINALS

Harvey Haddix

Bob Porterfield

Mickey Vernon

VIC POWER

first base KANSAS CITY A'S

Vic Power

AL ROSEN
third base CLEVELAND INDIANS

DON Newcombe
BROOKLYN DODGERS PITCHER

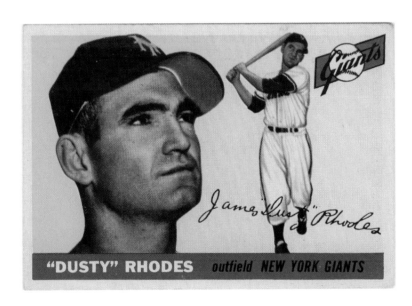

"DUSTY" RHODES outfield NEW YORK GIANTS

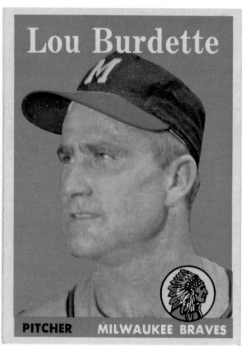

DICK GROAT
Shortstop
Pittsburgh Pirates

VERN LAW
Pitcher
Pittsburgh Pirates

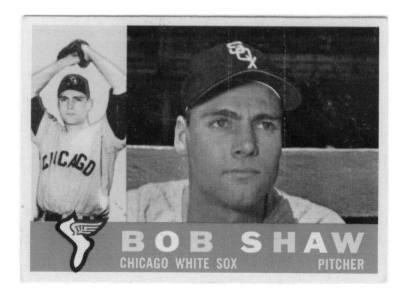

BOB SHAW
CHICAGO WHITE SOX   PITCHER

JOE
JAY
CIN. REDS   PITCHER

JIM
O'TOOLE
CIN. REDS   PITCHER

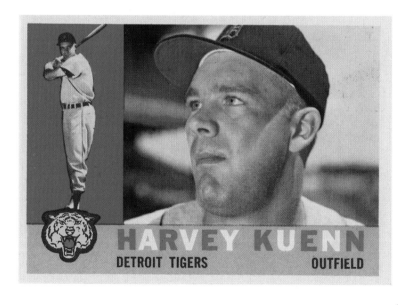

HARVEY KUENN
DETROIT TIGERS   OUTFIELD

9

1955: VIC POWER

KANSAS CITY ATHLETICS (NEW YORK YANKEES)

B y 1953, the National League combatants from New York City
had established themselves as perennial challengers for the
honors in that circuit. Their success was due largely to aggressiveness in signing high-quality black players, who quickly made a difference in the performance and depth of each team. Standouts such
as Roy Campanella, Hank Thompson, Willie Mays, and Monte Irvin
joined forces with Jackie Robinson to provide the New York Giants
and Brooklyn Dodgers with the virtual cream of the crop from the
Negro leagues. Pressure began to mount on the American League
Yankees to recruit blacks for promotion to the big team. In addition, the Bronx, home of the Yankees, had a growing population
of Negro and Latino families. The Yankees responded by signing
Vic Pellot Power, Elston Howard, and Ruben Gomez, along with a
handful of others.

Power was playing ball in Canada's outlaw Provincial League
and had attracted more than his share of attention, including some
not necessarily desired. His surname, Pellot, conjured up certain

sexual overtones in French-speaking Quebec. In order to ward off any trouble, Victor Pellot took a derivation of his mother's maiden name (Pove) and became Vic Power. Yankee scout Tom Greenwade, who had the distinction of discovering Mickey Mantle, signed Power to a New York contract. Vic quickly made it up the Yankees' minor league ladder, starting at Syracuse in 1951. There he hit .295 and rose to the Yanks' Kansas City American Association affiliate the following year. He became an immediate fan favorite in KC, batting .336 in 1952 and leading that circuit with a .349 average in 1953. In October of that year, the Yankees purchased his and Elston Howard's contracts, virtually assuring them both a trip to spring training.

During the 1953 season, the Yankee fans began to anticipate the promotion of Power to the parent club. After all, he was tearing apart the Triple A league and first base was not the talent-laden Yanks' strongest position. Joe Collins showed his age at the sack and was playing fewer and fewer games. Power could hit, was a slick fielder, and had a ready-made following. However, the season ended with another world championship, the fifth straight for the Bronx Bombers, and still no representative of the Negro race in the house that Ruth built.

The early 1950s brought the best black ballplayers into the major leagues and the teams that pioneered integration helped their own cause immensely in the standings. Robinson became the spark plug behind the Dodgers and a good deal of the Giants' success can be attributed to the contributions of Mays, Irvin, and Thompson. Cleveland's Indians added Larry Doby and the ageless Satchel Paige, and these two players were key to their 1948 championship. The Boston Braves quickly followed, and though their early recruits such as Sam Jethroe did not become household names, later additions like Hank Aaron and Wes Covington helped produce championship teams in their subsequent home of Milwaukee.

Power, a native of Puerto Rico, who had never known any form of discrimination, continuously left a burr on the seat of Yankee executive George Weiss. While in the minor leagues, he reputedly dated white women and drove a flashy Cadillac convertible despite subtle suggestions to act "appropriately." This flaunting of Yankee conservative standards and his questioning of authority led Weiss to keep him in Kansas City for the 1953 season. While Vic was also an especially adroit fielder around the sack, he brought innovations and a bit of flair to the art of playing first base. Being a right-hander took away some of the stretch that a lefty would naturally possess, so Power began playing the bag by catching with his gloved hand only, pointing out to critics that you would get two gloves if the rules required using two hands. In today's professional baseball, you would be hard pressed to find a player who does not catch anything higher than four feet with just one hand. Power was well ahead of his time with his defensive play.

Power usually answered his critics with logical responses, further infuriating them. On one occasion, when asked about his penchant for attractive white women, he answered, "I suppose if I told them I liked big mammas, they'd leave me alone." Another time, when the team was in the South for training and the bus stopped for the players to eat, Vic was informed by the owner of a restaurant that he did not serve Negroes. Power quickly let him know that he did not eat Negroes and that he would be satisfied with rice and beans.

Victor Filipe Pellot was born in 1931 in Arecibo, Puerto Rico. As a boy he showed talent as an artist, but when he was thirteen, his father died, the result of an industrial accident. The firm for which the elder Pellot worked had pledged to assist Mrs. Pellot and her children, but her lawyer abruptly dropped the case against the company. This infuriated the family and convinced young Victor that he should pursue the legal profession in order to make old wrongs right. He held that dream until he signed a contract to play with Caguas, in the winter league, in 1947. The skills and maturity he showed at first base convinced the regular thirty-five-year-old first-sacker to retire in favor of this enthusiastic and energetic young man. Power played the entire four-month season and earned $250 per month in the process. The following year, his salary was increased to five hundred dollars monthly and he was able to purchase a home for the family in San Juan, relieving his mother of the financial burden of providing for the family. He did this and completed high school, a shining example for his younger siblings, who all finished their secondary education. His success at baseball, however, eliminated his plans for pursuit of the law.

After playing baseball in Puerto Rico for two seasons, the seventeen-year-old Pellot signed a contract with Drummondville, a Quebec team in Canada's independent Provincial League, in time for the 1949 season. He suffered airsickness on the plane ride north and quickly became homesick, as he had never traveled away from the island. Here he was, fifteen hundred miles from home, with nary a clue as to the customs or the language. The fans embraced him immediately, however, and Quincy Trouppe, who signed him, took him under his wing, caring for him as a son.

He started in right field and after his first season was switched to first base. During the 1949–50 period, Victor Power batted over .330 and in 1950 drove in 105 runs in 105 games. This consistency brought Tom Greenwade of the Yankees to watch the league all-star game and Power in particular. Vic's performance included an error, so Greenwade rated his fielding as poor. Still, the Yankees bought his contract from Drummondville for seventy-five hundred dollars but the twenty-year-old showed that bit of independence that would annoy the Yankee brass in the future. He wanted a share of the purchase price, and got it. It was only five hundred dollars, but Power showed that he would be a force to deal with.

Up with the Yankees?

The New York Yankees, who acquired the contract of Vic Power, were born as part of a compromise between the warring professional major leagues of baseball after the birth of the American League in 1901. After a decade and a half of so-so baseball, in 1914 they became the property of one Jacob Ruppert. The new owner had inherited a large estate but was a success in his own right. He and his dollars presided over the birth of the Yankees dynasty. He purchased the best players available, among them Babe Ruth, in time for the 1920 season. The next twenty-three years saw fourteen Yankee pennants and ten World Series flags. Stellar Yankees besides Ruth included Lou Gehrig, Bill Dickey, Joe DiMaggio, and Red Ruffing.

World War II took its toll on all big-league teams and the Yankees suffered through a three-year stretch (1944–1946) in which other teams took championships. They resumed their winning ways in 1947, besting the Brooklyn Dodgers in a tough seven-game series for the world title.

Yankee general manager Larry McPhail shocked the baseball world by resigning immediately after the 1947 campaign, and George Weiss took over as general overseer. He replaced McPhail's choice of manager, Bucky Harris, after a near miss in the 1948 campaign and raised a few eyebrows when he announced his selection, Charles Dillon "Casey" Stengel.

Stengel had been seen as somewhat of a clown in his playing days, as well as in his previous terms as a manager. He had played well, albeit colorfully, in the National League but his managerial career had been less than successful. He led the Dodgers and the Braves over nine seasons, but his best effort produced a 77-75 record in 1938. His record in the Pacific Coast League was more Yankee-like, but he had not managed in the major leagues for six years. The press wondered if Weiss had been hit in the head with a fly ball, as had some of Stengel's "Daffiness Boys of Brooklyn" teammates of the 1920s. However, Stengel brought certain innovations to the game and implemented them with care and consistency.

Stengel seemed to read the classified ads of old ballplayers who had just a little bit more greatness in their systems. He picked up future Hall of Famers Enos Slaughter and Johnny Mize from the Cardinals and Giants, respectively. Pitcher Johnny Sain came over from the Braves and provided the Yankees with relief and a good spot starter. He later acquired former MVPs Bobby Shantz and Jim Konstanty, both of whom gave Stengel some very good and timely mound work. Stengel listened to his players but always made the final decisions. He implemented a platoon system and utilized his talent to play the percentages to the hilt, maximizing the lefty-righty confrontations.

Another Yankee transition began to take hold. DiMaggio called it quits at the age of thirty-six and Mickey Mantle was there to take his place in center field. Stengel coddled those who required coddling and disciplined those needing a talking-to. Casey, who never had children of his own, took well to the young newcomers. He taught everyone the necessity of playing ball with the brain, prompting a famous Yogi Berra quip: "Baseball is ninety percent mental, the other half is physical."

Stengel's Yankees won five straight World Series from 1949 to 1953, taking twenty games to the National League champs' combined seven. The New Yorkers produced Most Valuable Players in both 1950 (Phil Rizzuto) and 1951 (Berra with the first of three), but the minority fans of the Bronx began clamoring for players to whom they could relate. The National League had vigorously embraced Branch Rickey's experiment with Negro players, and they had cornered the best. As an aside, in the 1949–59 span all but two National League MVPs (Konstanty in 1950 and Hank Sauer in 1952) were black. The first teams to sign quality Negro players in the senior circuit dominated play from 1947 through 1959 with the exception of the 1950 Phillies. Pressure was being brought to bear on Yankee management from all sides.

Vic Power's performance on the field that season in the Yanks' American Association affiliate in Kansas City forced the Yankees to place him on the spring-training roster in the fall of 1953. He was twenty-four years old, a proven hitter in the minors' top echelons and a nearly flawless fielder. He had yet to play a game in the major leagues but already commanded a following. The growing black and Hispanic populations of New York anticipated his arrival and the press threw in additional support. First base was beginning to be the team's weakness. All signs pointed to the promotion of Vic Power to the Yankees.

The Yankees, however, would not bend to pressure from either the press or their fans. Venerable sportswriter Dan Daniel, of the *World Tribune Sun*, often criticized the team in his columns, specifically mentioning their treatment of Power. On several occasions during the 1953 season, pickets paraded around Yankee Stadium with signs insisting on the promotion of Power to New York. On August 16, catcher Gus Triandos came up from the Yankees' AA affiliate in Birmingham. With Triandos's promotion, the Power crowd grew larger and louder, but the front office continued to resist its demands. It seemed that the first Negro to play for the Yankees would have to be a black DiMaggio, with the same sophistication and quiet class. Vic Power would not be their man. On December 16, 1953, he went to the Philadelphia Athletics with four other players for pitcher Harry Byrd, first baseman Eddie Robinson, and three others. In 1954, the Yankees finished runner-up to the record-setting Cleveland Indians.

The 1954 edition of the Philadelphia Athletics was the final chapter for a storied franchise that had seen far better days. The team won only fifty-one games and Power did not play to expectations and press clippings, batting only .255. Wally Moses, the batting coach, felt that Vic could not handle a heavy, thirty-six-ounce bat so he forced him to hit with a lighter one. He played mainly in the outfield, as manager Eddie Joost needed his fielding skills in the outer confines of Shibe Park. Before the 1955 season, the Mack family sold its interests in the club to Chicago businessman Arnold Johnston, and Vic Power moved west back to Kansas City with the Athletics.

Vic Power and the
Kansas City Big League Debut

Unlike the Braves, who followed their final season in Boston with a rousing success in Milwaukee, the A's just did not possess the talent to rise in the standings. Their arrival in KC was exuberantly followed by the locals and the nation. The April 11, 1955, edition of the *New York Times* reported that more than 200,000 fans turned out to greet the A's and watched them as the players were paraded through the city. On opening day, no less of a dignitary than former president Harry S Truman threw out the ceremonial first ball. The

A's disappointed no one; they beat the Detroit Tigers 6-2 behind Alex Kellner in the first major league game played west of St. Louis, with attendance exceeding 32,000 fans.

On April 5, Winston Churchill stepped down as prime minister of Great Britain, preferring the role of a mere member of Parliament. The man who led the English through World War II and became an intimate of former president Truman happily ceded his role to Anthony Eden, thus ending an era of British history.

The world lost Albert Einstein on April 18. The great scientist, who came to America from the early days of the German Nazis, died in his sleep in Princeton (N.J.) Hospital at the age of seventy-six.

By April 18, the A's had dropped their next five games. On April 23, the Chicago White Sox buried them in a 29-6 barrage. After ten games, the new KC entry stood at 3-7. From this rubble Vic Power's star began to emerge. Manager Lou Boudreau returned him to first base, where his defensive skills contributed a great deal to tightening up the right side of the infield. His performance at the plate mirrored that of his play in the field and he was batting a torrid .425 with two home runs. The end of April saw him slip to .407, but he managed to lead the team to a 6-8 start before the beginning of May.

The first of May saw John Antonelli of the New York Giants pitch a sixteen-inning 2-1, complete-game victory over the Cincinnati Reds. The papers said he faced fifty-seven batters. Strange, no pitch counts were recorded for the stylish lefty.

While the citizens of the United States waited anxiously for the Salk vaccine to arrive in order to inoculate our schoolchildren, excitement was building at Kentucky's Churchill Downs as the mighty Nashua sought his seventh consecutive victory in the Derby, to be run on Saturday, May 7. Swaps and Willie Shoemaker would take care of that streak and upset the colt by one and a half lengths.

The A's were in the midst of a run of their own, albeit one without much success. During a 4-9 stretch, they absorbed three straight losses to the Red Sox. The A's split a doubleheader at Yankee Stadium, with Vic back in the lineup from an injury. Boudreau had moved him from leadoff to sixth to provide some punch in the middle of the order.

The University of Kansas Jayhawks announced that a seven-foot, two-inch schoolboy from Philadelphia named Wilt Chamberlain would be attending college there on a basketball scholarship.

The A's continued to flounder through May, although Power contributed his share of hits, collaborating with veterans Enos Slaughter and Elmer Valo to beat the White Sox 1-0 on May 20.

Walt Disney's Davy Crockett, King of the Wild Frontier opened in New York, creating a run on stores for coonskin hats.

Power drove in a run in a 4-2 loss to the Indians on May 29 in Cleveland. The A's then swept the Tigers in a holiday double-header at Detroit's Briggs Stadium, 5-4 and 8-6. Power knocked in four runs with three hits in the first game, virtually sealing the win single-handedly. While his batting average dropped slowly to .329 behind eventual bat champ Al Kaline and future 1959 champ Harvey Kuenn, both of the Tigers, his presence on the field gave the team a certain degree of credibility, despite their 16-25 mark at May's end.

On Memorial Day, two-time Indianapolis 500 winner Bill Vukovich was killed in his attempt to perform a three-peat in the race, prompting the criticism of using the event as an experimental lab for American auto manufacturers.

Elmer Valo, at the age of thirty-four, had been a fixture with the Athletics since 1940, with the exception of two seasons lost to World War II. He took the young Power under his wing and worked with him on various aspects of the game, also teaching him rudimentary English. Valo, who batted .282 over a twenty-year career, had a sense of humor that meshed with Power's. The two became good friends and enjoyed their best years in baseball in 1955. Valo hit .364 in 112 games but did not qualify for the bat title.

June 1955 continued to prove that the A's would not repeat the miracle of the Boston/Milwaukee Braves move due mainly to the fact that the quality of the personnel did not equal that of the Tribe. The team won twelve games while losing sixteen and Power hit .272

for the month to tail off to .304 by June 30. During the month, however, he produced some timely hits that resulted in much-needed run production. On June 9, he supplied a key double that drove in the second run of a four-run fourth inning. The four runs were all the A's needed and, in fact, all they got in a 4-2 win over the equally hapless Washington Senators.

On June 10, at Belmont Park, Nashua, a 3-20 pick, ran away with the third leg of racing's Triple Crown by nine lengths after having taken the Preakness weeks earlier.

By the end of that weekend, the major leagues hit a record fifty home runs in a nineteen-game schedule. Fans in Ebbets Field in Brooklyn and Municipal Stadium in Cleveland each saw a dozen clear the fences. The A's, at home that weekend, did not participate in the barrage although their guests from Baltimore contributed one round-tripper.

Attempting to salvage the third game of a set in Boston on June 16, Power, still batting leadoff, had gone three for five with a double and two runs scored as the A's led the Red Sox 6-5 going into the bottom of the ninth. Billy Klaus, a journeyman ballplayer who was enjoying his own *one glorious season* and thrilling Beantown fans to boot, hit a two-run homer off Johnny Sain to nail a comeback 7-6 win. That same day Harry Agganis, the young Boston first baseman and former All-American Quarterback from Boston University, was placed on the voluntary retired list due to what was thought to be pneumonia. He died of a blood clot in his lung eleven days later, at the age of twenty-five.

The A's moved on to New York, where, on June 21, Mickey Mantle, using a bat borrowed from teammate Hank Bauer, hit a first-inning, 488-foot homer into the bleachers in dead center field, the first person ever to clear that fence. The A's, possibly stunned by that blast, lost to the Bronx Bombers 6-2 despite two hits by Power, who had been shifted back to fifth place in the lineup by manager Boudreau, who hoped to shake up his personnel. The A's finished the month in sixth place with a 28-41 record and Vic Power was hitting .304 despite a weak June.

July started on a positive note when the A's overcame a 5-0 Tiger lead with a seven-run seventh before nearly 19,000 wildly enthusiastic fans in Kansas City. Vic sparked the rally with a leadoff home run, giving the team the impetus to turn defeat into victory.

The Tigers had two more games to play in Kansas City, and the A's accomplished a four-game sweep. The final game of the Sunday doubleheader saw Power go three for six with four RBI. He hit two home runs, one a fourteenth-inning shot that won the second game for the A's, 9-8.

By July 4, the A's had racked up six wins in their last seven games. The team appeared to be jelling and following the lead of their slick-fielding first baseman with clutch hits and late-inning victories, bringing thrills and enthusiasm to their new following. On July 3, Vic belted two home runs and knocked in four runs to pace a sweep over Detroit. The second round-tripper won the contest in the bottom of the fourteenth inning. The rest of July proved to be somewhat of a mystery, however, as the team suffered through a ten-game losing streak. They struggled to an overall 14-20 mark for the entire month although they provided some fireworks and good pitching in two four-game splits with the Yankees, one at home and one in New York.

Cleveland manager Al Lopez chose Power as a substitute for the midseason All-Star classic. Vic finished second to the Senators' Mickey Vernon at first base in the fans' voting and appeared in the contest, popping up as a pinch hitter for pitcher Early Wynn.

On July 20, the U.S. government announced it would be launching a rocket, most likely in 1957 or 1958. Plans called for the satellite to be the size of a basketball and travel at 18,000 miles per hour in orbit about 250 miles above Earth. James Hagerty, the White House press secretary, said that the United States would offer to share all scientific data with other nations.

At the end of July, the A's had a secure hold on sixth place with a 42-61 record and Vic Power showed more and more consistency as his bat mark stood at .311. On August 6, he went four for five against the Red Sox in Boston and started the winning rally with a timely single as the A's scored three in the ninth to win 6-5. The following day, the Bosox won 16-12 in a game that the *New York Times* noted took two hours and 54 minutes to complete.

Power continued to lead the team when he could: For example, on September 23, he hit a homer and drove in three runs in a 4-3 win over the Senators. Two days later he paced the team with three hits in a 9-2 victory over the Orioles. The A's kept the Yankees from establishing a permanent grip on first place, taking a 4-3 game from the New Yorkers. Power went two for four and hit his seventeenth home run of the year, spoiling Billy Martin's return from the Army. In that contest, Vic was brushed back and hit the deck on a Johnny Kucks pitch in the seventh inning and promptly charged the mound. His teammates restrained him and he stayed in the game, providing a different kind of punch.

The A's went 12-14 during August and Power hit .339, bringing his average back to .318 on August 31. The season went into the final stretch with just three games separating the first four teams on September 5 as Cleveland led the charge. Power's two for four included a two-bagger that helped the A's win the first game of a doubleheader with the Tribe before Indians rookie ace Herb Score beat them 9-2 for his fifteenth victory. Two days later, Vic made a throwing error at Yankee Stadium while trying to force Mickey Mantle at second base, and that led to an unearned run and a 2-1 New York win.

Over in the National League, Don Newcombe of the Dodgers won his twentieth game and hit home run number seven of the season, tying a record for pitchers. Three days later the Dodgers clinched the National League pennant by beating the second-place Braves, 8-2.

By September 13, the Red Sox had slipped to six games behind the Indians when the A's visited Fenway Park for a twin bill. Power went five for ten with two RBI as the teams split, sounding a death knell for Boston. The following day, he put another nail in the coffin with a home run in a 7-3 victory over the Bosox.

The government's Public Health Service finally announced the allo-cation of nearly four million doses of the Salk polio vaccine. This was very important to the baseball community, for one of its own, Indians first baseman Vic Wertz, had been stricken by the disease on August 24, 1955. Wertz, a gallant man who in the 1954 World Series against the New York Giants made what was generally acknowledged to be the most famous out in baseball history, came back to play in 1956 and would hit more than one hundred home runs before hanging up his spikes.

Back in Kansas City, the A's gave the White Sox hopes a lasting jolt when they took the final two games played in Kansas City in 1955. Power led the assault in game one with a double and two RBI in a 13-7 romp. The A's went on the road for the last week of the season and eventually finished with sixty-three wins and ninety-one losses. They finished third in attendance in the majors and drew nearly 1.4 million fans, more than a million over their attendance in 1954. Power finished second in the batting race at .319 behind Detroit's Al Kaline's .340 and among the top five in slugging (.505), total bases (301), doubles (thirty-four), and triples (ten). He hit nine-teen homers and drove in seventy-six scores. He led the league in most defensive statistics at his position and began virtually to re-create the fundamentals of first base.

Power played in the majors until 1965, when he retired after a season with the California Angels. In between, he played with Cleveland and Minnesota in the American League and did an eighteen-game stint with the 1964 Phillies. He retired with a .284 lifetime average and 126 home runs. In the process, he won seven Gold Gloves and played in the outfield as well as every infield posi-tion with expertise and finesse. He believed in entertaining the fans and they loved him for his bravado. Power was popular everywhere he went. If he had played longer and for a better team, he might have rivaled Brooks Robinson as the finest defensive player to walk through the portals of Cooperstown.

After his retirement from the game, Vic returned to Puerto Rico and served as a scout for the Angels. He also managed an amateur team and worked as a consultant regarding sports matters for the island's House of Representatives. He gives thanks today for his involvement in sports and encourages today's youth to play when and where they can. Vic, whose personality and confidence made him a positive force and thinker during his days in the majors, remembers his tour in the big leagues fondly. Any racism and disappointments are just faded memories deep in the recesses of his mind. He made it difficult to forget the excitement of a city's new team and a successful year, *that one glorious season.*

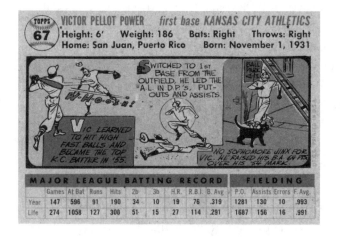

10

1956: DON NEWCOMBE

BROOKLYN DODGERS

A controversy surrounding the election of the major leagues' most valuable players (MVP) had stirred ever since the inception of the awards in 1931. It was that year that the Baseball Writers of America took over the process of choosing the MVP, and they have controlled it ever since. Certain elements called for the accolade to be restricted to everyday, position players, thereby eliminating pitchers. Others found the pitchers deserving. In the twenty-five-year period through 1955, eleven pitchers took the award, representing 22 percent of the fifty MVPs so elected from the American and National Leagues. The regular players felt slighted, as their feeling was that a player who appeared only every fourth or fifth day should not be considered for the MVP award.

Eventually, the powers that be offered a compromise in the Cy Young Award, an honor reserved for the best pitcher in the major leagues. Reason prevailed in this decision. After all, in 1952, Robin Roberts of the Philadelphia Phillies went 28-7 for a fourth-place team and finished second in the National League MVP voting to

Hank Sauer, a .270 hitter from a fifth-place entry. Roberts won no awards, but fellow Philadelphian Bobby Shantz took a 24-7 record to the voters, also for a fourth-place team, and walked away with MVP honors in the American League. In time the award would be expanded to bestow the honor on the best hurlers from both circuits.

The question, which was never answered as far as I was concerned, was: "For whom are they doing this? Pitchers or regulars?" In 1956, in the first year of dual trophies, Don Newcombe, the big Brooklyn Dodger right-handed pitcher, forever put the query to rest. For anybody! He not only took the first-ever Cy Young with a 27-7 record but he added the National League's Most Valuable Player Award to his trophy case as well.

Don Newcombe came into the world in 1926 in Madison, New Jersey, and by the time he turned thirteen years old he had grown into a young man whose size placed him on a semipro baseball team. In 1944, at the age of eighteen, he joined the Newark Eagles of the Negro National League and in the following year posted an 8-4 record. After pitching in an exhibition game in Brooklyn's Ebbets Field, legendary scout Clyde Sukeforth invited him back the following day. The Dodgers, eager to skim the cream of the crop from the Negro leagues, signed him and his cheery teammate, Roy Campanella, to contracts with their Nashua, New Hampshire, affiliate, in the New England League. Newcombe won fourteen games against four defeats in his first year in Nashua and followed up with a 19-6 mark in 1947.

Both Campanella and Newcombe found warm hospitality in that small New Hampshire city. By the mid-1940s, most residents of the Granite State had not seen many black men in real life, but the community embraced the six-feet-four-inch right-hander and the effervescent Campanella. The two became friendly with the local firemen and, in a *Boston Globe* article written by Lois Shea for the May 14, 1995, edition, Newcombe fondly remembered a barber who did not know where to start when it came to cutting the hair of a Negro man. After a few anxious moments and with their permission, the barber trimmed them to the scalp, setting them up for the remainder of the steamy New England summer.

Don's success in Nashua earned him a promotion to the Montreal Royals in time for the 1948 season. Montreal had been the starting spot for Jackie Robinson's foray into the big leagues and the Canadian fans eagerly cheered Newcombe as he went 17-6. He went to spring training with the Dodgers in 1949 and impressed the team fathers, but inexplicably went back to the Royals. After a month of frustration, he returned to the parent club in mid-May. He came up to a team that found itself in a seesaw battle with the St. Louis Cardinals for the league pennant. Newcombe responded with grace and confidence. In his first starting appearance, he shut out the Cincinnati Reds.

Joining the Dodgers

The Brooklyn Dodgers are probably America's most storied baseball team. Long after their departure from the urban confines of the city of New York for the gold of Los Angeles, they still command a following throughout the country. Old-time Dodger memorabilia is in demand. For example, the 1955 World Series mug sold out shortly after being introduced recently in the gift shop at the Baseball Hall of Fame. In 1972 Roger Kahn wrote the classic *Boys of Summer*, in which he revisited the members of the 1952–1953 pennant winners. In 1993, he followed up with *The Era*, a story of when New York City ruled the baseball world through the 1947–57 period. Royal blue baseball caps with a white *B* are worn up and down the East Coast with their beaks proudly forward. It is true that the hair beneath the caps is often as white as the *B* but the point is that the Brooklyn Dodgers live on. The Dodgers belong to many people who still have not forgiven Walter O'Malley for taking them away, far, far away.

Brooklyn joined the National League in time for the 1890 season and surprised sports fans nationwide by taking the championship, easily finishing first. After a pair of flags in the 1899–1900 period, they did not win another championship until 1916. They added one more in 1920, both under the tutelage of Wilbert "Uncle Robby" Robinson. Robby and his immediate successors brought home no more championships through 1938. The next year, shortstop Leo Durocher took over as field boss.

Durocher had a knack for getting his players to achieve at a level higher than their abilities called for. He took over a seventh-place team and played 113 games at short. The hustling Dodgers finished an astonishing third, winning fifteen games more than in the previous year. The following year they finished second to the Reds, setting the stage for the next decade and a half.

The Dodgers took the National League pennant in 1941 but lost the World Series to the New York Yankees in the first of seven inter-borough fall classics. The next year, Branch Rickey left the St. Louis Cardinals to join the Dodgers in the position of general manager, as World War II began to decimate big-league rosters.

The 1946 season brought the veterans back home, and the quality of baseball quickly improved over that of the war years. An exciting race between the Dodgers and the St. Louis Cardinals resulted in a tie at the end of the campaign. The Cardinals took the first postseason playoff in two straight games but the real fireworks were destined for the 1947 season, with the appearance of one Jack Roosevelt Robinson.

Major league baseball, influenced by commissioner Kennesaw Mountain Landis, had ignored and/or purposely stayed away from utilizing the talents of the black ballplayers. The Negro leagues had their following and, in the minds of many baseball executives, their place. There had been a few rumblings toward integration, but Landis usually had his way and crushed any uprising. In 1944, Bill Veeck made a bid to purchase the Philadelphia Phillies and stock the team with Negro league graduates. Landis got wind of the scheme, pur-portedly through the National League office, and forced the sale of the team to the Carpenter family. By 1945, Landis had passed away and been replaced by Albert B. "Happy" Chandler. Chandler sup-ported Rickey and the Dodgers' signing of Robinson despite a 15-1 vote by the owners against the deal. Chandler had been a governor of and U.S. senator from Kentucky and some said he sold out his southern heritage to Rickey. Instead, it was probably his finest hour.

Rickey signed Robinson to a contract with the team's International League affiliate in Montreal. He spelled out the rules of the game while calling him every vile name in the book and spewing racist invective totally out of character with his religious background. He then asked Robinson if he could stand to be vilified like that and not fight back for the first season of integration. Jackie agreed and, of course, the rest is history.

Robinson came up to the Dodgers in time for the 1947 season. He had been preceded in 1946 by outfielder Carl Furillo, whose strong and accurate arm would earn him the nickname "the Reading Rifle." In 1947, pitcher Ralph Branca arrived in Brooklyn, and Rickey's farm system began to bear fruit. Robinson played first base, batted .297, and led the league with twenty-nine stolen bases. Normally a second baseman, Robinson ceded that position to Eddie Stanky, who had clicked with Pee Wee Reese upon the latter's return from military duty to produce a sterling middle infield. For this performance and the courage he displayed throughout a difficult season, he was named baseball's first ever Rookie of the Year. Branca led the staff with twenty-one victories and Brooklyn's Bums once again made it to the World Series.

Durocher, however, did not accompany them to the fall classic, as Chandler had suspended him earlier in the season for allegedly associating with gamblers during spring training. Prior to his departure, however, Leo showed his strength in shutting down an internal revolt among a faction who saw the coming of Robinson and integration in baseball as a threat or an insult. The team had played a number of exhibitions in Havana, against the Montreal team, and Robinson, still with the Royals, had stolen the show as well as many bases. Dixie Walker, a southerner, had written Leo a letter informing him that he wanted to be traded for "personal reasons" and subsequently tried to rally other southern players into a team boycott of sorts. Reese, from Kentucky, openly opposed Walker, and pitcher Kirby Higbe got the word to Durocher. Leo called a team meeting in the morning's wee hours and made it clear that the big leagues would be integrated and that the Dodgers would lead the way. The performance was pure Durocher as he put it into a dollars-and-cents concept.

Burt Shotton then replaced Leo at the start of the season and guided the team to the pennant. They met the Yankees in a rematch of 1941. The Dodgers lost the first two games but bounced back to eventually tie the set and force a seventh game. In between, they deprived Bill Bevens of the first no-hitter in series history in game four and took the contest to boot on Cookie Lavagetto's pinch-hit double in the ninth inning. They lost the series in the seventh game; relief ace Joe Page of the Yanks gave up just one hit in the last five innings and the Yankees took the contest and the championship.

Durocher returned for the 1948 campaign, but after a 36-37 record, the stress of the suspension and his lifestyle had soured his relationship with Rickey. The other owners lobbied hard for his removal. Attendance was lagging and the team seemed to be on a trip to nowhere. After being ejected from a game on July 4, Durocher was encouraged to resign from the Dodgers. He took over as manager of the New York Giants; Mel Ott was given his walking papers. Once again, Shotton replaced Durocher. He guided the team to a 48-33 record and a third-place finish behind the Boston Braves.

During 1948, catcher Roy Campanella joined forces with Robinson while Larry Doby and the legendary Satchel Paige toiled for the world champion Cleveland Indians as Rickey's grand experiment in integration began to gain wider interest. In 1949, his planning and scouting paid off: Robinson enjoyed his finest season, winning the bat crown with a .342 mark and finishing second to Pittsburgh's Ralph Kiner with 124 RBI. He paced the majors in stolen bases and posted a high slugging percentage (.528) despite only sixteen homers. He was voted the league's Most Valuable Player for his solid achievements.

Jackie had moved over to second as Stanky went to the Braves prior to the 1948 season. Rounding out the infield were slugger Gil Hodges at first and slick-fielding Billy Cox at third. The outfield consisted mainly of Furillo in right and newcomer Duke Snider in center field, with Gene Hermanski getting the most time in the troublesome left-field position.

Don Newcombe came up to the Dodgers in mid-May 1949 and promptly took over as leader of the pitching staff. The American League 1949 pennant race has been glamorized in print by David Halberstam in his book *Summer of '49*. That the Dodgers played on the East Coast and the Cardinals on the other side of the Mississippi did not diminish the intrigue for the pursuit of the flag in the senior circuit. The Dodgers and the Cards were the National League's premier teams of the 1940s, taking seven of the ten available championships. The teams were in lockstep throughout the 1949 campaign, never more than a few games apart and constantly exchanging the lead. Shotton consistently called on Newcombe, who proved a glutton for work. On August 8, he beat the Giants to keep his team in the lead and later that month shut out St. Louis, 6-0, to bring the team to within one game of the Cards. With four games left in the season, on September 29, Brooklyn trailed St. Louis by a game but Newcombe shut out the Braves on four hits after a first-game victory by Preacher Roe. Shotton started him on the last day of the season with just two days of rest but he had to be relieved in the fourth inning, although the Dodgers took the pennant with a victory in that game.

Three days later, Newcombe started the first game of the World Series against the Yankees and held them to four hits, but the last one was a ninth-inning home run by Tom Henrich, and Newcombe lost 1-0. One more time, on two days' rest, he started in the series but did not have his best, losing 6-4. Thus, in the pressure-packed, ten-day, September 29–October 8 period, Don Newcombe started four games, won one, completed two, and pitched a total of twenty-six innings.

In 1949, Newcome showed that he belonged as he went 17-8 in a season that was for him a month short. He led the league in shutouts with five and during one stretch pitched thirty-one consecutive scoreless innings. He was evenhanded with his stinginess, beating patsies such as the Pittsburgh Pirates and contenders like the Cardinals. For his efforts, the writers elected him Rookie of the Year.

Newcombe, Campanella, and Robinson made the league All-Star team, and the game was conveniently played in Brooklyn. Larry Doby of the Indians played for the American League. This marked the first time that the Negro race was represented in that classic. Newcombe relieved Warren Spahn in the second inning and was robbed of a hit by Ted Williams in the bottom of that frame.

The 1950 season brought promise to Brooklyn, but the team was overshadowed by the Whiz Kids of Philadelphia. The Phillies played over their heads for the entire season and on September 6 held a seven-and-a-half-game lead. After losing the previous three games, Brooklyn met the Phils at Shibe Park for a doubleheader. Newcombe, who had won his last five starts, won the opener 2-0, yielding but three hits. Shotton, who had no idea who his second-game pitcher would be, asked Newk if he could start game two. Big Don was thrilled and took the ball to the mound, becoming the first pitcher since 1928 to start both ends of a doubleheader. Once the Philadelphia fans, no lovers of the enemy, realized what they were witnessing, they stood and gave him a rousing ovation. He pitched seven more innings and left trailing Curt Simmons 2-0 on runs tainted by a rare fielding miscue on the part of Furillo. The Dodgers pulled out the game in the ninth, reducing the Phils' lead to five and a half games.

The two teams continued to play equal baseball and met once again on September 23, Brooklyn's Bums still behind by seven games. This time Newcome bested Robin Roberts 3-2. The Phils began to fall apart while Brooklyn caught fire, and on the first of October, the Dodgers needed a victory in the season's final contest to force the teams into a playoff series. Roberts and Newcombe once again went head-to-head, this time at Ebbets Field, with both men seeking their twentieth victory. Early in the game, Snider and Robinson could not get together on a Texas leaguer by Del Ennis, and this resulted in the Phils' only score. After nine innings the game was tied 1-1, but in the tenth Dick Sisler propelled the Phils into the

World Series with a dramatic three-run homer off Newcombe, who wound up the year with a 19-11 record.

Spring training of 1951 brought a new manager to the Dodgers in the form of Charlie Dressen, as well as the departure of Branch Rickey for Pittsburgh. Dressen, a protégé of Durocher's, had coached under Leo, and exhibited a certain paranoia about him being better than his mentor. Many observers felt it affected how he managed the Dodgers. The absence of Rickey left a sort of void in the team although the Mahatma had left the club with a full pipeline of potential and a well-oiled organization. Dodger president Walter O'Malley had called in his chits among all other stockholders with the express purpose of replacing Rickey, who at the time was nearing the age of seventy. Rickey did not want to spend the rest of his life in an ineffective minority position, so when O'Malley offered to buy his stock at no profit, he outmaneuvered his tormentor by threatening to sell his shares to a partner whom O'Malley did not want nor felt he could control. Rickey got his price of $1.25 million and moved on to Pittsburgh, where he began to remake the Pirates' farm system in the mold of the Cardinals and Dodgers. O'Malley, the great manipulator, was outmaneuvered by Rickey, a greater manipulator.

The season started as expected, with the Dodgers quickly positioned in first place while the New York Giants found the cellar. On June 15, the Dodgers were six games up on the Giants and filled the left-field trouble spot with the acquisition of Andy Pafko from the Chicago Cubs. Meanwhile, the Giants, who had lost eleven of their first twelve games in April, continued to play good baseball, pulling to within five games of Brooklyn despite Newcombe's tenth victory of the season on June 26. On July 4, the Dodgers took a holiday doubleheader from the Giants, and Newcombe completed the three-game sweep with an 8-4 win on the following day. At the All-Star break, the Dodgers appeared to be the class of the league with a 50-26 record and an advantage of eight and a half games over New York.

By August 9, the lead had grown to twelve and a half games. It was after a Dodger sweep that an incident occurred that may have turned the tide in favor of the Giants. The Dodgers had won the game and proceeded to taunt the Giants through the clubhouse walls with shouts of "The Giants is dead." Dressen and Robinson led the assault aided, ironically, by Ralph Branca. Newcombe, who had great respect for Durocher as a manager, refused to join the fray but the damage was done and the bees in the hive, in the form of the New York Giants, were beginning to stir.

Brooklyn's lead peaked at thirteen and a half games. From that point on, the Dodgers played .500 baseball while the Giants took thirty-seven of their last forty-four games. Most baseball fans know that the two teams ended in a flat-footed tie with 96-58 records, setting the stage for what many people believe to be the greatest game ever played. During that stretch, Don Newcombe two-hit the Giants on September 8, winning 9-0, and got his twentieth win against Robin Roberts at Philadelphia in the must-win next-to-last game of the season. This victory secured a tie in the standings. The very next day, in the third inning, Dressen called upon Newcombe to pitch in relief of Preacher Roe, who had posted a 22-3 record over the season. Don responded with a clutch effort of shutout relief. The Dodgers won in the fourteenth inning and it was on to the playoffs.

The first game of the set took place at Ebbets Field and the Giants' Jim Hearn, behind home runs by Bobby Thomson and Monte Irvin, bested Branca and the Dodgers 3-1. The series moved to the Polo Grounds, and the Dodgers responded with a convincing 10-0 win, the shutout authored by young Clem Labine. The season had come down to one game and Dressen called on Newcombe.

Why did Charlie want Newcombe in this pressure-packed situation? It was Wednesday, October 3, and Don had just pitched nearly fifteen shutout innings over the September 29–30 weekend. Preacher Roe with his 22-3 record lasted only into the third inning on Sunday; Carl Erskine at 16-12 had not pitched since Friday; and Clyde King (14-7) threw a few innings before Newk's superb effort on Sunday. Again, why Newcombe? Because he was the best man Dressen had.

The Polo Grounds seated more than 55,000 fans. For some reason, only 34,320 saw the deciding game of the 1951 season. The Dodgers opened the scoring in the first inning when Robinson singled home Reese. New York tied the game in the seventh when Thomson scored Irvin with a hit to shallow center. In the top of the eighth, Brooklyn finally got to Maglie and came up with three runs. Reese and Snider both singled and Pee Wee scored on a Maglie wild pitch. Pafko and Cox brought two more home with singles of their own. The Giants went down one-two-three in the bottom of the eighth.

Durocher relieved starter Sal Magile with Larry Jansen. Both pitchers had been mainstays throughout the season, eventually accounting for twenty-three wins apiece. Jansen set down the Dodgers in order and the Giants were left with their last three outs. Newcombe took the mound and got two quick strikes on Al Dark before Dark hit a squeaker between first and second. Don Mueller singled him to third and the creaky ballpark in northern Manhattan began to wake up from the dirge played during the previous inning. Newk then got Monte Irvin to pop up to first baseman Gil Hodges. Whitey Lockman then poked a soft liner just over third baseman Billy Cox's head to score Dark and sending Mueller to third, where he pulled a tendon as his spikes got caught on the bag. Mueller had to leave the game.

Dressen had had enough even though Newcombe was not hit hard and appeared still to have his stuff, but Charlie called on Ralph Branca to pitch to Bobby Thomson. As we all know, Bobby promptly cleared the decks on Branca's second serving to propel the New York Giants into the World Series. As in 1950, Don Newcombe had been asked to perform over and above the call of duty and he did his best, going 20-9 with an earned run average of 3.28.

Newk missed the 1952 and 1953 championship seasons, spending those years in the Army. He came back in time for the 1954 campaign and Walter Alston had replaced Dressen as manager of the Dodgers. However, Don went a disappointing 9-8 as the Giants once again took the pennant, and also the World Series.

The Bums from Brooklyn still sought their first world title and were tired of "waitin' till next year."

In 1955, Newcombe regained his form. He won his first ten decisions of the season and was 18-1 on July 31. He finished with a 20-5 record and a 3.20 ERA. Newcombe started the first game of the World Series but Joe Collins of the Yankees sent him to an early shower with a two-run homer in the sixth, and he lost 6-5. Mysteriously, he never appeared in that series again. The Dodgers finally brought the borough of Brooklyn its only world championship with an exciting four-games-to-three victory over the Yankees.

It was during 1955 that Don showed that he could also wield a bat as he hit .359 with a pitchers record of seven homers in 117 at bats. Manager Walter Alston used him as a pinch hitter and he responded by batting .381 with an eight-for-twenty-one showing. Newcombe had a lifetime batting average of .271 in 878 at bats, and slammed fifteen homers and drove in 108 runs in the process. As a pinch hitter, he went twenty for eighty-seven over the course of his career.

Although the 1956 Dodgers consisted of the same personnel as the previous year's title squad, the teams did not resemble each other. The 1955 team won ninety-eight games and finished thirteen and a half games ahead of the Milwaukee Braves. As a team, they paced the league in batting, runs scored, and home runs (with 201), and the pitching staff posted the best ERA with 3.68. Duke Snider drove in 136 runs and Campanella contributed 107 to go with his third MVP award. In 1956, the Dodgers as a team led in no category but Snider led with forty-three homers, although his RBI production dropped to 101. The Dodgers, however, had Don Newcombe.

Don Newcombe and the 1956 Season

The new season started slowly for the Dodgers, as their triumph in the 1955 World Series seemed to be some sort of heavy collar. The team that ran away with the flag in the previous campaign was chosen by the Sunday, April 15, issue of the *New York Times* along with the Yankees to meet once again in the fall classic. However, the Dodgers started on the wrong foot when Newcombe gave up five hits in two and a third innings as Robin Roberts and the Phillies took the season opener 8-6. By the end of April, they were 7-4 and Newcombe improved to 2-1. On May 3, Newcombe won his third game, going eight innings to set back the Cardinals 7-3 in St. Louis and snap a four-game Dodger losing streak.

Needles, an 8-5 favorite with Dave Erb aboard, took the Kentucky Derby by less than a length over Fabius on Saturday, May 5. At the USC/ UCLA track meet in Los Angeles, Jim Bailey, a little-known runner from Australia, ran the first-ever sub-four-minute mile in the United States. He nosed out countryman John Landy by one-tenth of a second at 3:58.6.

Brooklyn traveled to Chicago, with Newcombe taking the mound on May 8. He shut out the Cubs on three hits for a 6-0 victory as the Dodgers evened their record at 9-9. Five days later, with help from Clem Labine, he beat the Giants 6-4 at Ebbets Field, one day after right-hander Carl Erskine tossed the second no-hitter of his career, winning against the Giants 3-0.

On May 13, Australian John Landy ran his sixth sub-four-minute mile at a meet in Fresno, California.

On May 15, the Dodgers did the unthinkable. They acquired the services of former nemesis Sal Maglie from the Cleveland Indians. Maglie had tormented the Dodgers as a pitcher for the New York Giants and dominated them with a lifetime 23-11 record. After six seasons with the Giants, he went to the Indians late in 1955. When he did not figure in the Tribe's plans, the Dodgers picked him up for cash. Maglie had captured only ninety-six victories at this point in his career. Nearly 25 percent of those wins came at the expense of Brooklyn. To give the Dodgers credit, they also accounted for 25 percent of his forty-four career losses. He went on to win thirteen games for the Dodgers in 1956 and was a key cog in the run for the flag.

American track-and-field hopes were dealt a strong slap in a New York Supreme Court decision. Marine 1st Lt. Wes Santee, a former miler from Kansas and the current U.S. record holder for that event, had appealed his amateur status. The Court upheld an earlier decision that he took fifteen hundred dollars more in expense money than was due him and thus he forfeited his chance to compete in the 1956 Olympics. It was unknown whether Santee would appeal this decision.

Later that week, in a fight in Los Angeles, thirty-five-year-old Sugar Ray Robinson retained his middleweight title with a TKO in the fourth round against Bobo Olson, eight years his junior.

On Saturday, May 19, Fabius and Needles reversed the Derby order in the Preakness. Fabius, guided by Willie Hartack, won the classic by one and three-quarter lengths. On that same day, Nashua, who had finished as runner-up in the previous year's Derby before taking both the Preakness and the Belmont, won the Camden Handicap at Garden State Park. This remarkable four-year-old had appeared in twenty-four races to date, winning nineteen. He finished second thrice and third once. He finished out of the money (fifth) just one time.

Newcombe started against Cincinnati on May 19, and was hammered by the Redlegs, leaving in the third inning and absorbing his second setback. The next day, he relieved Ken Lehman in the third inning of the second game of a twin bill against Chicago. Newk stayed until the end and picked up his sixth win in a 5-3 sweep of the Cubs. The Dodgers had bounced back to second place with a 16-11 mark.

Dale Long, first baseman for the Pittsburgh Pirates, had gone on a home-run-hitting rampage, getting one round-tripper in each of seven games. On May 28, his Buccaneers faced the Dodgers at Forbes Field and beat them 3-2 as Long extended his streak to eight. The next day, Newcombe ended Long's record-setting run with a 10-1 win over the Pirates, and ended May at 7-3.

In Texas, Don January won his first tournament in the Professional Golfers Association tour, taking the Dallas Centennial Open with a 268. He nosed out both Dow Finsterwald and Doug Ford by one stroke with an eagle on the par-four eighteenth hole. January recorded three eagles during his final round and took home six thousand dollars for his efforts.

The Dodgers started June on a sour note, dropping three to the Cubs in Chicago. Newcombe lost 5-4 despite banging two hits and driving in a run. The Dodgers had fallen back to a 19-19 record, three and a half games behind the league-leading Milwaukee Braves. On

June 6, Newk went the distance and improved to 8-4 with a five-hit, 5-2 victory over the Braves. Newcombe started only three more games in June, beating the Cards and dropping one to Milwaukee, and wound up at 9-5 on June 30. The Dodgers were 37-28, in second place.

By July 4, the Dodgers were a mere one and a half games behind the Braves and the powerful and surprising Cincinnati Redlegs. On the holiday, Newk beat the Giants at the Polo Grounds behind a nasty 15-2 attack. Brooklyn held a 40-30 mark and Newcombe sported a 10-5 record. On Sunday, July 8, Don picked up win number eleven by beating the Phillies 9-2 while newly arrived old rival Sal Maglie lost the nightcap 3-2. The All-Star break saw the Dodgers in third place two games behind Cincy with a 42-32 record. The midsummer classic found another National League victory, by a score of 7-3.

The New York Times *ran an advertisement for A&P Supermarkets touting a carton of cigarettes for $2.09 and two twenty-eight-ounce bottles of Canada Dry Ginger Ale for forty-five cents.*

After the break, the Dodgers continued their downward slide and on Friday, July 13, dropped two games to the Braves. Newcombe started the first contest but was not tagged with the loss. The Reds continued to keep pace with Milwaukee, propelled by Brooks Lawrence, who at this point in the season had not lost in thirteen decisions, and by a young rookie outfielder named Frank Robinson. Cincinnati's Robinson would go on to hit thirty-eight home runs in 1956. By July 19, Brooklyn had fallen to six games behind the Braves and seemed to be on a trip to nowhere. The next day, Newcombe won his thirteenth decision with a five-hit, 4-1 victory over the Cardinals in the seventeenth game of a nineteen-game road trip. Sandy Koufax and Carl Erskine took a twin bill from the Cards on the last day of the journey to give the Dodgers a marginal 10-9 record over the stretch.

On July 25, Newcombe beat the Reds 2-1 in one of seven games the Dodgers played in Jersey City that season. O'Malley had scheduled the games in hopes of generating additional attendance and as a teaser to New York's politicians. He had been lobbying for a modern stadium in Brooklyn for a number of years and found resistance in the form of Robert Moses, who had done most of the postwar planning for the city of New York. Moses, who is cast as the villain in Michael Shapiro's *The Last Good Season*, forced O'Malley's hand. With the Jersey City games, he was beginning to make preparations for the move to Los Angeles.

The Italian luxury liner Andrea Doria *collided with the Swedish ship* Stockholm *off the coast of Massachusetts, forty-five miles south of Nantucket, in dense fog. Fifty-one lives were lost in the tragedy.*

Newcombe finished July with another win over the Cubs, shutting them down 1-0 for his fifteenth win in 1956 and one hundredth of his career. He followed that with shutouts against the Braves on August 2 and the Pirates on the seventh. His record now showed seventeen wins with just five losses, and four days later he was a 5-2 winner over the Phillies. At 18-5, he had won nine straight, and pitched thirty-nine and two-thirds consecutive scoreless innings in the process.

The ides of August proved to be unkind to Don Newcombe, as John Antonelli and the last-place Giants beat him 1-0 at Jersey City. Since the Independence Day doubleheader, Newcombe had produced a 9-1 mark whereas the Dodgers scratched out a 24-16 record over that stretch trying to keep up with the Braves. On the nineteenth, Newk beat the Phillies in Philadelphia 3-2 to improve to 19-6.

Four days later, Big Newk put the Dodgers two games up on the Reds with a 6-5 complete-game win over them at Crosley Field to improve to 20-6. Don helped his own cause with a double and a run scored, keeping Brooklyn only two games behind Milwaukee. On August 27, he started against the Braves and left the game trailing 3-0 in the fifth, although the Bums pulled out a ninth-inning win with a Campanella three-run homer. The next day he pitched an inning and two-thirds of relief against the Cubs and picked up victory number twenty-one. On the last day of August he beat the

Giants at the Polo Grounds 7-3, but the Dodgers remained an elusive two and a half games behind the front-running Braves.

Due to a series of rainouts, Newcombe did not pitch again until September 7, but on that date he salvaged the second game of a twin bill with a 3-1 victory in anticipation of a crucial two-game series with Milwaukee. He and Maglie were scheduled to pitch against the Braves' Lew Burdette and Bob Buhl. In the opener, Maglie gained his tenth win, besting Buhl 4-2. The second game saw neither Burdette nor Newcombe by the third frame as the Braves took that game 8-7 and maintained their lead over Brooklyn by a game and a half.

On September 15, Newcombe shut out the Cubs 3-0 for his twenty-fourth win and the Dodgers finally attained the top of the league by .002 percentage point. On the nineteenth, he became only the fifth National League pitcher to win twenty-five games in the past twenty seasons, joining Carl Hubbell and Robin Roberts, among others. The previous day, the Yankees had clinched the American League flag with a 3-2 win over Chicago ace Billy Pierce on Mickey Mantle's fiftieth home run of the year.

During the season's last week, the tension grew as the Dodgers and the Braves ran neck-and-neck. Newcombe took the second game of a Sunday doubleheader against the Pirates in Pittsburgh although he had to wait until Monday to make it official because of Pennsylvania's Sunday laws, which suspended the game in the eighth inning. On two days of rest he then lost to Robin Roberts on September 26, falling victim to a Sandy Amoros two-run error in the second inning. Victory number twenty-seven came on the last day of the season, and it clinched the pennant for Brooklyn by one game over the Braves.

Newcombe had posted a 27-7 record for the season. He was 17-2 over the last eighty-four games while the Dodgers went 53-31 during that span. His ERA for the campaign was a fifth-best 3.06 but after the All-Star Game he gave up a stingy 2.20 per game. He completed eighteen of his thirty-six starts and held the opposition to just over one and a half walks per game.

Two horrific World Series appearances marred Don's greatest season. Yogi Berra touched him for three home runs and he left both his starts in the early innings. He had a verbal and physical run-in with an unsympathetic and ignorant parking lot attendant who obviously was unaware that Brooklyn would have watched the World Series on television had it not been for Don Newcombe. Attention had been showered on Maglie the Barber, the archenemy who came from nowhere to save the day with his 13-5 mark. However, Newcombe was named Most Valuable Player by the National League sportswriters, garnering 223 points to Maglie's 183. As noted earlier, he also bagged the first-ever Cy Young Award.

The following year he slumped to 11-12, and by mid-1958, he was no longer a Dodger. The team, which had been moved to Los Angeles before the 1958 season, traded him to Cincinnati. He had a good 1959, going 13-8 for the Reds, but was finished as a player by 1960.

Nerwcombe's troubles began to accelerate. He had always been a big drinker, but his size and overall performance masked any problems he might have had with demon rum. After his playing days, he owned a bar and a liquor store. Neither made it, nor did his first marriage. His second wife was ready to leave him, for she could not handle raising a family along with a drunken husband. That did it. In 1966 Don Newcombe became sober, and since then has been a crusader against the excesses of alcohol. His honesty about his experiences has most likely saved the career of more than one athlete. He has been employed by the Dodger organization as a counselor for substance abuse.[17]

Don Newcombe is the only man ever to win the Rookie of the Year, Cy Young, and Most Valuable Player awards. He won a total of 149 games against ninety losses. He posted twenty victories three times and may have been baseball's best-hitting pitcher besides

---

17. *Big Newk Is Winning the Big One*, Dave Anderson, *New York Times* November 6, 1975.

Babe Ruth. He enjoyed a splendid career, although it was tainted by a number of poor performances while in the national spotlight.

Don Newcombe started five World Series games for the Brooklyn Dodgers and had a record of 0-4 in postseason competition. Critics have often targeted him for his record in so-called clutch games, but in reality, Newcombe was a key reason for the success the Dodgers enjoyed in the era during which New York City just about dominated major league baseball.

Newk's reputation of not winning the big ones came despite the fact that during the 1949–51 period the Dodgers won the first pennant by one game and lost the next two on the last day of the season. Newcombe happened to start each of those final-day contests. In 1949, only two days after a complete-game, four-hit shutout, he was cruising with a 5-0 lead after four innings against the Philadelphia Phillies but third baseman Willie "Puddin' Head" Jones cracked a three-run homer and the game was soon tied. Newcombe was yanked, but the Dodgers won in extra innings. In 1950, he lost to the Phillies 4-1 on a tenth-inning Dick Sisler home run as they stormed to their "Whiz Kids" pennant. In 1951, after his team blew a thirteen-and-a-half-game lead, he went into the ninth inning against the Giants in the final playoff game and left leading 4-2, with Bobby Thomson coming to the plate and Ralph Branca trudging in from the bullpen.

In the opening game of the 1949 World Series, Don—the first black man to start a Word Series contest—gave up five hits and fanned eleven, but lost to the New York Yankees 1-0 in the ninth inning when Tommy Henrich clubbed a home run. Where were the Brooklyn hitters during this game? They had slugged a league-leading 152 home runs in the regular season and led the circuit in runs batted in but were among the missing when Newk needed only a couple of runs, getting just two hits off the Yankees' Allie Reynolds. Two days later, Dodger manager Burt Shotton started Newcombe in the third game and Don responded with three shutout innings before faltering in the fourth, giving up three runs and suffering his second loss in the series. People have a tendency to ignore the fact that the Dodgers would not have achieved such success were it not for Don Newcombe, who won fifty-six games in the 1949–51 years.

It is also convenient to forget that without Newcombe, the situation in 1950 would not have been do-or-die. Going into that final game, both he and opposing pitcher Robin Roberts were gunning for their twentieth victory. Only three weeks earlier, Newcombe had started both games of a twi-night doubleheader in Philadelphia against the then faltering Phillies. He shut out the Phils on three hits in the first game and went seven innings in the second, giving up eight hits. He left with the score 2-0 in favor of Curt Simmons and the home team. Brooklyn came back to win in the top of the ninth, but the win went to reliever Dan Bankhead. Newk's effort that evening gave the Dodger relief corps a boost and brought Brooklyn to within five and a half games of the first-place Phillies.

No pitcher was ever more responsible for leading his team into a World Series than was Big Newk in 1956. For his 27-7 performance in the regular season, he was named both the National League's Most Valuable Player and the first-ever Cy Young pitching award—certainly for him, *that one glorious season.*

DONALD NEWCOMBE   pitcher BROOKLYN DODGERS
Ht: 6'4"   Wt: 220   Bats: Left   Throws: Right
Born: June 14, 1926; Madison, New Jersey

Don was voted the N.L. Most Valuable Player in '56 for chalking up the most victories and leading the Dodgers to the pennant. He turned in 5 shutouts including a 2 hitter and two 3 hit games. Against Chicago, Pittsburgh and St. Louis he was a one man wrecking squad compiling a 16-1 record against the three teams.

HOW MANY GAMES DID THE DEAN BROS WIN IN 1934?

COMPLETE MAJOR LEAGUE PITCHING RECORD

YEAR	CLUB	LEA.	G	IP	W	L	PCT	SO	BB	ERA
1949	Brooklyn	N. L.	38	244	17	8	.680	149	73	3.17
1950	Brooklyn	N. L.	40	267	19	11	.633	130	75	3.71
1951	Brooklyn	N. L.	40	272	20	9	.690	164	91	3.28
'52-53	Brooklyn	N. L.					(In Military Service)			
1954	Brooklyn	N. L.	29	144	9	8	.529	82	49	4.56
1955	Brooklyn	N. L.	34	234	20	5	.800	143	38	3.19
1956	Brooklyn	N. L.	38	268	27	7	.794	139	46	3.06
Major League Totals 6 Yrs.			219	1429	112	48	.700	807	372	3.41

11

1957: LEW BURDETTE

MILWAUKEE BRAVES

On October 10, 1957, Lew Burdette, of the Milwaukee Braves, took the mound in Yankee Stadium for the ninth inning of game seven of the World Series. He had already won twice in the series. Braves manager Fred Haney had given him the assignment of starting the final contest with just two days' rest after he beat the New York Yankees in Milwaukee with a 1-0, seven-hit game. Nursing a 5-0 lead, which could be wiped out in a flash by the powerful Yanks, he quickly dispensed with the ever-dangerous Yogi Berra, but gave up a single to shortstop Gil McDougald. Rookie Tony Kubek, a native of Milwaukee, whose third-inning error paved the way for four Braves runs, hit a drive to right field, but Hank Aaron swiftly put it away.

That left one out to go for the ultimate victory, and Gerry Coleman stood between Burdette and immortality. Coleman postponed the celebration with a hit to right field, advancing McDougald. Pitcher Tommy Byrne, a good hitter, then singled to right, loading the bases. Bill Skowron hit a vicious shot down the third-base line, which looked like a certain two-base hit into left field, bringing the crowd to its feet. But what they witnessed was a spectacular grab on the part of Braves third baseman Eddie Mathews, who promptly stepped on the bag and forced Coleman, ensuring Milwaukee's first and only world championship and Burdette's second shutout of the fall classic.

Lew Burdette had won his third game of the series and shut out the Yankees twice in three days, becoming the first man since Harry "the Cat" Brecheen of the 1946 Cardinals to take three in a series. Brecheen, however, got his third win with a two-inning relief stint to achieve his feat. The last man before Burdette to win three complete games in a series was Stan Coveleski of the 1920 Cleveland Indians, and he did it in a best-of-nine series although the Indians took the series five games to two. The next to snare three would be Bob Gibson of the 1967 St. Louis Cardinals and then Mickey Lolich of the 1968 Detroit Tigers. None but the New York Giants' Christy Mathewson ever threw three shutouts in one series, and that happened in 1905 against the Philadelphia A's in the all-shutout series.

The postseason proved to be a fitting cap to the Braves' and Burdette's 1957 season. The Braves made up for a horrific loss during the final days of 1956 by taking the National League pennant, and Burdette helped immensely with a regular-season record of 17-9 and an earned run average of 3.72.

During a major league career that effectively spanned the period 1952–66, Lew Burdette won more than two hundred regular-season games. Even today he is revered in the city of Milwaukee for the three games he won in the fall of 1957, bringing the Midwest brewery town its first—and what would be only—world championship.

Selva Lewis Burdette Jr. was born in 1926 and raised in the West Virginia company town of Nitro, which manufactured explosives as its primary product. The town grew exponentially during World War I, supplying American troops with ammunition. After the war, things seemed to grind to a halt, but chemical plants took over the existing engineering infrastructure and Nitro once again bustled with activity.

The Burdette family settled there just before Lew's birth, and as a youngster he roamed the hills and fields that bordered the town. He grew to be a six-foot-two-inch high schooler, but his creativity on the football field led him to disagreements with the powers that be in secondary-school sports. This resulted in a falling-out with the gridiron coach, but Lew's reinstatement became a key component in the team's eventual success.

His introduction to baseball came about because of a shortage of players for his father's company team. Burdette had not played much baseball, but his reputation for having a strong, accurate arm grew with each telling. The youngsters in Nitro engaged in all kinds of sports that were invented as a result of the Depression, and competitive rock throwing grew to be an important activity. Lew Burdette became the town's uncrowned champion and his accuracy was legendary. He could throw higher, farther, and for longer periods than any of his contemporaries and in doing so earned a spot on the American Viscose Chemical baseball team. He often pitched while his brother Gene was crouched behind the plate.

After a summer of playing ball and working as a messenger, Lew Burdette signed on with the Army in the hopes of becoming a pilot in World War II, but the conflict was coming to an end. Burdette was released from the service in the fall of 1945. After returning to Nitro, a local clergyman convinced him to attend the University of Richmond and play baseball. While at Richmond, a scout for the New York Yankees watched him pitch and offered him a minor league contract. After accepting a two-hundred-dollar bonus, Burdette moved on to their Norfolk affiliate, where he posted a 1-1 record. He was soon sent down a notch to Amsterdam, New York, of the Canadian American League.

He hit his stride during this stretch in the low minors, and although he suffered ten losses to go with nine victories, his 2.82 ERA impressed the Yankees enough to promote him to Quincy, Illinois, of the Three-I League. In 1948, Burdette won sixteen games and allowed a mere 2.02 earned runs per game for Quincy. He struck out 185, gave up only seventy-two walks, and threw six shutouts. Good control would become a Burdette trademark. The Yankees wanted another look at him and this time they assigned him to their top farm team, the Triple A Kansas City Blues of the American Association.

Between seasons, Lew had met a young woman named Mary Ann Shelton in a Charleston bowling alley; the couple were married in June of 1949. Over the years, they had four children and five grandchildren.

Burdette spent the next two seasons with the Blues, posting records of 6-7 and 7-7 over 1949 and 1950. During the 1949 campaign, he toiled primarily as a reliever and in the following year he resurfaced as a starter, earning a trip to New York to pitch for the parent club late in the season. He appeared in two games and seemed destined for a return to Kansas City, but after a spring training in which he allowed only one run in nineteen innings, he was shocked when he was told that he was being sent to San Francisco, of the Pacific Coast League, far from New York. The Yankees had a wealth of pitching talent and Burdette did not seem to be a part of their plans.

However, the Yankees needed pitching support in the waning days of 1951 as they roared to their third consecutive flag, but Casey Stengel did not want to take a chance on a rookie. Casey felt that he had to have Johnny Sain, the four-time twenty-game winner of the floundering Boston Braves. Sain, of "Spahn and Sain and pray for rain" fame, was in the midst of his worst year and the Braves willingly peddled him to New York for the sum of $50,000 and a quality prospect. Thus did Lew Burdette became a member of the Boston Braves of the National League.

Life with the Braves

The Boston Braves began life as the Red Stockings in the National Association and joined the National League as one of its charter members in 1876. They finished in first place eight times in the next twenty-five years. The advent of the twentieth century brought a reversal of fortunes and the Boston representative of the league took only one flag in the next forty-three seasons, finishing in the second division on thirty-six occasions. However, things were about to change for the better.

In 1944, three Boston-area contractors, headed by Lou Perini, took controlling ownership of the club, having been previously relegated to minority positions. Nicknamed the "three steam shovels," they brought energy and a fierce desire to forge a winning team for Braves Field. They fired manager Casey Stengel and replaced him with Bob Coleman, who did no better in 1944 than to match Casey's most recent sixth-place finish. The following season, despite outfielder Tommy Holmes's .352 batting average and league-leading home-run total, they still could not manage to improve on that sixth-place position.

Perini and his partners sought the best man to instill discipline and produce a team who played fundamental, winning baseball. John Quinn, the newly appointed general manager, thought that St. Louis Cardinals skipper Billy Southworth could resurrect the Braves' fortunes. Southworth had led the Redbirds to three pennants and two second-place finishes in five and a half seasons. Southworth accepted Perini's offer and came to Boston.

Southworth's presence had an immediate effect on the franchise, as it improved by fourteen victories over 1945 and placed fourth. Holmes batted a solid .310 and led the team with seventy-nine RBI. Johnny Sain, a twenty-eight-year-old right-handed pitcher, went 20-14 with a 2.21 ERA to pace the pitching staff. Mort Cooper had been acquired in May 1945 from the Cardinals after a contract dispute, and he added a 13-11 mark. They were joined late in the season by a stylish left-hander named Warren Spahn, who had been a late release from military service. Spahn appeared in twenty-four games, winning eight and losing five while registering a 2.94 ERA.

The Braves generated interest and set a team record, drawing nearly a million war-weary fans. It helped that they played night games and that they preceded other big-league teams with self-promoting materials such as the first team book, complete with pictures and statistics. Their marketing-savvy owners also had produced a team movie that appeared in theaters throughout New England.

In 1947, the team advanced to third place on the shoulders of third baseman Bob Elliot. Elliot, who had been acquired from the Pittsburgh Pirates after the 1946 season, batted .317, knocked in 113 runs, and earned Most Valuable Player honors. Spahn and Sain each contributed twenty-one victories and Holmes added a .309 average to the cause as the team geared up for 1948 with its best showing since 1916.

Quinn, who virtually had an open checkbook with a direct order from Perini to produce a winner, continued to seek out talent. He acquired an aging outfielder, Jeff Heath, from the St. Louis Browns for cash in December 1947. Quinn's most controversial acquisition proved to be a pesky second baseman named Eddie Stanky, who combined with rookie-of-the-year shortstop Al Dark to tighten the middle infield. Stanky had played a key role for the Brooklyn Dodgers champions in 1947, but for an inexplicable reason was seen as expendable. Stanky, unfortunately, broke his ankle in June after appearing in only sixty-six games.

In 1948, Heath batted .319 and had produced twenty homers and seventy-six RBI, until he too broke an ankle, in August. Elliot continued to produce, driving in one hundred runs while first baseman Earl Torgeson provided defensive stability and occasional power to the lineup. Spahn and Sain (and a day of rain) anchored the staff; Sain had the year of his life, winning twenty-four games with a 2.60 ERA. Spahn added another fifteen wins and newcomer Vern Bickford went 11-5. The Braves reached first place in June and fought off both the Dodgers and the Cards, taking the flag by six and a half games. Ironically, the Tribes from both leagues each won the second pennant in their modern team histories and both looked for their second World Series victory.

The Cleveland Indians took the series in six games; the Braves could muster just three runs in the first four games although they won the opener 1-0. The Indians took the finale in Boston 4-3 but only after the Braves pulled to within one run in the eighth inning.

For the next three seasons, the Braves took up residence in fourth place, barely showing a .500 record for the duration. Spahn continued to sparkle, winning sixty-four games over the period and adding to his reputation as one of the finest left-handers ever to take the mound. He went on to record a 363-245 career mark with an ERA of 3.09. He won more games than any other southpaw in the history of the game. In 1963, at the age of forty-two, he went 23-7 with twenty-two complete games in thirty-three starts.

The success of the Braves in the early Southworth years brought a cheerful atmosphere to the club, and imperfections in both the manager and the players became secondary issues. With the gradual decline of the team, the warts began to show. In 1950, rumors flew around the Hub that Southworth frequently hit the bottle. The players lacked any semblance of self-discipline off the field, eventually affecting their on-field performances.

Sain slipped to 10-17 in 1949 but rebounded to record his fourth twenty-game season in 1950. At the end of 1951, the Yankees acquired him late in the season. As noted earlier, he was exchanged for pitcher Lew Burdette.

Southworth was replaced by Holmes, who made it through thirty-five games into 1952 before being replaced by Charlie Grimm. The Braves headed downhill in a hurry and the trip could be traced to the trade that sent Stanky and Dark to the New York Giants for sluggers Willard Marshall and Sid Gordon after the 1949 campaign. The slightly improved offense gave way to a leaky infield and slowness of foot. The Braves gave up much more than they received. Stanky had been feuding with Southworth and this lack of respect gave the manager an excuse to be rid of him. Stanky and Dark became key ingredients to the successful Giant teams of the early 1950s.

In 1950, the Braves purchased the contract of Sam Jethroe from Brooklyn. Jethroe had starred in the Negro leagues and won three bat crowns in the 1940s. With Jethroe, a speedy base runner who could hit with power, on the roster, the Braves became the third National League team (behind the Dodgers and the Giants) to employ a Negro ballplayer. His showing in 1950 earned him the Rookie of the Year award, the third black man in four seasons to take that prize. In the 1951–59 period, no other senior circuit squad other than these three would win a pennant. Over that span, Hank Sauer, in 1952, was the only white man elected Most Valuable Player in the National League. It would not be until 1963, when the Yankees' Elston Howard was elected, that the American League had a black MVP.

The 1952 squad finished seventh with a 64-89 record, but that mark did not indicate the potential of the personnel on the roster. Spahn suffered through a 14-19 season despite a 2.98 ERA, and the supporting cast consisted of newcomers such as third baseman Eddie Mathews and shortstop Johnny Logan. Burdette remained in the shadows of the dugout posting a 6-11 mark with a creditable 3.61 ERA. The team drew only 298,000 fans and Perini and his partners were at wits' end trying to devise ways to meet expenses.

The team started spring training in 1953 as the Boston Braves and finished as the Milwaukee Braves. Perini saw Bill Veeck making overtures toward Milwaukee as a location for his hapless St. Louis Browns. Veeck had been an owner of the Milwaukee franchise during World War II and saw the city as ripe for big-league ball. Perini, who owned Milwaukee's American Association franchise, acted before Veeck could make his move. He requested and won support from his fellow owners, and the Braves relocated to the Midwest.

The team arrived in Wisconsin in April 1953 to the cheers of delirious fans who were unaware of the caliber of their new neighbors. The players, accustomed to small, nonchalant crowds, became instant celebrities and provided thrills beyond expectations. Jack Dittmer joined Logan and the two became an adequate keystone combination. Mathews blossomed into a genuine slugger, belting forty-seven homers to go with a .302 batting average. Del Crandall rejoined the team after a military stint and went on to supply excellent catching skills and a steady bat for the better part of a decade. Bill Bruton, a swift center fielder, took over from the fading Jethroe as the key to the outer pastures, further strengthening the middle. Joe Adcock relocated to Milwaukee from Cincinnati via a four-team trade to play first base and hit gargantuan home runs.

The team could hit and run, and enjoyed a tight defense. It displayed an eager enthusiasm and had the guiding hand of manager Charlie Grimm to maintain order. And they had pitching. Spahn tied with the Philadelphia Phillies' Robin Roberts for the league lead in wins, going 23-7. Four other hurlers tossed in another fifty-one wins, led by Burdette with a 15-5 mark and a 3.24 ERA. The Braves stormed to second place, improving to 92-62 and finishing thirteen games behind the Dodgers. The staff led the circuit in pitching with a 3.30 ERA and completed seventy-six games. Milwaukee fans turned out in droves and the team drew more than 1.8 million paying customers.

The Braves made two trades during the off-season to improve the club. The first, with the Pirates, brought second baseman Danny O'Connell into the fold, giving Logan a capable partner and the team a fine catcher/second base/center field alignment. The departure of Sid Gordon in the O'Connell deal left a void in left field and Quinn moved to fill that hole by trading left-hander Johnny Antonelli and three others to the Giants for the 1951 "shot heard 'round the world" author Bobby Thomson.

The citizens of Wisconsin could not wait for the season to begin. However, on March 13, 1954, during a spring training game, Thomson jammed his ankle while sliding into third base and was lost for months. Grimm called on a twenty-year-old outfielder from Mobile, Alabama, to help the team. Henry Aaron had been destined to play at either Toledo or Atlanta but he took Thomson's place in the lineup the very next day. For the season, he batted .280 and had thirteen home runs until he, too, tore up his ankle, in early September.

The Braves did not achieve any greatness in 1954; the Giants took all the honors that season. However, Milwaukee proved that

1953 had been no flash in the pan and played very respectable baseball, finishing third at 89-65, eight games out. Mathews contributed forty more home runs and Spahn posted a 21-12 season. Burdette went 15-14 and his 2.76 ERA was second in the league.

By now, Burdette had enjoyed two good seasons, and he began to take on the reputation of a pitcher who had mastered the outlawed spitball. Old-time spitball pitcher Burleigh Grimes once tutored Lew in the art of pitching and it had been widely rumored that the Hall of Famer had imparted the secrets of tossing and hiding the wet pitch. Both Grimes and Burdette vehemently denied any transfer of knowledge and to this day the mystery remains. Burdette had a variety of pitches and had control of them all, whether he threw overhand or sidearm.

The Dodgers ran away with the flag in 1955 and took their only Brooklyn World Series in the process, while the Braves finished a distant second. The fans continued to turn out in record numbers as they drew more than two million in both 1954 and 1955. Second base was still a trouble spot, for O'Connell began to decline. Grimm became desperate and even played Aaron at the position for twenty-seven games in 1955 in his search for a solution.

While the Dodgers basked in their glory, the rest of the league was becoming acutely aware that the team had aged. The Braves, on the other hand, still had a young lineup with an outstanding pitching staff. They made no move to strengthen a mediocre bullpen, however, or to improve the middle infield.

The 1956 season started slowly for the team, and on June 15, after a 24-22 fifth-place start, Charlie Grimm resigned in favor of coach Fred Haney. Immediately after ascending to the skipper's position, Haney led the Braves on an eleven-game win streak. By the All-Star break they had risen to second place, a game and a half behind the surprising and power-laden Cincinnati Reds. The three days off in mid-July seemed to energize the team and they went on a 15-2 tear that saw them in first place five and a half games up on the Reds. They stayed in first place through September 15, but only by percentage points.

They went into the season's final weekend in first place with three games scheduled with the Cardinals in St. Louis. The Braves needed to win two to clinch a tie and a sweep to ensure a trip to the World Series. They did neither, with Bob Buhl and Spahn pitching well but losing as Brooklyn won two. On Sunday, now a game behind, Burdette took a 4-2 win, but it came too late.

Burdette went 19-10 and led the league in ERA, giving up only 2.70 runs per game. He completed sixteen games and struck out 110 batters, yielding just fifty-two walks in 256 innings. The Braves staff once again reigned supreme in the National League, leading in ERA, complete games, and shutouts. Spahn and Buhl contributed another thirty-eight wins. Aaron took the bat crown at .328 while Adcock and Mathews finished two, three in home runs.

The Memorable 1957 Campaign

The players who took the field to inaugurate baseball in Milwaukee in April 1953 looked remarkably similar to those who started the team's fifth season in 1957 as the young cast of characters developed. Dittmer had departed in 1956 and, of course, Aaron arrived in 1954, eventually taking over for Andy Pafko in right field.

The 1957 season opened on April 16 with Spahn on the mound in Chicago against the Cubs, who meekly succumbed to the veteran left-hander, 4-1, on four hits. Two days later, in Milwaukee, Burdette shut out the Reds 1-0 and the Braves lengthened their at-home opening-day win streak, posting their fifth straight victory (in five tries) since moving west. Milwaukee continued to play winning baseball and held on to first place through April 30 at 9-2, even though Buhl had dropped the month's final contest to John Antonelli and the Giants, 4-0.

The merry month of May saw the IRS relieve Sugar Ray Robinson of $23,000 of his May 1 purse for back taxes owed. He had just knocked out Gene Fullmer to gain the middleweight title when the feds appeared. On May 4, Iron Liege, driven by Willie Hartack, took the Kentucky Derby over Gallant Man with Willie Shoemaker aboard.

Burdette beat the Pirates on the second of May with his second shutout of the young season, 1-0, and Milwaukee advanced to a league-leading 11-2 mark. The Braves stayed in first place until May 16, when they lost to Bob Friend of Pittsburgh 2-1 at home, dropping a game behind Cincinnati.

On Saturday, May 18, at Pimlico, Derby favorite Bold Ruler beat Iron Liege by two lengths to capture the Preakness, ensuring another year without a Triple Crown winner in horse racing.

On May 22, Burdette beat Robin Roberts and the Phillies 4-3 at home, but the Braves still lingered in second, a game and a half in back of Cincinnati with a 19-10 record. The remainder of May proved to be no picnic: Milwaukee played 4-5 baseball, ending the month at 23-16.

The Tribe entered June on a sour note, dropping a home game to the St. Louis Cardinals, dipping to three and a half games behind. They would not drop further behind for the duration of the long campaign. In the meantime, Perini, who had suffered through an attendance drought in Boston, reverted to the owners' mentality of the 1930s and withdrew all televised games from the local area, even road games. This prompted fans to jeer manager Haney during the May–June home stand, in which the team went a mere 4-4 and they dropped to their season low point.

Despite Perini's uncharacteristic and miserly actions, the fans continued to pour into County Stadium for home games in record numbers and the Braves did not disappoint them. After that mediocre stay in Milwaukee, they headed back to enemy territory and regained their winning ways. They reclaimed first place on June 13 with an 8-5 win over the Dodgers at Ebbets Field. In that contest, Logan and Brooklyn pitcher Don Drysdale were ejected after Drysdale plunked the Braves' shortstop with a fastball.

On June 15, racing's Triple Crown became evenly divided as Gallant Man took the Belmont stakes in record time.

The Braves' principal weakness was corrected on June 15 with the acquisition of second baseman Red Schoendienst from the New York Giants for O'Connell and Bobby Thomson. Schoendienst, a young thirty-four, immediately stepped into the Braves infield and combined with shortstop Johnny Logan to give the club a good-hitting, good-fielding second-base combination. Schoendinst, who had finished second to Carl Furillo for the batting title in 1953 with a .342 mark, hit .310 for the Braves for the duration of 1957. Overall, for the entire season, he led the majors in base hits with two hundred and batted .309.

Injuries dotted the landscape at County Stadium and were pervasive throughout 1957. Besides Bruton, who missed the remainder of the season due to a July 11 collision with Felix Mantilla, Adcock broke his leg on a slide into second and had to sit out for nearly three months. Logan missed three weeks with a shinbone infection and Mantilla was out for nineteen games after his bump with Bruton. The pitching staff joined in the infirm with Burdette out for nearly a month and Buhl for three weeks. Both these hurlers failed to pick up twenty victories, most likely because of these lost starts.

The team received help, however, from its rich farm system. Left fielder Wes Covington came up from Wichita on June 19 and filled the void in the outfield left by Thomson's departure and went on to hit .284 with twenty-one homers. On July 28, Bob "Hurricane" Hazle was rushed up from Wichita to cover for Bruton and had a *"Shining Season."*[18] He appeared in forty-one games and batted .403 with seven home runs and twenty-seven key RBI. He was back in the minors for the 1959 season and soon retired from the game.

From the time of Schoendienst's arrival through the All-Star Game on July 9, Milwaukee played cat and mouse with first place, never letting the prize out of sight but making no serious attempt to claim the position as its sole possession. At the time of the break, they trailed the Cardinals by two and a half games with a 44-34 record. Although picked for the midseason-classic roster, Burdette had not put together a particularly impressive first half. He had but six victories against six losses and his ERA hovered around four

---

18. Michael Fedo, *One Shining Season*, New York: Pharos Books, 1991.

runs per game. However, Dodger skipper and All-Star manager Walt Alston saw Lew as one tough pitcher and was well aware that Burdette had missed nearly a month's action. Burdette relieved starter Curt Simmons of the Phillies in the second inning of the game and proceeded to pitch four frames, giving up two hits and no runs in a 6-5 American League victory.

All sports took a back seat to tennis star Althea Gibson of Manhattan, as she enjoyed a ride up Broadway in honor of her magnificent triumph at England's Wimbledon tournament.

On July 11, the Braves renewed their quest for baseball's Holy Grail. Two days later, Burdette took a 4-3 win over the Pirates in the Steel City and the Braves pulled to within a game and a half of the Cardinals.

The U.S. Senate voted 71-18 to take up debate on the Civil Rights Bill presented to them by the Eisenhower administration. Staunch southerners were shocked by the defection of four of their colleagues who voted in favor of debate, vowing revenge on future election days. However, Senators Johnson and Yarborough of Texas and Senator Gore of Tennessee would have no problem in getting reelected, whereas Senator Kefauver of Tennessee retired after his current term.

Warren Spahn, a notorious slow starter, on July 15 picked up victory number ten over the Phils 6-2 and Burdette followed with a 10-3 win the next day to improve to 8-6. Both games drew more than 24,000 fans into Shibe Park as they watched the Braves gain a tie with the pesky Phillies.

While Horace Stoneham honestly admitted to Arthur Daley of the *New York Times* that he had all but resigned himself to leaving New York with his Giants, most likely to the reaches of San Francisco, Billy Graham gathered more than 100,000 people into Yankee Stadium for an evening of repentance. Stoneham showed no remorse, as he could not explain why the Giants did not attract fans in droves. Even in the best of times, such as the championship years of 1951 and 1954, the team barely reached the break-even, one million mark in attendance. In 1957, with a team headed for obscurity as well as California, a good crowd approached 10,000 on a given day.

The Braves, however, displaying the best baseball in the National League, overcame the lethargy of the Giants fans and drew nearly 14,000 into the Polo Grounds on July 21, splitting a double-header with the home team. After Spahn dropped the opener 5-4, Willie Mays touched Burdette for a home run and Lew departed after the fourth inning in the second game, having given up four runs. Milwaukee came back to win 7-4, but Burdette did not figure in the decision. Back home five days later, he failed again in his quest for his ninth victory although he went eight innings against New York. He allowed only three runs on seven hits but the Braves held on to first place with an eventual 6-3 win over Ruben Gomez. July ended with the Braves winning their fourth straight but still in second place, a half game out at 60-41.

On August 1, Milwaukee enjoyed a day off and the Cardinals regained a tie for first, beating the Giants with an 8-0 whitewash. That same day saw Gil Hodges of the Dodgers hit his league-record thirteenth lifetime grand slam, helping a young left-hander named Sandy Koufax complete the second game of his career and take a win over the Cubs. Those same Dodgers dropped the Braves into second place on August 3, when they beat Burdette. They knocked him out of the game with a four-run uprising in the seventh inning before 39,000 fans at home.

The Cards and the Braves continued to share the lead, but by August 6 Milwaukee had secured the top spot. Two days later, Burdette, assisted by a clutch Schoendienst eighth-inning single, helped widen the lead over St. Louis with a 5-3 decision over Cincinnati. Lew stood at 10-7 with an ERA of 3.93 on that date. His team then went on a rampage, eventually winning ten straight games while the Cards lost nine in a row. Bob Buhl sported a 15-6 mark and Spahn had begun to hit his groove at 11-8. Hank Aaron, who would ultimately be elected the league's Most Valuable Player, led in all hitting categories with a batting average of .334, with thirty-two homers and eighty-seven RBI.

During the win string, Burdette added to the home-run output with two fence-clearers in a 12-4 rout in Pittsburgh. After losing to the Cards on August 15, snapping both teams' streaks, he started again two days later against the Redbirds but gave way to none other than Warren Spahn in the ninth. Spahn took the extra-inning win in relief as the Braves increased their lead over St. Louis to eight and a half games. Lew then handcuffed the Dodgers and Sal Maglie 6-1 in a game at Ebbets Field. Two days later, Burdette took his thirteenth victory in a relief effort over Brooklyn, boosting the Braves to 75-46. On August 27, he won the next-to-last contest played between the Giants and the Braves in New York, before nearly 15,000 fans. He reached 14-7 and his team stood at 77-47 with thirty games to go.

Nobody said it would be easy. On September 2 and 5, Burdette got knocked around by both the Cubs and the Cardinals, respectively, getting tagged by the Redbirds with his eighth loss.

On September 7, Arkansas governor Orval Faubus went to court to avoid having to allow blacks to attend classes in Little Rock's Central High School.

The Giants beat the Dodgers 3-2 on September 8 in what would be the final game played at the Polo Grounds by these ancient rivals. During the 1900–1957 period the teams tangled 1,256 times, with the Giants holding a 650-606 edge.

On the tenth, Burdette recorded win number fifteen in a 4-3 squeaker over the Pirates, preserving the team's lead at five and a half games, the smallest since August 11. On September 14, the lead dropped to four games as Lew lost to Brooklyn 7-1 and the Cardinals trounced the Giants 6-1. Four days later, with the lead a precarious three games, Burdette responded with a four-hit, 8-2 win over the Giants at home for his sixteenth success. Don Drysdale of the Dodgers made his sixteenth victory worthwhile, beating St. Louis.

On September 23, 1957, at Milwaukee's County Stadium before 40,926 ecstatic fans, Lew Burdette took the mound against the Cardinals. He went ten innings, departing for a pinch-hitter with the bases loaded. Frank Torre bounced sharply into a double play, depriving Burdette of the eventual victory, which went to Gene Conley. In the bottom of the eleventh, Hank Aaron lined Billy Muffett's first pitch toward center field. The ball cleared the fence by six feet, assuring the Braves fans of a well-deserved pennant.

Although he did not nail the clinching victory, Lew kept the team in the game with a well-pitched effort. He wound up the season at 17-9 with an ERA of 3.72. It was not his best overall effort, but we must consider that he lost a month in the spring and went 9-3 over the last nine weeks of the season, while the Braves played at a 35-18 pace. Unbeknownst to anyone, though, the best was yet to come, in the 1957 World Series against the Yankees of New York.

The 1957 World Series

The Braves went into the series as underdogs and rightfully so. Casey Stengel's Bronx Bombers were appearing in their eighth post-season classic in nine years and boasted the most potent offense in the American League as well as the stingiest pitching staff. Milwaukee enjoyed a well-balanced offense and had led the National League in home runs. Hank Aaron, who had paced the circuit in round-trippers and RBI with forty-four and 132, respectively, was complemented by Eddie Mathews's thirty-two homers. Spahn had taken twenty-one wins during the season and Bob Buhl went 18-7. The pitching staff, as a whole, had completed sixty of their starts and posted a team ERA of 3.47, second in the league.

The World Series began in New York with lefty Whitey Ford besting Spahn 3-1. Burdette, who had become a father for the third time just prior to the series, got the call to start game two and responded with a 4-2 win over Bobby Shantz. Yankee outfielder Tony Kubek, a Milwaukee native whose dad had played with the minor league Brewers, helped the cause with an error in the fourth inning after Wes Covington singled to break a 2-2 tie. Covington had also made a spectacular catch off Shantz, saving two runs in the second inning and quashing a Yankee uprising.

That victory over the Yankees broke an overlooked streak of victories. The last time a team from other than New York City had won a World Series game was in 1948, the series that featured the Boston Braves versus the Cleveland Indians. In the ensuing eight classics, the only non-Gotham teams to appear in the fall classic had been swept away. The 1950 Phillies and the 1954 Indians went home empty-handed at the mercy of the Yankees and Giants, respectively, while the other six series became the exclusive domain of the city of New York.

The series moved to Milwaukee. The Yankees took the third game 12-3 as Buhl lasted only two-thirds of an inning. The next contest went into overtime but Spahn held the fort for a complete-game, ten-inning, 7-5 victory. In the bottom of the tenth, Haney sent Nippy Jones to hit for Spahn. Yankee pitcher Tommy Byrne threw a low, inside pitch that got past catcher Yogi Berra. Umpire Augie Donatelli called it a ball but Jones insisted that the pitch had hit his foot. A close examination of the baseball revealed shoe polish on the ball, so Donatelli granted Jones first base. Jones scored on Johnny Logan's double, which set up Eddie Mathews's game-winning home run.

Game five saw Burdette back on the mound, and he won a nail-biter beating his former Yankee teammate Whitey Ford 1-0 as he allowed the Yankees seven hits and no free passes. Covington again provided the game's fielding gem as he robbed Gil McDougald of a home run in the fourth inning, holding the ball tight as he hit the fence. The game's only run came on a series of sixth-inning singles by Braves strongmen Mathews, Aaron, and Joe Adcock.

Back in New York, Buhl once again left the game early, this time in the third. The game proved a delight although the win wound up in the Yankee column. Bullet Bob Turley gave the sports world a preview of his 1958 performance with a neat four-hit, 3-2, complete-game effort. The series was now tied at three games. All the marbles came out and went on the line for a showdown between Lew Burdette and Don Larsen.

On October 10, 1957, Spahn had been penciled in to start the series decider; however, he came down with the flu. Haney was forced to start Burdette on only two days' rest but Lew responded with a 5-0 victory, bringing home Milwaukee's only world championship. Larsen, the hero of the 1956 series with his perfect effort in the fifth game, left in the third frame as Mathews sent two runners home with a double, the key hit in a four-run inning. Burdette required no more than those initial two tallies as he shut out the Yankees for the second straight time. In accomplishing that feat, he also extended his consecutive series scoreless streak to twenty-four innings and won his third complete game of the series. Lew Burdette became only the fourth man to win three games in a seven-game World Series. Ironically, the Yankees suffered only two whitewashes during the entire 1957 season. Then Burdette did the deed twice in a seventy-two-hour span.

The Braves took the pennant again in 1958, and Lew once again started three games in the World Series. This time he dropped the finale, however, and could muster just one victory as the Yankees came from a 3-1 deficit to take the championship. The Braves finished second in 1959, losing a playoff to the newly transplanted Dodgers, now of Los Angeles. Burdette enjoyed twenty-victory seasons in both 1958 and 1959. He opposed Harvey Haddix in the "greatest game" ever pitched, and won it. He beat the Pirates 1-0 after Haddix threw twelve perfect innings against the Braves, only to lose the contest in the thirteenth frame.

Burdette went on to win 203 games against 144 losses over his career. His lifetime ERA settled in at 3.66 and he walked only 628 batters in 3,068 innings. He stayed with Milwaukee until 1963, when he was traded to St. Louis. He wound up with California in the American League and there he proved to be an effective reliever before retiring in 1967.

During his playing days, Lew and Mary Burdette had decided on Florida as a permanent residence. From that location, Lew managed and coached in the minors and served as pitching coach for the Atlanta Braves in the 1972–73 era. He also returned to Milwaukee as a spokesman for a brewery but eventually returned to Florida full time. He worked in cable television in its infancy and is now retired in Sarasota. Like many of the other ballplayers described in this book, he certainly enjoyed a great career, but 1957 had to be his crowning achievement, his *one glorious season*.

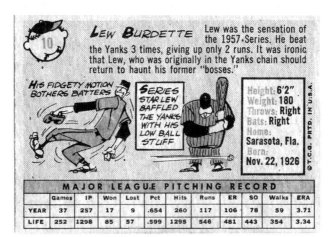

LEW BURDETTE Lew was the sensation of the 1957 Series. He beat the Yanks 3 times, giving up only 2 runs. It was ironic that Lew, who was originally in the Yanks chain should return to haunt his former "bosses."

HIS FIDGETY MOTION BOTHERS BATTERS

SERIES STAR LEW BAFFLED THE YANKS WITH HIS LOW BALL STUFF

Height: 6'2"
Weight: 180
Throws: Right
Bats: Right
Home: Sarasota, Fla.
Born: Nov. 22, 1926

© T.C.G. PRTD. IN U.S.A.

	Games	IP	Won	Lost	Pct	Hits	Runs	ER	SO	Walks	ERA
MAJOR LEAGUE PITCHING RECORD											
YEAR	37	257	17	9	.654	260	117	106	78	59	3.71
LIFE	252	1298	85	57	.599	1295	546	481	443	354	3.34

12

1958: JACKIE JENSEN
BOSTON RED SOX

The arrival of Jackie Jensen in New York as a rookie with the Yankees marked the emergence of one of baseball's first true glamour players. Born in San Francisco in 1927, he rose from the youngest of three boys raised in a fatherless home to become the finest athlete to graduate from Oakland (California) High School. He was pursued by a number of colleges, but with World War II winding down yet still very much a factor, he enlisted in the Navy upon graduation from high school in June 1945. He married Zoe Ann Olsen, who had won a silver medal in diving in the 1948 Olympics, and was blessed with three children.

On release from the service, his instincts were to play professional sports. Ralph Kerchum, a former coach of Jackie's, encouraged him to continue his education. He attended a Brooklyn Dodger tryout camp but impressed no one in particular. He then decided to enter college, matriculating at the nearby University of California, Berkeley. He enjoyed a fine football career at Cal, leading the Golden Bears to an undefeated 1948 season and into the Rose Bowl, where they bowed to favored Northwestern 20-14. Jackie had been injured early in the third period. That injury, along with a number of serious professional baseball offers, convinced him to forgo his senior year and turn pro.

He signed with the New York Yankees' Oakland affiliate in 1949 and made it to the big team in 1950 at the age of twenty-three. He was in the running with Mickey Mantle and Bob Cerv to replace Joe DiMaggio, another Bay Area native, his boyhood hero, a Hall of Fame member, and, in the minds of many fans, baseball's only near perfect player. Manager Casey Stengel quickly realized that Jackie did not have the ability of Joltin' Joe to pull the ball or to place it strategically all over the field. He was truly hindered by the dimensions of Yankee Stadium. Jackie's abilities in the field, on the bases, and at bat commanded plenty of attention from others. While Casey waited for Mantle to harness and control his overall raw ability, he traded Jensen and right-hander Spec Shea to the Washington Senators for veteran center fielder Irv Noren early in the 1952 season. While with the Yankees, Jackie Jensen did appear in the 1950 World Series, becoming the first man to play in both the Rose Bowl and the fall classic.

Washington's Griffith Stadium was a pitcher-friendly ballpark. It measured 386 feet from home plate to the left-field wall. It could have been the only baseball park in the world in which the left-field power alley was closer to the plate, at 372 feet, than a dead pull down the line. That did not help would-be sluggers who toiled for the Senators. From 1903 through 1953, only one Senator stroked more than twenty home runs in a season. Zeke Bonura, of the 1938 edition of the Senators, hit twenty-two round-trippers.

The Washington Senators were the butt of many a joke over the first half of the twentieth century. "First in war, first in peace, last in the American League" had a bit of truth to it. The Senators occupied the first division in only twenty of the first fifty years through 1950 with just three pennants to show for their efforts. Walter Johnson, also known as "the Big Train," was the main reason they performed as well as they did. He pitched for only the Senators, amassing 416 victories over a twenty-one-season span encompassing 1907 through 1927. That means he notched twenty wins per season for a team that averaged seventy-four wins over that same period. The Senators won two of their flags during these years and finished fourth or higher eleven times in the Johnson era.

Other Washington baseball notables were child managers Bucky Harris and Joe Cronin, both of whom guided the club to its only pennants while playing regularly in the infield. They were inducted into baseball's Hall of Fame in Cooperstown, New York. Goose Goslin and Sam Rice patrolled the spacious outfield during the team's heyday in Griffith Stadium, and are also enshrined at Cooperstown, having been elected during the 1960s.

The Senators that Jackie Jensen joined in the spring of 1952 had finished seventh the previous season. Griffith had convinced Bucky Harris to return to the helm of the club for his third stint as manager in 1950. Bucky was able to cajole a fifth-place finish from his troops, who had come up last in 1949, improving seventeen games over that year's finish. The team returned to more familiar surroundings in 1951.

Jackie Jensen played nearly two full seasons with the Senators and performed well and with consistency. He had the speed to roam the huge center field and finished among the league leaders in stolen bases and doubles. He hit ten home runs each season and averaged eighty-two runs batted in for the Nationals. The Senators finished fifth both seasons, winning two more games than they lost in total. A reasonably talented cast lent support to Harris's managerial skills with Mickey Vernon winning the batting title at .337 and Bob Porterfield leading the league with twenty-two victories in 1953.

As in New York, Jackie Jensen was not especially well suited for Griffith Stadium. Jensen had power but was not as strong or as fast as was Mantle. He was not a pure hitter like Ted Williams, nor did he have the wrist action of Hank Aaron. He was a better-than-average baseball player who, so far in his career, had the misfortune of playing in home fields completely at odds with his style of hitting.

The Boston Red Sox, however, saw in Jensen a player of abilities that were a good match with their cozy Fenway Park. He had good left-field power and sufficient speed to turn a line drive hit off the famous thirty-seven-foot wall from a single into a two-bagger. His fielding skills were well above average and his arm was strong enough to reach the plate from both deep right and center fields. In December 1953, the Boston Red Sox traded Mickey McDermott, an eighteen-game winner that year, and Tom Umphlett, a rookie who hit .283, to the Senators for outfielder Jackie Jensen.

Jensen joined the Boston Red Sox, a team that had a lot of history. The Red Sox had been the American League's dominant team from the circuit's birth in 1901 through 1918, capturing six pennants and five (of five tries) World Series. Then, coincident with the sale of Babe Ruth after the 1919 season, the Red Sox spent the 1920–1933 period mired deep in the second division, often in last place.

On February 25, 1933, Thomas A. Yawkey, a thirty-year-old southern baseball fan, bought the Boston Red Sox. He promptly set out to acquire quality ballplayers with the objective of building a winning team. The team improved to second place by 1938 and finished there in four of the next five seasons. The U.S. entry into World War II took many of the team's stars, among them Ted Williams, Bobby Doerr, and Dom DiMaggio.

The return of these players produced a pennant in 1946, which was followed by a disappointing loss to the St. Louis Cardinals in the World Series. The next six years brought a lot of excitement but only two near misses to show for it. The 1948 edition of the Bosox finished in a dead heat with the Cleveland Indians, forcing a single-game playoff. The Indians took the contest and proceeded to win the World Series from the Red Sox's hometown rivals, the Braves. In 1949, Boston traveled to New York for a season-ending two-game series with the Yankees, ahead of the Bronx crew by one game. The Yankees took both contests and embarked on a five-year stretch of consecutive world championships.

The 1950 and 1951 seasons proved to be continuing disappointments—the Red Sox finished third both years, with declining victory totals. Their slow sluggers got slower, and the pitching, which revolved around the fortunes of crafty Mel Parnell, slowly deteriorated. The Red Sox did hit .302 as a unit in 1950, the last major league team to accomplish that feat. The decline accelerated in 1952 when Ted Williams was recalled by the Marines to fly in the Korean conflict. The Red Sox finished sixth that season, the first second-division finish since the war-skewed years. When the Boston Braves left Boston for the frenzy in Milwaukee in March 1953, the Red Sox rebounded to a respectable fourth as ace left-hander Parnell won twenty-one games and Mickey McDermott, a wild but fireballing lefty, picked up another eighteen victories. Tom Umphlett, a rookie center fielder, batted .283 and teamed with the colorful Jim Piersall to give Boston a good defensive though not power-laden outfield. Williams returned from Korea late in the season and proceeded to hit .407 and thirteen home runs in only ninety-one at bats. Excitement ran high as fans looked with anticipation to 1954.

The trade that brought Jackie Jensen to Boston generated a good deal of grumbling among the Boston faithful. Umphlett had finished behind Harvey Kuenn of the Detroit Tigers in the Rookie of the Year voting and McDermott had seemed to find himself. There was some concern about trading two good players for a guy who had batted only .266 with a mere ten home runs. Overlooked was the fact that Griffith Stadium had the dimensions of a small city and that Jackie had driven in more than eighty runs in each of his seasons in the nation's capital. The Red Sox needed consistent right-handed power and neither Piersall nor Umphlett was about to provide it. A great deal was expected from the new outfielder, and Boston's reputation as a demanding sports town was about to be verified.

Jensen's first days presaged the year that was to be. He reluctantly reported to camp because he had developed a fear of flying. As the major leagues began to shed its two-team cities in 1953 with the move of the Braves from Boston to Milwaukee, it was evident that the distances between cities would increase. The trains were losing popularity and air travel was becoming quicker and more efficient with each passing year. Jackie sensed that he would be forced to fly with increasing frequency and he shuddered at the thought. General manager Joe Cronin finally convinced Jensen to report to Florida. Meanwhile, Ted Williams had slipped in the outfield and broken his collarbone on the first day of spring training and was lost until the middle of May. Jackie Jensen began the process of becoming a Red Soxer.

Jensen started strong and was flirting with .400 as the young season entered May. Perhaps the return of Williams relieved too much pressure. Ted came back on May 16 and went eight for nine in a doubleheader at Briggs Stadium in Detroit. Jensen soon entered his first slump as a Beantown ballplayer and quickly became the replacement goat for Williams, who had reentered baseball as an elder statesman. In the last three weeks of May, Jackie had a six-for-sixty stretch and watched his average dip all the way to .225.

The Boston woes did not end with Williams's early injury or Jensen's late-May slump. Ironically, on April 24, Mel Parnell had been hit by an errant Mickey McDermott fastball, breaking a bone in his pitching arm. He did not start again until mid-June. The man who had won 109 games over the previous six seasons would win only fourteen more in his abbreviated career. His 21-8 season in 1953 became a nightmarish 3-7 in 1954. The stylish lefty was never the same again.

The early-season pressures continued to fall on Jensen's shoulders. The Fenway boo-hounds had found a more than suitable replacement for Williams. Jensen, who led the American League that year in stolen bases with twenty-two, also set a record by hitting into thirty-two double plays. The fans constantly reminded him of the fact, conveniently forgetting that he followed some of the slowest batters in the league such as Williams and the lumbering first baseman Dick Gernert.

On July 9, the Sox were mired in last place and twenty games under .500. Jensen had hit ten home runs and driven in forty-six, but struggled with an average in the .240s. After the midseason break, he began to hit and the team followed his example. The second half of the season saw the Red Sox post a 41-37 record and Jensen hit .276 for the full year, belting twenty-five homers and driving in 117 runs. He was an important cog in the Red Sox machine, finally edging out the Detroit Tigers for a fourth-place, 69-85 finish in the American League's 1954 five-team second division.

Jensen paired with Jimmy Piersall to give the Bostons an excellent defensive outfield. He played center field during the 1954 season but moved to right next year and never went back. Fenway Park's unusual contours proved to be no mystery to him: He always ranked among the league leaders in assists and double plays as he utilized his speed and accurate throwing arm to his advantage. Although he was a skilled defensive outfielder, he committed more errors than most, because he was not afraid to take a chance on a daring play, the kind that has the potential to turn a spectacular out into a triple. As an example of his abilities in the field, in 1957 Jensen led all American League outfielders in assists and double plays as well as miscues.

Jensen continued to drive home runs as the Sox posted 84-70 records in both 1955 and 1956. He led the league in RBI in 1955 with 116 and in triples with eleven in 1956. He batted .315 that year, the only time in his career that he hit over .300. Ironically, it marked the only year in the 1954–59 span with the Red Sox that he failed to reach one hundred runs batted in, missing the century mark by three.

The American League had sort of a strange makeup to it during the 1950s. The Yankees dominated the junior circuit, winning nine of eleven flags over the 1950–60 period. The Cleveland Indians and Chicago White Sox each took one pennant, in 1954 and 1959, respectively. Those three teams virtually made up the first division. The Red Sox and Tigers jockeyed for fourth much of the time and it could be said that they were in the race early in the season but eventually made no difference. The other three teams, the Philadelphia/Kansas City A's, the St. Louis Browns/Baltimore Orioles, and Washington Senators, were usually in the running for last place and, with the exception of 1952, had a lock on that position. Boston fielded respectable teams but always had a glaring weakness, usually on the mound, in the field, on the base paths, or in various combinations.

Boston's trademark was hitting. Led by the Hall of Famer Williams, the Red Sox produced five of the thirteen batting champions during the 1950–1962 period while generating only one twenty-game winner. The pitching staff had a few temporary bright lights such as Frank Sullivan and Tom Brewer in addition to the star-crossed Parnell, but it lacked the depth and consistency to challenge the league's front-runners over a complete season. The outfield was strong defensively, with Williams the weak link in left. However, his years of experience in playing the Wall and the relatively short throw from left to the infield minimized his shortcomings. With Piersall and Jensen sharing center and right fields, their speed and defensive skills assisted Ted in left center.

The infield, on the other hand, became a revolving door. First baseman Harry Agannis, a local product from Boston University and the Boston suburb of Lynn, enjoyed a successful rookie year in 1954, but met an untimely death in June of the following year at the age of twenty-five. He was succeeded by Norm Zauchin, Mickey Vernon, and Dick Gernert over the next four years. Second base and shortstop proved to be more of the same as such non–household names as Ted Lepcio, Milt Bolling, Don Buddin, and Billy Klaus filled those spots. Handyman and former American League batting champ (1950) Billy Goodman also appeared around the infield. To be fair, Goodman continued to be a dependable leadoff hitter and Klaus and Bolling also enjoyed good individual seasons, but once again the Red Sox sorely lacked the consistency and defensive skill required in the up-the-middle positions.

Third base, on the other hand, received a much needed boost with the emergence of slick-fielding, hard-hitting Frank Malzone in late 1956. Malzone, who experienced the death of a child at that time, concentrated on his job as a means of coping with the tragedy and put together nine solid seasons for the Red Sox. Malzone was a fixture at the hot corner through 1964 and batted in more than eighty-five runs five times. He appeared in at least 143 games annually over that span and usually ranked at or near the top in all defensive categories.

The 1957 season provided the fans of New England with a third-place finish at 82-72, sixteen games behind the Yankees. Jensen hit a steady .281 and shared the team RBI lead with Malzone at 103. It was a year that many players would be proud to call their own, but it was not Jensen's best effort. His presence in the lineup batting fourth or fifth made most opposing hurlers think before they pitched to Boston's number three hitter, Ted Williams. In that season, Williams flirted with .400, eventually finishing at .388, six hits shy of the mark. It was a spectacular achievement for anyone, let alone a thirty-nine-year-old whose legs had been left in the cockpit of his U.S. Marine Corps jet in 1953. Controversy arose when the baseball writers chose Mickey Mantle as the league's Most Valuable Player. Boston fans, who had hooted and booed Williams in the past, suddenly took up his cause and demanded a recount and revote with a committee made up entirely of Hub sportswriters. It looked like 1958 would be a very interesting season!

A Most Valuable Season

The 1958 version of the Red Sox typified the teams put on the field by Boston during the fifties. The outfield was its strong point and its inhabitants continued to perform consistently in the field and at bat. The pitching remained suspect and the infield, other than third base, did not inspire confidence in either the fans or the press. Sammy White, the primary catcher for the Red Sox throughout the fifties, lent a steady hand behind the plate but had seen better days.

Just before the opening of the championship baseball season on April 14, Rutgers beat St. John's University 4-3 in a college game played at Ebbets Field in Brooklyn. Two days earlier, the St. Louis Hawks, led by Bob Pettit's fifty tallies, took the National Basketball Association title from the Boston Celtics 110-109. Celtic center Bill Russell spent the last twenty minutes on the court with his ankle wrapped and taped and tried valiantly to retain the championship attained the previous year.

Baseball writers throughout the country picked the Yankees and Braves to win the pennants of their respective leagues. The *New York Times* saw the Red Sox as a dark-horse contender.

Boston dropped its first two games of the season. On April 16, Jensen gave Dave Sisler a two-run shot in a 3-1 win over the Yankees at Fenway Park. They then lost five more to the Senators and Yankees, and on April 22 stood at 1-7, in sole possession of last place. Boston snapped out of its tailspin with two close wins over the Baltimore Orioles. Jensen had suffered a zero-for-ten spell against the Yanks but bounced back to go four for eight with three RBI against the Birds.

Meanwhile, Indian ace Herb Score, who had missed most of the 1957 campaign after being struck in the eye by a Gil McDougald line drive, struck out thirteen White Sox en route to a 2-0 complete-game victory on April 23.

The season had started very slowly for Boston. Williams did not take up where he had left off the previous year, and although Jensen ranked second behind former teammate and Kansas City outfielder Bob Cerv in both home runs and RBI at April's end, he was hitting a meager .196. He had hit four home runs but the Red Sox continued to struggle through the end of the month, as they had a hold on seventh place at 4-10.

Boston winter-sports fans suffered another setback as the Montreal Canadians took their third straight Stanley Cup by beating the Bruins 5-3 before a sellout crowd in the Boston Garden. They won the series four games to two. Down south in Louisville, Gary Player, a twenty-two-year-old South African golfer, won the $20,000 Kentucky Derby Open. He finished fourteen strokes under par at 274 for seventy-two holes. He took home twenty-eight hundred dollars for his fine effort.

In early May, the eyes of the sports world remained in Louisville and focused on the Kentucky Derby. In earlier races, fans had watched in awe as Silky Sullivan, a three-year-old colt, would fall way back into the crowd and make a move, often with less than three-eighths of a mile to go, and come out in the winner's circle. Alas, given the quality of the competition on May 3, 1958, Silky and his jockey, Willie Shoemaker, could not maintain that pace at Churchill, and wound up a distant twelfth, having been boxed in and unable to make his usual move. Tim Tam, ridden by substitute jockey Ismael (Milo) Valenzuela, took the honors and would follow up with a win at the Preakness two weeks later, evoking thoughts of a Triple Crown. Jockey Willie Hartack, who had ridden Iron Liege to victory in the 1957 Derby, suffered a broken leg when his horse reared in fright at the starting gate the previous week. Hartack, twenty-five years old, had been expected to ride Tim Tam at the Derby.

Jackie Jensen usually made contact with the ball. Over the course of his major league career he struck out in about 10 percent of his at bats. His raw ability led him to hit all over the field. He had the natural right-hander's tendency to hit to left field, but was not a true pull hitter. He usually hit the ball hard, and if he went into a slump, he would hit it hard and into the ground toward the shortstop, often resulting in the dreaded double play. During the early part of 1958, he began to consistently and purposely hit to the opposite field. In May 1958, his efforts began to show results.

Jackie sat out a few games in early May due to an injury but by the sixth, he returned to the lineup and began to hit. He went three for five with an RBI to secure Murray Wall's first big-league triumph. On May 9, he hit a double and had an RBI to lift Dave Sisler to a 4-1 record with a victory in Baltimore. The Red Sox traveled down the road to our nation's capital, and on May 13, Jensen poked a grand slam and had two other hits to pace the Red Sox to a 9-5 win over the Senators.

The Sox returned home to face the Orioles and Jackie hit away, going seven for twelve with two homers and four RBI as Boston took two of three in a weekend series. With the Indians moving in, he did not relent. He drove in two runs, including a game-tying solo blast in the ninth inning on May 21. Unfortunately, Minnie Minoso won the game in the twelfth inning with a similar hit. Jensen finished off the home stand with a five-for-eleven performance as the Red Sox swept three games from Kansas City.

On May 27, President Dwight D. Eisenhower signed a bill increasing the price of first-class postage from three cents to four.

Jackie Jensen finished up with three hits and an RBI in a two-game split in Chicago on the twenty-seventh of May. On Memorial Day he paced a 2-0 win in the first game in Baltimore and garnered another hit in a 2-0 nightcap loss as the Red Sox bounced back with a successful May.

Jensen hit .379 to lead the Bosox to a 16-12 month despite the team's 1-7 stretch over the last eight games. On May 31, Jackie was hitting a very cool .301 with nine homers and twenty-seven RBI, but still trailed Cerv in the latter categories. Ironically, Cerv had also been traded by New York when it became apparent that Mickey Mantle would replace DiMaggio in the stadium for as long as his legs held out.

Boston floundered around the .500 mark as Ted Williams continued to struggle, batting a mere .267 at May's end. Williams had been unable to get untracked after his remarkable 1957 season and Jensen had assumed the responsibility for keeping the Red Sox respectable. The team's record at that date stood at 20-22, and the Sox trailed the Yankees by nine games.

The Red Sox hosted New York on the first of June and lost to Bob Turley 10-4 despite Jackie's bases-clearing, game-tying double. Two days later, the Indians overcame his two-run homer to win 7-5. On the fifth, he hit another two-run homer and drove in the winning score via a sacrifice fly in the eighth to pace a 5-3 win over Hoyt Wilhelm and the Orioles at Fenway.

On Saturday, June 7, in the Belmont Stakes, Cavan and jockey Pete Anderson spoiled Tim Tam's attempt to win racing's Triple Crown. In a neck-and-neck race, Tim Tam began to slow with about a quarter of a mile to go and eventually finished five and a half lengths back. A subsequent examination revealed that the three-year-old had fractured the sesamoid, one of two small bones running down the back of the ankle joint, ending his competitive career.

After evening their record on the seventh, Jensen and the Red Sox took two from Chicago on Sunday with Jackie supplying the winning runs in the first game on a two-run fence-clearer in a 6-5 thriller. He contributed a single in the 4-1 nightcap win. The Red

Sox then beat the Tigers 9-4 on June 9, assisted by Jackie's three hits and four RBI. The team had just won its sixth game in a row. After a rainout, Detroit promptly burst that bubble with a twin-bill sweep on June 11. Jensen got Boston back on track with his fifteenth home run the next day in a 4-2 win, giving the Sox a series split and pitcher Dave Sisler a 6-2 record.

That weekend, Oklahoman Tommy Bolt won the U.S. Open at Tulsa's Southern Hill Country Club with a 283, four strokes under Gary Player's effort. The often volatile Bolt calmly hit a 141 in the tourney's final thirty-six holes.

On June 18, Boston trounced Chicago, 13-9, hitting five home runs in the process. Jensen's seventeenth was among them as the Red Sox climbed into second place, eight games behind the Yankees.

The world watched as two Australians, Herb Elliot and Marv Lincoln, pursued both the four-minute mile and John Landy's record of 3:58 at a meet in Bakersfield, California. Elliot finished first, coming in at 3:57.9, six-tenths of a second ahead of Lincoln.

That followed a pair of losses to the A's in Kansas City. Then, in the final game of a three-game series, Jensen hit a screamer that A's second baseman Hector Lopez picked off, saving the go-ahead run. Lopez then came up in the bottom of the inning and won the game 2-1.

Boston trekked north to Cleveland, where Jensen tied the game at three on June 24 with a ninth-inning sacrifice fly and watched as Vic Power, usually a sure-handed first baseman, muffed a grounder hit to him by Lou Berberet, allowing Gene Stephens to score. Jackie then drove in four runs in a 6-5 win over the Tigers at Briggs Stadium. He belted two home runs in the process. The next day, he tied the game at five-all in the sixth with a three-run blast, setting up Ted Williams's game winner in the top of the ninth.

June 1958 ended with the Red Sox sporting a 35-34 record. They had reached second place; however, they trailed the Yankees by nine and a half games. Without Jensen's efforts, the Red Sox would surely have lost more than they won. During June, Jackie batted .299 but slugged fourteen homers and drove in thirty-three runs.

His last home run of the month and twenty-third of the year beat Detroit 10-7 on June 29. That game saw him take over the league RBI lead for good as he drove in his sixtieth run.

Alaskans rejoiced as the U.S. Senate voted 64-20 to admit the territory as the forty-ninth state in the Union. The House of Representatives had previously approved the measure. It now required the president's signature and approval in a territorial referendum.

Jackie continued to carry the team as Ike Delock opened July and improved his record to 6-0 with a complete-game effort. Jensen scored three times and contributed a three-run homer in a 10-5 win over the Senators before nearly 24,000 fans at Fenway Park. The Orioles came into town to celebrate the Fourth of July and the teams split a twin bill. Jensen contributed an RBI in both games. The next day, Jensen sent three men home to lead a 10-4 win over the Yankees and aided Delock in improving to 7-0.

On the fifth, American Althea Gibson took the women's tennis final at Wimbledon for the second straight year. She followed up that performance to team with Brazilian Maria Buena to take the women's doubles.

The All-Star break saw the Red Sox in second place at 38-37, but ten and a half games behind the Yankees. Jensen's heroics placed him among the league leaders in batting at .311 and heading the pack in both home runs and RBI at twenty-four and sixty-eight, respectively. Bob Cerv closely followed with twenty-two homers and sixty-two RBI, but was hitting a higher .323.

Jensen and Cerv joined Mickey Mantle as outfield starters in the 1958 midseason classic, held that year in Baltimore. The three competitors for the Yankees' center-field slot from the first part of the decade displayed the quality of the New York scouting and farm programs as well as the overall strength of the team itself. The Yankees let go two high-caliber players from their system to other teams and perform at an all-star level, but still won the majority of the era's pennants.

During the previous two seasons, the madcap fans of the Cincinnati Redlegs had stuffed the All-Star ballot box so full of votes for their players that Commissioner Ford Frick intervened and inserted other starters over some of the elected players. In 1958, it was agreed that the players themselves would elect the teams. The feeling was that the players really saw what their colleagues accomplished and would vote accordingly. Jensen said as much in an interview when the news of his election reached him: "It's a wonderful honor," he told Arthur Seigel of the defunct *Boston Traveler*. "Your fellow players are not governed by sentiment or headlines. When they mark your name in their book, you've made the grade." Jackie had been selected by Casey Stengel in 1952 and elected by the fans in 1955.

After going hitless in the All-Star Game, which was won by the American League 4-3, Jensen broke up a 1-1 tie against Chicago with a fourth-inning grand slam to start off the second half of the season on July 10. The next day he added four runs batted in to his total, providing Delock with all the scoring he needed to rack up his eighth victory. The White Sox, who had been mired in the league's nether regions, then shook off their demons to salvage a series split before leaving Beantown. Ironically, Jensen went for the collar in the last two games.

Facing the Indians two days later, Jensen flubbed Gary Geiger's liner, allowing him to make it to third base. The ever-dangerous Minnie Minoso nailed a single to score Geiger and tie the game 3-3, thus sending it into extra innings. In the tenth, Jackie walked to start the bottom of the inning and scored the winning run. The next day he paced a 5-2 win over the A's with a three-run homer and a double and helped big Frank Sullivan to his eighth victory. He followed that performance on July 16 by breaking up a 2-2 game with a two-run double in the bottom of the sixth before nearly 27,000 home fans. Boston went on to beat the A's 5-2 to hold second place. They won again over the Orioles the next day to extend their win streak to six games.

Detroit's Jim Bunning then spun a no-hit game against the Red Sox on July 20, striking out twelve in the opener of a doubleheader. Boston came back to secure Delock's tenth success in the nightcap, 5-2. Jensen contributed a pair of singles and an RBI. Boston then moved on to Kansas City, where Jensen poled a two-run homer in the sixth inning to put the Sox ahead, 3-2. However, nemesis Hector Lopez came through with a two-runner of his own in the last of the ninth to win it for the A's, 4-3.

After a trio of losses in Chicago, the Red Sox remained a distant second behind the Yankees at 47-45. Chicago had begun to awaken from its snooze in the cellar area and nailed Ike Delock with his first loss of the year on July 26. Jensen salvaged the series finale with a two-run shot in the sixth inning to put Boston up 4-3 en route to a 7-3 triumph. Boston ended July holding on to second place at 49-48 but began to feel the White Sox creeping up. Jackie Jensen batted .318 in July, hit six homers, and drove in thirty-one runs. He still led the American League in the latter categories with twenty-nine and ninety-one, respectively, while maintaining a .305 bat mark.

The Red Sox dropped two to Cleveland to open August and relinquished second place the next day after a 4-1 loss in which Jensen smacked a solo homer in the fourth to bring Boston to within two runs. On Sunday, the Sox swept a twin bill to regain second with a 51-51 record. After more than one hundred games, the Yankees were the only team in the American League to boast a winning percentage. Five days later, Jensen hit a three-run homer and Ted Williams scored career run number 1,700 with a rare triple in an 8-2 win over the Senators at Fenway. They won again the following day as Jackie hit home run number thirty-one.

On August 6, five milers broke the four-minute barrier; four of them shattered the existing world's record in a meet in Dublin. Herb Elliot, who had run a 3:57.9 mile in June, led the field with a 3:54.5 performance. The next day, Albert Thomas, who finished fifth in the mile during Elliot's record dash, broke the world's record for the two-mile, covering the distance in 8:32.

After being shut down 3-0 by Whitey Ford at Yankee Stadium on August 8, Boston came back to overtake the Bombers 9-6, with Jensen starting the scoring with a fourth-inning RBI single and poking another hit later in the contest. They then split a twin bill with New York as Jackie went five for eight with one RBI in the two games. The team took the train to the nation's capital. Jensen reached one hundred RBI for the fourth time in his five seasons with Boston as he drove in all the runs in a 6-3 loss to the Senators.

The White House revealed that the nuclear submarine Nautilus *had traveled from the Pacific to the Atlantic Ocean by crossing the Arctic and sailing under the North Pole.*

On August 15, the Sox hosted the Yankees and rookie left-hander Ted Bowfield beat Bullet Bob Turley 6-2 before more than 30,000 fans. Turley, on his way to twenty-one victories and the Cy Young Award, allowed Jensen and his teammates to break open a 3-2 game with three runs in the fifth. After Tom Brewer went the distance the next day with a 7-4 win, Jensen got the scoring going on Sunday, August 17, in a 6-5 victory, to finish a sweep of the pennant-bound New Yorkers. After a pair of losses to the streaking White Sox, Boston took two of three from Cleveland and swept the A's in a Sunday doubleheader. Jackie knocked in the winning run in the bottom of the eleventh to win the nightcap 3-2, securing the victory for Murray Wall after seven and two-thirds innings of one-hit relief.

On August 29, the Minneapolis City Council voted 11-2 to borrow nine million dollars in order to expand the existing Metropolitan Stadium. The city fathers hoped to snare a major league team and had their eyes on the long-suffering Washington Senators. The next day, Boston lost to the Orioles, then beat them 3-2 on August's final day. With less than a month to go in the season, the Red Sox were in third place at 66-61, twelve and a half games behind the Yankees. Jackie Jensen had hit thirty-three homers and driven in 110 runs to go with his .309 average.

September started in New York with the Yankees taking three of four and Jensen hitting a stone wall. He endured a two-for-thirteen drought with no RBI. Boston journeyed to Baltimore and took three of four as Jensen drove in three runs over the series.

At Forest Hills Tennis Club, Althea Gibson added the U.S. Open to the British crown she had taken in July. Ashley Cooper, a twenty-two-year-old Australian, earned the men's championship. Golfer Charlie Coe

took his second U.S. Amateur title, beating twenty-one-year-old Tommy
Aaron at San Francisco's Olympic Country Club.

After the Red Sox dropped a trio in Chicago, Rocky Colavito hit a grand slam to power the Indians to 5-4 decision in Cleveland. Boston clung to third despite having evened their record at 70-70. Warren Spahn, of the Milwaukee Braves, at age thirty-seven, achieved twenty victories for the ninth time in his career. He would attain that pinnacle four more times over the next five years.

On Sunday, September 14, Detroit swept the Red Sox as the Yankees clinched their twenty-fourth pennant at Kansas City. Two days later, Frank Lary of the Tigers beat New York for the seventh time in 1958. Lary, who went 7-1 against the Bombers that season, could muster only a 9-14 mark against the others in the American League. Boston then lost two of three to Kansas City, as Jensen could manage only two hits in the series. The Red Sox had now dropped to fifth place and Jackie Jensen had cooled down.

The batting race between defending champion Ted Williams and Boston first baseman Pete Runnels, however, had sparked intense interest in Boston. Williams, as noted earlier, had started slowly and did not reach .300 until late July. On September 18, at .318, he trailed Runnels by a mere .001.

On September 20, Jensen drove in both runs to give Frank Sullivan all the offense he needed in shutting out the Senators 2-0 for his twelfth win. The following day, in another 2-0 victory, Williams threw his bat in disgust after striking out and hit the housekeeper of Boston's general manager Joe Cronin. She spent the night in the hospital but suffered no lasting effects. On September 23, Boston handed the Yankees their sixth straight loss, 9-8, as Jensen and Williams drove in six of the tallies.

Boston swept the Senators in the final three games of the 1958 season and wound up third at 79-75. Williams took the batting title by six points and Jensen's 122 RBI easily beat runner-up Rocky Colavito's 113. The Yankees went on to face the Braves in the World Series and avenged the loss of the previous fall. In November,

Jackie Jensen was voted the Most Valuable Player in the American League.

Jensen's consistent play throughout the season supported that election. His batting average did not drop below .300 until early September, and he wound up at .286 with thirty-five home runs. He posted a slugging average of .535 and was responsible for starting rallies and supplying key hits throughout the campaign. He drove in sixteen runs in May, thirty-three in June, thirty in July, and twenty in August before tailing off to twelve in September. He took over the RBI lead in June and was never again challenged in that department.

The Red Sox have often been a team whose lineup was tailored for the dimensions of Fenway Park, and their home–away statistics reflect that. The 1958 season saw the Sox boast the league's best home record at 49-28 while playing at a 30-47 clip on the road. An eleven-game trip in June resulted in a creditable (for this team) 5-6 record. They were 1-5 after stops in Chicago and Kansas City but then won four of the last five games on that haul. Could they have done it without Jackie Jensen? Jackie hit .325 with seven round-trippers and fourteen RBI on that trip. Of his first twenty-three home runs, Jackie hit a dozen away from home, displaying his all-around ability and versatility.

With Boston teams of that era, the pitching came up weak and inconsistent. Tom Brewer and Frank Sullivan, a pair of right-handers who had produced fifty-six and sixty-one victories, respectively, over the previous four years, had combined for a mere thirteen victories by the end of July. Ike Delock, who in the two prior seasons started a total of ten games, was resurrected from the bullpen and wound up at 14-8 for the season; Brewer and Sullivan finally began to earn their pay and finished the year at 12-12 and 13-9, respectively.

Jackie Jensen had taken the riding from the fans over the years in stride. His attitude was that the folks had paid good money to see him perform and if he was not up to their standards, they had a right to heckle or boo him. His 1958 season changed that, as the demanding

Boston fans finally appreciated their All-Star right fielder. To demonstrate the change in the fans' attitude, during a game against Baltimore, Jackie swung at a bad pitch with runners on base and the Red Sox down by a run. Rather than the jeers from the old days, he was encouraged by calls such as "You can do it, Jackie." Jensen called time and left the batter's box, and then heard the Oriole catcher Gus Triandos murmur in a low voice, "Booooo." Jackie laughed, thanked Triandos for the memory, and promptly hit the next pitch over the left-field wall for a game-winning home run.

Sportswriters appreciated Jackie Jensen. He never shied away from the fourth estate and was always candid, sometimes brutally so. He would speak of his resentment of being away from his family almost to the point of complaining to anyone who would listen. Still, he was sincere. When he first arrived in Boston, he made the comment that baseball was a job, albeit a good job, but merely another way to make a living. Jackie never had an inflated ego, but in the supercharged Beantown sports arena, his remarks did not go over well. He was just being candid, more candid than the majority of his peers, but the public resented the "Golden Boy" and his honesty.

In addition to his Most Valuable Player award, the *Sporting News* named him the player of the year. The sportswriters who followed the major leagues finally put into perspective his importance to the Red Sox. Jensen could now add his All-Star starts and his MVP to his earlier appearances in the Rose Bowl, the East–West football game, and the 1950 World Series, being the only athlete to achieve all these honors.

Although prospects were not exactly bright for the Red Sox in 1959 due to a lack of depth, defense, and pitching, it was felt that they would hold up the first division and contend for third. That, in fact, was what they did, and their most notable opponents just happened to be the New York Yankees. The Chicago White Sox broke the Bronx Bombers' four-year hold on first place and finished five games ahead of the Cleveland Indians and fifteen ahead of the Yankees. The Detroit Tigers and Red Sox jockeyed for fourth, with the Tigers prevailing in the first-division chase. Ted Williams failed to hit .300 for the only time in his career and was determined to go out in glory, so he made plans to return in 1960. Jensen hit a respectable .277 while smacking twenty-eight homers and leading the league in RBI for the third time in six years, with 112.

In January 1960, Jensen dropped a bombshell, saying that he was retiring from the game. The reasons he gave—his fear of flying and his dislike of family separations—made perfect sense to most people, but certainly generated many questions. Why would a guy with the record he had put together over the last six years want to give up such a career? Well, there were easy answers. Jackie had been in sports' spotlight since his college days. He pursued a college education and, unlike many of his peers, had various sources of income other than baseball. He opened a restaurant, the Bow & Bell Restaurant in Oakland, with a childhood friend, Charles "Boots" Erb. The eatery had become successful and Jackie believed that they could expand into the Lake Tahoe area, where the Jensens lived at the time. Imagine, another Bow & Bell, but a mere five-minute commute! He truly dreaded the opening of training camp, for it took him away from his three children, who were approaching the ages where they needed their dad more than ever. Jackie loved the game but continued to sustain the destructive fear of flying that he felt resulted from a near miss while he was touring in Japan years before with a team of Americans led by former Yankee lefty Ed Lopat.

During the 1954–59 stretch with the Red Sox, Jensen had averaged .285 along with twenty-eight homers and 112 runs per season. He was also an outstanding defensive player, having won the 1959 Gold Glove for American League right fielders. This award had been established in 1957 to honor defensive achievements.

Jackie sat out the 1960 season and watched as the Red Sox fell with a resounding thud into seventh place. There were some individual achievements. His good friend Pete Runnels took the first of two batting titles at .320 and Ted Williams retired with a flourish, rebounding to .316 and smashing a home run in his last at bat. Mike Fornelies stood out in relief, leading the league in appearances and saves while compiling a 10-5 record with an ERA of 2.64. The rest of the team continued its decline and Boston management brought back Mike (Pinky) Higgins as manager. Higgins had run the team from 1955 through mid-1959.

Jackie had enjoyed a good relationship with Higgins during Mike's earlier stint managing the Red Sox. Higgins knew from the outset of the 1960 season that he was going to really miss his hustling right fielder. Higgins left subtle hints with Jackie and made timely phone calls, often with former teammates joining in on the conversation. Jensen eventually got the hint, and just before the end of the season he made plans to fly from Nevada to Boston for the opening of Bosox catcher Sammy White's bowling alley in Brighton, a Boston suburb. While in Boston, Jackie met with Red Sox management and accepted their offer to return to baseball.

Jensen had conquered his fear of flying with the assistance of a hypnotist. The fear did not originate from the near miss mentioned before, but from dreams and experiences from his childhood. Once his system had rid itself of these demons, Jackie approached airplane travel as a normal thing.

The demons returned, however, and he temporarily left the team in April 1961 and went back to hypnosis. He finished the season but the sequel, as is often the case, did not match the original. His home-run output dropped to thirteen and he hit just .263. Jackie Jensen retired from baseball for good in September 1961, at the age of thirty-four.

Jackie's great fears of family instability because of his absences were unfounded. In fact, after a few years together, he and Zoe were divorced, in 1963. They reconciled awhile later, but eventually split for good. Oakland's Bow & Bell continued to be successful and Jack sold his share to his partner. Their plans for Tahoe Bow & Bell never completely jelled, due mainly to a problem in the local water supply. He worked for an auto dealer in anticipation of establishing his own Volkswagen franchise in Nevada's capital, Carson City. However, the city's population experienced a decline and the corporate fathers decided against locating a dealership amid a decreasing populace.

He designed and built a golf course in Truckee, California, and worked as sports director for Harrah's in Lake Tahoe. He also toiled for a Reno television station.

Jackie had married Katherine Cortesi in 1968. The following year, he suffered a heart attack. After recuperation, he returned to school to complete his degree in physical education. He worked as a baseball coach at the Reno branch of the University of Nevada and was an administrator for the Nevada Office of Economic Opportunity, reporting directly to the governor. In 1971 he received a request from his alma mater, the University of California, to return as baseball coach. Jackie jumped at the offer and couldn't wait to report. However, he was not adequately prepared for the change in the attitude of college athletes. He coached baseball at Berkeley for five years and left that position when his methods, disciplinary requirements, and standards were not compatible with those of his players or of the university. Jackie expected his players to mirror the image of a gentleman, as he had been taught.

In 1976, he and Katherine moved to Scottsville, Virginia. They purchased an old tobacco plantation whose soil had been sapped by the continual harvesting of the weed. They considered various crops but decided on a Christmas tree farm.

The farm was just what the Jensens needed. Jackie kept himself in condition, and on May 1, 1982, he returned to Boston to appear in a Red Sox old-timers game. The sporting world was shocked when he collapsed and died of a heart attack just two months later, on July 14.

Jackie Jensen was an excellent baseball player who did not stay on the sports scene long enough to achieve any degree of immortality. Would he have been Cooperstown material? I don't know, but he gave Boston fans some great moments over the years. I had the thrill of meeting Jackie while I was sitting in the Red Sox dugout as an eleven-year-old in 1954. As he was with the press, he was very honest with me. I believe that he keenly observed my non-athletic physique and figured that I had little sports potential, for I remember distinctly that he advised me to study hard and do well in school.

Jackie Jensen was a quality gentleman, a consistent ballplayer, and a fine individual. He enjoyed many excellent years, but none as productive or as memorable as 1958, *that one glorious season*.

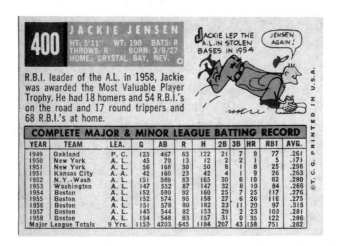

JACKIE JENSEN • 400
HT: 5'11"　WT: 190　BATS: R
THROWS: R　BORN: 3/9/27
HOME: CRYSTAL BAY, NEV.

R.B.I. leader of the A.L. in 1958, Jackie was awarded the Most Valuable Player Trophy. He had 18 homers and 54 R.B.I.'s on the road and 17 round trippers and 68 R.B.I.'s at home.

JACKIE LED THE A.L. IN STOLEN BASES IN 1954

JENSEN AGAIN!

© T. C. G. PRINTED IN U.S.A.

	COMPLETE MAJOR & MINOR LEAGUE BATTING RECORD										
YEAR	TEAM	LEA.	G	AB	R	H	2B	3B	HR	RBI	AVG.
1949	Oakland	P. C.	125	467	63	122	21	7	9	77	.261
1950	New York	A. L.	45	70	13	12	2	2	1	5	.171
1951	New York	A. L.	56	168	30	50	8	1	8	25	.298
1951	Kansas City	A. A.	42	160	23	42	4	1	9	26	.263
1952	N.Y.-Wash.	A. L.	151	589	83	165	30	6	10	82	.280
1953	Washington	A. L.	147	552	87	147	32	8	10	84	.266
1954	Boston	A. L.	152	580	92	160	25	7	25	117	.276
1955	Boston	A. L.	152	574	95	158	27	6	26	116	.275
1956	Boston	A. L.	151	578	80	182	23	11	20	97	.315
1957	Boston	A. L.	145	544	82	153	29	2	23	103	.281
1958	Boston	A. L.	154	548	83	157	31	0	35	122	.286
Major League Totals	9 Yrs.		1153	4203	645	1184	207	43	158	751	.282

13

1959: BOB SHAW
CHICAGO WHITE SOX

The largest crowd ever to watch a World Series game gathered in the Los Angeles Coliseum on October 5, 1959, to witness a classic pitchers duel between two young hurlers. Right-hander Bob Shaw of the Chicago White Sox in a do-or-die situation faced lefty Sandy Koufax of the hometown Dodgers in the series' fifth game. Shaw rose to the occasion and pitched a gut-wrenching seven and a third innings to beat Koufax and the recently transplanted Dodgers 1-0 before 92,706 fans. Shaw had started the second series contest but between his generosity in giving up three home runs and some poor baserunning on the part of his battery mate Sherman Lollar, he took a 4-3 loss in the Windy City.

Bob kept his team in the series with his second effort, bringing the White Sox to a 3-2 deficit. The Dodgers, however, took all the marbles in the sixth and final game in Chicago with a 9-3 victory over the Pale Hose in what was a remarkable and memorable season for the Chicago entry. Much of the Sox's success came as a result of Shaw's efforts. Shaw's intelligence, self-confidence, and outright chutzpah resulted in his arrival with the White Sox in 1958. His tenure, while short-lived, contributed to the team's success in 1959. He was a most unconventional young pitcher.

Bob Shaw came into the world in the Bronx, one of the five boroughs of New York City, in June 1933, the younger of two children. Shortly thereafter, his family moved to Garden City, Long Island, and Bob quickly established himself as an all-around athlete, cut in the mold of his father, who had excelled in sports as a youngster. Bob played virtually all sports as a student but baseball and football took precedence. He graduated from Kimball Union Academy in Meriden, New Hampshire, and played guard for the team that took the New England basketball championship in 1951. Ironically, he attended St. Lawrence University in upstate Canton, New York, on a football scholarship. He hurt his knee on the gridiron, however, and that prevented him from becoming a varsity hoopster. Thus, he was forced to concentrate on baseball.

He continued to hone his skills on the diamond and caught the eye of a number of scouts, among them Ray Garland of the Detroit Tigers. Garland pursued the young right-hander and soon won him over, as the pathetic pitching staffs of the early 1950s Tigers gave many a youngster a sense of optimism along with hopes of an early arrival in the big leagues.

Bob reported to the Tigers' Pony League entry in Jamestown, New York, in time for the 1953 season and went 10-3, but with a whopping 5.58 earned run average. It would be a precursor of a typical Bob Shaw season: some relieving, some starting, and a respectable number of complete games. While at Jamestown, he appeared in twenty-six games, started fourteen, and completed six. He moved up to Durham in the Carolina League the following season and went 6-13. The next year found him at the Augusta, Georgia, entry in the South Atlantic (Sally) League. In one and a half seasons at Augusta, he located and mastered his control and also brought down his ERA into the low threes while going 12-8. He spent the second half of 1956 in Syracuse, of the Class A Eastern League, and although he recorded a nondescript 6-7 mark, he completed six of his twelve starts and posted a good 3.26 ERA.

The following year, in August, the Tigers brought Bob up to the American League. He had toiled in Toronto and Charleston (West Virginia) of the International League and the American Association, respectively, going 9-6 combined. He appeared in just seven games for Detroit, losing his only decision. He spent the winter of 1957–58 playing in the Cuban League, where he went 17-3 and was named the circuit's most valuable player. He went to spring training determined to stick with the team and, in fact, headed north with the Tigers.

After appearing in eleven games, the Tigers optioned Shaw back to Charleston, as they had developed some good young arms in Jim Bunning, Frank Lary, Paul Foytack, and Billy Hoeft and felt that Bob could use more seasoning and, perhaps, bring a player of value in a trade.

Bob Shaw took this decision sitting down. Refusing to report to Charleston, he went home to Long Island and gambled that his actions, or lack thereof, would force a trade. Less than two weeks later, on June 15, 1958, on the eleventh hour of the trading deadline, he and infielder Ray Boone moved on to Chicago in exchange for Tito Francona and Bill Fischer. It turned out to be a great deal from both his perspective and that of the White Sox.

Bob reported to manager Al Lopez, who was known for a no-nonsense style of leadership. Lopez promptly turned him over to pitching coach Ray Berres. Berres, an eleven-year veteran of the National League, had been employed primarily as a defensive backup catcher during his playing days. He worked closely with Shaw and Lopez, another former backstop. They concentrated on his mechanics and had him throw strictly from a three-quarter sidearm position. Shaw did not possess an overpowering fastball and had the reputation of experimenting with his delivery, throwing from various arm positions. Berres put an end to his tinkering and helped him concentrate on a single style. The three-quarter motion began to work effectively when linked with his low-ball sinkers and sliders.

Shaw was essentially a sweetener in the Boone deal but appeared in twenty-nine games for the White Sox, going 4-2 with a 4.64 ERA. Bob went to spring training enthusiastic; however, he did not impress anyone and his performance rated a basic "ineffective." Nonetheless, Lopez kept him with the team and put him in the bullpen at the start of the season.

The Chicago White Sox of the late 1950s were one of three teams that had placed in the American League's top three since 1952. The New York Yankees and Cleveland Indians rounded out the trio. The White Sox had previously not been one of the junior circuit's more notable franchises despite its existence since the inception of the league in 1901. The club did take the league's first flag in 1901, and in 1906 produced the world champion "hitless wonders." They played respectable baseball and won another World Series in 1917. The 1919 entry, dubbed the "Black Sox," did serious damage to the sport with their sellout to gamblers during the World Series. However, the "perfect-storm" arrival of Babe Ruth, the lively ball, and Judge Kennesaw Mountain Landis restored the integrity and popularity of the game.

The White Sox then embarked on a thirty-year journey during which they were among the top four finishers a mere three times. In that period, men such as shortstop Luke Appling and pitcher Ted Lyons graced the field for the Sox. Neither Appling, who batted .310 over a twenty-year career, nor Lyons, who won 260 games for mediocre teams, ever played in a World Series or for another team, but both were inducted into the Hall of Fame.

After World War II, the White Sox continued to flounder, finishing in the cellar in 1948. Charles Comiskey, a grandson of the team's first owner, took the reins and hired Frank Lane as general manager. The 1949–50 squads both finished sixth but a core of solidarity began to appear. A second baseman named Nellie Fox came to Chicago by way of the Philadelphia A's just before the 1950 campaign. He followed Billy Pierce, a crafty left-hander who would do his best to make the long drought since Ted Lyons appear to be shorter. Lane became famous as a frenetic trader. There would be no sacrosanct players on his team and the turnover was torrid. Lane, however, had a plan, and he and Comiskey hired Paul Richards to implement the first phase of the rebirth of the Chicago White Sox.

Paul Richards had been a so-so player in the majors and enjoyed his most memorable season as a member of the 1945 Detroit world champions. Richards spent his playing days either behind the plate or on the bench, observing the movements of managers and fellow players. He had managed in the International and Pacific Coast Leagues and built a reputation as a solid thinker. He and Lane combined to produce the go-go White Sox.

Lane had been active since appearing on the scene, and on April 30, 1951, he engineered a trade for a twenty-eight-year-old Cuban jack-of-all-trades named Orestes "Minnie" Minoso. In Minoso, Lane brought the first man of color to the Chicago Americans and that man proceeded to hit .324 for the Sox while playing four positions over the course of 1951. He paced the league in triples and stolen bases and, though he hit only ten homers, he still managed a slugging percentage of .500. Paced by Minoso and first baseman Eddie Robinson, who had twenty-nine home runs and 117 RBIs, the White Sox finished a respectable fourth at 81-73, seventeen games behind the Yankees.

The White Sox were dubbed the go-go Sox due to their speed and aggressiveness on the base paths. The team brought fans to the ballpark and thrilled their long-suffering patrons by actually holding first place on June 10. The Pale Hose had not enjoyed so lofty a position that late in the season since 1920. The team drew more than a million fans for the first time in its history and the interest in the Windy City began to shift from Wrigley Field and the Cubs to the south side.

Richards built his infield around Fox and the outfield around Minoso. Fox, at second, was complemented by Chico Carrasquel, a slick-fielding shortstop who came to the White Sox via Caracas, Venezuala, and Brooklyn, New York. Luke Appling, the longtime resident at shortstop, took it upon himself to work with Chico and make him a big-league shortstop. He succeeded. The team's main strength, however, centered on the pitching. Richards, the old catcher, worked with Pierce and turned him into the ace of the staff. The crafty lefty produced solid win totals and low ERAs, eventually retiring with more than two hundred career wins. Richards taught Pierce the slider and Billy responded with a string of fine performances.

Richards hung around for four seasons, producing a fourth- and three third-place finishes, a great career by White Sox standards, but relations began to strain between him and trader Lane. Richards left for Baltimore with nine games to play in 1954 to build the newly rehatched Orioles. Comiskey, considered by Lane to be as green as a Granny Smith apple, poured fuel on the fire by sticking his nose into the fray. Lane followed Richards out the door after a seven-year sojourn in which a total of 353 players changed uniforms. In the meantime, former St. Louis Cardinals slick-fielding shortstop Marty Marion relieved Paul Richards late in 1954 and stayed through 1956, producing two more third-place finishes.

Lane's wheeling and dealing generated interest and hope for the fans of the Windy City. Unlike men such as Tom Yawkey of the Red Sox who tried to purchase a title, Lane attempted to deal for one. On his departure, however, he left Chicago with a creditable group of players unseen on the south side in years. Carrasquel had been dealt to the Cleveland Indians in exchange for center fielder Larry Doby, and Chico was replaced at short by another Venezuelan, future Hall of Famer Luis Aparicio. Luis was virtually the only homegrown product in the lineup, and Marion, probably the classiest shortstop in the 1940s, helped him along, polishing his play in the field. As a result, Aparicio was selected Rookie of the Year in the American League in 1956.

Marion's two third-place results did not endear him to Comiskey and his new partner, John Rigney. When a sweep of the Yankees in a four-game series in June 1956 stirred emotions and dreams of October grandeur, the team went into a tailspin from which it never recovered, winding up in third for the fifth straight season. Marion did not seem to have much job security, particularly in light of the rumors emanating from the Indians' front office that management had tired of skipper Al Lopez. Lopez had produced five seconds and a pennant. His greatest sin, though, had been the shocking World Series sweep of his record-setting 1954 edition of the Indians by the New York Giants. He joined the White Sox in time for the 1957 campaign.

Lopez, the "Señor," like Richards before him, had spent his playing days behind the plate. He liked the White Sox, as they played his brand of baseball. They had good pitching and strength up the middle. Sherman Lollar had been a stable and capable catcher for the Sox since Lane obtained him from the now defunct St. Louis Browns after the 1951 campaign. Fox, who would join Aparicio in Cooperstown, combined with Luis to give the team a tight second base. Doby, who had played for Lopez in Cleveland, had seen better days in his Hall of Fame career, but he still had a few hits left in his bat besides being a capable center fielder.

Lopez guided the White Sox to a second-place finish in 1957. In the off-season, the White Sox obtained pitcher Early Wynn and outfielder Al Smith from the Indians for Fred Hatfield and fan favorite Minoso. Wynn, another future Cooperstown inhabitant, had struggled through a tough season, going 14-17 with an ERA of 4.31 for the sixth-place Indians. Still, he mustered enough gumption to lead the league in strikeouts while pitching 263 innings. He was, however, thirty-seven years old, and in the 1950s, that spelled ancient in baseball annals. Still, Lopez knew Wynn and had confidence in his abilities. No pitcher could surpass Wynn for meanness, according to Ted Williams, who always joked that he would not go fishing in the Everglades with Wynn because he wasn't sure that he'd emerge from the mysterious swamp intact, or even alive.

Lopez racked up another second in 1958, albeit a poor runner-up at 82-72, ten games behind the world champion Yankees. The "go-go" team of the early fifties that so took the league and the fans by storm seemed to be aging and running out of steam. They lacked a slugger and Wynn had not returned to his former self, going 14-16 with an ERA of 4.13. Still, the old boy paced the circuit in strikeouts once again, posting 179 whiffs. Pierce had won twenty games in both 1956 and 1957 but dropped to a 17-11 mark in 1958. Righty Dick Donovan rounded out the top three at 15-14. The Yankees had breezed to their fourth consecutive flag and their ninth in ten tries. Although they no longer appeared invincible, no one in the American League seemed ready to take away the role of league leader from Stengel and company.

Winds of change blew rather fiercely in the 1958–59 off-season, even for the Windy City. The Comiskey family spent substantial amounts of time in the Cook County Probate Court as the younger generation fought for control of the White Sox. Son Chuck thought the team belonged to him, growing up believing that to be a fact. However, his sister Dorothy, who held a controlling interest in the team, would not relinquish that power. Enter Bill Veeck, who had cut his teeth as a seller of wares in the stands of cross-town Wrigley Field and was a man of the people in both Cleveland and St. Louis. The battle in court dragged on through most of spring training, until a judge's decision allowed Veeck and his partners to take over the team.

The Chicago White Sox and Bob Shaw's 1959 Season

Lopez assured Veeck that the White Sox could take it all, as he felt that New York had weak spots and no other team could match Chicago's strengths. Lopez discouraged Veeck from trading for Senators slugger Roy Sievers, as he thought that Sievers's power would be offset by his fielding lapses. Chicago power? In 1958, Sherm Lollar hit twenty home runs and drove across eighty-four runs. The team led the majors in stolen bases and was a cinch to do so again. But nothing else seemed to be much more than merely adequate. Could Lopez perform magic?

Chicago started the season with a 9-7, fourteen-inning victory over the Tigers in Detroit on April 10. Fox paced the attack with five hits in seven tries and won the game with a two-run homer off Don Mossi. Nellie would hit one more home run during his Most

Valuable Player season. Twelve days later, the White Sox trounced the A's in Kansas City, 20-6. Fox had garnered four more hits and two bases-loaded walks in the eleven-run seventh inning. The team ended April at 10-6 and in second place.

As mentioned earlier, a little noted trade took place in June 1958 between the White Sox and the Tigers. Bob Shaw arrived in Chicago with Ray Boone. Shaw did not play a key role with the 1958 Sox; he went 4-2 in twenty-nine games and 5-4 overall. During this apprenticeship, however, Lopez monitored his skills, studying his excellent control, and assigned him to pitching coach Ray Berres. Berres worked on his delivery, mechanics, and technique. By early May he had appeared in fourteen games and allowed only three earned runs in twenty-five innings and was rewarded with his first start of the year.

So on May 13, 1959, Bob Shaw got the nod in Boston and recorded a neat five-hit, no-walk, 4-0 victory over the Bosox, keeping the Pale Hose one game behind the Indians. Four days later, Shaw started against the Washington Senators and gave up six earned runs. He hung on long enough to prevail in a 10-7 victory in the second game of a doubleheader. More than 22,000 fans had flocked to Griffith Stadium to make up the largest crowd in the Capital City ever to watch the White Sox play baseball. The hometown Nationals had beaten the Sox in the opener to snap Chicago's eight-game win streak. Bob faced the Athletics in Kansas City on May 22 and the White Sox pulled off a 2-1 win, beating former Yankee Bob Grimm.

On May 23, Royal Orbit took the Preakness at Pimlico Raceway in Maryland, thus assuring racing fans of another year without a Triple Crown winner. Tomy Lee, an English-bred colt, with Willie Shoemaker aboard, had taken the Kentucky Derby handily on May 2.

After returning home and just before a game with the Indians on May 26, a rogue helicopter suddenly landed in shallow center field and four very short spacemen hopped out, "captured" the Chicago keystone combination of Fox and Aparicio, and armed them with ray guns. Eddie Gaedel of St. Louis Browns fame and a former (and most likely current) Veeck employee led the "spacemen." Gaedel allegedly "did not want to be taken to their leader, as he already knew him well."[19]

Nearing the end of May, Bob Shaw had improved his record to 4-0 but ran into a bump in the log on May 29 as he lost to Detroit 4-1 at Comiskey Park. Along with his 2.05 ERA, he had thus far let up a mere ten bases on balls in fifty-seven innings. The White Sox, one game behind the Indians in second place, stood at 25-19 at the end of May. On June 2, during the same home stand, Shaw lost 3-2 to future Hall of Fame knuckleballer Hoyt Wilhelm and the Baltimore Orioles. Wilhelm, who would go on to pitch in a record 1,070 games, started only fifty-two games in his twenty-one-year career. Forty-nine of these starts came under the tutelage of Paul Richards. Richards, who was known for having an inventive side, had designed an oversized catcher's mitt when he observed the trouble catcher Gus Triandos had in being the recipient of Wilhelm's pitches. Richards soon had his team playing like the White Sox, with an emphasis on pitching, speed, and defense. The Orioles, for so long the doormat St. Louis Browns, began to rise like the phoenix in 1959, but would remain contenders only through mid-year.

On the fourth of June, Shaw relieved against Baltimore in the twelfth frame of a seventeen-inning game and finished up, picking up his fifth win. The Senators roughed him up a bit on June 9, touching him for four runs in seven innings in an eventual no-decision for him. Billy Pierce, who fared better against Washington than did Shaw, pitched Chicago into first place on June 12 with his fourth career one-hitter, winning 3-1.

On June 13, Sword Dancer, ridden by Bob Ussery, captured the Belmont Stakes in a race that saw Eddie Arcaro suffer a concussion when his horse, Black Hills, broke a bone in his leg and fell, taking Arcaro with him. That same day, Tomy Lee, the Derby winner, who did not compete on Long Island in the Belmont, finished out of the money at California's Hollywood Park.

---

19. www.baseballlibrary.com/baseballlibrary/ballplayers/G/
    Gaedel_Eddie.stm

By June 20 the White Sox had hit a nasty streak, falling to a fourth-place tie at 33-30, although they remained within one and a half games of the first-place Indians. And where were the Yankees? The reigning world champs trailed the Sox by mere percentage points at 35-32. The Stengelmen all seemed to swoon at once and found it hard getting up to speed in the early season. Yet they surely could not be counted out with such everyday players as Mickey Mantle, Yogi Berra, and Bill Skowron and a pitching staff headed by Whitey Ford and 1958 Cy Young winner Bob Turley.

On June 26, Sweden's Ingemar Johansson emerged victorious against world heavyweight champion Floyd Patterson in Yankee Stadium. He knocked Patterson to the canvas seven times in less than three rounds before referee Ruby Goldstein stopped the fight.

The Yankees beat the White Sox and Billy Pierce in Chicago on Friday night, June 26. The following day Shaw took the mound against the Yanks and went eight innings for a 5-4 decision and his sixth victory. Harry "Suitcase" Simpson abetted Bob's effort with a grand slam in the bottom of the eighth.

Bob went four innings against Detroit on July 2, giving up three runs. He did not figure in the decision although the Bengals took the contest 9-7. On Independence Day, in Kansas City, Bob relieved starter Dick Donovan in the fourth inning with the White Sox behind 4-2. He earned his seventh win with a fine five-inning effort, giving up but one hit.

The All-Star break saw Chicago very much in contention with a 43-35 mark, two games behind the front-running Indians. The Yankees, although always a threat, trailed by five games at 40-38. Turley, who had gone 21-7 in his 1958 Cy Young season, was a mediocre 7-8 at this juncture in the season. The New Yorkers endured key injuries to Bill Skowron and Bobby Richardson. At the same time, Mickey Mantle suffered through a mild loss of production. The Bronx Bombers did not seem to want to win the pennant in 1959.

On July 7, the National League took the first All-Star game by a 5-4 score on a run-scoring, eighth-inning triple by San Francisco

Giant Willie Mays. During the three-day break, rumors had it that Al Lopez would be taking over for Casey Stengel as skipper of the Yankees and that former Giant manager Leo Durocher was in line for the Señor's job in Chicago. Lopez, who knew only what he read in the papers, stated that he had every intention of staying at the helm of the White Sox for the remainder of the season.

The major leagues went back to the work of determining a winner, and on July 12, Bob Shaw took the ball and went six good innings to beat the A's in the second game of a twin bill. Two days earlier he had relieved for one frame but was tagged for three runs. On July 13, Pierce evened his record at 10-10 with a 7-3 decision over the Red Sox before more than 20,000 fans at Fenway Park, snaring a tie with the Indians for first place. Two days later, they inched ahead of Cleveland, splitting a doubleheader with the Red Sox while the Tribe lost a pair to the Yankees. The Yankees, under .500 at 42-43, still trailed the White Sox by only six and a half games.

Chicago left Boston for a series with New York at Yankee Stadium. Early Wynn, in perhaps the best season in his illustrious career, took the first game 2-0 while giving up only two hits. The White Sox could manage to scratch out two singles against loser Ralph Terry but both came in the ninth inning and sandwiched a failed fielder's choice and an intentional walk. The next day, Bob "Buck" Shaw went eight and a third innings to beat the Yanks 2-1, securing his ninth win. Shaw aided his own cause by going two for four at the plate, driving in the second Chicago run in the fourth. Left-fielder Al Smith made a great throw to nail Hector Lopez, who tried to score from second on a Richardson single. The White Sox then lost the last two to the Yanks but left New York still tied for first with the Indians.

On July 20, the city of Havana swelled from its normal million residents to about 1.5 million. Devotees of former ballplayer Fidel Castro waited to join him in celebrating the sixth anniversary of his attack against deposed dictator Batista's Moncado Barracks in Santiago de Cuba.

Back in Chicago, Billy Pierce beat the Orioles 2-1 before more than 29,000 fans. At this point in the season the White Sox stood

22-4 in one-run decisions. For the entire campaign, their record in squeakers was 36-14. The next day, July 25, Bob Shaw pitched the first eleven innings of a seventeen-inning game in which the White Sox eventually overcame the Orioles. Bob let up just one run but could not come up with his tenth victory. On Sunday, July 26, Early Wynn won his thirteenth with a 4-1 decision over the Orioles, but the Sox dropped the second game of a doubleheader while the Indians swept theirs, resulting in a half-game lead for the Tribe.

The Continental League, a brainchild of Branch Rickey, announced on July 28 that it would be ready to play in time for the 1961 season. Five cities had signed up and the roster looked like the majors of the future: Minneapolis–St. Paul, Toronto, Denver, Houston, and New York. The Gotham entry's ballpark would be built in the Flushing section of Queens. Its ownership was headed by Joan Payson, the future owner of the Mets. At the end of July, Rickey and respective league presidents Warren Giles and Joe Cronin met in Washington with Sen. Estes Kefauver regarding the proposal of a third circuit. Kefauver warned the major leagues that Congress would be keeping an eye out for any indication of roadblocks put in the way of the Continental. Through a spokesman, Commissioner of Baseball Ford Frick promised complete cooperation.

After a 4-3 victory by Pierce over the Yankees on July 28, the next day brought rain to Chicago. Shaw faced Ralph Terry in an abbreviated game that ended in a six-inning, 4-4 tie. During the delay, Bill Veeck treated the fans to a fireworks display. The next day Wynn followed with his fourteenth victory, and at the end of July, the White Sox held the top position at 59-40 and were one up on Cleveland. The Yankees battled with .500 at 49-51 and pursued the league leaders, behind by ten and a half games. With fifty-five games remaining, Bob Shaw could boast a 9-3 record, along with a 2.98 ERA.

On August 2, Shaw picked up his tenth victory, going seven and two-thirds innings against the Senators in the nightcap of a doubleheader swept by Chicago 3-2 and 9-3. Shaw lacked his normal pinpoint control, allowing six walks, and gave way to relief ace Gerry Staley for the duration of the game. Staley, who had gone 54-36 as a starter for the Cardinals over the 1951–53 seasons, had found a home in the White Sox bullpen during the 1957–60 stretch. He appeared in more than two hundred games and accumulated thirty-nine saves in addition to thirty wins and a four-year earned run average under 2.50.

The 1959–62 years saw two All-Star Games played each season. In 1959 the first, won by the Nationals 5-4, took place in Pittsburgh in July at the regular interval. The second was played in Los Angeles on August 3. The junior league won that contest 5-3, with Chisoxer Nellie Fox driving in the go-ahead run in the fourth inning.

On August 7, Bob Shaw went the distance to beat the Senators 4-1 in Washington, improving his record to 11-3. The White Sox got ten hits, all singles, and were paced by handyman Billy Goodman, who accounted for three hits and three RBI. Goodman, the league's bat champ in 1950 with a .354 mark, three times came up to the plate with an identical situation: a man on second and two outs. Each time he produced an identical result: a single and an RBI.

The White Sox stood at 64-42 with a one-and-a-half-game lead over the Indians. In the National League, the San Francisco Giants headed the pack with a similar game-and-a-half spread over the Los Angeles Dodgers. The newly transplanted West Coast teams appeared to be in a position to continue their rivalry, albeit over an interstate freeway rather than an intracity subway. Scribes began to question who would appear in the World Series, as the Yankees continued barely to flirt with .500 and the defending National League champion Milwaukee Braves could not mount a consistent winning period.

Bob Shaw picked up win number twelve with another complete game on August 14, this time a 5-1 victory over the Athletics in Kansas City. This followed on the heels of Early Wynn's sixteenth win, a 9-0 whitewash of the Tigers. That same day, the Indians suffered through an 11-1 trouncing at the hands of the Tigers, dropping to three and a half games behind. The Red Sox traveled to the Bronx over the August 14–16 weekend and proceeded to take three games of a four-game series with the Yankees, putting New York twelve and a half games down with thirty-seven to play, an almost impossible distance to make up. Despite losing the last two games to the A's, the White Sox emerged from Kansas City still three games up on Cleveland.

After losing to the Orioles on August 19, Shaw faced New York in the nightcap of a doubleheader on Sunday, August 23, and improved to 13-4 with a complete-game, 5-0 win before 44,000 fans at Yankee Stadium. In the borough of Brooklyn, fans ventured to Ebbets Field to watch a Negro league exhibition game featuring Satchel Paige pitching for the Havana Cubans.

On August 26, the New York Times *featured a remarkable story about Marine Corps Lt. Col. William Rankin, who ejected from his jet fighter at about 48,000 feet. He then free-fell for more than seven miles as his parachute was preset to open at the two-mile altitude mark. His fall lasted over forty minutes and he remained conscious for the entire time. He suffered a broken hand during the ejection process and hit his head on the trunk of a pine tree when his chute was caught in the branches as he reached terra firma. He then walked to a road where a passerby recognized his flight uniform and gave him a lift to town.*

On August 28, on earth and in Cleveland, Bob Shaw took the mound before some 70,000 fans and increased the Chisox lead over the Tribe to two and a half games with a route-going 7-3 victory. He had gone 5-1 during the month of August while his team posted a 21-10 record, lengthening their lead over the Indians to five full games. On September 1, he lost to Jim Bunning and the Tigers 4-0, lasting only five innings and allowing all the runs.

Four days later, Shaw lost to the Indians in Chicago, 6-5. Cleveland was aided by an error by Goodman that resulted in an unearned run. Bob had just suffered his last regular-season defeat in 1959 and showed a 14-6 mark. Despite the loss, the White Sox maintained a five-and-a-half-game lead over the Indians.

On the tenth of September, Shaw regained his winning ways, beating Washington 5-1 the day after Early Wynn improved to 19-9 with a 3-2 victory over Kansas City. The following day, Senators ace Camilo Pasquel beat Chicago 8-2, but no ground was lost; the Indians dropped their contest to Hoyt Wilhelm and the Orioles. Two days later, those same Orioles became Wynn's twentieth victim as they submitted meekly to him in Baltimore by a score of 6-1. Bob followed that performance with a steady seven-plus innings against the Red Sox, as Goodman redeemed himself for his earlier miscue with his first home run in two years. Shaw gave up only two hits through the first seven innings, but when Boston touched him for three in the eighth, Lopez brought in Pierce to squelch the flames and preserve Buck's sixteenth win.

Billy Pierce took on the Yankees at the stadium on September 15. This time Shaw provided the relief in a 4-3 win that had many hearts pounding back in the Windy City. In the bottom of the ninth, Mantle touched Shaw for his second home run of the night and Berra fouled out. Elston Howard wound up on second base as his drive to center was misplayed by novice Jim McAnany. Bobby Shantz ran for Howard and was off with the crack of the bat when Hector Lopez screamed a sinking liner into right field. However, speedy flychaser Jim Rivera nailed it with a shoestring grab. Rivera then doubled up Shantz with the help of heads-up backup by third baseman Bubba Philips, thus preserving the win and reducing Chicago's "magic number" to four.

Shaw's 1-0 effort against the Tigers further reduced the number of White Sox victories (or Cleveland losses) required for a trip to the World Series to two. He went the distance and gave up only five hits before more than 37,000 fans at Comiskey Park. At the same time, Joe Gordon, the Indians' manager, announced his resignation, to be effective at season's end.

Nevertheless, the season still had life in it as the White Sox dropped a twin-bill to the Tigers on September 20 and the Indians closed the gap to three and a half games. Two days later, Wynn put the lid on the Cleveland coffin with a 4-2 triumph over the Indians at Municipal Stadium before more than 54,000 fans, all hoping for a miracle. Bob Shaw had a hand in that celebration with nearly three innings of shutout relief as Wynn departed in the sixth. To mark the occasion, the Chicago City Council, along with Mayor Richard Daley, had authorized the city's air-raid whistles to sound upon clinching of the pennant. They went off at 10:30 in the evening, without warning, frightening residents and sending a good many to their backyard bomb shelters.[20]

The last day of the season saw Bob pick up win number eighteen in a five-frame tune-up in anticipation of the World Series. Chicago took the American League flag with a record of 94-60, five games up on the Indians. The White Sox hit fewer homers than any other team in the league but the pitching staff led with an ERA of 3.29 and thirty-six saves. They also led in stolen bases with 113, with Aparicio pacing all baserunners with fifty-six steals. Over in the National League, the Dodgers and the Braves tied for first and entered a playoff to decide who would face the White Sox. Los Angeles took both games and earned the right to represent the senior circuit. As noted earlier, they won the series but it took them six games to overcome the White Sox. Bob Shaw started games two and five and split the two decisions. He pitched well into the seventh inning of his first start but then gave up two home runs before being relieved by Turk Lown. He won his second outing in the nail-biter against Koufax. He posted a 2.57 ERA in fourteen innings and was Chicago's most effective starter.

Wynn took the Cy Young Award that season in recognition of his 22-10 record, but Bob Shaw played a very important role in helping Chicago get to the fall classic. He went 18-6 with a 2.69 ERA and finished third in the Cy Young ballots, and was named American League Sophomore of the Year. He appeared in forty-seven games, completed eight of his twenty-six starts, and relieved in twenty-one games, picking up two wins and three saves. The sportswriters voted second baseman Nellie Fox the American League's Most Valuable Player; Aparicio and Wynn placed second and third, respectively.

20. *Encyclopedia of Major League Baseball*, Richard Lindberg.

The White Sox slipped to third in 1960 as the Yankees regained their foothold on the top rung of the American League ladder. Bob went 13-13 and was traded to Kansas City the following year. In 1962, he found himself back in the nation's heartland with the Milwaukee Braves and provided them with a 15-9 mark and a 2.80 ERA, representing them in the All-Star Game. In 1965 he went 16-9 for the San Francisco Giants with an ERA of 2.64. He retired from baseball after a combined 3-11 for the Mets and Cubs in 1967. He went 108-98 with a lifetime ERA of 3.52.

During his days with the White Sox, Bob Shaw recognized the value of coastal property in the state of Florida, getting into the citrus-packaging business and eventually specializing in real estate. He has been involved in the design and management of office buildings and shopping centers. He spent many years managing in the American Legion and in 1986 coached the Jensen Beach, Florida, entry to the National Championship. He also coached for both the Dodgers and the Milwaukee Brewers and managed in the Oakland A's system.

In 1972, he wrote *Pitching*, published by Viking Press. The book is a composite of the lessons learned from Lopez and Berres and articulated in the words of Bob Shaw, who certainly took them seriously. In addition, he has been very helpful in supplying me with a résumé and various specifics for this project.

He has spent most of his post-baseball days in the Sunshine State, where he lives and works in Tequesta. He has been married to Asta since 1963 and they have three children, Karen, Linda, and Glenn.

I had the pleasure of spending a couple of hours with Bob on a Sunday afternoon in January 2000. At the end of our visit, I asked if pitching and winning a World Series game before a huge crowd in the Los Angeles Coliseum was his greatest thrill in baseball. He quickly replied, "No, it was when Gaylord Perry entered baseball's Hall of Fame in Cooperstown." Apparently, after thanking his family and coaches and so on, Gaylord made the comment that he surely would not be standing there were it not for Bob Shaw. Bob then followed up with "You see, I taught him how to throw the spitter."

Interestingly, at a recent book sale at my hometown Lunenburg (Massachusetts) Public Library, I spotted a paperback titled *Me & the Spitter,* by none other than Gaylord Perry. Gaylord told of being a struggling young pitcher trying to win a permanent job with the San Francisco Giants when he learned of the arrival of a seasoned hurler named Bob Shaw via a trade with Milwaukee. On page 129, he writes, "I was sorry to see Shaw and [Bob] Hendley coming to San Francisco. I should have rejoiced." He explains why in the following chapter, but I'm sure you know the rest.

Bob Shaw took his risks as a young ballplayer and continued with the challenges of business and family. His careers have had many more ups than downs and he might well agree that it all started back in 1959 with *that one glorious season.*

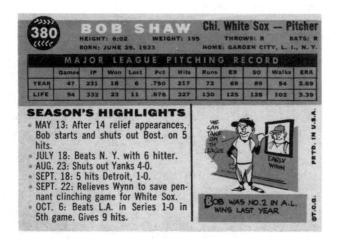

14

1959: HARVEY KUENN

DETROIT TIGERS

On April 17, 1960, on the eve of the new baseball season, the Detroit Tigers and the Cleveland Indians executed a blockbuster trade. The Tigers' Harvey Kuenn went to Cleveland in exchange for Rocky Colavito. On the surface, it was a normal exchange of outfielders, but the reality is that the league's batting champ was traded for the league's home run leader. Kuenn had hit a hefty .353 and Colavito had scored forty-one home runs. Both had good fielding skills, but Colavito could nearly penetrate a brick wall with his rocket for an arm while Kuenn had the range of a former shortstop along with an accurate, if not overpowering, arm.

Both players had spent their entire careers to date with one organization and Colavito had garnered extraordinarilyy strong fan support among the youngsters along Lake Erie. Cleveland general manager Frank Lane was hanged in effigy after the trade. Detroit fans were not all that happy either, as they had come to appreciate the solid consistency of Harvey Kuenn, a quality he carried until his death in 1988.

Harvey Kuenn was born in Milwaukee on December 4, 1930, the only child of Harvey and Dorothy Kuenn. He began playing baseball at a very early age as his father, a shipping clerk for a local lithographing firm, had some success with the sport and managed to play at a high amateur level. The elder Kuenn led the Milwaukee City League in batting in 1945 with a mark of .387.

Harvey, the son, graduated from Lutheran High School in June 1949 and had earned ten athletic letters, four in baseball. He played the infield and batted and threw right-handed. Scouts from six major league clubs had watched him during his schoolboy days but none offered much encouragement or money, so the Kuenn family made a decision and Harvey went off to Luther College in Decorah, Iowa.

Kuenn had concentrated on baseball every summer during his high school career, playing with the West Allis Highway Beer Depot squad. He had grown to six-feet, two inches and weighed a solid 185. He was built more like a football lineman than a baseball player, with the strong square frame that represented the Midwest and its unique mid-century ethnic groups. Steve Balish managed the Depot team and Ron Unke pitched. Harvey and Unke went on to Luther College, but both became disenchanted and left before completing a year. Together, they enrolled at the University of Wisconsin at Madison in February 1950. Kuenn moved in to the university baseball team's shortstop position and Unke pitched. Ron Unke eventually spent time as a St. Louis Cardinals farmhand but never made it to the big leagues.

Kuenn immediately hit college pitching hard in the spring of 1951 but had trouble in the field, committing fifteen errors in twenty-three games. He tied a Big Ten record for ineptitude with four miscues in one contest. By his second year, he had become much steadier in the field and his bat was red-hot. In 1952, he hit .436 for the college season and led the Big Ten in virtually all categories except home runs.

Scouts lurked around every corner and this time they brought with them various contracts and loads of money. Harvey and

Wisconsin baseball coach Art (Dynie) Mansfield had frequent con-
versations and Mansfield agreed with Kuenn that the big-league
offers were too good for him to play that last year of eligibility.
Amateurs at best at this sort of thing, the Kuenns asked Mansfield to
help in negotiating with the major leagues. Mansfield performed his
duties in a very fair, unselfish, and professional way. He realized
that his best player would be departing but he also realized that if
Harvey had the skills to play professional baseball, he might as well
start as soon as he could.

Mansfield handled the bids on a one-shot, highly ethical, confi-
dential basis. There would be no leaks to drive up the price for this
sterling prospect. Kuenn came to the attention of nearly every team
and seven clubs exhibited serious interest. A few teams had become
shy; Kuenn disclosed that he had suffered a knee injury in high
school and had been rejected for military duty as a result. The final
decision was up to Harvey, who analyzed his prospects for advancement and chose the Detroit organization, which was mired in the
American League's second division. More important, the Tigers had
embarked on a youth movement. Detroit offered a $55,000 bonus,
purportedly not the highest bid but the most creative. The bonus
money was to be doled out over a four-year period with no restrictions as to injury. Harvey took it and became a Detroit farmhand in
time for the summer of 1952.

Kuenn reported to Davenport, Iowa, in the Three-I League and
batted .340 in sixty-three games. He struck out only sixteen times in
256 at-bats, a skill he brought with him to the major leagues. While
at Davenport, his manager, Marv Owen, who played short for the
powerhouse Tiger teams of the 1930s, took him under his wing
and they worked to smooth the rough edges in the field. Harvey
improved his weaknesses and by the time he arrived at Briggs Stadium, on September 6, 1952, he had made considerable progress. In
his first game, he mishandled an eleventh-inning grounder to give
the Chicago White Sox a 4-3 victory. Ironically, that was his twelfth
chance of the game and his only miscue. He hit .325 in nineteen

games for the hapless last-place Tigers and committed three more errors for a fielding average of .962.

The Tigers went to spring training in 1953 with few expectations. Virgil Trucks, a 5-19 pitcher, had been traded to the St. Louis Browns for hard-hitting Bob Nieman, but besides the addition of Kuenn, no one anticipated much improvement in the team's fortunes. Kuenn arrived with the reputation of being shaky in the field. Johnny Pesky, in the last stages of an excellent career spent on the infields of the Boston Red Sox and the Tigers, began to work with Harvey on the finer aspects of work around second base. He complemented the lessons taught by Owen at Davenport, and Kuenn began to develop into a good major league shortstop.

The baseball players who attended the training camp that spring did not truly represent the history of the Detroit Tigers. The Tigers entered the American League in 1901 and won three consecutive pennants in the 1907–09 period. They fielded respectable teams over the next quarter century, led by the indomitable Ty Cobb. They took flags in both 1934 and 1935, winning their first world championship over the Chicago Cubs in the latter year. The Tigers made it to the World Series in both 1940 and 1945, taking the title in 1945. The immediate postwar years resulted in three second-place finishes, highlighted by a 95-59 record in 1950. Third baseman George Kell and pitcher Hal Newhouser, both Hall of Famers, paced the squad.

Newhouser, who had enlisted in the military during the war, was found to have a heart murmur, and that kept him from active duty. His pride forced him to report for night work in a local defense plant as his share in the war effort. Burning both ends of the candle might have helped "Prince Hal," as he went 29-9 during the 1944 season. Dizzy Trout contributed another twenty-seven wins. The remainder of the staff could manage only thirty-two victories. The Tigers settled for second place behind the surprising St. Louis Browns, who captured their only modern flag. Detroit took the pennant the following year as Newhouser added another twenty-five wins. They were aided by the late-season return of veterans Hank Greenberg and Virgil Trucks and took the seven-game World

Series over the Cubs. Newhouser became the only pitcher to win two consecutive Most Valuable Player awards as he copped both the 1944–45 honors.

The Tigers entered the 1946 season bolstered by the full-time status of Greenberg and Trucks, but fell twelve games short of the Red Sox. Newhouser picked up another twenty-six wins, giving him a three-year record of 80-27 and ERAs under 2.00 runs per game in both 1945 and 1946. He was elected to the Hall of Fame in 1992 amid the controversy of being a wartime pitching ace. However, in the five immediate postwar seasons, Hal Newhouser notched ninety-seven victories.

The Tigers followed up with another second place in 1947 but slumped to fifth the next year. They rebounded to a strong fourth in 1949. Vic Wertz and Walter "Hoot" Evers both hit over .300 and roamed the left and right sides of the outfield. Wertz developed into an RBI machine and drove home 133 tallies. Newhouser and Trucks won eighteen and nineteen games, respectively, and Fred Hutchinson went 17-8. The Tigers played the best baseball in the American League over the last two months of the season.

The team ran up to second in 1950, falling just three games shy of the Yankees. Kell, Wertz, and Evers each contributed more than one hundred RBI and the Tigers batted .282, led by Kell's .340. This marked the end of an eight-year stretch of .500-plus finishes. After a fifth in 1951 and a 23-49 start in 1952, both under Red Rolfe, Hutchinson took over as skipper. Hutch, at thirty-three, was pretty well finished up as a pitcher, but he had had no managerial experience. He was immediately placed in charge of his former peers. The Tigers plummeted to the cellar with a resounding thud, winning only fifty games and winding up fourteen games behind the Browns. For the first time in the club's history, the Detroit Tigers finished last. Virgil Trucks became the third pitcher in major league history to throw two no-hitters in a single season. He won only three other games, however, going 5-19 in 1952 with a 3.97 ERA. Three of his five victories were shutouts. In his five wins, he gave up a total of nine hits. Besides his no-hitters he threw a one-hitter, a two-hitter, and a six-hitter. The following year he turned a 20-10 mark with an ERA of 2.93 in a season spent with the Browns and the White Sox.

Team owner Walter Briggs had passed away just before the start of the 1952 campaign. His son, Spike, took over the team and by June had begun to replace some of the stalwarts who had served the Detroit franchise so well over the years. Kell, Evers, and Trout went to the Red Sox and Briggs began to concentrate on fresh prospects to fill the pipeline. Late that season a twenty-one-year-old "bonus-baby" shortstop named Harvey Kuenn came up from the Three-I League for a look. He played in nineteen games and batted .325.

Kuenn arrived at spring training in 1953 and quickly convinced Hutchinson that he was in the majors to stay. Kuenn led the league's shortstops in putouts and all hitters with with 209 base hits. He batted .308 in the process and won the Rookie of the Year honors. The Tigers reached sixth place, winning ten games more than in their previous effort.

Kuenn hammered out another 206 hits in 1954 and averaged .306. Ray Boone provided some offense with his second straight twenty-home-run season. Steve Gromek went 18-16 and Ned Garver contributed a 14-11 record, as Detroit climbed another notch into fifth. Bucky Harris replaced Hutchinson as manager when Hutch insisted on a two-year contract.

In 1955, Al Kaline, a twenty-year-old outfielder, who had hit .276 in 1954 for the Tigers, startled the baseball world by capturing the American League bat crown with a .340 average. Both he and Boone drove in more than a hundred runs, with Boone tying for the league lead with 116. Kuenn poked another .306 (he was nothing if not consistent) with 190 base hits, lefty Bill Hoeft went 16-7 with a 2.99 ERA, and the Tigers edged above .500 at 79-75.

They improved to 82-72 in 1956 but had to settle for another fifth. Kuenn soared to .332, banging out 196 hits in the process. He led the circuit in hits for the third time in his four-year career. Kaline settled in at .314 with 128 RBI while Boone and newcomer Charlie Maxwell combined for fifty-three home runs. Frank Lary and Billy

Hoeft gave Detroit two twenty-game winners for the first time since Newhouser and Trout turned the trick in 1944.

Kuenn had torn ligaments in his knee during the 1956 season and the injury failed to heal properly. In the off-season he began to learn the intricacies of banking in the event that his legs gave out prematurely. In 1957, his average plummeted to .277 and he led all shortstops in errors. Despite his shortcomings, the team managed to make it to fourth place under rookie manager Jack Tighe. Jim Bunning, in his first full season, won twenty games for the only time in his Hall of Fame career. The next year Harvey rebounded to .319 and was switched to center field, where he led the league in putouts. The Tigers maintained their status as a .500 team with a consistent fifth-place, 77-77 result. The next year would be more of the same except that Harvey Kuenn enjoyed the best year of his playing career.

1959: The Batting Title

Despite their fifth-place finish in 1958, the Tigers were well regarded going into 1959. Indeed, they had two of the league's best right-handed batters in Kuenn and Kaline. Charlie Maxwell had proved to be a consistent power threat from the left side and Frank Bolling, a classy-fielding second baseman, helped tighten up the middle. Kaline and Kuenn switched positions and Harvey soon settled in right field. Detroit was picked by the sportswriters as the team most likely to challenge the Yankees. How right they would be. The battle would not be for the American League flag, however, but instead for third place.

After thirteen games, the Tigers had won only one game and had the cellar all to themselves. Kuenn and Kaline were hitting well but the team continued to falter. The bottom hit at 2-15 and while Herb Score of the Indians was beating the Yankees 5-2, the inimitable Jimmy Dykes replaced the beleaguered Bill Norman. Norman had succeeded Tighe in June 1958. Dykes, whose baseball career spanned forty-three years, had been a favorite of Philadelphia A's manager Connie Mack. In 1950, he replaced Mr. Mack as only the second manager of the Philadelphia Americans. Before that he had skippered the White Sox for thirteen seasons, serving as player-manager for six.

Dykes immediately set about to light a fire under the team. They took on the faltering Yankees before a home crowd that exceeded 43,000 fans and swept the New Yorkers. Kuenn had been injured in a 9-1 loss to the Senators on April 30, and returned on May 8 to drive in a run and go two for three in a 5-4 win over Kansas City. The next day Kuenn contributed two hits in another triumph over the A's. On May 10, Dykes pushed his record to 7-1 since taking over, and Kuenn continued his streak of two-hit games in a 7-6 conquest of the ever-handy A's.

On May 8, Ray Norton, a San Jose State football halfback, tied the world record for the 100-yard dash by clocking out at 9.3 seconds in a semi-final heat. He then proceeded to win the finale with a 9.4 time over Bobby Morrow, who had been the 1956 Olympic sprint champion. On May 15, Glenn Davis of Ohio State ran the 440-yard race in a record 46.5 seconds at the Coliseum Relays in Los Angeles.

On Friday, May 15, Harvey Kuenn banged out two more hits in a 2-1 loss to the Baltimore Orioles to boost his batting average to a league-leading .402. He followed that up with a two-for-four performance against Hoyt Wilhelm but his team dropped another to the Birds, 6-1. He had reached a mark of .407. He then suffered a knee injury against the Red Sox in Boston and was forced to skip a few games. When Kuenn returned to play, it appeared that he had lost his batting touch. He endured a number of nothing-for-four games and watched his league-leading batting average drop to .387 by May 25.

The U.S. Supreme Court drove another spike into the heart of segregation when it decided that Louisiana laws prohibiting interracial boxing violated the Constitution.

The following evening, in Milwaukee, Harvey Haddix, of the Pirates, spun his twelve-inning perfect game against the Braves and lost. Kuenn suffered another none-for-four night against the Athletics and was thankful for two consecutive rainouts. On the eve of

Memorial Day, Kuenn scored a run and banged out a single in a 4-1 win over the White Sox at Comiskey Park. By the end of May, his average had settled at .354 and the Tigers stood in fifth place, just ahead of the stumbling Yankees. During Jimmy Dykes's brief reign, Detroit had put together an 18-8 run with an overall mark of 20-23. The Tigers kept winning under Dykes's easygoing hand but Kuenn continued his slide, dropping all the way to .347, though still on top in the bat race.

On June 3, the United States sent up a fifty-four-ton rocket to propel four one-ounce mice into space. The object was to retrieve living objects from orbit for scientific analysis.

Kuenn snapped out of his batting doldrums and promptly went on a six-for-fourteen tear, helping to push the Tigers to .500, at 25-25, on June 7, increasing Dykes's run to 23-10.

Detroit moved into fourth and trailed the White Sox by a mere two and a half games after a 6-3 win in Boston. Kuenn contributed a two-for-three game on June 8. Two days later, Harvey poked a double in four tries and drove in a run while scoring three in a come-from-behind win over the Red Sox. That same day, Rocky Colavito hit four home runs, driving in six scores to lead the Indians to a victory over Baltimore. He became the eighth player to slam four round-trippers in one game.

The Tigers moved on to New York and advanced to third place with a 3-1 win over the Yankees. The loss dropped the defending champs to a game below .500. The two teams played three more contests, with Detroit taking two. Kuenn went seven for seventeen in the series, including a home run. He trailed teammate Al Kaline in the batting race, .354 to .356. In the meantime, Ted Williams, the 1958 batting champ, was benched when his average dropped to an anemic .175 with one home run. Williams would struggle through the worst season of his illustrious career, missing .300 for the only time.

In Mamaroneck, New York, golfer Billy Casper took the U.S. Open at the Winged Foot Golf Club. He recorded a two-over-par 282 and beat the likes of Ben Hogan and Sam Snead as well as a young Arnold Palmer, who carded a 286. Casper took home the $12,000 first prize.

After dropping two of three in Baltimore, the Tigers split a four-game series with the Senators as Kuenn went eight for eleven. When Detroit left the nation's capital, Harvey was back in first in the batting race at .359 and the Tigers held down fourth place at 35-30. They then lost four games in a row, but Kuenn kept hitting. In Boston, on June 23, Williams appeared back in left field. He along with Jackie Jensen and Frank Malzone homered to crush Kuenn and company by a 10-4 score. Two days later, Harvey contributed a double and an RBI as Detroit snapped its losing streak with a 10-5 win over Boston.

While Ingemar Johansson upset Floyd Patterson at Yankee Stadium for the world heavyweight crown on June 26, President Dwight Eisenhower teamed with England's Queen Elizabeth to dedicate the St. Lawrence Seaway at the St. Lambert, Quebec, locks. St. Lambert locks, located just outside of Montreal, were the first steps in a journey that would exceed two thousand miles to the Atlantic Ocean through the Great Lakes.

By the end of June, the Tigers sported a 38-36 record, a mere four games behind the front-running Indians. Kuenn still led the field, now with a .356 mark.

At Wimbledon, in Great Britain, Alex Olmedo of Peru gained the final in the men's tennis singles by beating Roy Emerson of Australia. Olmedo, playing for the United States, eventually justified his top seed by defeating Rod Laver for the title.

As the league approached the All-Star break, the Tigers continued with their 1950s trademark .500 play. They ended the first part of the season at 40-40 in fifth place, a mere six games behind the front-running Indians. Kuenn, at the top of the American League batting chart at .356, was chosen as a substitute for the midseason classic and went hitless in one at bat.

The U.S. Senate debated a rise in the minimum wage to $1.25 per hour.

On Sunday, July 12, Kuenn went two for seven in a doubleheader split with the Indians. He drove across two runs in the firstgame, 6-2 victory and poked a two-bagger in the second-game loss. The Tigers did not fare well over the next week: They continued to flounder against the lowly Senators and Orioles. By July 17, a loss to Baltimore gave them their fifth straight defeat. They had compiled a woeful 2-13 over their last fifteen contests. That same day, a seventeen-year-old youngster named Darold Knowles struck out thirty-two batters in a thirteen-inning game in the Ban Johnson League, based in Missouri. Knowles later played in the majors over a fifteen-year period and appeared in 765 games, only eight of which he started. He retired after the 1980 campaign with a career 3.12 ERA and 143 saves.

The Tigers' miseries began to rub off on Kuenn as he went one for eight in a Saturday split with the Orioles and watched his batting average drop to .342. Frank Lary bested Hoyt Wilhelm 2-0 in the nightcap.

Shot-putter Parry O'Brien set a world's record of sixty-three feet, two and a-half inches in a dual track meet with the USSR at Franklin Field in Philadelphia.

The Tigers happily arrived back home on July 21 and met up with the Senators, taking a quick three games. Kuenn regained his stride, going seven for twelve with a home run and five RBI. The team appeared to be rejuvenated in time for the arrival of the Yankees. Don Mossi took the mound against New York and picked up his season's fifth win against the Bombers. The Tigers improved their record to 9-3 over New York with ten games to go in the season series.

Vice President Richard Nixon visited the American National Exhibition in Moscow, where he participated in the famous "kitchen debate" with Premier Nikita Khrushchev. The two high-ranking officials discussed the differences between capitalism and communism, with washing machines as a backdrop.

The Tigers and Yankees split the next two games as Frank Lary won his fourth against the Yanks, 1-0, in a ten-inning game. Kuenn, injured in the Saturday game, fell behind an upstart named Roger Maris of the Kansas City Athletics in the batting race by a point, with Kuenn at .343. Kuenn did not return to the lineup until the seventh of August. The Tigers visited Fenway Park and dropped a pair of 4-3 decisions to Boston on consecutive days. Harvey went five for ten in the series and drove the go-ahead tally in a four-run outburst in the top of the ninth inning on Sunday to take the finale 7-3.

The Tigers returned home for a series with the pennant-bound White Sox, and on August 11 Kuenn drove in a run in an 8-1 win over Billy Pierce. The Tigers lost the next day, 11-6, despite Kuenn's home run and two RBI. Detroit pitching gave up eight free passes to the Pale Hose and five of these walkers scored. The Indians arrived on August 14 and Detroit struck a mortal blow to their pennant hopes with three wins that weekend. Kuenn rattled six hits including a home run. His five RBI in the series included the game winner in a 5-4 decision over Gary Bell.

The Yankees came to town and took the first two contests. On August 19, they beat Frank Lary for the first time since July 1958. Third baseman Eddie Yost committed an error in the fourth inning and Yankees ace Whitey Ford threw five and two-thirds innings of shutout relief to nail down the victory. The next day, Kuenn had an eighteen-game batting streak broken, going none-for-six while Jim Bunning continued the Tigers' mastery over the Yankees with a 14-2 victory.

On August 21, the United States accepted its fiftieth member state when Hawaii joined the union. Alaska had been admitted earlier in 1959, marking the first new member since 1912. Two states, New Mexico and Arizona, had joined that year also.

Kuenn went three for three in Boston and scored the winning run in a 2-0 victory over the Red Sox. During the last ten days of August, Detroit regained its winning ways and finished the month at 65-65, while Kuenn remained atop the league in the batting race with a .351 mark.

September started with a 4-0 win over Bob Shaw and the flag-bound White Sox. Harvey contributed mightily with a four-for-five day, including a pair of two-baggers. The Pale Hose quickly recovered the next day with a twin sweep, 7-2 and 11-4. All the runs in the nightcap came in the fifth inning.

In Cleveland, on September 7, the Indians took two from Detroit, 15-14 and 6-5, scoring three runs in the bottom of the ninth in each game to come to within four and a half games of the White Sox. Harvey could manage only two hits in eight trips to the plate. On September 12, Don Mossi won his sixth game against New York with a 4-0 shutout as Kuenn led the way with two hits. The season series ended in Detroit's favor, fourteen games to eight. Mossi went 17-9 that season to post the highest win total in his twelve-year career. Lifetime, he won 101 games against eighty losses. He was used primarily as a reliever during his first five seasons with Cleveland and became a starter after arriving in Detroit in 1959.

The country was once again shocked by the Soviet Union's early success in the space arena. The Russians hit the moon's Sea of Tranquillity with a rocket estimated to be traveling at about seventy-five hundred miles per hour. The spaceship contained many flags depicting the USSR's hammer and sickle. U.S. officials quickly rejected the notion that the Soviets held any ownership rights to the moon.

The season began its final descent and it became evident that unless a complete collapse occurred, the White Sox would take their first flag since the ignominious season of 1919. On September 15, Mossi took win number fifteen as Kuenn contributed three hits and an RBI in a 3-1 decision over the Orioles. Harvey and company then took two from the White Sox, and continued to place obstacles in their road to the title. Chicago had just played its final game at home and now faced the task of clinching on the road. Kuenn had gone six for twelve in the final three games in the Windy City and now stood at .356. Rocky Colavito, of the second-place Indians, had just belted his forty-first home run and battled Boston's Jackie Jensen for the league lead with 106 RBI.

On September 22, Kuenn picked up two more hits, including a three-run homer in a 6-4 win over the A's. In the season's final series, he drove in two against the White Sox to pace the Tigers to a 6-5 win. The White Sox, who finally clinched the flag in Cleveland, took the campaign's last two games from Detroit and carefully watched events unfold in the National League. There, the Braves and Dodgers tied at season's end. The playoff was taken by Los Angeles.

Harvey Kuenn won his only batting crown in 1959 with an average of .353, and displayed a remarkable consistency. At the end of each month, his batting averages were: May .354, June .356, July .343, August .351, and, of course, the final .353. He pounded out 198 hits despite missing fifteen games because of injuries. He led the league in doubles with forty-two and, though hitting only nine home runs, compiled a .501 slugging percentage. In addition, he scored ninety-nine runs and drove in seventy-one, providing fellow flychasers Kaline and Maxwell with a fine setup man as they knocked in ninety-four and ninety-five runs, respectively.

Dykes brought in the Tigers at 76-78 with his record a respectable 74-63. Frank Lary and Jim Bunning joined Mossi with seventeen wins each, and all three posted an ERA under 3.90. Detroit finished with the second worst team ERA , however, at 4.20. To his credit, Jimmy Dykes got a lot from his players in 1959.

Detroit had enjoyed a good deal of success against both the Yankees and the White Sox in 1959, and traveled to spring training with hopes for a better result in 1960. The team's starting pitching was respectable, and the Tigers enjoyed the consistent bats and gloves of Kuenn and the great Kaline. As noted earlier, everything changed on April 17, 1960, on the eve of the new season. Neither the Tigers nor the Indians fared as well in 1960 as in 1959. Dykes and Cleveland manager Joe Gordon were traded for each other at about the season's two-thirds point. Both squads suffered losing records: The Tribe fell to fourth and the Tigers dropped to sixth.

Kuenn batted .308 in his one year with the Indians, and then moved on to the San Francisco Giants in exchange for pitcher Johnny Antonelli and outfielder Willie Kirkland. He spent a bit more than four seasons in the Bay Area and hit .304 in the Giants' pennant-winning season of 1962. He appeared in four World Series games but could manage only one hit for an anemic .083 batting average. He left active playing after hitting .296 in eighty-nine games for the Cubs and Phillies in 1966, retiring with a lifetime .303 average with 2,092 base hits.

Harvey Kuenn journeyed home to Milwaukee, where he joined the Brewers organization shortly after their move from Seattle, in time for the 1970 season. He became the team's hitting coach and eventually its manager in 1982; that season, after a 23-24 start, Harvey replaced manager Buck Rodgers in June. Kuenn supplied the low-key leadership that led them to the American League title and into the World Series. There they succumbed to the St. Louis Cardinals, in their only series appearance. The players enjoyed a relaxed club-house and dubbed themselves "Harvey's Wallbangers."

Kuenn endured open-heart surgery in 1976, a serious kidney ailment in 1979, and the amputation of his right leg in 1980. Still, Harvey plodded along, ever the loyal soldier who gave his all to his team and the game of baseball. He managed the Brewers through 1983 and continued to work for them as a scout. Harvey Kuenn died in 1988 at the young age of fifty-seven, leaving his wife, Audrey, and a son and daughter. His legacy as a favorite son of the city of Milwaukee is further enhanced with the memory of *that one glorious season* he put together as a member of the Detroit Tigers back in the year 1959.

15

1960: Dick Groat & Vern Law

Pittsburgh Pirates

When baseball fans consider the 1960 World Champion Pittsburgh Pirates, the image of second baseman Bill Mazeroski, with a full-faced grin, his hat his hand, rounding third base and heading for home, pops up first and foremost. Mazeroski had just hit a home run that won the world title for the Pirates over the New York Yankees in a most unusual series. The Yankees' three victories, 16-3, 10-0, and 12-0, came easily; Pittsburgh's first three triumphs were the result of good pitching and timely hitting.

Although Mazeroski became the Steel City's man of the hour with his last-of-the-ninth homer that turned a 9-9 tie into a one-run Pirate victory, the rally that got the team going was sparked by a mere single, a hit in the eighth inning. With his team trailing 7-4, Pirate shortstop Dick Groat hit that single off Bobby Shantz to drive in one run. That hit ignited a rally for four more and a 9-7 Pittsburgh lead. In the top of the ninth, the Yankees came back to tie the game 9-9, setting the stage for Mazeroski's leadoff heroics.

That game epitomized the kind of year Dick Groat enjoyed. He produced when the team needed a boost and provided the charge required to stir things up. Groat led the league in batting with a .325 average but hit only two home runs to go with his fifty runs batted in. By the time the World Series began, the National League sportswriters had already decided that Dick Groat would be the Most Valuable Player in the National League. On November 16, Dick Groat officially received that honor, the first Pirate since Paul Waner, of his counterpart 1927 National League champions, to win the award. Like Groat, Waner's Pirates faced the Yankees in the World Series. Unlike Waner, Groat's Pirates overcame long odds to conquer the bullies from the Bronx and take all the marbles back to western Pennsylvania.

Dick Groat was born in Wilkinsburg, Pennsylvania, in 1930 and grew up in the shadow of Pittsburgh in the town of Swiss-vale. His father encouraged Dick and his other sons to partake in sports as youngsters. After starring in baseball and basketball in high school, Dick left home to attend Duke University in Durham, North Carolina, where he played both sports. On the court in his junior year, he set a record for points scored in one season and earned All-American status in both his junior and senior years. He worked diligently at his game and made himself into an exceptionally accurate shooter under the tutelage of assistant coach Arnold "Red" Auerbach, compensating for his smallish, five-foot, eleven-inch height in a game of big men.

Auerbach, the soon-to-be legendary coach of the Boston Celtics, taught Groat backcourt moves and defense and worked on his shooting. Red once lamented to a sportswriter that, in his opinion, the second best shooter in America (his own Bill Sharman was the best) was not even playing basketball.[21] That shooter happened to be Dick Groat. Groat perfected the jump shot and also rebounded well,

---

21. *Sport Magazine, The Sport Special,* Myron Cope, May 1961, page 68.

considering his size. The Fort Wayne Pistons, of the National Basketball Association, drafted him—and therein lies a spectacular tale.

Groat had finished up his athletic career before his college graduation. Recognizing the importance of a degree, Dick enrolled in classes to fulfill his requirements. The Pistons asked him to play with them for a few exhibition games and he agreed. He had never practiced with the team, and coach Paul Birch inserted him sparingly until the final minutes of a game. He made a key rebound and scored the final four points on a field goal and two free throws. The next night he scored twenty points and the Pistons begged for his services, if only on weekends. He played for the Pistons through the middle of February 1953, averaging twelve points a game. He then entered the Army, putting his professional athletic career on hold.

While at Duke, Dick had played shortstop for the baseball team and, here again, took All-American honors during his final two years in school. He hit over .300 both seasons and worked the field with skills beyond his age and experience. Although he committed numerous errors, he grew adept at turning the double play and drew various scouts to the campus. He impressed Branch Rickey, who at that time was engineering the rebuilding of the Pirates and saw an important cog in the process.

In the meantime, Groat had a job waiting for him with the Pistons, but he succumbed to the lure of Rickey and joined the Pittsburgh Pirates at the end of the spring semester in June 1952. In his rookie year, he appeared in ninety-five games and batted a respectable .284 for a team that went 42-112 and finished dead last, more than fifty games behind the pacesetting Brooklyn Dodgers and more than twenty games behind the seventh-place Boston Braves. He spent the next two seasons with Uncle Sam at Fort Belvoir, Virginia, and led his baseball and basketball teams to Army championships.

While Groat played college sports, Vern Law was toiling in the depths of the Pirate organization. He, like Groat, was born in 1930 but in Meridian, Idaho. He starred in high school and American Legion baseball, leading the Boise team to the regional championship in 1947. A future U.S. senator, Herman Welker, had attended college with singer Bing Crosby, who now held an ownership interest in the Pirates. Welker contacted Crosby, and Pirate scout Babe Herman joined eight other teams in pursuing the talented right-handed pitcher.

The Law family devoutly followed the Mormon faith, so Herman refrained from smoking and dugout jokes. (Vern was affectionately known as the Deacon during his tenure in the majors.) A follow-up phone call from Bing the Groaner merely sealed the deal with the Pittsburgh club. Vern Law and his catcher, his brother Evan, reported to the Pirates' Class D squad, of the Far West League, in Santa Rosa, California.

Law went 8-5 with an earned run average of 4.66 in a partial season after graduation from high school. Evan hung up his spikes before the start of the next season and Vern proceeded to the Class B Three-I League, where he won five and lost eleven but posted an ERA of 2.94. In March 1950, he married VaNita McGuire, and the couple eventually produced five sons, all of whose names began with *V*. He split the next year between the Pirates' affiliate in the Double A Southern Association and the parent club in Pittsburgh, going 6-4 and 7-9, respectively. He was in the majors to stay by 1951 and spent the 1952–53 seasons in the Army, where he played ball for the Fort Eustis, Virginia, team. Ironically, he had experienced some arm troubles during 1951 and did not pitch while in the service. He played first base, and the hiatus from the mound chores apparently cured his arm problems.

The Pirates had fallen on meager times with the cessation of world hostilities in 1945. In the 1900–27 period, they had taken six pennants and two of the three World Series in which they participated. Through 1945, they had never finished last and wound up in seventh place only once. They represented their city well, always there and ready, rarely spectacular and never an embarrassment.

During the 1942–45 war years, a total of thirty-five Pittsburgh players served in the armed forces, and with the end of the conflict they returned home in time for the 1946 baseball wars. Slugger Ralph Kiner, who had served as a Navy pilot, joined the team and led the league in home runs; the Pirates finished seventh, however. By 1950, Kiner had led the league in home runs in each of the years he played but the Pirates had fallen into last place.

The Pirates continued to flounder, but in 1951 principal owner John Galbreath hired Branch Rickey as general manager. Rickey, who had supervised the creation of the Cardinals' vaunted farm system and was responsible for the resurgence of the Dodgers, spoke of a five-year plan to fly a pennant over Forbes Field. The Pirates finished seventh in 1951, two games ahead of the Cubs, led again by Kiner in home runs and by Murray Dickson's 20-16 record on the mound. The following season saw the nadir, as the team won but forty-two games.

Groat paced the team in average in his rookie year in a season in which Kiner once again led the league in homers, tying Hank Sauer of the Cubs with thirty-seven. Kiner accomplished the feat of leading (or tying for the lead) the league in home runs for seven consecutive seasons. He did this without the advantage of a backup hitter to preclude pitchers from pitching around him. Dickson went 14-21 but posted a respectable ERA of 3.57. The team would soon turn to Frank Thomas for its run production, as Kiner went to the Cubs in June 1953. Thomas would hit at least twenty-three home runs annually for the next six seasons.

Groat returned to the Pirates in 1955 and, although he came back to the last of four consecutive cellar-dwellers, he saw a great improvement over the 1952 edition. The staff included young arms belonging to Vern Law, Elroy Face, and Bob Friend. Law had settled to a 10-10 record, dropping his ERA to 3.81. Friend went 14-12, leading the National League with an ERA of 2.83. A young right-handed hitter from Puerto Rico named Roberto Clemente moved into right field and would remain there for eighteen seasons.

In November 1955, Dick Groat married Barbara Womble, the daughter of an avid New York Giants fan. They are the parents of two daughters.

By 1956, the team had increased its victory total to sixty-six and made an upward movement to seventh place. In May of that year, Pirate fans believed they had another Kiner in the form of first baseman Dale Long. Long hit home runs in an unprecedented eight straight games and finished the year with twenty-seven. Groat batted .273 and Clemente hit .311. Friend went 17-17 with a 3.46 ERA but Vern Law slipped to 8-16 and an ERA of 4.32.

Manager Bobby Bragan could not maintain the forward motion of the team, and after a miserable 36-67 record, former Pirate second baseman Danny Murtaugh took the reins as manager. Murtaugh cajoled a 26-25 record from the squad over the remainder of the season and tied the Cubs for seventh. Groat batted .315, and Friend, while going only 14-18, continued to hold the line in allowing runs with a 3.38 ERA. Law contributed a 10-8 record with a stingy 2.87 ERA.

Murtaugh began to put together the pieces in 1958. With Thomas clubbing thirty-five homers and driving in 109 runs, Groat hit .300 to lead the offense. Friend went 22-14 to pace the pitching while Face led the league in saves with twenty. Law won fourteen games with an ERA of 3.97. The team finished a nimble second at 84-70, eight games behind the Braves. The next year they slipped to 78-76 but held on to fourth place. Slugger Dick Stuart took over at first base and hit twenty-seven home runs while leading all first-sackers in errors. Groat batted .275, Law went 18-9 with an ERA of 2.98, and forkballer Face went an incredible 18-1 with ten saves and an ERA of 2.70. The ingredients were there, but it was up to Danny Murtaugh to create the magic potions.

1960: It All Comes Together

John Drebinger, of the *New York Times*, in his column of April 10, picked the San Francisco Giants to win the National League pennant and the Pirates to finish fifth. *Sport Magazine*, in its annual poll of ballplayers, chose the Bucs to repeat as fourth-place finishers in the senior circuit. The season opened on April 12, and after an opening-day loss to the Braves in Milwaukee, the Pirates began their quest for a flag with a 13-0 drubbing of the Reds at Forbes Field. Vern Law took his first victory and Dick Groat contributed three hits to the cause. On April 20, Law defeated the Philadelphia Phillies, 4-2, for his second success. The Phils were destined for the cellar in 1960, a familiar position.

In the meantime, the baseball world buzzed with anticipation as Branch Rickey unveiled his plans for a stadium to be constructed for the New York entry in the yet-to-be-formed Continental League. The ballpark would be in the Flushing Meadows section of the borough of Queens. With Rickey in the photo was the chairman of Mayor Robert Wagner's baseball committee, one William Shea. Competing with the plans for the stadium were the Cleveland Indians, who made two major player deals in two days. On April 17, one day before the American League opener, they sent 1959 home-run champ and fan favorite Rocky Colavito to the Detroit Tigers in exchange for 1959 batting champ Harvey Kuenn. The next day, star-crossed lefty Herb Score headed to the Chicago White Sox for pitcher Barry Latman.

On Sunday, April 24, President Eisenhower entertained France's President Charles de Gaulle at his Gettysburg, Pennsylvania, farm.

The Pirates, behind Harvey Haddix, moved into first place on the twenty-fourth with a 7-3 home win over the Braves. Three days later, Law won his third game, beating the Phillies 3-2 in the first contest of a seventeen-game road trip. Groat went three for five, including a double. Pittsburgh ended April at 11-3 with a ten-run, second-inning outburst against the Reds at Crosley Field, winning its eighth consecutive game. Groat, batting a healthy .345, aided the offense with two hits, one of them a double.

At Philadelphia's Franklin Field, a nineteen-year-old Boston University sophomore, John Thomas, reached for the stars as he established a record for the high jump, an incredible seven feet, one and a half inches, during the Penn Relays.

The Pirates' win streak ended at nine games as Elroy Face, virtually unbeatable in 1959, walked in the winning run in the bottom of the ninth to lose to the Cardinals 4-3 on May 2. The next day they went north to Chicago, only to come up short when Dick Ellsworth emerged with his first major league victory for the Cubbies. The next day the Pirates spoiled Lou Boudreau's debut as Chicago manager with a come-from-behind, 9-7 triumph over his new charges. The Cubs led going into the seventh 7-2, but Groat singled in Bob Skinner, who had gained second base via an error. Clemente followed with a one-on homer and Bill Virdon won the game in the ninth by poking a pinch-hit triple with two aboard.

With a high-level, multination conference scheduled in Paris on May 16, an American spy plane, a U-2, was shot down over Russia on May 5. Russian leader Nikita Khrushchev used the U-2 incident to snub President Eisenhower in Paris and force the cancellation of Ike's scheduled visit to the Soviet Union in June. The next day, with the nation focused on the fate of pilot Francis Gary Powers, Bill Hartack rode Venetian Way to victory at Churchill Downs to take the Kentucky Derby.

The Pirates took a trip to the West Coast and proceeded to lose four straight games until Law pitched a complete 3-2 win over the Dodgers on May 10. They followed up with another victory on the eleventh.

On May 10, the junior senator from Massachusetts, John F. Kennedy, scored a decisive win over Minnesota Sen. Hubert H. Humphrey in the West Virginia primary. This election finally put the religion concerns on the back burner of American politics and paved the way for Kennedy's nomination for and eventual election to the presidency of the United States. The next day, philanthropist John D. Rockefeller Jr. died at eighty-six.

On May 13, in an 8-2 rout of the Braves in Milwaukee, Groat went six for six with three doubles and two runs batted in and followed up with two hits the next day as Pittsburgh won again, this time by a 6-4 margin in eleven innings.

Back home on May 18, Groat drove what would be the winning run in the seventh inning of Law's 4-2 victory over the Cardinals. Two days later, more than 39,000 fans watched the Pirates beat the Giants 5-4 in twelve frames. Dick punched in the tying run as San Francisco had gone up 3-2 in the top of the inning. Clemente promptly singled him in to notch the win. At this point, the Pirates led the second-place Giants by one and a half games, with a 22-10 record. The next day, the Giants beat the Pirates 3-1. Groat and

Skinner once again teamed up to start a ninth-inning rally against Johnny Antonelli, but Bud Byerly came in to shut things down and preserve the win.

Saturday, May 21, saw Ballache take the Preakness. Just one week earlier the horse had been sold for $1.25 million. That same day, John Thomas broke his own high jump mark, this time soaring to seven feet, one and three-quarters inches.

By the end of May, the Pirates held first place by one and a half games over the Giants with a 27-14 mark. They won their last four games of the month with Law improving his record to 7-1 at the expense of the Phils, 8-5, on the twenty-ninth with the help of Groat's three-for-five effort. Dick had suffered through a batting slump that dropped him to below .290. The following day, Groat's four-for-five performance spurred the Bucs to an 8-3 win over the Braves. Groat finished off the month sparking an eleventh-inning, game-winning rally with a bunt single as part of a five-for-six day as Pittsburgh eked out a 4-3 win over the Reds. Dick Groat entered the month of June batting .324.

Amid great fanfare, New York Mayor Robert Wagner introduced meter maids to the city on June 1.

Groat, with two hits, and Bob Friend, with a neat 5-0 whitewash of the Reds, produced another Pirate victory on June 1. After an off day, Law followed suit, shutting out the Phils in the City of Brotherly Love, 3-0, for victory number eight. Groat abetted the cause with two hits and a key sacrifice, helping generate the team's first score in the three-run third. The next day, the cellar-dwelling Phils knocked off the Pirates with a twin-bill sweep, halting their six-game win streak. Pittsburgh then moved on to Chicago, where the Cubs blew them and Vern Law out of Wrigley Field with a 13-2 drubbing. The Bucs snapped their three-game skid the next day, 5-3 over Chicago.

On June 11, Bill Hartack won the Belmont to go with his Derby victory in May. However, this time he was aboard Celtic Ash, who outdistanced Derby winner Venetian Way by more than five lengths.

In St. Louis, the Cardinals rallied for three runs in the ninth to register their second straight win over Pittsburgh. The next day, Law took the finale 13-2. Of the National League's top ten batters on that same day, four belonged in the Pirate batting order, headed by Clemente with Groat holding up the rear at .324.

On June 15, a play titled The Apartment, *starring a young actor named Jack Lemmon and his female counterpart, Shirley MacLaine, opened at the Astor in New York. The next day, an Alfred Hitchcock thriller,* Psycho, *opened at two theaters in Manhattan.* New York Times *movie critic Bosley Crowther gave* Psycho *a mediocre review, although he had to admit it could scare you.*

Harvey Haddix won his fourth game of the season, beating the Giants 14-6 on June 15. Both he and Groat went four for five with a pair of RBI. As was becoming common, Groat started the team's first rally, this time in the third inning with a single. He later scored on Clemente's double.

After a three-game sweep of the Giants in the City by the Bay, the Pirates ventured to the Los Angeles Coliseum for a three-game series with the Dodgers. Law took the opener on Friday, June 17, for his tenth victory. Groat scored the first run in a 2-1 victory. They returned home two days later after completing a 9-7 road trip that had taken them to five cities.

The next day they beat the Dodgers again, this time in a 4-3 ten-inning game. That same day, Ted Williams of the Red Sox became the fourth man to hit five hundred career home runs. He did so in a 3-1 Bosox win over the Indians at Cleveland.

On the links, Arnold Palmer won the U.S. Open at Denver's Cherry Hill Country Club with a 280. Palmer scored a scorching thirty on the back nine and a thirty-five coming in during the final round. An amateur named Jack Nicklaus finished an unprecedented second with a score of 282.

Boxer Floyd Patterson helped draw nearly 32,000 fans into the abandoned Polo Grounds and became the first man to regain a heavyweight title. He scored a fifth-round technical knockout over Ingemar Johansson, of Sweden, to whom he had lost the crown in June 1959.

On June 21, Vern Law beat the Cards, 3-2. Groat knocked in Mazeroski with the first run off Bob Gibson. He later added another RBI. The following day, Friend threw his fourth shutout of the season as Groat tallied four hits. By the end of June, the Pirates led the league with a 42-25 record and were three games up on the Milwaukee Braves. Groat, at .334, was third in the batting race behind Willie Mays of the Giants and Norm Larker of the Dodgers.

John Thomas opened July with another assault on the high jump record, this time at Stanford University in the trials for the Summer Olympics in Rome. This time he soared to nearly seven feet, four inches. This man could clear Wilt Chamberlain's head with room to spare.

The Pirates played the Dodgers on the first three days of July, but dropped two of the three contests at Forbes Field. From there they headed to Milwaukee, where they took two of three and proceeded to win three of five over the Reds and Phillies. The Pirates reached the All-Star break in first place, sporting a 49-30 mark, five games up on the Braves.

Vern Law, 11-4 at the break, started the clash of the titans, which was played in Kansas City. Seven other Pirates including Dick Groat joined Law, who went two innings and picked up the win in a 6-0 National League triumph. Groat batted for the Cubs' Ernie Banks in the eighth inning and hit into a double play.

Sen. John F. Kennedy of Massachusetts won the presidential nomination of the Democratic Party on July 14 at the Los Angeles convention. Fifteen days later, in Chicago, Vice President Richard M. Nixon became the presidential nominee of the Republican Party.

Official play resumed on the fourteenth, and Pittsburgh began a 4-7 streak, dropping to second place by Sunday, July 24. Law had picked up win number twelve on the twenty-first with a 4-1 success over the Dodgers. Meanwhile, on July 22, over in the American League, the White Sox finally put a run together to tie the Yankees for first. The next day the Giants picked up a game on Pittsburgh as a young right-hander from the Dominican Republic named Juan Marichal won his second big-league start 2-1 over the Pirates out on the West Coast.

With Milwaukee breathing down the Pirates' necks and a mere half game off the top, Groat, who was inserted at third in the batting order, went three for five with an RBI in a 7-3 win over the Cubs. The next day he nailed two more hits as Vinegar Bend Mizell, a Cards castoff, whitewashed the Cubs 4-0 for their eighth straight setback. The Pirates' streak stopped there on July 30 as Friend lost, 6-1, for his seventh setback of the year. At the end of July, Pittsburgh still held first place with a 57-39 mark, two games up on the Braves. Dick Groat was batting .308.

On August 2, a Miami jury ruled that smoking caused the death of Edwin Green but refused to hold the American Tobacco Company responsible. The big news in the sports world was the collapse of the Continental League and the announcement that the American and National Leagues would each expand to ten teams by 1962.

August began positively for the Pirates with a 3-0 win over the Dodgers at Forbes Field. Groat and Mazeroski knocked in all the runs to bring Law's record to 14-5. The teams split the next two contests. On August 5, in the bottom of the eighth inning of a scoreless game with the Giants in Pittsburgh, center fielder Bill Virdon walked and Groat attempted to sacrifice him to second. Pitcher Sam Jones threw to first but the ball sailed over Don Blasingame's head. Groat and Blasingame collided and Virdon scampered home with the winning run. The next day, Groat beat the Giants, this time knocking in the winning run in the tenth inning. It was his only hit in six at bats. On Sunday, August 7, the Pirates completed their sweep of the Giants 4-1 and 7-5 with Groat bunting home Mazeroski with the go-ahead tally in the nightcap.

The Cardinals stayed within five games of the Pirates and came into Pittsburgh determined to make up some ground. They shocked the Pirates, winning the first two contests, and snapped the Bucs' seven-game win streak in the process. Pittsburgh came roaring back, sweeping a Sunday doubleheader, and the Redbirds left the Steel City no better off than when they arrived. The Pirates continued to achieve success on the home stand, going 14-4 and winning in bizarre ways. For example, in the eighth inning of the second game of a doubleheader against the hapless Phillies on August 16, Groat, Skinner, and Rocky Nelson all bunted safely to load the bases in a 3-3 game. Clemente then walked and Groat scored the winning run. As they departed Pittsburgh for the Midwest, they held a commanding seven-and-a-half-game lead over St. Louis.

On Thursday, August 18, Law defeated the Reds 3-2 in the first game of the trip. He won again six days later against the Cubs, 10-6. On August 26, the Pirates dropped a 3-1 decision to the Cardinals as Stan Musial beat them with a seventh-inning two-run homer. The next day, the Man did it again, this time in the ninth, to win it for St. Louis 5-4. The Cards finished a sweep of the Pirates, but though Pittsburgh limped out of St. Louis, the team still led the Cardinals and Braves by five and a half games. Law snapped that string with a 10-2 win at Los Angeles. The Pirates went 4-0 on a western swing. Groat provided Bob Friend with the go-ahead run with his second homer of the year in a 5-2 decision over the Dodgers. On August 31, he went two for five and the Pirates took the Giants at Candlestick Park by a 7-4 score. The month ended: The Bucs had increased their lead to six and a half games over St. Louis and went 21-10 for August. Groat batted .373 for the month and clearly led the way with timely hits and clutch plays.

In Williamsport, Pennsylvania, twelve-year-old Joe Mormello Jr. of Levittown, Pennsylvania, threw a no-hitter in the Little League World Series finale and shut out the Fort Worth, Texas, entry 5-0 to bring home the crown. He also hit a two-run homer in the first inning.

On September 1, the American sports world was jolted when high jumper John Thomas earned only a bronze medal at the Rome Olympics, finishing behind two Russians in the event. He failed to jump higher than seven feet one-quarter inch while the Soviets both surpassed seven feet one inch.

Back in the States, the Pirates continued to hold their lead. They hosted the Braves and split a doubleheader on September 6 before more than 34,000 fans. The next day, Lew Burdette of the Braves let a slider get away in the first inning and the pitch broke Groat's left wrist. Dick played until the third frame, when the swelling forced him out. X-rays revealed a fracture, and he was sidelined for at least four weeks. Dick Schofield replaced Groat at shortstop and banged out three hits to finish the game as the Pirates resumed their quest and won 5-3. Over the rest of the season, Schofield did a creditable job at short. The next day, the Pirates overcame the Cardinals as Law improved to 19-6. At that point Pittsburgh stood at 82-51, seven games up on the Cards. Groat was hitting .325 but trailed the Dodgers' Norm Larker by .006 in the batting race.

On Sunday, September 18, Vern Law entered the twenty-victory club, taking the first game of a Crosley Field doubleheader, beating the Redlegs 5-3. The following Sunday, the Pirates lost their third straight game in Milwaukee but backed into the pennant when the Cubs shut out the Cardinals 5-0 with a week to go in the regular season.

Larker faded to .323 and Groat became the National League bat champ. The Pirates won the pennant by seven games over the Braves and prepared to take on the Yankees in the World Series.

The World Series

The series opened in Pittsburgh on October 5. The city was in a frenzy, as it had not seen postseason action since facing these same Yankees in 1927. Groat's wrist had healed and he was back in the lineup. Law took the mound for the first game and beat the Yanks 6-4 with relief from Elroy Face. Bill Mazeroski poled a two-run homer in the fourth inning to provide a cushion, but Face nearly let it go when Yankee catcher Elston Howard drove in two runs with his round-tripper in the ninth.

The next day the Yankees got even with a lopsided 16-3 victory. In New York for the third game, the Bronx Bombers kept up the barrage with a 10-0 shutout capped by Bobby Richardson's grand slam. Law took the fourth game, helping his cause with a double that tied the game in the fifth inning. Harvey Haddix won the next contest and Face earned two more saves. The Pirates headed home leading three games to two.

On October 12, Whitey Ford threw his second shutout of the series, blanking the Pirates 12-0 to set the stage for perhaps the most exciting finale ever to a World Series. The Yankees led 7-4 as Pittsburgh came up to bat in the home half of the eighth inning. With Gino Cimoli on first, Bill Virdon hit a ball squarely at short-stop Tony Kubek, but a bad bounce struck Kubek in the neck and everyone was safe. Groat, who batted only .214 in the series, poked a clutch single between short and third and Cimoli scored the first of five runs. The Pirates went into the ninth leading 9-7. The Yan-kees scored two runs in the top of the inning and, as any student of baseball can tell you, Bill Mazeroski took Ralph Terry's first pitch for a ball, then brought the Pirates the world championship for the first time since 1925 with a fence-clearer to left for a 10-9 victory.

The Pirates won the World Series but certainly lost the statis-tical contest. The team batted .256 and the pitching staff gave up a horrendous 7.11 earned runs per game. The Yankees, as a team, hit .338 and posted an ERA of 3.56. Yankee second baseman Rich-ardson hit .367 with twelve RBI and was named the series Most Valuable Player.

On November 3, Vern Law was named the winner of the Cy Young Award. He had gone 20-9 with an ERA of 3.08. He completed eighteen of his thirty-five starts and allowed a paltry forty bases on balls in 266 innings. Lost in the euphoria of the World Series vic-tory, however, was a little-known item: Law had suffered an injury to his foot in a post-pennant-clinching ride to the Milwaukee air-port. Although he won two games in the World Series, he struggled against the Yankees.[22] Vern said that he changed his pitching style to favor his ankle, which had suffered torn ligaments, and tore muscles in his shoulder.[23] He struggled through 1961 with a 3-4 mark.

He won ten games in 1962 but retired temporarily, and spent time in the minors the following season as his shoulder still bothered

---

22. *The 1992 Baseball Engagement Book,* by Michael Gershman, March 15, 1992 *"The Deacon."*

23. Ibid.

him. After a 12-13 record in 1964, he bounced back to 17-9 with an ERA of 2.15 the following year. The Pirates challenged the Dodgers for the flag but came up seven games short. Law took the honors as the National League's Comeback Player of the Year. He retired after the 1967 campaign with a career 162-147 and an ERA of 3.77.

He stayed on with the club and served as pitching coach in 1968 and 1969. He later coached at Brigham Young University and managed the Denver Zephyrs before entering the corporate world as a sales representative.

On November 16, 1960, Groat was voted the Most Valuable Player in the National League. He hit only two home runs and drove in just fifty runs but his scrappy leadership helped blend a group of men into baseball's finest for the year. In 1961 the magic moved to Cincinnati and the Pirates plummeted to sixth with Groat dropping all the way to .275. In 1962, the team advanced to a strong fourth, but Dick's days appeared numbered in Pittsburgh. On November 19, 1962, he moved on to the Cardinals in exchange for pitcher Don Cardwell.

Groat spent the next three years in St. Louis and played a key role in the Cardinals' 1964 world championship. He played in 161 games and batted .292 and, once again, participated in a series that went seven games. For the second time in two tries, his team emerged the winner.

In 1966 Groat moved on to the Phillies, and then to the Giants in mid-1967. He stayed with the team for that summer and retired at the end of the season. He batted .286 lifetime and accumulated 2,138 base hits. He then applied for the position of manager of the Pirates but an inability to agree with general manager Joe L. Brown on certain points led the team to hire Larry Shepherd as skipper.

During Dick's final years as a player, he realized that even shortstops have to diversify. In 1966, he and former teammate Jerry Lynch opened a golf course that they had built in Ligonier, Pennsylvania. Champion Lakes took many more years to perfect, and by 1977 it was a highly rated challenge in the world of golf. During the lean building years, Groat and Lynch performed all tasks, from janitorial to financial management.

Dick Groat was one of the Commonwealth of Pennsylvania's finest athletes. He starred in college and professionally in two sports and reached the pinnacle in baseball not once, but twice. Both he and Vern Law achieved success in baseball and beyond, but I'm sure that when they look back, they remember especially *that one glorious season* of 1960.

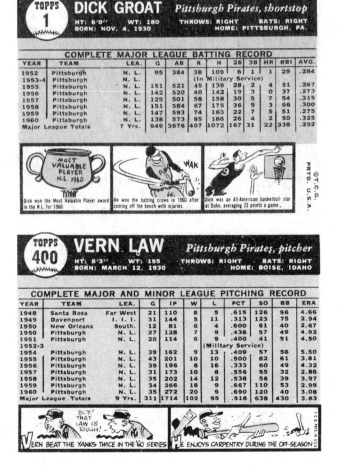

16

1961: JOEY JAY & JIM O'TOOLE
CINCINNATI REDS

On October 5, 1961, Joey Jay, a twenty-six-year-old pitcher who had earlier earned his fame as the first Little Leaguer to make it into the majors, started the second game of the World Series for the upstart Cincinnati Reds against the New York Yankees. Joey fared well against the Yanks and threw a complete-game 6-2, four-hit victory as the Reds tied the series after two games in New York. That victory followed a tough 2-0 loss the previous day as Jim O'Toole gave up only six hits (two home runs). However, Whitey Ford won his eighth career World Series game with a two-hitter against the Reds. Satisfied with a split in the Big Apple, the Reds headed back to the Ohio Rhineland to lose three (and the series) at home to the men from the Bronx.

Although Jay lasted only two-thirds of an inning and lost the fifth and final game to the Yankees, the Reds would not have made it to the fall classic had it not been for the effectiveness of Jay's right arm and the left arm of fellow pitcher Jim O'Toole. Jay turned in a sparkling 21-10 record in 1961 along with an earned run average of

3.53. O'Toole complemented him very nicely, winning nineteen and losing nine, pacing the Reds starters with an ERA of 3.10.

Jay and O'Toole came to the Reds via very different routes. Joey had been signed by the Milwaukee Braves as a seventeen-year-old bonus baby after graduating from Woodrow Wilson High School in Middletown, Connecticut, in 1953. Jay was born in August 1935 and grew so rapidly in his preteen years that he was excluded from pitching in Middletown's inaugural Little League season of 1948. Jay, who eventually grew to six feet, four inches, was forced to play the infield, primarily first base. He led the league in home runs with two, as he told Arthur Daley of the *New York Times* in a 1958 interview while with the Braves.[24]

Jay's father, Joseph, had also pitched in the Braves organization. He reached the club's International League affiliate in Rochester, New York, and received a look-see at the 1938 spring training sessions. However, a bad back got in the way of further progress and the elder Jay headed back to Connecticut and his family.

Joey Jay switched to pitching in the senior leagues and in high school. He starred in the Babe Ruth League, in American Legion baseball, and in high school, throwing twenty no-hit games. A dozen clubs followed his progress but the Braves convinced him to sign with them for $40,000. At the time, the major league fathers had enacted a rule requiring any "bonus baby" to remain with the parent club for two years before becoming eligible for seasoning in the minors. This rule no doubt hurt the Braves, as they vaulted into a contender on their arrival in Milwaukee and Jay took the place of a more experienced player who could have helped the team. Instead, Joey spent the 1953 and 1954 seasons on the bench, appearing in a total of eighteen games, and utilized his time mainly picking splinters from his uniform. He started one game in each year; ironically, both were against the Redlegs. In 1953, he three-hit his future team, but they knocked him out in his next start a year later.

---

24 "Sports of the Times," *New York Times*, June 15, 1958.

Joey's initial reaction to being in the majors was predictable. As the youngest player in the big leagues, he felt awed and overwhelmed. As his first season progressed, he felt alone and unwanted. The veterans resented his bonus and his lack of contribution, although some realized he was a victim of the rules. Manager Charlie Grimm ignored him and Jay retreated into a shell. His father convinced him to try again in 1954. Finally, his two-year stint in oblivion ended in mid-1955 and he was assigned to Toledo, of the American Association.

The next two seasons began the transformation of Joey Jay into a pitcher. While at Toledo, he befriended Carl Willey, another right-handed pitcher, who would eventually join him in Milwaukee. Both had recently married (Joey in 1954), their wives became fast friends, and life became fun again for Joey Jay.

The next season the Braves switched Triple A teams. Both pitchers moved to Wichita, where Jay began to experience control problems, and he went down to Atlanta in the Southern Association. There he proved too much for the batters, spinning two one-hitters in three starts. He quickly found himself back in Wichita for the 1957 campaign, but once again he had trouble locating the plate. Because of his emphasis on control, the hitters dug in and had a field day, resulting in his unimpressive 2-6 record.

Manager Ben Geraghty, who had a total of seventy major league games to his credit, mainly as an infielder and pinch runner, took the youngster under his wing. He instilled a confidence that quickly paid dividends. Jay had heretofore attempted to blow his fastball past the batter. Under Geraghty's tutelage and encouragement, Joey began to mix up his pitches and developed an assortment of curve balls; his slow variety was the most effective. He won fifteen of his last nineteen decisions, striking out 199 men in 223 innings, thus meriting a trip back to the major leagues.

This time he earned his place on the Braves, who happened to be defending a world championship. He went to spring training and was treated not as an unwanted appendage, but instead as a fine prospect. He was also back with his pal Carl Willey. He stuck with the team but skipper Fred Haney experienced trepidation about adding Jay to a staff that boasted Warren Spahn, Lew Burdette, and Bob Buhl. An injury to Buhl early in the season forced Haney to go with his untried youngsters, and he called on Jay on none other than Friday, June 13. Jay responded with a four-hit shutout against the St. Louis Cardinals. That gave Haney the impetus to turn to Willey and Juan Pizarro for spot starts. The three youngsters contributed twenty-two wins to the Braves' second consecutive National League championship.

Jay went 7-5 in 1958 and posted a sparkling 2.14 ERA. He threw three shutouts and kept the team in the race with six victories by August 1. He broke a finger on his pitching hand later in August and was lost for the remainder of the season, including the World Series. His statistics for the next two years showed only fifteen wins against nineteen losses. Spahn, Burdette, and Buhl kept cranking out the victories, to the detriment of the youngsters. Chuck Dressen had replaced Haney as field boss after the 1959 playoff loss to the Los Angeles Dodgers and the Braves then finished second to the Pittsburgh Pirates in 1960. Dressen wanted slick-fielding shortstop Roy McMillan of the Cincinnati Reds to bolster his infield. He traded Jay and Pizarro to Cincinnati for McMillan. The Reds then sent Pizarro to the Chicago White Sox for third baseman Gene Freese, who was also about to embark on the season of his life.

Jim O'Toole grew up on Chicago's south side and had no real schoolboy experiences; his high school, St. Leo, had no baseball program. He took part in the Sherman Parks summer programs, however, and his pitching caught the attention of a number of big-league scouts in the summer of 1955. One, George Moriarty, a former teammate of Ty Cobb, worked for the Detroit Tigers, and he was able to convince the University of Wisconsin to offer an athletic scholarship to the eighteen-year-old left-handed pitcher. Moriarty stayed in touch with O'Toole. Jim pitched with the varsity for one season and played the summer in the Basin League, which comprised college players, going 9-1.

The Reds were vaguely aware of O'Toole but on a trip to

Chicago, Paul Florence, a Reds executive, stopped to visit a relative and was inundated with stories of a police officer's son who
looked like a good prospect. Upon his return to Cincinnati, Florence
checked the files. He indeed found O'Toole and also discovered that
those who had seen him rated him highly. He spoke to general manager Gabe Paul, who called Jim and invited him to Cincinnati, where
he worked out and talked to Paul and then manager Birdie Tebbetts.
Tebbetts advised him to sign with a pitching-poor organization.

O'Toole went back to Wisconsin but the Reds thought he might
slip away into the hands of Moriarty if they did not solidify their
position. Florence visited the O'Toole family during the Christmas
holidays and convinced Jim to drop out of school and join the Reds
organization for a $50,000 bonus. O'Toole would not sign with
Cincinnati until he spoke with Moriarty, who had hoped that Jim
would complete his education.

O'Toole signed with Cincinnati. His first stop was Plant City,
Florida, where he attended the Reds' rookie school. The book on
him was that he had an excellent fastball but experienced trouble
with consistency. His first-season assignment was Nashville of the
Southern Association, where he went 20-8 with no control problems
and was the *Sporting News'* minor league Player of the Year. He
moved up to the majors for good in time for 1959, but felt that manager Mayo Smith had no confidence in him. By midseason Smith
had departed and Fred Hutchinson was in his place. O'Toole went
5-8 in 1959 but improved to 12-12 in 1960 with a 3.80 ERA in a small
ballpark. He pitched 196 innings, striking out 124 and walking just
sixty-six batters.

During that season, Jim married a former girlfriend, Betty Jane
Murphy, who had reappeared in his life. As a bachelor, he had
gotten into the normal scrapes associated with being single. Getting
married calmed him down although he suffered his first loss ever to
the Cubs in his first start after the wedding.[25]

---

25. Roy McHugh, "Ask O'Toole, He'll Tell You," *Sport Magazine,*
   August 1962, page 62.

The arrival of Hutchinson as Reds manager could not have been better timed. Hutch, at that moment, was the only former pitcher among all big-league skippers. He took great pains to analyze the pitching staff and sought to maximize its strengths and improve its weaknesses. By the end of 1960, only three pitchers—O'Toole, Bob Purkey, and Jim Brosnan—survived Hutch's in-depth scrutiny.

Paul had acquired Brosnan from the St. Louis Cardinals in 1959 before Smith's departure. Brosnan, known more for his literary works than for his mound exploits, had had trouble getting past the fifth or sixth inning as a starter, and the mental strain of not succeeding began to weigh on him. Hutchinson soon convinced him of his value as a reliever. Hutch then acquired the Cubs' Bill Henry to secure the left side of the relief corps. The next step was the acquisition of Joey Jay.

The team Joey Jay joined in the spring of 1961 had a long history in the annals of baseball lore. An English cricket star, Harry Wright, took over a team of amateurs in 1868 and renamed them the Cincinnati Red Stockings. He paid salaries to four of his players. He was determined to make the entire 1869 team one of paid professionals. Over a chorus of amateur dissenters, he did just that and so the first fully paid team became a reality.

The Red Stockings did not belong to a league; there was none at the time. They were, basically, a barnstorming crew much like basketball's Globetrotters and Magicians. They traveled from city to city and toured from coast to coast. In their first season, they won sixty-five consecutive games with one 17-17 tie sandwiched somewhere within their schedule. As they left one town, the upcoming host assembled the best players with the sole idea of beating the mighty Red Stockings. They finally lost to the Atlantics of Brooklyn in an eleven-inning squeaker, 8-7, after going undefeated for nearly two years and 130 contests. In 1876, they joined seven other cities to form the National League.

After years of so-so play, the Reds won their first National League flag and World Championship in 1919 under manager Buck Moran, but were tainted by the Chicago White Sox and their performance in the World Series. Their next flag came in 1939 and the powerful New York Yankees humiliated them in four straight games. The following year, the Reds brought a fully legitimate World Series title to Ohio's Queen City, overtaking the Detroit Tigers in a seven-game set.

The postwar years brought mediocre squads, but in the mid-fifties a group of sluggers arrived to provide the fans with exciting baseball. Led by skipper Birdie Tebbetts, the 1956 Redlegs (a temporary name for six seasons, the result of America's anti-Communist attitude) slammed a record-tying 221 home runs. Rookie Frank Robinson paced the team with thirty-eight round-trippers while four other starters each hit twenty-eight or more. The Cincinnati entry finished a surprising third with a 91-63 record, a mere two games behind the Brooklyn Dodgers.

The Redlegs dropped to fourth in both 1957 and 1958 and Tebbetts departed during the latter campaign. Robinson was on the verge of becoming a superstar, belting twenty-nine and thirty-nine homers, respectively, over those two years en route to the Hall of Fame. Brooks Lawrence, who won nineteen games in 1956, went 16-13 in 1957 and right-hander Bob Purkey came over from the Pirates in time for 1958. He picked up a knuckleball and became a mainstay on the Redleg staff, going 17-11 with seventeen completions.

Jimmy Dykes, fresh from a three-year hiatus during which he did not manage, succeeded Tebbetts. His 1953 Philadelphia Athletics and 1954 Baltimore Orioles had racked up a total of 195 losses and two seventh-place results. He took over the Redlegs and guided them to a 24-17 finish. His stay was temporary and Mayo Smith, who had been fired as the Philadelphia Phillies' skipper, took over the recently re-renamed Reds. New Reds general manager Frank Lane, who had started in Cincinnati but made his reputation in the American League as a fearless trader of ballplayers, fired Smith after a 35-45 start and brought Fred Hutchinson aboard as field boss for the duration of the 1959 season.

Hutchinson had been a good starting pitcher for the Detroit Tigers, having averaged more than fifteen victories in the 1946–50 span. He took over in mid-1952 as manager of the worst Tiger team ever to take the field and struggled to a 27-56 mark. He had the team in fifth place within two years. He left to take the helm of the Cardinals, delivering a second-place finish in 1957. After arriving in Cincinnati in the middle of the 1959 campaign, his gentle but firm persuasion coaxed a 39-35 result and an eventual tie for fifth place. The Reds paced the league in most offensive categories: batting, slugging, and run production. Frank Robinson, who hit .311 with thirty-six homers and 125 RBI, was joined by Vada Pinson, who added a .316 average to the mix. The pitching staff had the league's second worst ERA. Purkey slumped to 13-18 but Don Newcombe contributed a 13-8 effort with an ERA of 3.18 for his last hurrah before retirement.

In 1960, the Reds suffered a form of malaise. Robinson and Pinson both dropped below .300 and the team, so offensively oriented over the past half-dozen years, could not produce a .300 hitter. Purkey bounced back with a 17-11 mark to go with his 3.60 ERA but the Reds fell to sixth. Jim O'Toole, a young lefty, went 12-12, also with an ERA of 3.60, completing seven of his thirty-one starts.

Hutchinson sought to strengthen both pitching and defense. He traded fan favorite and defensive whiz Roy McMillan to the Braves in exchange for a former bonus baby named Joey Jay. He acquired Gene Freese, a solid-hitting third baseman, from the White Sox and took a chance by moving Eddie Kasko permanently into McMillan's old spot. These three moves and the foundation put in place in earlier years set the stage for a dream season for the Cincinnati Reds.

1961: The Cincinnati Reds' Pennant Season

Events from the preseason did not bode well for the Reds of Fred Hutchinson. Reds general manager Gabe Paul left spring training to join the new Houston franchise and supervise the stocking and management of the expansion team to be formed in 1962. Owner Powell Crosley passed away suddenly just before the club's departure from the South. The Reds' off-season acquisitions impressed no one and the consensus was that the team was destined for the middle of the second division.

Bill Russell of the Boston Celtics put on a total show of his basketball prowess on April 11. He scored thirty points, blocked eight shots, and snatched thirty-eight rebounds to lead the Green to their fourth championship in five years. Russell, known primarily for the magnificent defense he brought to the court, showed his offensive skills as well.

On April 11, Jim O'Toole opened the campaign at home with a four-hit victory over the Cubs. After the Reds won their next two games, Joey Jay made his debut on April 15. Jay lasted only four innings in a five-inning, rain-delayed game and gave up two runs in a 4-0 loss to the Cardinals. Ernie Broglio, who had won twenty-one games in 1960 for the Redbirds, got the win. The next day the Cards hammered O'Toole in the fifth inning and won 5-3 behind Ray Sadecki.

A crisis in Cuba was heating up. Cuban anti-Castro insurgents, supported by the United States, were executing attacks on Castro loyalists. Meanwhile, the Soviet Union offered help to the island nation in beating back the rebels. The United States warned the Soviets against intervention. This eventually led to the ill-fated Bay of Pigs, where insurrectionary forces seeking to overthrow Fidel Castro were not given the promised American support and were repelled by Cuban forces. Many of the invaders were captured and executed.

O'Toole took the mound again on April 20 in San Francisco and suffered his second straight setback, 2-1. The Reds traveled south and Jay faced the Dodgers, seeking his first win as a Red. He pitched well, giving up only four hits and one run, but the punchless Reds managed none and lost 1-0.

On April 26, the Dodgers' Don Zimmer belted a home run in the bottom of the eleventh to beat the Reds 3-2, spoiling O'Toole's six innings of one-run ball. After another setback at the hands of Chicago, the team returned to Cincinnati with Jay scheduled to start on April 28, but cold weather forced a postponement. That same night, Braves ace left-hander Warren Spahn tossed his second career no-hitter to beat the Giants 1-0. Spahn, who had come up to stay with the Braves in 1946 at the age of twenty-five, had thrown his first hitless gem only seven months earlier, in September 1960, against the Phillies.

On April 29, the crew from MIT overcame an eleven-year drought and beat the Yale rowers on the Housatonic River in Connecticut.

Joey Jay started against the defending world champion Pirates on the twenty-ninth. He gave up five earned runs in six innings and dropped to 0-3 with a 4.00 ERA, and the Reds suffered their seventh straight loss. The next day, in Milwaukee, Willie Mays, of the San Francisco Giants, slammed four home runs in one game and became only the ninth man ever to accomplish that feat. Back in Cincinnati, Bob Purkey, the mainstay of the Reds staff, broke the team's losing streak at eight, winning the nightcap of a twin bill to boost his record to 3-1. At the end of April, the Reds languished in last place at 6-10. So far, the prognosticators were on target.

May 1961 commenced on a bright note when lefty O'Toole went the distance at home and beat the Phillies 3-2. He gave up only six hits in the process while striking out nine batters. In that same series, Jay finally picked up win number one as he one-hit the Phils and struck out seven. Johnny Callison reached Joey for a first-inning single. The Reds took their fifth straight contest and reached the .500 mark at 10-10.

On Friday May 5, a Navy commander and test pilot from Derry, New Hampshire, Alan Shepard, became the first American in space as he enjoyed a ride 115 miles above Earth. Russian cosmonaut Yuri Gagarin had actually orbited Earth earlier in the year, but he had been simply a passenger; on the other hand, Shepard actually took control of the craft while cruising at forty-eight hundred miles per hour.

That same historic weekend, Carryback, a 5-2 favorite ridden by Johnny Sellers, came from eleventh in a field of fifteen to win the Kentucky Derby at Churchill Downs by three-quarters of a length.

The Reds continued their winning ways with O'Toole taking the nightcap of a Sunday doubleheader in Milwaukee. He shut out the Braves on five hits and struck out seven to record his third win of the young season as the Reds extended their streak to eight victories. Three days later, back in Cincinnati, Jay scattered six hits in seven innings to beat the Cardinals 3-2. Vada Pinson helped his cause with a two-run homer.

The Pirates then came into town and hammered both Purkey and O'Toole, ending the skein of victories at nine. The team moved on to Philadelphia and the Phillies, who were destined for the cellar in 1961, proved ever handy as Jay got the Reds back on to their winning ways with a 4-2 complete-game victory over the home team. He struck out seven, and Freese and Robinson supplied all the runs with fence-clearers. Purkey followed up with a 2-1 win the next day.

Back at home for a weekend series with the Braves, O'Toole started off by winning his fourth game 3-2, giving up just five hits. Gus Bell and Freese again brought in all the necessary runs with homers.

Jay picked up his fourth win on Sunday with a complete-game, 7-6 win. Bell once again provided the heroics and won the game with a last-of-the-ninth double with a man on. The Braves took the second game of the twin bill before nearly 26,000 fans at Crosley Field.

Carryback, under Sellers again, won the Preakness on Saturday, May 20. The placid American landscape we all knew as the 1950s was beginning to metamorphose into the tumultuous '60s. In Montgomery, Alabama, a mob attacked a busload of Freedom Fighters who had arrived in that city to assist local Negroes. On May 22, martial law was declared and twenty people were injured.

In Cincinnati, the Giants overcame the Reds with three unearned runs against O'Toole and won 5-4 despite a three-run homer by Pinson in the bottom of the eighth. Two days later, Jay beat the Phillies for his fifth straight success, 5-4. He went eight innings and gave up only four hits and two runs while striking out six.

The Reds flew out to the West Coast and met the Giants for a Memorial Day doubleheader. O'Toole and Jim Maloney earned the wins as the Reds swept the Giants 7-6 and 6-4 before nearly 42,000 fans. Pinson went four for ten in the two games with three runs batted in, and the two victories propelled the Reds into a tie for first with San Francisco at 25-16. Jay finished off the month in

Los Angeles and went seven and a third innings to escape with his sixth straight victory despite allowing six runs. Gene Freese hit a tie-breaking home run in the top of the seventh frame to give Joey the boost he needed for the win. It was Freese's second round-tripper of the game. The Reds went 20-6 during the month of May and Jay contributed six wins without a setback.

On June 3, Carryback went to the post as a 9–20 favorite to take the Belmont Stakes, the third leg of horse racing's Triple Crown. The colt had become a fan favorite with his come-from-behind victories, but this time it was not to be. Sellers got wedged between two other horses and Carryback finished a dismal seventh of nine entries. Sherluck, mounted by twenty-one-year-old Panamanian native Braulio Baeza, went off at 65-1 and took the race by two and a half lengths, paying $132.10 for a two-dollar bet.

That weekend, the Reds faced Chicago at Crosley Field, but the Cubbies snapped their six-game win streak, 7-6, and took Saturday's game as well. On Sunday, June 4, the Reds split a doubleheader with the Cubs. Jim Maloney won the opener 3-1 but O'Toole got hammered in the nightcap, 8-2, dropping his record to 5-5. On Monday, Jay followed up with a no-decision although the Reds beat the Braves 5-3 on Frank Robinson's two-run homer in the bottom of the eighth. Purkey improved to 6-3 the next day, when Freese's tenth home run powered a 7-3 win. Maloney won his fourth game as the Reds took the series finale 10-8 in a slugfest that included eight home runs, six of which were poked by Milwaukee. The tribe set a record that day by hammering four consecutive round-trippers in the top of the seventh inning. Maloney was cruising along with a 10-2 lead when Eddie Mathews and Hank Aaron cleared the fences. Marshall Bridges relieved Maloney and promptly gave up homers to Joe Adcock and Frank Thomas.

Forty-four- (or forty-seven; it depends on with whom you spoke) year-old light-heavyweight Archie Moore went fifteen rounds to beat twenty-six-year-old Guilio Rinaldi of Italy on points before ninety-five hundred fans at New York's Madison Square Garden.

The Reds journeyed to St. Louis, and on June 9, Jim O'Toole took a pounding, giving up six runs in three and a third innings. Jay got the Reds rolling again the next afternoon with a 4-2 victory over the Cards. Second baseman Don Blasingame pounded out four hits against his former mates and accounted for two of the scores with a two-run single in the fifth. Jay actually entered the ninth having given up only four hits, but Hutchinson promptly replaced him with Bill Henry after Joey gave up two quick hits while getting but one out. The Reds swept the Sunday twin bill and moved back into a tie with the Dodgers. Bob Purkey picked up win number seven in the 9-3 nightcap. Freese batted in six runs over the two games.

After O'Toole's no-decision loss to the Pirates, Jay once again righted the team, this time with an 8-1 win over the Buccaneers at Forbes Field. He was the beneficiary of Freese's largesse one more time, as the third baseman continued to drive in runs. He got the game going, clearing the bases with a double in the top of the first.

Jim O'Toole, struggling of late, had fallen to 5-6. On June 18, the Reds swept the Phillies in Philadelphia, 7-2 and 10-0. O'Toole evened his record at 6-6 with the second-game whitewash.

The Reds came home and split a midweek doubleheader with the Cardinals. Despite Jay's loss in the second game, 6-3, the Reds maintained their lead by one and a half games with a 39-24 mark. The loss snapped Joey's eight-game win streak and he dropped to 8-4. Two days later, Frank Robinson drove in three runs to lead the team past the Redbirds 7-5 and help Purkey to his ninth win. Robbie, who had started slowly but would eventually earn the league's Most Valuable Player award, had driven in twelve runs in the past five games. He had now tallied seventeen homers.

O'Toole was stymied in his quest for his seventh win on June 23 but the Reds beat the Dodgers anyway, 5-4. Light-hitting Eddie Kasko drove in the ubiquitous Freese with the winning tally. Freese had doubled in the bottom of the ninth to start the inning. The Reds went three games up on Los Angeles with their ninth triumph in ten games.

At New York's Downing Stadium, college star athletes treated track-and-field fans to a series of outstanding performances. Frank Budd of Villanova ran the one-hundred-yard dash in 9.2 seconds to set a new mark while

Ralph Boston equaled his own record of twenty-six and a quarter inches in the broad jump. At the same meet, John Thomas lost the high jump to Bob Avant despite Thomas's seven-foot leap.

The next day Jay set back the Dodgers 3-2 to improve to 9-4. He required help from Jim Brosnan for the final inning and a third. Cincinnati struck right away, scoring all its runs in the home first. Jay had held the Dodgers scoreless through the sixth inning, when shortstop Chico Cardenas threw wildly to first in a double-play attempt and allowed a run to score. That miscue set up the second run and rattled Jay, prompting Hutch to take Brosnan away from his typewriter and bring him on in relief.

The Cubs came to town and went on a binge that must have been the highlight of their dismal season. They swept the Reds in a two-day, three-game series and scored thirty-two runs in the process. Over the three games, they banged out forty-two hits and hit nine home runs. Chicago nailed Purkey for eight runs in four innings in a 16-5 first-game rout. O'Toole became the Cubs' victim in the nightcap when he gave up six more runs. He was relieved by Purkey, who merely verified that he had no stuff that day either, giving up one more score in a one-inning appearance.

On June 30, the Reds once again invaded Milwaukee, but this time they were wounded and shell-shocked from the pounding they had received at the hands of the Cubs. They turned to Jay, and once again he provided the lift to get them on a positive track. He shut out the Braves 4-0, despite giving up eleven base hits. He halted their streak of ten straight games in which they had hit at least one homer per game, twenty-two round-trippers in all. The Reds, with a 45-28 mark, were still in first place by two and a half games over Los Angeles; in the American League, Detroit led the Yankees by two. In the junior circuit, Mickey Mantle and Roger Maris had been clearing the fences with amazing regularity. Together they banged out fifty-one home runs, with Maris accounting for twenty-seven of them. People were beginning to discuss the possibility of someone beating the Babe's magical sixty.

On Sunday, July 3, The Reds took a twin bill from the Braves, 8-5 and 4-3, after a 5-1 setback the previous day. O'Toole had started the opener but gave up all five runs in five innings, but because the game went thirteen frames, he was not involved in the decision. Purkey took the second game to go 10-4. First-sacker Gordy Coleman went eight for ten in the doubleheader and boosted his bat mark to .303 in what would be the season of his life. Jay followed up with his second shutout in a row, doing in the Pirates 2-0 on three hits. Freese again supplied all the scoring Jay needed, with a solo shot in the fifth.

The team journeyed to the West Coast, and O'Toole, going the distance, stopped the Giants 3-2 for his seventh win. Coleman hit a home run and Pinson contributed two defensive gems to rob Harvey Kuenn and Orlando Cepeda of base hits.

In Ketchum, Idaho, Ernest Hemingway was buried in a cemetery near the Saw Tooth Mountain Range and the Wood River, where he used to fish.

On Friday, July 7, Reds rookie right-hander Ken Hunt improved to 9-4 while lowering his ERA to 3.38. He was the beneficiary of four unearned runs as the Dodgers' Frank Howard dropped a fly ball in the fourth inning of an 11-7 Cincinnati victory. Hunt had given the staff a tremendous boost in the first half of the season, but he would never win another major league game. In the contest that followed as part of a doubleheader, Purkey captured his eleventh win, 4-1. The Dodgers took Saturday's game and Jay again reversed the team's fortunes, with a 14-3 win on the last day before the All-Star break.

At the midseason interlude, the Cincinnati Reds led the National League by five games over the Dodgers. The pitching had surpassed all expectations with Jay and Purkey 12-4 and 11-4, respectively. O'Toole stood at 7-7 but had a good ERA of 3.45. Frank Robinson placed in the top echelon in all offensive categories and was hitting .328 with twenty-three home runs and seventy RBI. The Tigers still led the American League by half a game, while

Maris and Mantle had hit thirty-three and twenty-nine home runs, respectively.

After the Nationals beat the Americans 5-4 in the first of two All-Star games in 1961, the leagues got back to the business of championship baseball. O'Toole started the season's second half on July 13 with a complete-game, 4-3 win over the Cubs in Cincinnati. Jay raised his record to 13-4 at the expense of the Cubs two days later with another route-going outing. He had a 2-0 shutout until Ron Santo hit a solo home run in the bottom of the ninth.

Valery Brumel of Russia jumped a record 7'4" to beat John Thomas by two inches before 55,000 track enthusiasts in Moscow's Lenin Stadium. In that same event, Ralph Boston, of the United States, set a world record in the broad jump at 27'1¾."

Hunt started on the sixteenth and went down to the Cubs 4-2, to initiate a Cincinnati losing streak that would reach six games. On July 20, the Dodgers hammered Jay with a 10-1 rout. He gave up nine runs in five innings as the Reds suffered their fifth straight setback. Two days later, the winless span increased to six when Hunt lost to Jack Sanford and the Giants 8-3. The Reds then swept the Giants in a twin bill 6-5 and 10-1, Purkey and O'Toole both going the distance. Jerry Lynch, playing in the outfield, hit two home runs in the opener; Robinson and Pinson provided the fireworks in the second.

The Reds left home and headed to Milwaukee, where Jay won his fourteenth game with a 9-3 win over the Braves. He beat Warren Spahn, who, at this point in the season, was struggling with a 9-12 record. However, the forty-year-old left-hander would finish at 21-13, a twenty-game winner for the twelfth, and not last, time in his career. In defeating the Braves, the Reds led the Dodgers by two games.

On July 25, golfing great Walter Hagen was picked by the Golf Writers Association to receive the first Walter H. Hagen Award on the eve of the Professional Golf Association tournament, which was to be played in Chicago. Hagen had won the PGA each year from 1924–27 and had taken the British Open four times.

The Yankees swept a doubleheader from the White Sox on the twenty-fifth while Maris slugged four home runs, giving him forty for the season. The Yanks took over the American League lead when the Tigers dropped a game to the fledgling but surprising Los Angeles Angels and fell to second. Back in the National League, Hunt pitched well but lost to Lew Burdette 2-0 in Milwaukee. The Reds' lead shrank to one game as the Dodgers whipped the futile Phillies 7-2.

In the series finale at Milwaukee, Purkey beat the Braves and Joey Jay's buddy Carl Willey 2-1 to gain win number thirteen. In the top of the ninth, with the bases full, Pinson attempted a steal of home. He was able to knock the ball from catcher Sammy White's hand, and scored the eventual winning run.

The Reds moved on to Wrigley Field. O'Toole opened the series with a 4-3 win over the Cubs. Frank Robinson hit two home runs and contributed three RBI. The Dodgers kept pace, beating Pittsburgh 6-4. The next day was Old-Timers Day at Yankee Stadium and Whitey Ford helped honor the retired ballplayers with a 5-4 win over the Orioles, increasing the Yankees' lead to a full two games when Detroit fell to the Minnesota Twins by the same score. Meanwhile, the Cubs routed Jay in the sixth inning and nailed him for six runs, winning 7-6. The Dodgers, for their part, overcame the Pirates 5-4 and took over the league lead. The next day, the Reds split with the Cubs and the Dodgers won over the Buccaneers 7-3, edging one and a half games up. The Reds took a 63-40 record into August.

On Monday, July 31, the major leagues played the season's second All-Star Game in Boston. The game ended in a 1-1 tie, and the score seemed appropriate for this four-year experiment. The extra games, played to raise pension funds for the older ballplayers, succeeded in their objective, but taxed the players with an onerous travel schedule.

Seventy-one Air National Guard and Reserve units received advisory notices of a pending callup due to increased activity in Berlin by Soviet troops. The notices affected about 28,000 part-time air personnel.

On August 2, the baseball wars resumed and O'Toole and Jay each won an end of a doubleheader over Philadelphia. The hapless Phillies were in the midst of a twenty-three-game losing streak. Coleman, Robinson, and Freese helped in the 3-2 and 4-2 victories. The next game saw the Reds regain possession of first place with a 7-1 win over Philadelphia, giving them fifteen wins against no losses to the boys of the City of Brotherly Love.

Still at home, Brosnan relieved Purkey and was the beneficiary of Robinson's ninth-inning, game-winning double to beat the Pirates 5-4. The next day, the Reds and Hunt lost to the Bucs, 11-7, and the Reds were back in a tie with Los Angeles. On Sunday, August 6, the Dodgers took over the lead as Jay dropped the first game of a twin bill to the Pirates 9-4. O'Toole salvaged the second but Brosnan again got the win when Pinson ended the contest with a ninth-inning home run.

After two losses to the Cardinals in St. Louis, Jay shut out the conveniently scheduled Phillies 5-0 on August 9, giving up six hits. However, the Reds had slipped to three games behind Los Angeles. By the eleventh, the Reds had dropped five of their previous seven games as the Giants and Juan Marichal beat O'Toole 4-2 at Candlestick Park. Purkey suffered another loss to the Giants, but the Reds finally got back to the business of chasing a flag with an 8-1 rout of San Francisco. They now trailed the Dodgers by three and a half games.

They ventured to Southern California and on August 15 Jay came through in his role as a stopper, winning 5-4 for his seventeenth success. He celebrated his twenty-sixth birthday by beating Sandy Koufax, giving up six hits. Kasko also donned the hero uniform by poking four singles to annoy and disrupt Koufax. The next day, while Maris hit home runs number forty-seven and forty-eight, O'Toole and Purkey did a double whitewash of Los Angeles for wins fourteen and twelve, respectively, before more than 72,000 fans. The Reds left Los Angeles in a first-place tie.

They traveled home for the start of a weekend series with St. Louis. Ken Johnson, who had been let go by the Kansas City

Athletics, won his fourth game as a Red, beating the Cards 6-3, the team's fifth consecutive success. Jay threw the staff's fifth straight complete game and beat the Cards 3-1 for win number eighteen. The Dodgers lost, and Cincinnati was now three games up. Both the Reds and the Dodgers suffered losses on Sunday, August 20.

The Reds had Monday off and prepared to host the Giants and Dodgers for four games apiece in a six-day stretch. At this point, Cincinnati led by three games over Los Angeles and seven over San Francisco. The Giants took the first three games of their series, hammering Jay in the second game. He had retired nineteen straight batters from the first inning through the eighth but was behind 2-0 entering the ninth. In that frame, the Giants hopped on him and his relief for twelve runs and ran away with a 14-0 victory. Two days later, O'Toole salvaged the final game 8-5 for his thirteenth win.

Los Angeles came into town after dropping two of three at St. Louis and split the four-game series with the Reds. Jay started the third contest but left, behind 5-1. Reliable Gene Freese got the home team rolling with a three-run homer in the seventh, narrowing the gap to 5-4. In the bottom of the eighth, Chico Cardenas scored the winning run after sending Jerry Lynch home with a triple. Ken Johnson won the nightcap 8-3. At the end of the crucial home stand, the Reds led Los Angeles by three and a half and the Giants by six and a half.

In Pittsburgh, O'Toole beat the Pirates 3-0 on August 29 with help from Jim Maloney in the ninth. Purkey took his tenth loss the following day, falling to Tom Sturdivant 3-1. The Reds enjoyed an off day but increased their lead as the Braves defeated the Dodgers. August came to a close and Cincinnati led the National League by three games with a record of 79-53.

Because the American League expanded to ten teams in time for the 1961 season and the senior circuit waited until 1962, the Nationals played a 154-game season versus the Americans' 162 contests. The seasons began and started together, so the National League had extra time off during the year. Thus, the Reds took a second day off and started their final push for the flag on September

2. Jay faced the Phillies at Shibe Park and came away winning his nineteenth game 7-4, with assistance from Bill Henry in the ninth. Pinson and Lynch also helped with home runs.

The next day, the Phillies stopped the Reds' mastery of them at seventeen consecutive games. Jim O'Toole started and was pitching well when he slipped trying to field a sacrifice bunt and could not make a play. He then walked Jim Owens, the opposing pitcher, and after a run-scoring double play, Johnny Callison banged a triple and the Phils were on their way to victory. A twin bill followed and the teams split, Ken Johnson winning his sixth and Ken Hunt losing his tenth.

The team met St. Louis on September 5 and Purkey won number fifteen 5-2, taking a shutout into the ninth inning. Jay started against the Cards the next day and lasted a mere third of an inning in his quest for his twentieth victory. He emerged unscathed as the Reds tied the score before eventually losing. In an unusual home-and-home series, O'Toole followed up with an eight-inning outing at Crosley but was not involved in the decision when the Reds overcame the Cards in the bottom of the tenth on Kasko's game-winning single. Brosnan earned the win in relief. The Dodgers were splitting a pair with the Giants, so the Reds' lead stayed at two games.

On September 12, Jim O'Toole gave up ten hits and went the distance in a 7-2 win over the Cubs, improving to 15-9. Wally Post hit his nineteenth home run and Darrell Johnson drove in three runs to boost the Reds' lead to four and a half games. In the American League, the Yankees won their thirteenth straight and one-hundredth game of the year while surging to an eleven-and-a-half-game lead over Detroit.

On September 13, President John F. Kennedy was slated to nominate Thurgood Marshall to one of three new judgeships in the second (New York) district Court of Appeals. Marshall, chief counsel for the National Association for the Advancement of Colored People (NAACP), had to be confirmed by the U.S. Senate. Prior to that, he had to face the Senate Judiciary Committee, which was chaired by Sen. James O. Eastland of Mississippi, an ardent foe of desegregation.

Jay finally won number twenty, beating the Braves and his old friend Carleton Willey 1-0 at Crosley. The Dodgers fell behind another game, losing to the Pirates 8-2. On September 15, the Yankees broke the team home-run record of 221 shared by the 1947 Giants and 1956 Redlegs by hitting two fence-clearers to reach 223. Oddly enough, neither homer was hit by Maris or Mantle.

September 16 saw a twenty-one-year-old golfer named Jack Nicklaus win the U.S. Amateur tourney at Pebble Beach in California. Nicklaus, from Columbus, Ohio, and a senior at Ohio State University, took the prize for the second time.

That same day, O'Toole won his sixteenth game. He had entered the game in relief as the fourth of five Cincinnati hurlers in a 3-2 victory over the Phils. The Reds scored all three runs in the bottom of the seventh. Philadelphia first baseman Don Demeter muffed a double-play ball hit by Pinson, and that resulted in one run. Pinch hitter deluxe Jerry Lynch drove in the next two with a double to secure the win. Lynch picked up nineteen hits in forty-seven pinch-hit at bats in 1961, a .404 clip.

After Purkey suffered his eleventh loss of the season at the hands of the Phillies, O'Toole won his seventeenth game on September 19 by beating the Pirates 10-1. Gene Freese hit homers twenty-five and twenty-six and drove in four runs. Jay followed with his twenty-first victory, giving up seven walks but still beating Pittsburgh 3-2. Post sealed the win with a two-run homer in the home eighth.

O'Toole lowered the Reds' magic number to three and won his eighteenth game in the process with a sloppy 10-6 victory over the Giants. Blasingame hit three doubles and Coleman two home runs to pace the attack. Jay was even sloppier the next day as he gave up seven runs in three and a third innings in a loss to San Francisco, 12-5.

After a day off, on September 26, Brosnan relieved Purkey and won his tenth game. He clinched the flag to boot, as the Reds beat the Cubs in Chicago 6-3 and the Dodgers lost to the Pirates. O'Toole won his nineteenth against those same Pirates after two more days off. The season ended and the Reds won their first pennant since 1940. They boasted a 93-61 record and bested second-place Los Angeles by four games.

It was a definite team victory. The position players shared the hero-a-day honors and Frank Robinson earned the MVP by hitting .323 with thirty-seven homers and 124 RBI. Freese seemed always to fill the void with his twenty-six round-trippers. Pinson finished second in the batting race with a .343 mark and Coleman contributed twenty-eight home runs. The trio each batted in eighty-seven runs to nicely complement Robinson. The team led the league in shutouts with twelve and saves with forty and lowered its ERA from 4.00 in 1960 to 3.78. Jay tied Spahn for the most victories with twenty-one and O'Toole placed second in ERA with 3.10. Together, the righty-lefty duo completed twenty-five games.

While Jay slipped to 9-6 in the second part of the season, O'Toole won twelve of his last fourteen decisions. The Reds went 39-30 after the first All-Star Game but the Dodgers could gain only one game. It was truly a great team effort.

The Yankees went into the World Series as 5-2 favorites, but then the Reds had been 60-1 longshots to take the pennant. O'Toole started the first game at Yankee Stadium. He pitched creditably but lost 2-0 to Whitey Ford as Elston Howard and Bill Skowron hit solo home runs. Jay started the second and threw a complete game, winning 6-2, assisted by a Coleman two-run shot.

The series moved to Cincinnati. Purkey also went the distance but came up short 3-2 as Johnny Blanchard hit a pinch home run in the top of the eighth and Maris won the game with a homer in the ninth. In the fourth game, Ford broke Babe Ruth's forty-three-year-old mark of twenty-nine and two-thirds consecutive scoreless innings and won 7-0. O'Toole went five innings, giving up two runs.

Jay came back in the hopes of taking one game at home but lasted only two-thirds of an inning. He gave up four runs and the Yankees regained the world title with a 13-5 smashup of the Reds.

In 1962, under the new ten-team format, the Reds won five more games but finished third to the Giants by only three and a half games. Jay went 21-14 with an ERA of 3.76 while O'Toole slipped to 16-13, giving up an average of 3.50 earned runs. Purkey enjoyed his finest effort, 23-5, while posting an ERA of 2.81. The next year the team slipped to 86-76 and a fifth-place result. O'Toole was his consistent self with seventeen victories but Jay and Purkey plummeted to 7-18 and 6-10, respectively. In 1964 Hutch left the team in August; he had been diagnosed with terminal cancer. The Reds tried to win it for him but came up two games short of the Cardinals. O'Toole once again led the staff, at 17-7, and Jay rebounded to 11-11.

Joey Jay retired from baseball after the 1966 season, during which he was traded to the Braves, who by then occupied Atlanta. He spent some time in the Phillies organization and voluntarily took a trip to the Carolina League in hopes of a big-league return. It was not to be.

Jay became involved in the oil business and other ventures.[26] He is a very private man and, in an article in *Inside Sports* in 1981, requested that no one disclose his residence.

Jim O'Toole retired after spending the 1967 season chasing the American League flag with the White Sox. Once he hung up his spikes, he returned to Cincinnati, where he worked in the real estate and waste-disposal industries.

Jay's lifetime marks amounted to 99-91 with a 3.77 ERA; O'Toole cashed in at 98-84 and 3.57. They were two guys from different sides of the mound who had similar careers, but in a short six-month span they complemented each other perfectly and the result was *one glorious season* for them and for the 1961 Cincinnati Reds.

26. *The Sporting News*, March 7, 1962.

J O E   J A Y
pitcher   Cin. Reds
440

HT: 6:04   WT: 225   BATS: Both
THROWS: Right   BORN: August 15, 1935
HOME: Lutz, Fla.

Acquired from the Braves before the '61 season, Joe developed into the N.L.'s winningest pitcher last year. The big righthander, a former Milwaukee bonus baby, spun four shutouts in 1961. Joe's best game was a one-hit victory over the Philadelphia Phillies.

©T.C.G. PRINTED IN U.S.A.

BIG VICTORY FOR JOE
Joe beat the Yanks in the 2nd game of the 1961 World Series.

MAJOR LEAGUE PITCHING RECORD										
	Games	IP	Won	Lost	Pct	Hits	Runs	ER	SO	BB	ERA
YEAR	34	247	21	10	.677	215	102	97	157	92	3.53
LIFE	149	661	45	34	.570	585	282	253	429	292	3.44

JIM O'TOOLE
pitcher   Cin. Reds
450

HT: 6:00   WT: 192   BATS: Both
THROWS: Left   BORN: Jan. 10, 1937
HOME: Chicago, Illinois

The 19-game winner of 1961 was a key factor in the Reds' surprising pennant victory last year. Jim pitched 3 shutouts and led the staff with a low E.R.A. The righthander won 12 games in 1960.

©T.C.G. PRINTED IN U.S.A.

CRAFTY LEFTY
Jim was a 20 game winner in his rookie minor league season in '58.

MAJOR LEAGUE PITCHING RECORD										
	Games	IP	Won	Lost	Pct	Hits	Runs	ER	SO	BB	ERA
YEAR	39	253	19	9	.679	229	101	87	178	93	3.09
LIFE	102	585	36	30	.545	575	275	245	374	237	3.77

Bibliography

1950: Jim Konstanty& Del Ennis, Philadelphia Phillies

Baumgartner, Stan. "The Brains Behind the Phillies," *Sport Magazine,* January 1951.

———. "The Philadelphia Phillies," *Sport Magazine,* August 1951.

Bjarkman, Peter C. "Philadelphia Phillies, Swooning in the Shadow of the Miracle Whiz Kids," *Encyclopedia of Major League Baseball, National League,* New York: Carroll & Graf, 1993.

Daley, Arthur. "Miracle in Philadelphia," *New York Times Magazine,* September 9, 1950.

Davis, Russ. "King of Swing," *Collier's Magazine* May 1947.

Duncan, Andy. "Jim Konstanty, All-Time Fireman," *Sport Magazine,* May 1951.

Microsoft Corporation. *Total Baseball,* 1994.

Silverman, Al. "The Del Ennis Puzzle," *Sport Magazine,* August 1952.

Williams Edgar. "Comeback Jim Konstanty," *Baseball Digest,* September 1955.

1951: Ned Garver, St. Louis Browns

Bisher, Furman. "How Ned Garver Found His Arm Again," *Sport Magazine,* July 1955.

Burnes, Bob. "The St. Louis Browns," in *Sport Magazine,* April 1951.

Fedo, Michael. *One Shining Season,* New York: Pharos Books, 1991.

Felber, Bill. "St. Louis Browns-Baltimore Orioles: One of the Very Worst and One of the Very Best," *Encyclopedia of Major League Baseball, American League,* New York: Carroll & Graf Publishers, 1993.,

Garver, Ned, as told to Al Silverman, "Life in Last Place," *Sport Magazine,* August 1951.

Golenbock, Peter. *The Spirit of St. Louis: A History of the St. Louis Cardinals and Browns,* New York: Avon Books, 2000.

Lardner, John. "The Man Who Hypnotized the Browns," *Sport Magazine,* July 1950.

Reidenbaugh, Lowell. "Veeck's Midget Steals the Show," The Sporting News *Selects Baseball's 50 Greatest Games,* St. Louis: The Sporting News Publishing Co., 1986.

1952: Bobby Shantz, Philadelphia Athletics

Bricker, Charles. "Ferris Fain's Story a Complicated One," *San Jose Mercury News,* April 20, 1986.

Kiersh, Edward. *Bobby Shantz,* book section from *Where Have You Gone, Vince DiMaggio,* New York: Bantam Books, 1983.

Macht, Norman L. "Philadelphia Athletics-Kansas City Athletics-Oakland A's, Three Families and Three Baseball Epochs," *Encyclopedia of Baseball, American League,* New York: Carroll & Graf, 1993.

Ross, John. "Mighty Mite of the A's," *Sport Magazine,* July 1952.

Shantz, Bobby. As told to Ralph Bernstein, *The Story of Bobby Shantz,* Philadelphia and New York: J. B. Lippincott, 1953.

Stump, Al. "Fearless Ferris Fain," *Sport Magazine,* July 1953.

1952: Hank Sauer, Chicago Cubs

Ahrens, Art. "Chicago Cubs: Sic Transit Gloria Mundi," *Encyclopedia of Major League Baseball, National League,* New York: Carroll & Graf, 1993.

Golenbock, Peter. *Wrigleyville: A Magical History Tour of the Chicago Cubs,* New York: St. Martin's Press, 1996.

Hofman, John C. *Hank Sauer: Most Valuable Player Series,* New York: A. S. Barnes and Company, 1953.

Richman, Milton. "The Sauer Surprise," *Sport Magazine,* October 1952.

Sexauer, Chuck. "Old Man Sauer," *Sport Magazine,* May 1958.

Stump, Al. "Sauer Can't Win," *Sport Magazine,* June 1953.

1953: Harvey Haddix, St. Louis Cardinals

Carlson, Stanley W. "St. Louis Cardinals, Baseball's Perennial Gas House Gang," *Encyclopedia of Major League Baseball, National League*, New York: Carroll & Graf, 1993.

Golenbock, Peter. *The Spirit of St. Louis: A History of the St. Louis Cardinals and Browns*, New York: Avon Books, 2000.

Johnson, George. "Haddix Has IT!" *Sport Magazine*, March 1954.

Reidenbaugh, Lowell. "Haddix Discovers Perfect Way to Lose," *The Sporting News Selects Baseball's 50 Greatest Games*, St. Louis: The Sporting News Publishing Co., 1986.

Stockton, J. Roy, "The St. Louis Cardinals," *Sport Magazine*, January 1951.

1953: Bob Porterfield & Mickey Vernon, Washington Senators

Bjarkman, Peter. "Washington Senators-Minnesota Twins: Expansion-Era Baseball Comes to the American League," *Encyclopedia of Major League Baseball, American League*, New York: Carrol & Graf, 1993.

Furlong, Bill. "The Silent Senator," *Sport Magazine*, October 1953.

Furlong, William Barry. "The Senators' Prize Castoff," *The Saturday Evening Post*, August 8, 1954.

Hann, Ralph. "The Making of Blue Ridge Bob," *Sport Magazine*, February 1954.

1953: Al Rosen, Cleveland Indians

Benson, John, Tony Blengino, and Fred Matos. *Baseball's Top 100: The Best Individual Seasons of All Time*, Wilton Conn.: Diamond Library, 1995.

Cuddy, Don, "Big Chief Rosen," *Sport Magazine,* April 1954.

Eckhouse, Morris A. "Cleveland Indians, Recent Wahoo Woes Overshadow Cleveland's Baseball Tradition," *Encyclopedia of Major League Baseball*, New York: Carroll & Graf, 1993.

Gershman, Michael. *Indians Greats, Total Indians*, New York: Penguin Books, 1996.

Hoynes, Paul. *The Indians History, Total Indians*, New York: Penguin Books, 1996.

Kahn, Roger. *How the Weather Was*, New York: Harper & Row Publishers, 1973.

Ribalow, Harold U., and Meir Z. Ribalow. *The Jew in American Sports*, 4th edition. New York: Hippocrene Books, 1966.

Rosen, Al (as told to Milton Richman). "They Pay Off in Runs Batted In," *Sport Magazine*, October 1954.

Torry, Jack. *Endless Summers: The Fall and Rise of the Cleveland Indians,* South Bend, Ind.: Diamond Communications, 1996.

1954: Dusty Rhodes & Johnny Antonelli, New York Giants

Bisher, Furman. "The Dizzy Dean of Pinch-Hitters," in *Sport Magazine,* February 1955.

Daley, Arthur. "It's Not Done With Mirrors," the *New York Times,* October 1, 1954.

Frommer, Harvey. *New York City Baseball: The Last Golden Age,* San Diego, New York, London: Harcourt, Brace, Jovanovich, 1992.

Gershman, Michael. *Baseball Engagement Book,* Boston: Houghton Mifflin Co., 1992.

Graham, Frank. "The New York Giants," *Sport Magazine,* July 1951.

Greene, Lee. *The Baseball Life of Willie Mays,* New York: Scholastic Book Services, 1955.

Hano, Arnold, "The Four Days of Dusty Rhodes," *Sport Magazine,* October 1959.

Hirschberg, Al. "Johnny Antonelli, From Bonus Baby to Big-Leaguer," *Sport Magazine,* June 1955.

Hynd, Noel. *The Giants of the Polo Grounds,* Dallas: Taylor, 1995.

Kiersh, Edward. "All-Stars of Yesterday, Johnny Antonelli Owns Prosperous Tire Company," *Sporting News,* July 12,1982.

Madden, Bill. "Dusty Rhodes, Colossus to Tugboat," *Sporting News,* October 20, 1979.

Noble, John Wesley. "What they Say in the Dugouts about the San Francisco Giants," *Sport Magazine,* June 1958.

Stein, Fred. "New York Giants—San Francisco Giants A Tale of Two Cities," *Encyclopedia of Major League Baseball—National League,* New York: Carroll & Graf Publishers, 1993.

1955: Vic Power, Kansas City Athletics (New York Yankees)

Lebovitz, Hal. "The True Story of Vic Power," *Sport Magazine,* August 1959.

Orr, Jack. "Were the Yankees Wrong on Vic Power?" *Sport Magazine,* September 1954.

Peary, Danny. "Interview with Vic Power," *Cult Baseball Players,* New York: Simon and Schuster, 1990.

Peary, Danny. "Vic Power Remembers His Playing Days," *Sports Collectors Digest,* March 9, 1990.

Schecter, Leonard. "Vic Power's Wonderful New World," the Sport Special, *Sport Magazine*, May 1963.

"Vic Power: He's Top Banana in Cleveland Now," *Sport Magazine*, July 1960.

Williams, Joe. "Negro Player Yanks Traded Set as Regular," *New York World Tribune Sun*, March 3, 1954.

1956: Don Newcombe, Brooklyn Dodgers

Bjarkman, Peter C. "Brooklyn Dodgers—Los Angeles Dodgers: From Daffiness Boys to the Boys of Summer and the Myth of America's Team," *Encyclopedia of Major League Baseball, National League*, New York: Carroll & Graf, 1993.

Foorman, Ross, *"Don Newcombe Makes Pitch for HOF"* (Hall of Fame), *Sports Collectors Digest*, June 3, 1994.

Frommer, Harvey. *New York City Baseball: The Last Golden Age*, Orlando, Fla.: Harcourt, Brace, Jovanovich, 1992.

Kahn, Roger. *The Era 1947–1957, When the Yankees, the Giants, and the Dodgers Ruled the World*, New York: Ticknor and Fields, 1993.

Newcombe, Don (as told to Milton Gross). *"I'm No Quitter,"* Saturday Evening Post, March 9, 1957.

Shapiro, Michael. *The Last Good Season*, New York: Broadway Books, 2003.

Snider, Duke, with Bill Gilbert. *The Duke of Flatbush*, New York: Zebra Books, 1988.

Waterman, Guy. "Racial Pioneering on the Mound, Don Newcombe's Social and Psychological Ordeal," *A Journal of Baseball History and Social Policy Perspectives*, vol. 1, no. 2, spring 1993.

———. "Grace Under Pressure," *The Baseball Research Journal*, no. 23, 1994.

1957: Lew Burdette, Milwaukee Braves

Buege, Bob. *The Milwaukee Braves, A Baseball Eulogy*. Milwaukee, Wisc.: Douglas American Sports Publications, 1988.

Burdette, Lou (as told to Lou Chapman). "What the Spitball Has Done for Me," *New York Journal American*, June 30, 1957.

Driver, David, "The Pride of Nitro," *Goldenseal*, fall 1998.

Eckhouse, Morris. "Boston Braves–Milwaukee Braves–Atlanta Braves: More Woes Than Wahoos for Baseball's Wanderers," *Encyclopedia of Major League Baseball, National League*, New York: Carroll & Graf, 1993.

Kahn, Roger. "Lew Burdette, Professional Pitcher," *Sport Magazine*, February, 1959.

Silverman, Al. "Man of the Year," in *Sport Magazine*, March 1958.

Walfoort, Cleon. "Forget Burdette? Bombers Can't Do It," *The Sporting News*, October 16, 1957.

1958: Jackie Jensen, Boston Red Sox

Hirschberg, Al. *The Jackie Jensen Story.* New York: Julian Messner, 1960.

————. "What Do They Want from Jackie Jensen?" *Sport Magazine*, September 1958.

Ivor-Campbell, Frederick. "The Boston Red Sox: Their Foot Shall Slide . . . Baseball's Most Potent Myth," *Encyclopedia of Major League Baseball—American League*, New York: Carroll & Graf Publishers, 1993.

Martin, George. *The Golden Boy: A Biography of Jackie Jensen.* Portsmouth, N.H.: Peter E. Randall Publisher, 2000.

Povich, Shirley. "Jackie Jensen, The Yankees' Greatest Mistake," *Sport Magazine*, December 1952.

Stump, Al. "How Jackie Jensen Found Himself," *Sport Magazine*, February 1955.

1959: Bob Shaw, Chicago White Sox

Hines, Rick. "Bob Shaw Was Big Man for '59 Chisox," *Sports Collectors Digest*, March 8, 1991.

Isaacs, Stan. "Nobody Laughs at Bob Shaw Now," *Sport Magazine*, July 1960.

Kremenko, Barney. "They Always Holler When I'm Winning," *Sporting News*, July 30, 1966.

Lindberg, Richard C. "Chicago White Sox: Second Class in the Second City," *Encyclopedia of Major League Baseball, American League*. New York: Carroll & Graf, 1993.

"Bob Shaw: All He Wanted was a Chance," *Sport Magazine*, July 1960, page 65.

1959: Harvey Kuenn, Detroit Tigers

Cope, Myron. "Baseball's Biggest Trade Two Years Later," *The Sport Special, Sport Magazine*, August 1962.

Eckhouse, Morris A. "Detroit Tigers, the Cornerstone of Detroit Baseball is Stability," *Encyclopedia of Major League Baseball, American League*. New York: Carroll & Graf, 1993.

Paxton, Harry T. "This Bonus Boy Was A Bargain," *Saturday Evening Post*, May 8, 1954.

Middlesworth, Hal. "Call Him 'Keen,'" *Sport Magazine*, April 1954.

1960: Dick Groat & Vern Law, Pittsburgh Pirates

Adomites, Paul. "The Pittsburgh Pirates: The Art of the Comeback," *Encyclopedia of Major League Baseball, National League*. New York: Carroll & Graf, 1993.

Biederman, Les. "A Long road Back—But Law Made It." *The Sporting News*, September 4, 1965.

Bingham, Walter. "Dick Groat and His Hitting Machine." *Sports Illustrated*, July 22, 1963.

Cope, Myron. "Can Dick Groat Fire Up the Pirates Again?" *The Sport Special, Sport Magazine*, May 1961.

Devaney, John. "Hey Dick, Do You Do This?" *Sport Magazine*, October 1963.

Gershman, Michael. *"The Deacon,"* March 15, 1992 *Baseball Engagement Book*. Boston: Houghton Mifflin, 1992.

Groat, Dick, with Frank Dascenzo. *Groat, I Hit and Ran*. Durham, N.C.: Moore Publishing Company, 1978.

Klein, Larry. "Vern Law: The Predictable Pirate." *Sport Magazine*, September 1960.

McCollister, John. *The Story of the Pittsburgh Pirates*. Lenexa, Kans.: Addax Publishing Group, 1998.

1961: Joey Jay & Jim O'Toole, Cincinnati Reds

Bjarkman, Peter C. "Cincinnati Reds: Cincinnati's Hometown Game, from the Red Stockings to the Big Red Machine." *Encyclopedia of Major League Baseball, National League*, New York: Carrol & Graf, 1993.

Furlong, Bill. "How the Reds Built a Pitching Staff." *Sport Magazine*, January 1962.

Lawson, Earl. "Jay First Red Hurler Since Blackwell in 1947 to Cop 20 Wins." *The Sporting News*, September 27, 1961.

McHugh, Roy. "Ask O'Toole, He'll Tell You," *Sport Magazine*, August 1962.

Index